IN THE GAME

IN THE GAME

Race, Identity, and Sports in the Twentieth Century

Edited by Amy Bass

First published 2005 by
PALGRAVE MACMILLAN™
175 Fifth Avenue, New York, N.Y. 10010 and
Houndmills, Basingstoke, Hampshire, England RG21 6XS.
Companies and representatives throughout the world.

PALGRAVE MACMILLAN is the global academic imprint of the Palgrave
Macmillan division of St. Martin's Press, LLC and of Palgrave Macmillan Ltd.
Macmillan® is a registered trademark in the United States, United Kingdom
and other countries. Palgrave is a registered trademark in the European Union
and other countries.

ISBN 1–4039–6570–6

Library of Congress Cataloging-in-Publication Data
In the game: race, identity, and sports in the twentieth century/ edited by Amy
Bass.
    p.   cm.
  Includes bibliographical references and index.
  ISBN 1–4039–6570–6
  1. Racism in sports—History—20th century. 2. Discrimination in sports—
History—20th century. 3. Sports—Social aspects—History—20th century.
4. Ethnic relations—History—20th century. I. Bass, Amy.

GV706.32.I62   2005
796'.089—dc22

                                                                2004060108

A catalogue record for this book is available from the British Library.

Design by Letra Libre, Inc.

First edition: August 2005
10 9 8 7 6 5 4 3 2 1

Printed in the United States of America

Contents

IN THE GAME

INTRODUCTION

"No Compromise with Slavery! No Union with Slaveholders," or "Who was the *Last* Team to Integrate?"

Amy Bass

The student, as I remember, had what could only be described as a wry smile on his face when he asked the question. He already knew the answer. "Professor Bass, who was the *last* team to integrate?"

A good question? Well, not for discussion purposes. Not if you want your class to interact with the texts and each other. Too cut and dried for any kind of real pedagogical use, I surmised.

Who was the last team to integrate?

A good question? Well, its answer, I have to admit, does have a substantial context in terms of civil rights, immigration, integration, busing, basketball and, yes, the 1918 World Series.

Who was the last team to integrate?

I answer the question, failing to mention that it technically should be *what* was the last team to integrate. My answer, as always, is accompanied by the fact that they actually gave Jackie Robinson a tryout before Branch Rickey ever did.

Who was the last team to integrate?

The Boston Red Sox. Some twelve years after Robinson stepped up to the major league plate. But. . . .

There is always a "but" to the answer to the question that is always asked during my lecture about Jackie Robinson's historic breaking of a color line that had existed in major league baseball for well over half a century. That lecture, which uses Jules Tygiel's exceedingly readable and immensely teachable *Baseball's Great Experiment* as its main source, is not part of the upper-division seminar that I occasionally offer entitled "Race, Sport, and Society." Rather, it is part of my post–World War II lecture in the U.S. Survey (Reconstruction to Present) that I teach on a fairly regular rotation. I find that Robinson's debut and Branch Rickey's push to make the Brooklyn Dodgers the team that would transform baseball's color line are among the best ways to teach the visible rise of civil rights movements in the immediate postwar period, and the role of culture in it. It is not *sports* history. It's history.

There are many, many (many) burdens—well-known burdens—that come along with being a Red Sox fan (and, for clarification, I am not from Boston, but rather Richmond, Massachusetts, a small town outside of Pittsfield that has recently taken ownership of inventing the game from Cooperstown—and no, I am not being defensive). But as a cultural historian who has spent a lot of time writing about race and sports and civil rights, the drain of being a fan can be almost unbearable. The first time the question was posed in my class—*Who was the last team to integrate?*—the student knew why the question would plague me. During office hours, he had seen the 1986 World Series banner that I boldly displayed in my graduate student space at a large university on, yes, Long Island, not too far from Shea Stadium (but far enough for me), and not that much farther from that place in the Bronx where rumors have it that a local team plays baseball rather well. So, with his Yankees hat turned into "rally" position, he eagerly awaited my anguish, not necessarily knowing the degree to which it stirred my own memories of sitting in Fenway during Game 3, 1986, and watching Oil Can Boyd futilely try to change history.

Who was the last team to integrate?

The answer is complex. While the Boston Red Sox did not bring Elijah "Pumpsie" Green on board until 1959, technically they tried (well, "*tried*" is likely not the right word—I used to say "tried" but then Howard Bryant's wonderful book, *Shut Out: A Story of Race and Baseball in Boston,* changed my mind on employing that particular verb to describe the Red Sox's integration efforts) to integrate before anyone else.

In 1945, Red Sox General Manager Eddie Collins came under fire from Boston city councilor Isadore Muchnick, who wanted Collins to take the lead in the push to integrate baseball. Collins pleaded innocence to charges that Boston had prevented black players from trying out in the past, claiming that for the duration of his tenure with the team, he had "never had a single request for a tryout by a colored applicant."[1] However, Muchnick continued his quest, at one point threatening Collins that if an integrated tryout did not occur in Boston, he would block the required unanimous City Council vote for the team to play on Sundays. Further weight landed on Collins' shoulders when *Boston Record* columnist Dave Egan, reiterating the charge that black columnists such as Wendell Smith and Sam Lacy had been leading in the black press, began a campaign urging both of Boston's baseball teams—the Red Sox and the (now Atlanta) Braves—to consider Boston's historical responsibility to equality and to do the right thing. Between Muchnick's unyielding pressure and Egan's hype, the Red Sox agreed to be the first major league baseball team in the twentieth century to hold an integrated tryout.[2]

On April 14, 1945, Marvin Williams, Sam Jethroe, and, indeed, Jackie Robinson arrived at Fenway Park for their tryout, only to find it delayed for two days because of the death of Franklin Delano Roosevelt. When the tryout finally took place, few are sure what exactly happened. Many versions of what went down that day still circle history, largely because few folks deemed it worthy of their attention. According to Bryant, the relatively confirmed course of events include the fact that the team itself was not there. Manager (and former Red Sox great) Joe Cronin had given the players the day off because the season was beginning the next day in New York. Former Red Sox outfielder Hugh Duffy oversaw the tryout, while Cronin sat and watched. The *Boston Record* reported that Robinson did well and impressed Cronin, while others claimed that Cronin barely looked at the field. At the conclusion of the tryout, Collins told the trio they would hear from him soon. None did.[3]

Much more, of course, has been whispered about what occurred in Fenway Park that day. While Robinson, for one, generally refused to discuss it, *Boston Globe* reporter Clif Keane lent the tryout what Bryant calls "its historical significance." Keane claims that he heard someone shout from the stands, "Get those niggers off the field."[4] While many have been credited with the affront, most conclusions point toward Red Sox owner Tom Yawkey (of Yawkey's Way, the street outside of Fenway where I have purchased countless hats, shirts, beers, and so on).

As we know, and as Tygiel details, as a member of the Montreal Royals, the Brooklyn Dodgers' farm team, Jackie Robinson enjoyed a stunning summer season in 1946, making a name for himself in the small venues of America's favorite pastime. He went on to his major league debut in 1947, and was named Rookie of the Year. Sam Jethroe went to the Boston Braves in 1950, integrating Boston baseball, but not the Red Sox, and replicated Robinson's feat by taking the Rookie of the Year title. Having declined to sign either player, Red Sox management went back to work against integration. Tom

Yawkey, for example, served on a committee formed by baseball owners to study integration. On August 27, 1946, the committee submitted its notorious conclusions, which were apparently so distasteful that readers were asked to destroy their copies when finished. The tried and tired reasons were presented up front: baseball was being used by activists, Negro Leagues players did not have the skills to be competitive in the majors and did not know the game well enough, the contractual obligations players had to the Negro Leagues had to be observed. The real reason, of course, was made more subtly: Major league baseball profited from segregation. Integration meant, for example, that the Negro Leagues would no longer rent their parks from the majors. And it meant that more African Americans would come to major league games, isolating white fans and thus lowering the value of teams in major urban areas.

Who was the last team to integrate?

The Boston Red Sox. And not only did they decline to sign Robinson, in 1949 they shunned the advice of the general manager of their AA team in Alabama, the Birmingham Barons, that a star on the Birmingham Black Barons could be acquired for a mere $5,000. The team's scout, Larry Woodall—a Texan—could not fit the kid into his schedule. "I'm not going to waste my time," he said, "waiting on a bunch of niggers."[5] Thus, just as the Red Sox passed on Jackie Robinson, the team missed out on Willie Mays.

Say hey, indeed.

By the time the Red Sox called up Pumpsie Green from the minors in 1959, some 128 years after William Lloyd Garrison (who declared my title quote) opened the *Liberator* offices in what is now Government Center in Boston, Mays was a standout on the Giants, Robinson was retired, stars such as Hank Aaron, Ernie Banks, and Frank Robinson were shining for their teams, and journalists Lacy and Smith had confirmed in the black press that the Red Sox were a racist club. Rosters changed dramatically in terms of who played the game in the decades that followed World War II, and while the battle for racial integration moved toward center stage in the United States for a variety of reasons, it was perhaps most dramatically imagined in its initial stages on baseball diamonds. The Red Sox, however, kept their eyes closed to the cornucopia of talent that descended from the legacy of the Negro Leagues.

Rather than consider the impact that the refusal to integrate has had on the team's record, in Boston it was the "Curse of the Bambino" that had allegedly plagued Fenway Park, preventing the ultimate victory from ever gracing the likes of some of the game's greatest individual players—Ted Williams, Jimmy Collins, Duffy Lewis, Tris Speaker, Jim Rice, Carl Yastrzemski, Carlton Fisk, Jimmie Foxx, Bobby Doerr, Dom DiMaggio, and so on. Of course, the history of the Curse is completely convoluted. The short story? In 1920, less than two years after a World Series victory, Red Sox owner Harry Frazee needed cash to finance his girlfriend's play, so he sold Babe Ruth's contract to the Yankees. The real-er story? According to Yankees chronicler Glenn Stout, the "tidy package known as 'the Curse of the Bambino'" is grossly misrepresented, piling undue blame on Frazee, who was actually an astute businessman, and removing it from the "shenanigans elsewhere in the American League" that actually cost Boston the Babe.[6]

Regardless, the conclusion of the legend of the Curse is that the Yankees have gone on to an unmentionable number of championship seasons and the Red Sox—well, it took a while. But the legend of the Curse, which dutifully followed the Red Sox into the twenty-first century (it is apparently, as one insightful—ugh—Yankee fan in the stands pointed out on a poster in 1999, Y2K compliant), serves as a sort of Boston sports fan's version of claiming that the Confederate flag stands for "states rights," largely masking the impact that history might have had on the team. Few sports fans claim to have a better understanding of history than those in Boston. Yet Red Sox fans, as Howard Bryant summarizes, are "often frustrated by history but rarely by the people . . . who made the history."[7] We know, but do not often discuss, that many black stars over the course of the past several decades have ensured, contractually, that they never have to play for the home team in Boston. And those who sit in the visitors' dugout at Fenway Park claim a special satisfaction in victory. "I used to love to play the Red Sox, just to beat them," admitted former Yankee Willie Randolph. " . . . As a black player, the Red Sox brought out that little something in all of us."[8]

As Bryant succinctly understands, "the Red Sox more than other franchises have always found themselves linked with the larger Boston story of abolition, opportunity, politics, and clannish insularity."[9] Bottom line? It ain't easy being a Red Sox fan. Yet hope springs eternal, and one now has hope that under the watchful eye of Robinson's retired #42, which resides next to the retired numbers of great Red Sox players on the right field façade in Fenway, things are different. In February 2002, a new ownership group took over the Red Sox, and with it what president and CEO Larry Lucchino calls the team's "undeniable legacy of racial intolerance." For the first time, the team directly confronted its history, beginning a series of outreach programs into black Boston. The team started, equipped, and sponsors, for example, a 16-team Boston church league that fields 500 teenage players. According to principal owner John Henry, the effort has been a deliberate and terribly self-conscious one: "I think we have to make a statement not just in baseball but in our community that diversity is an issue that hasn't been fully addressed in the past and certainly has to be fully addressed," he says. "I think it's important what your actions are. That will really define the franchise going forward."[10] In a conversation with Henry, Howard Bryant found his perspective to be a refreshing one. "What John Henry wanted to know wasn't if the Red Sox live in racism's shadow, for he knows his new franchise most certainly does," Bryant recalls. "With that recognition, he stood already quantum leaps ahead of his predecessors, who often seemed to believe that forceful, impassioned denial could somehow alter the facts."[11]

The Red Sox that I fell in love with from my home in the far western reaches of Massachusetts was the same team that Bryant, who grew up in Dorchester, cheered for: Jim Rice, Freddy Lynn, Dewey Evans, El Tiante, Yaz, the Spaceman. I have never left them, loving Marty Barrett as a teenager (I was a girl and he was, like, *so cute*), and thinking that Mo Vaughan, Tom Gordon, Oil Can Boyd, and Nomar Garciaparra held keys to modern salvation, or at least could bring home a World Series ring.

And now that time has arrived: the coveted championship flag was raised in Boston on Opening Day of the 2005 season—the first time Boston had seen it in 86 years. Did Henry's efforts have an effect? Did the Curse end, as New York and Boston newspapers alike determined, when the Red Sox came back from a 0–3 deficit—the only team ever to do so in baseball history—to win the 2004 pennant, defeating the Yankees in the House that Ruth Built in Game 7? Did it happen, as many believe, on August 31, 2004, when Manny Ramirez pounded a foul ball past the Pesky Pole in Fenway and hit 16-year-old Lee Gavin, who lives with his family in Babe Ruth's former house in Sudbury, in the mouth and knocked out two of his teeth, making him THE KID WHO BROKE THE CURSE in his high school? Did it happen, as my friend Sarah speculated, when Alex Rodriguez slapped the ball out of Bronson Arroyo's hand in a feeble attempt to make it to first base in Game 6? Or did we have to wait until 11:38 pm on October 27, 2004, in St. Louis, when Keith Foulke gently tossed the ball to Doug Mientkiewicz and, well, it was done?

As the Red Sox Nation, as we now call ourselves in an interesting construction of inclusiveness that maintains age-old regional borders while acknowledging the global diaspora of fandom, assembled at Fenway Park for the first game of the 2004 World Series, fan paraphernalia—posters, banners, buttons, and shirts—emblazoned with the phrase "WE BELIEVE" solidified how being a Red Sox fan is, indeed, a faith-based occupation. It is one that even goes beyond life on earth, evidenced by those in Boston who placed balloons and pennants on the graves of their grandfathers and grandmothers, uncles and aunts, telling them what had happened—that *it* had finally happened.

But perhaps more important to consider when wondering when the Curse went away are the cheers of "PAPI-PAPI-PAPI" that filled the stadium of the faithful of this mismatched band of, in the words of hirsute outfielder Johnny Damon, "idiots." Throughout the Series, it was clear to the country: David "Papi" Ortiz, named Most Valuable Player of the American League Championship Series, was loved in Boston. Ramirez, named Most Valuable Player of the World Series, was loved in Boston. And with those chants, and with fond memories of George Scott, it is possible that the Curse lifted in a way that members of the Nation were not even aware of.

It can be a problem when our personal and professional lives collide. Liking a movie with characters derived from the minstrel stage. Liking a Mel Gibson movie. Being a Red Sox fan when you have just told your undergraduates that they were the last team to desegregate and you know why Mo Vaughan or Jim Rice often hated playing there. Those of us who think about the power structures and cultural legacies of ideas of race know well the personal liabilities of such knowledge. It magnifies things in your daily routine that many people do not deal with, whether when admitting that "your" team has a history more racist than most or when watching the African American actor in the "buddy" role die first and realizing that you still like the movie.

Discussing sports can, in particular, be a liability, but that is what those who signed onto this project agreed to do. It is territory where many have tried and failed—or perhaps flailed—from a variety of different perspectives. Marge Schott. Jimmy the Greek. Sir Roger Bannister. Al Campanis. Rush Limbaugh.

Ahhhh, Rush. What a week it was. When ESPN announced in July 2003 that Limbaugh would join its *NFL Countdown* show as "the voice of the fan and to spark debate on the show," I do not think I was alone in thinking *which fan is that?* ESPN, for its part, seemed pleased with its choice. "Rush is a great communicator and a fan's fan," said ESPN executive vice president Mark Shapiro. "His acute sense of what's on the minds of his listeners combined with his ability to entertain and serve as a lightning rod for lively discussion makes him the perfect fit for this new role." Limbaugh, too, appeared enthusiastic about his transition to television—especially sports television. "I am a big fan of the NFL and now I get to do what every football fan would love to do," he stated at the press conference that announced his new role. "I get to take my observations from the living room couch to the ESPN studios and talk football with the best journalists and players in the business."[12]

He lasted, as we all know, approximately one month because of those revered observations. "RUSH SACKS SELF," screamed the *New York Post* on October 2, 2003, in its announcement that Limbaugh "resigned" from his post at ESPN after accusations of racism. Those charges emerged, of course, in regard to his on-air comments about Philadelphia quarterback Donovan McNabb: During the network's "Sunday NFL Countdown" show before an Eagles/Bills game, Limbaugh said, "The media has been very desirous that a black quarterback do well. There is a little hope invested in McNabb, and he got a lot of credit . . . that he didn't deserve."[13] The uproar that followed was expected by everyone except Limbaugh. "My comments this past Sunday were directed at the media and were not racially motivated," he stated in his own defense. " . . . I love 'NFL Sunday Countdown' and do not want to be a distraction to the great work done by all who work on it."[14] Limbaugh's defense, then, read as a sacrifice for the good of the show, rather than an apology for an unquestionably racist analysis of football. McNabb, for one, understood this, disregarding any kind of statement from Limbaugh. "An apology would do no good because he obviously thought about it before he said it," McNabb pointed out. "It's somewhat shocking to hear that on national TV from him. It's not something that I can sit here and say won't bother me."[15]

Conversely, the statement itself, it seems, did not bother Limbaugh, who felt that the entire episode was "a mountain out of a molehill."[16] And in a way, he was right: Why was there so much of an uproar that Rush Limbaugh had made racist remarks in a national forum? Who, we must ask, was *surprised* that he could be perceived as racist? Certainly not those who felt compelled to create a petition to boycott ESPN "due to hiring of Rush Limbaugh." Those who signed the online document—before, mind you, Limbaugh waxed poetic on McNabb—committed to "refrain from watching, listening to, logging on to, reading, or gaining any information directly from ESPN, ESPN Radio, ESPN.com, ESPN Magazine, and all other ESPN affiliates (including ABC Sports) until ESPN terminates the contract of Rush Limbaugh. . . ." And why, pray tell, did the undersigned feel the need for such a petition? Because, in the words of the petition, they understood that

Mr. Limbaugh continues to discharge venomous, vindictive, inaccurate, and erroneous statements daily against anything and everything that he has a dislike for. Giving a man such as him an additional forum unrelated to his purported expertise only serves to further insult and anger millions of football fans, and undermines the legitimate professionals in this field, all of whom are more qualified. . . . Most of all, the mere selection of such a controversial political figure for a sports show indicates that ESPN does not value its audience, or at least highly underestimates the intelligence of much of its audience. As a commercial enterprise, ESPN stands to lose significant amounts of money for such a bizarre hiring that alienates half of its consumers. While this one move does reflect badly on the whole organization of ESPN, the company can still salvage some respect and integrity by releasing Mr. Limbaugh of his Sunday Night Countdown duties immediately.[17]

Limbaugh's resignation from ESPN was followed by accusations that he illegally used prescription painkillers. This latter episode made famous OxyContin and Wilma Cline—Limbaugh's maid and alleged drug supplier—and thus overshadowed the McNabb/ESPN debacle, destining his words to join the many of what are considered anomalous misfires regarding race in the sports world. However, Rush's "Jimmy the Greek" moment held a particularly disturbing vein that we should not let vanish from public record: his defense that he had been forced to resign for speaking *truth*. As the clamor regarding his McNabb remarks began to grow, Limbaugh's explanation for the uproar became more disturbing than the initial comment itself. "There's no racism here; there's no racist intent whatsoever," Limbaugh insisted. "This has become the tempest that it is because I *must have been right about something*. If I wasn't right, there wouldn't be this cacophony of outrage that has sprung up in the sportswriter community."[18]

According to this line of reasoning, any dialogue regarding issues of race within the sports world is, first, to be commended as brave and, second, must yield truth as measured by the reaction/attention to it. Is that why sports remains a rarely touched realm within the broad and brave field of cultural studies? It is not that no one writes about sports in a meaningful way. Some of the best contemporary writers on race, including Robin D. G. Kelley, Henry Louis Gates Jr., Michael Eric Dyson, and Gerald Early, have devoted essays in this manner, making obvious the bountiful intellectual fodder to be found in sports topics. In 1997, an issue of *Social Text* devoted itself to sports, producing a wide variety of smart pieces that probed pertinent issues—particularly, perhaps, race—into which sports provides windows. Edited by Toby Miller, author of the compelling *Sportsex*,[19] the issue determined that what could be called "the politics of sport" created "a key component of nationalism and discrimination, as well as an integral part of everyday oppositional culture."[20] This issue of *Social Text,* while not completely unique, represents a rare attempt by a diverse collection of scholars to pull so-called sports history out of its relatively isolated intellectual location, understanding the way in which this mass cultural format—which sport categorically is— provides an incredibly fertile ground to examine the always complex nature of racial operations, as well as demonstrating how the relationship between sports and race work as an umbrella over other critical themes of cultural projects, particularly—but not limited to—gender, sexuality, transnationalism, postcolonialism, and national identity.[21]

As always, the roots of such an examination lie with C. L. R. James. In his decisive analysis of cricket, *Beyond a Boundary,* which I have used elsewhere in a similar manner, James illustrates how sport subsists as a fundamental model for other forms of social existence.[22] His oft-cited query—"What do they know of cricket who only cricket know?"— demonstrates the need to take sports away from those who best know it— and perhaps only it—and hand it over to those who ask different questions with an alternative charge. It is an attempt, in part, to push forward a paradigmatic shift in a cultural study of sport, impart an interdisciplinary gaze in an accessible manner, and probe the cardinal questions deeply embedded in cultural studies, in general, and on race, often most broadly defined, in particular. As well, this charge seeks to examine the historical, ideological, and cultural imperatives contained within sport, firmly situating it as a significant, if not commanding, element of studies that engage with ideas of racial identity, hopefully embodying a pioneering way of looking not only at sports and popular culture, but the examination of race and ethnicity writ large.

With James' worthy influence clearly in sight, then, the following essays attempt to encompass a new arena of study for those who focus their work on ideas of race, ethnicity, and nation, incorporating not only the more standard scholarly research articles, but also more reflective pieces that encompass intellectual insight, observation, and personal memoir. Together, these essays demonstrate the increasingly transnational reach of sports culture, allowing thought-provoking perspectives on race to be considered without cordoning off ideas of culture, gender, nation, globality, class, and so on, possibly serving as a springboard that will connect studies of the ever-important subject of sports with those who have serious concern about and interest in ideas of race and identity. Again, these writers plunge into waters in which many—whether Jimmy or Al or Rush—have drowned before. They also acknowledge that there are few who do not think about race and sports in terms of being *fans* of some sort. But these essays are not merely about people's hobbies, which has often been the case when academics who do not normally write about sports take the time to do so. These are not professors who box in their spare time. Rather, those whose work follows took frameworks that they excel in—immigration history, postcolonialism, African American aesthetics, gender constructions—and applied them to sports, stretching their own intellectual centers of attention to an arena that saturates our daily lives, whether fans or not.

In the first section, entitled "Heroes," we begin with Matthew Frye Jacobson. Jacobson's innovations in immigration history have contributed greatly to the study of race, nation, and ethnicity, and one of his greatest skills throughout his previous works has been his ability to find where race exists in our cultural worlds and reveal just how powerful that existence is. Jacobson has demonstrated throughout his scholarship the multitude of lines that are crossed at all levels and in all aspects of American society in terms of race and ethnicity, thoughtfully and persuasively revealing how race works as both a social and cultural construction, and the numerous—and very real—consequences that follow. Here, he has applied his abilities to baseball, with a particularly personal focus on Dick "Richie" Allen, the focal point for his boyhood love of the game. In "'Richie' Allen, Whitey's Ways, and Me: A Political Education in the 1960s," Jacobson shows how the athlete battles—literally—against those who watch the game, own the game, and play the game. His soul-baring take on how Allen's career has been constructed demonstrates how—in similar fashion to C. L. R. James—what goes on in baseball quite often has nothing to do with baseball, and reveals much about the impact racialized perception can have on sport, nation, and a kid watching in Colorado.

Like Jacobson, Theresa Runstedtler also focuses on an individual, Joe Louis, not only challenging the popular mythos surrounding Louis, but also investigating his iconography to explore larger questions about the relationships among race, gender, and resistance. Rather than engage in the familiar scenario of Louis as the savior of American democracy, in "In Sports the Best Man Wins: How Joe Louis Whupped Jim Crow," Runstedtler considers Louis in the role of "Race Man." Examining the public commentary regarding Louis's successes, both in and out of the ring, in a variety of sources—from blues songs to political cartoons—Runstedtler locates Louis within the 1930s context of the "New Negro," a trend of engendering blackness—dignity, strength, defiance, nationalism, and so on—as a particularly male construction. Her analysis of the "Brown Bomber," which she offers with great detail regarding some of Louis's most important bouts, demonstrates how, as African Americans from all walks of economic life critiqued a lack of social justice by using discursive strategies that promoted black male ascendancy, broadly conceived popular ideas of racial progress became increasingly intertwined with the redemption of patriarchal black manhood. This engendering of blackness, then, is another reason why sporting men have become icons of the black community.

The next section moves from the figure of the athlete to the ideas that envelop those who watch the game—"Fans." Grant Farred, a scholar of postcolonialism, and especially of James, leads off, pondering ideas of how the athlete is received by the nation. When asked to join this project, Farred's immediate response was to write about soccer (which he insists, despite living in Durham, North Carolina, on calling "football") and, more specifically, soccer in Argentina, because he finds it to be the most significant and public roundtable for any conversation about race and identity. In his piece "Race and Silence in Argentine Football," Farred focuses on soccer star Juan Sebastian Veron, not as a sports hero in the manner of Jacobson and Runstedler, but rather as a way to explore the manner in which Argentina has manipulated racial perceptions of the self. According to Farred, Argentina has, indeed, denied the existence of blackness, while simultaneously elevating a decidedly black athlete, in order to put on its most modern (read: European) face, creating a stage that formally denies color while its people, conversely, push it toward a postcolonial state more in line with both its neighbors and Europe. As such, it is with a soccer star—Veron—that Argentina begins to understand the demand for acknowledging color, regardless of its self-identity that refuses to do so.

Jen Scanlon and Michael Arthur approach cricket in a similar style, from the perspectives of both ardent fan and scholar, investigating what they consider to be the stark reality of contemporary West Indian cricket, a sport that once provided colonial subjects with hope of liberation through their dexterity on the pitch. Their examination forces the question of what it means to be Caribbean or West Indian in the postcolonial moment, and what role cricket plays within such struggle of identity. Theirs, then, is a call for what they consider to be a new cricket, one that considers the particulars of a historical moment that is not cultivated by ideas of national identity or anti-British attitudes, but rather speaks to a broader understanding of island life in postcolonial society and maintains its necessity in creating a sense of belonging for people of the Caribbean as a whole.

For Tony Clark, the idea of belonging is central to his article about the use of "Indian" mascots by teams and fans, and their perpetuation by mainstream media. Clark situates the use of these so-called Indian representations as definitively racist, a seemingly easy argument to make, but goes further to explore how these active symbols stifle the creation of useful or respectful narratives regarding Indigenous Peoples in American society. Via the various media channels that reproduce them, mascots, whether an Atlanta Brave or Chief Wahoo, come to speak for the people they allegedly represent, removing any kind of voice from the people themselves. With this, the ability of American Indians to engage in society as United States citizens is suppressed, as well as any kind of autonomy they might have as sovereign nations within an empire, removing the actual people for the sake of the image created by athletic teams and their fans.

Beginning the section entitled "Aesthetics," Joel Dinerstein's take on 1970s football culture, "Backfield in Motion: The Transformation of the NFL by Black Culture," extends his own broader work on black aesthetics and movement. Dinerstein, whose award-winning book *Swinging the Machine* focused on how music and dance in the interwar "machine age" aided an increasingly urban and technologically advanced society deal with modernity, examines the black aesthetic in the academically oft-neglected world of football. While basketball has consumed the public's attention for the past few decades regarding the dominance of black style and substance, Dinerstein, focusing on the 1970s, demonstrates how black culture transformed football, providing what he considers to be paradigms of "aesthetic excellence." Locating these innovations in the style and performance of football in this era, Dinerstein does more than merely demonstrate that black cultural traditions find their way into a mainstream and decidedly American culture: He begins to unpack how this path is forged, by whom, and to what consequence for those that created the style, those that imitated it, and those that co-opted it into a global flow.

In a different vein, Latin American historian Eric Zolov focuses on the Mexico City Olympic Games in 1968, paying particular attention to how the host country celebrated its own alleged transcendence of racial and political conflicts in order to fully embrace its role as the first "developing" nation to serve as host. To do so, Zolov examines what we would now call "the look of the Games." At the Athens Olympics in 2004, the look was defined by Barcelona architect Santiago Calatrava, mixing ideas of antiquity and modernity in stark white architecture and red clay grounds. In Sydney in 2000, it meant the melding of an aboriginal past with a metropolitan future, symbolized most dramatically by Cathy Freeman's emotional lighting of the Olympic cauldron. For his part, Zolov examines the generally overlooked "Cultural Olympics" that accompanies the sporting program of each Olympic Games as well as the colors, pageantry, and imagery that Mexico put forth during its two-week stint as global host. In 1968, the Mexican Olympic Organizing Committee utilized a program of colors, pageantry, art, and imagery designed to erase Mexico's tired stereotype of being "lazy," as well as to mask the domestic contradictions of a repressive authoritarian regime—whose harshness became public with the massacre of student protesters of the eve of the Opening Ceremony. With the cultural agenda of the Olympics in 1968, two contradictory versions of Mexico were to come together—one that portrayed the nation as one of folk culture and tradition, and another that portrayed Mexico as a bastion of modernity, a nation with a future. Zolov uses this dualistic sensibility to explore the problematics of channeling domestic criticism, on one hand, and managing national reputations on a global stage, on the other, making clear the limitations of strategies of aesthetic containment in silencing civil struggle and reshaping foreign opinion.

While both Dinerstein and Zolov deal with ideas of modernity and aesthetics in sports, in the last section, "Futures," Tracie Church Guzzio demonstrates where a viable window lies into the postmodern, postindustrial moment of basketball. Using the oeuvre of novelist John Edgar Wideman,

Guzzio investigates the long-standing representations of black masculinity and physicality, focusing specifically on Wideman's autobiographical work *Hoop Roots.* In *Hoop Roots,* Wideman argues that sports can be viewed as a form of resistant expression, one that both addresses and contests black male stereotypes and reveals the instability of such cultural constructions, as well as a critical African American source of unity and celebration. As such, according to Guzzio, Wideman, a writer, professor, Rhodes scholar, and basketball player, argues for a different image of the black male via basketball, one that contests and re-creates commonly accepted views of black masculinity while maintaining connections to the racial past and providing space for a contemporary moment in which negative imagery can be deconstructed, but never forgotten.

Carlo Rotella, however, leads in a bit of a different direction. According to Rotella, whose celebrated work has ranged from surveys of urban literature to afternoons with heavyweight boxer Larry Holmes, an eagerness to make sports be "about race" constrains our access to the full range of what sports can mean. Academics and many journalists often treat boxing, in particular, as racial drama. The examples are obvious, whether one begins with Johnson versus Jeffries or Louis versus Schmeling. But Rotella provocatively argues that portraying boxing in this manner is a reductionist effort, one that throttles other meanings made available by the complex theater of the ring. To make his point, Rotella recasts the last great black-white heavyweight title bout of the twentieth century: Larry Holmes versus Gerry Cooney, 1982, a fight that brought together two very different fighting styles at cultural center stage within a context orchestrated by master showmen (including Don King) and media organs enthralled with the bout's many parallels to *Rocky.* With his examination of this fight and its historical moment, Rotella leaves us with perhaps the next step in a critical examination of this thing we call sports.

To have writers of this caliber assemble in one place makes working on such a project an absolute pleasure, so a great deal of thanks goes to each and every one of them for their attention to the project, their timeliness in facing some serious deadlines, and their generosity in their advice and support to me. Many of these contributors have served as mentors to me in the past, and to have them as colleagues on such a project has been an absolute delight. As well, thanks to Rachel Buff and Michel Willard, who provided critical feedback at a very early stage, and Brendan O'Malley, whose support, detailed and constructive criticism, and shared devotion to the Boston Red Sox enabled this project to flourish. From a personal angle, thanks to my family for their constant counsel, especially my mother for her fine editorial eye, my father for his enthusiasm, my sister for her humor, and my brother for his ACLS tickets. Most important, thanks to Evan, who willingly relinquished the remote control and his Metrocard so that I could experience baseball from a variety of seats during the historic 2004 postseason.

Notes

1. Quoted in Howard Bryant, *Shut Out: A Story of Race and Baseball in Boston* (New York: Routledge, 2002), 29.
2. Bryant, 24–28.
3. Bryant, 30–31.
4. Bryant, 32.
5. Quoted in Bryant, 1.
6. Glenn Stout, "When the Yankees Nearly Moved to Boston," ESPN.com, July 18, 2002, accessed on July 6, 2004. For a detailed explanation as to how Babe Ruth ended up in New York, see Stout, *Yankees Century: 100 Years of New York Yankees Baseball* (New York: Houghton Mifflin, 2002). For the impact of the Curse through the decades in Boston, see Dan Shaughnessy, *The Curse of the Bambino* (New York: Penguin Books, 2000).
7. Bryant, 23.
8. Quoted in Bryant, xii.
9. Bryant, xi.
10. Juan Williams, "The Boston Red Sox and Racism," *Morning Addition*, National Public Radio, October 11, 2002, accessed at http://www.npr.org/programs.morning/features/2002/oct/redsox/, April 17, 2004.
11. Bryant, xiii.
12. ESPN.com, July 14, 2003; accessed October 3, 2003.
13. Quoted in Todd Venezia, "Rush Sacks Self," *The New York Post*, October 2, 2003, 17.
14. Venezia, "Rush Sacks Self."
15. Quoted in Venezia, "Rush Sacks Self."
16. Quoted in Venzia, "Rush Sacks Self."
17. http://www.petitiononline.com/no2espn/petition.html, accessed October 3, 2003. The petition was written by David August and hosted by PetitionOnline, which provides petitions for public advocacy free of charge. At the time it was accessed, the signatures on August's petition totaled 3,220, most with extensive commentary.
18. Quoted in Venzia, "Rush Sacks Self," emphasis mine.
19. See Toby Miller, *Sportsex* (Philadelphia: Temple University Press, 2002).
20. "The Politics of Sport," *Social Text* 50 (Spring 1997).

21. Another collection in this vein is John Bloom and Michael Willard, *Sports Matters: Race, Recreation, and Culture* (New York: New York University Press, 2002).

22. See Amy Bass, *Not the Triumph but the Struggle: The 1968 Olympic Games and the Making of the Black Athlete* (Minneapolis: University of Minnesota Press, 2002).

PART I:
HEROES

ONE

"Richie" Allen, Whitey's Ways, and Me: A Political Education in the 1960s

Matthew Frye Jacobson

I wouldn't say that I hate Whitey, but deep down in my heart, I just can't stand Whitey's ways, man.

—*Dick Allen,* Ebony, *1970*

"Disrespect" would be a euphemism. Dick Allen was unanimously re-named "Richie" in 1960 by a white press wholly indifferent to the young ballplayer's protestations that everyone from his mother on down had always called him "Dick." Later, when Allen finally did insist upon his rightful name after several years of patiently accepting what he thought a vaguely racist diminutive, the press variously ignored his request, spitefully granted it ("Dick 'Don't Call Me Richie' Allen"), or—worse—depicted the "name-change" as an emblem of Allen's unstable character (as in: "in mid-career he became, adamantly, 'Dick.'" *Sports Illustrated* referred to this as Allen's "first name sensitivity.")[1] Fans in Philadelphia delighted in throwing objects at Allen—pennies, chicken bones, batteries, bolts, half pints—and when he took to wearing a batting helmet in the field, the press intimated that he needed the protection because he was bad with a glove. Allen twice appeared on the cover of *Sports Illustrated:* once in 1970 under the heading "Baseball in Turmoil" (a reference to Curt Flood's challenge to baseball's reserve clause, but Allen was the sport's better poster boy for "turmoil"), and once in 1972, smoking what remains the only cigarette in the history of *SI* covers.

Nor has Allen's treatment mellowed over the years. The current entry for Allen on BaseballLibrary.com ("The Stories behind the Stats") begins this way: "Talented, controversial, charming, and abusive, Allen put in 15 major league seasons, hitting prodigious homers and paying prodigious fines. He was praised as a money player and condemned as a loafer." The site does duly note Allen's Rookie of the Year season in 1964 and his MVP season in 1972; but its overall flavor tends fairly decisively toward "loafer" rather than "money player." (The account of his stellar rookie season opens on the odd—but for Allen, familiar—note, "He made 41 errors at third base. . . .")[2] *Total Baseball,* the baseball encyclopedia, ranks Allen as the eighty-eighth best player of all time in an entry that begins, "Dick Allen feuded with writers, fans, managers, and teammates, earned many suspensions and behaved and fielded erratically."[3]

In American political life, the phrase "Black Power" will always bring to mind Stokley Carmichael, H. Rap Brown, Huey Newton, Bobby Seale, the Black Panther Party, and other black radicals who came to prominence in the latter half of the 1960s. In the too-clever parlance of '60s- and '70s-era baseball writing, however, its appropriation conjured figures like Hank Aaron, Willie Mays, Willie McCovey, Frank Robinson, and Richie Allen—the 1.5 generation of baseball's integration after Jackie Robinson had broken the color bar, black sluggers whose speed and playing style and might were transforming the national pastime. (Absent its black stars, Hank Aaron points out, the National League's stand-out player of the 1960s would have been *Ron Santo.*)[4]

But the two meanings of "black power" were not unrelated, as Dick Allen's career demonstrates perhaps better than most. The social drama of the Civil Rights movement constituted the inescapable context within which black ballplayers of this generation were understood and measured in the white media—most often, if tacitly, located along an imagined political spectrum of "good" and "bad" Negroes (Willie Mays at one end of the spectrum, Richie Allen, Bob Gibson, and Dock Ellis at the other). "If [Allen] had been white," writes Gibson, "he would have been considered merely a free spirit. As a black man who did as he pleased and guarded his privacy, he was instead regarded as a trouble-maker."[5] It is only in the context of the wider political and social world of the 1960s, not of the clubhouse and diamond, that one can comprehend Allen's becoming "a dart-board for the press," in Pirate outfielder Willie Stargell's phrase.[6]

Thus the sports page served as a site of oblique but significant social commentary on the racial questions of the day (indeed it was in relation to the sports page that whites seem to have first acknowledged and accepted that there might even be such a thing as a "white press"). It is not just that the world of Orval Faubus, Martin Luther King, Jr., Strom Thurmond, and Malcolm X supplied the cues for writing about a figure like Richie Allen, but also, contrariwise, that commentary on the likes of Allen—or Muhammad Ali or Cookie Gilchrist or Lew Alcindor—was by its very nature a genre of *political* writing whose significations reached beyond the diamond, the ring, or the gridiron, to the roiling racial world of a nation in unrest.

By the time Allen's autobiography appeared in 1989, vernacular polit-ical discourse was better equipped to deal with the experience of someone "enormously talented and black in a game run by white owners, executives, and managers," as one reviewer put it.[7] Across the arc of his career in Philadelphia, however, from 1964 to 1969, the *political* truths of the sports world were grasped and analyzed chiefly by athletes and writers on the black side of the color line, and only very occasionally by a white com-mentator like Robert Lipsyte or Jack Olsen. Most often, black analyses of how race mattered—along with black protestations that race did matter—were simply folded into white power's already-scripted tale of the "bad Negro," as when Cookie Gilchrist mounted a boycott of the AFL's 1964 All-Star Game in Jim Crow New Orleans, when Tommie Smith and John Carlos raised their gloved fists on the dais in Mexico City in 1968, or when Dick Allen or Frank Robinson raised the issue of Major League Baseball's racist hiring practices. Bad boys all. By suggesting that race had anything to do with his image as "the bad boy of baseball," in other words, a figure like Allen could only *prove* himself the "bad boy of baseball."

This essay is not primarily about Dick Allen, but—quite deliberately—about *Richie* Allen, a creation of the white press, a negative icon of the Civil Rights era, "just about the premier bad boy in sports."[8] It is also about Richie Allen as a persona who—against the odds, one has to con-clude—became a positive icon to me, a white kid growing up in the subur-ban setting of Boulder, Colorado. The sports pages of this era constituted my political education. I was six years old and just beginning to pay atten-tion to baseball during Allen's phenomenal rookie year. If "black power" signified anything to me at age nine, around the time when the term entered political parlance, it signified Allen's towering home run to straightaway center in the All-Star Game in Anaheim. But by age ten, always hungry for another story, another AP wire photo, another stat on Allen, I could not help but notice that most of what I found was some brand of vilification.

My fourth-grade teacher Miss Harms could lecture on Reverend King and the freedom struggle; but what I learned about the injustices and the slanders of racism, I learned mostly by following Richie Allen in the *Denver Post*, waiting in vain for someone to write something good. ("Richie played with fire in his eyes, always," says Orlando Cepeda. "Never read that in no newspaper."[9])

Reflecting on the odd oasis of adulation that his own fame provided him amid a wider, uglier world of racism, harassment, and danger, Bob Gibson once told baseball writer Roger Angell, "It's nice to get attention and favors . . . but I can never forget the fact that if I were an ordinary black person I'd be in the shithouse, like millions of others."[10] Allen never did quite get out, even despite his talent and his fame and the awed respect he earned inside the lines. Here, in what stands as both a historical and a personal reflection, I seek to discover what that might say about politics and sport in the 1960s, and also to recover what it *did* mean to one white fan, thousands of miles and many worlds away from the Philadelphia shithouse called Connie Mack Stadium.

1. Philadelphia

"No baseball season in my fifteen-year career had the highs and lows of '64," wrote Allen in his autobiography, *Crash*. "The Temps said it best baby, I was a ball of confusion."[11] Allen was the National League Rookie of the Year, hitting .318 with 201 hits, 29 home runs, and 91 RBIs. He also had 38 doubles and 13 triples, a single-season combination that the likes of Mays, Aaron, Roberto Clemente, and Pete Rose never matched. Or Jackie Robinson, for that matter. (Joe DiMaggio bested it back in 1936, with 44 doubles and 15 triples). But Phillies fans found ways to sour on him nonetheless, many blaming him for the team's spectacular September freefall that cost them what had seemed a sure pennant. Fans' merciless booing became so common at Connie Mack Stadium in ensuing years that by the end of his tenure in Philadelphia, Allen had taken to scratching messages during the game—such as the word "boo"—in the infield dirt with his spikes.[12]

Jackie Robinson and the magical date of 1947 seem to have long passed by the time Allen cracked the majors, but the key to his bitter experience in the 1960s lies precisely in how little had happened in the intervening years. When one thinks of baseball's falling racial barriers, the players who come to mind in addition to Robinson are people like Larry Doby, Roy Campanella, and Monte Irvin, a generation born in the teens and twenties, who came of age in the forties and played in the Negro

Leagues before entering the newly integrated majors directly on the heels of Branch Rickey's "great experiment" in Brooklyn. The intervening glory years make it hard enough to recall that Willie Mays and Hank Aaron played their first pro ball in the Negro Leagues (Mays with the Birmingham Black Barons, Aaron with the Indianapolis Clowns); but even the players slightly younger than they—players with no Negro League experience at all—spent the early part of their careers in a baseball environment no less white and no less hostile than Jackie Robinson's Ebbets Field.

Hank Aaron himself refers to them as "second generation black players," though *1.5 generation* would be more accurate—Willie McCovey, Billy Williams, Bill White, Orlando Cepeda, Bob Gibson, Curt Flood, Lou Brock. Though associated with the 1960s and a baseball era far removed from the Jackie Robinson moment, "most of them came through the minor leagues in the 1950s, and almost all of them had their own horror stories."[13] In *October 1964*, David Halberstam writes of this generation,

> If they were not the black players of the pioneer generation, they had come up right behind them: most had grown up in ghettos, and their way into the big leagues had been difficult, often through a still-segregated minor-league system. This obstacle course remained the foundation of big-league baseball, and it was rife with prejudice. Playing on minor-league teams in tiny Southern towns meant the crowds—even the home crowds—were usually hostile. Worse, most of their fellow players were rural country white boys, who, more often than not, seemed to accept the local mores.[14]

"I didn't know anything about racism or bigotry until I went into professional baseball in 1953," writes Frank Robinson, who grew up in West Oakland and whose initiation in the taunts of "Nigger, go back to Africa" came in Sally League towns like Augusta, Macon, and Savannah.[15] As Dock Ellis—ten years younger still than Robinson—put it, "You learn more than baseball in the minor leagues." For his own part, Ellis recalls going into the stands in a game against the Geneva Senators, swinging a leaded bat at a fan who had called him Stepin Fetchit, or standing defiantly on the mound, middle finger extended to a hostile crowd, after striking out the last batter in a game in Wilson, North Carolina.[16]

Such incidents—Aaron's racial "horror stories"—punctuate the biographies of virtually every player of the 1.5 generation. Bill White spent 1953 as the only black player in the Class-B Carolina League, serving, in Halberstam's words, as "a kind of beacon to local rednecks, who would come out to the ballpark and, for a tiny amount of money, yell at this one young black player, who symbolized to them a world beginning to change." He sometimes carried a bat with him as he left the clubhouse, according to Bob

Gibson, in order "to get through the hostile crowds that stood between him and the team bus."[17] Aaron and Wes Covington broke the color barrier up north in Eau Claire, Wisconsin (Aaron: "We didn't exactly blend in"; Covington: "I felt like a sideshow freak") before Aaron was sent to the Jacksonville Braves to break the color line in the Sally League.[18] The president of the Sally League, Dick Butler, later claimed to have "followed Jacksonville and sat in the stands to keep a lookout. You were never sure what was going to happen. Those people had awfully strong feelings about what was going on."[19] John Roseboro endured taunts of "chocolate drop" in Sheboygan; Felipe Alou was barred from the Evangeline League because of Louisiana segregation statutes (and shipped instead to the more hospitable Cocoa Indians of the Florida State League, "a class D menagerie").[20] In Fayette, North Carolina, Curt Flood "heard spluttering gasps, 'There's a goddamned nigger son-of-a-bitch playing ball with those white boys! I'm leaving'"; and in Greensboro, Leon Wagner faced an armed fan by the outfield fence, issuing a warning, "Nigger, I'm going to fill you with shot if you catch one ball out there." "What kind of country is this?" Vic Power wanted to know, upon confronting racial mores so different from those that obtained in his native Puerto Rico.[21]

Even after they had safely reached the majors, far from the redneck sneers of the Sally League circuit, most of the 1.5 generation had to negotiate the southern racial climate and the segregated facilities of Florida sites like Bradenton, Vero Beach, Clearwater, or Tampa during the months of spring training. Most also had to deal with some element of segregation in their team's travel, lodging, rooming, or eating arrangements in cities like St. Louis and Cincinnati during the regular season; many, like Reggie Smith, had epithets and more dangerous objects hurled at them at one time or another, even by the "fans" in their home ballparks. Some joined major league teams that were themselves deeply divided by race. Gibson and White broke into the majors playing for an overtly racist manager named Solly Hemus: "either he disliked us deeply or he genuinely believed that the only way to motivate us was with insults," remembers Gibson. During one clubhouse meeting, in the presence of the full team, Hemus referred to an opposing pitcher as a "nigger." Orlando Cepeda, for his part, attributes the perennial also-ran fortunes of the Giants during the early '60s to the breakdown of team feeling along ethnoracial lines. (Among other things, though his lineup featured Cepeda, all three Alou brothers, Jose Pagan, and Juan Marichal, manager Alvin Dark tried to ban the Spanish language in the clubhouse. Dark— who, ironically, had grown up in Lake Charles, Louisiana, the very town that barred Felipe Alou—also openly questioned the "mental alertness" of his "Negro and Spanish-speaking players.")[22]

Dick Allen drew a cruel hand, even by the standards of such a deck: after brief stints in Elmira (New York), Magic Valley (Utah), and Williamsport (Pennsylvania), in 1963 and at the age of only 20, Allen landed with the Arkansas Travelers, the Phillies' AAA team whose home park was in Little Rock (of Central High fame) and whose lineup had, to that point, been white only. (As Lou Brock, who had been born there, liked to say, Arkansas was indeed "the land of opportunity"—at the very first opportunity he had gotten the hell out.[23]) "When I arrived at the park," Allen recalls, " . . . there were people marching around with signs. One said, DON'T NEGRO-IZE BASEBALL. Another, NIGGER GO HOME. . . . Here, in my mind, I thought Jackie Robinson had Negro-ized baseball sixteen years earlier." As if to underscore the militant whiteness of this white world, the season's festivities began with the ceremonial throwing out of the first pitch by *Governor Orval Faubus*. Afterward Allen found a note on the windshield of his car: "DON'T COME BACK AGAIN, NIGGER." "There might be something more terrifying than being black and holding a note that says 'Nigger' in an empty parking lot in Little Rock, Arkansas, in 1963," Allen comments, "but if there is, it hasn't crossed my path yet." That AAA season was filled with this sort of menace and danger; and it was also exceptionally isolating, as off the field Allen was removed from the rest of the team by the maze of segregationist civic codes and social rituals of pre-Civil Rights Act Little Rock.[24]

This was perhaps the beginning of bad blood between Allen and both the Phillies' white officialdom and Philadelphia's white press. For one thing, Allen felt that he was ready for the majors already (his nine spring-training home runs in 1963 seemed to argue in his favor), and he saw himself as a sacrificial lamb to the organization's imperative to desegregate its farm system. This might have been workable if, for another thing, the Phillies had handled Allen's situation with some of the forethought and sensitivity that the Dodgers had shown Jackie Robinson. But the organization was quite calloused in its general disinterest in Allen's Arkansas experience. As *Ebony* wryly noted in 1970, "During [the] 1963 season with Philadelphia's minor league team in Little Rock, . . . he complained about racial injustice (Philly writers say they found no prejudice there)."[25] Most telling, perhaps, was Arkansas manager Frank Lucchesi's nonchalance toward the social burden that Allen was made to carry that season: "Richie was upset one night because one person said, 'Come on, Chocolate Drop, hit one out. . . . That's not in taste but the fan didn't realize it. They say worse things to white ballplayers. Richie is sensitive and he is self-centered."[26]

And so, one might have thought, the trip north to Philadelphia the following year would be an improvement. But Philadelphia baseball had a fairly spectacular history of racism of its own: though Connie Mack had tried to smuggle talented black players into Shibe Park as Italians or Indians earlier in the century, the Philadelphia stadium—like the Phillies lineup—remained the most stubbornly anti-integrationist in the National League. The black press of the 1940s reported that Mack himself was among the owners "most bitterly" opposed to integration; and according to historian Bruce Kuklick, when Jackie Robinson joined the Dodgers in 1947, "the cruelest taunts he received at Ebbets Field came from the visiting Phillies. . . ." As for Brooklyn's visits to Shibe Park, Phillies GM Herb Pennock pleaded with Branch Rickey not to bring Robinson at all: "Branch, you can't bring the nigger here. Philadelphia's not ready for that yet." When Robinson did turn up in Philadelphia, pitchers threw at him, infielders purposely spiked him, and Phillies players once lined up on the dugout steps, pointing their bats at him and making gunshot sounds. By the mid-1950s, the Phillies were the only remaining all-white team in the National League; and even after the team finally did integrate, it remained among the last major league teams to end segregated housing during spring training.[27]

Over and above the racialized traditions of Philadelphia baseball, the city itself was entering a heated and dangerous period in black-white relations—it was a "racial tinderbox," as the head of the city's Urban League described it.[28] In 1964 Allen arrived in a Philadelphia wracked by racial violence over issues of job discrimination, housing, school segregation, and police brutality, and in which an aggressive (and aggressively white) former beat cop named Frank Rizzo was rising rapidly through the ranks toward the commissioner's office, which he attained in 1967.[29] (Faubus and Rizzo: two-thirds of some weird, depressing hat trick. Later Allen worked for Al Campanis.) There had been violent clashes over the integration of Philadelphia construction in 1963; and in August 1964, during Allen's rookie season, three days of rioting engulfed a 125-block area of Lower North Philadelphia, one boundary of which was marked by Connie Mack Stadium. Players had to pass through a "police state" to get to the ballpark during those days. One black resident lamented, "The only thing I regret about the riot . . . was that we didn't burn down that goddamn stadium. They had it surrounded by cops, and we couldn't get to it. I just wish we could've burned it down and wiped away its history that tells me I'm nothing but a nigger." Two died and 339 were injured in the rioting.[30]

Although Philadelphia fans might indeed "boo the losers in an Easter egg hunt," as Bob Uecker once quipped, and even white outfielder Johnny Callison had objects thrown at him, still these fans found a very special—vitriolic—place in their hearts for the new arrival from the Arkansas Travelers. Even his Rookie of the Year stats (.318, 29 HR, 91 RBI) were not enough to shield Allen from the tense, racial hatreds of

mid-'60s Philadelphia.[31] Fan animosity toward Allen seems a compound
of garden variety racism; scapegoating for the Phillies' 1964 tailspin;
venting on the larger race questions facing the city; and a misappre-
hending response, as *Sports Illustrated* noted, to Allen's expressionless
playing style, which to many whites made him look "arrogant." (Manager Gene Mauch's more generous observation of Allen's demeanor was
that "He doesn't get way up when things are going good, or way down
when things are going bad. And that's the best approach to any professional sport.") All of which was further fueled by "some of the harshest
press in the city's sports history."[32]

Allen was in fact booed for the first time in the fifth inning of the Phils'
home opener in 1964, and he was booed plenty as the Phillies squandered
their six and a half game lead in the final 12 games of that season. But the
mutual bitterness began in earnest the next season, in July 1965, when a
pregame fight between Allen and Philadelphia favorite Frank Thomas resulted in Thomas' departure from the Phillies.[33] The fight, by most accounts, was itself "racial." Thomas was already well-known among his
teammates for his derisive comments toward Allen, Johnny Briggs, and
other black players. One thing that particularly enraged Allen was when
Thomas would approach a black player, pretending "to offer his hand in a
soul shake," and then "grab the player's thumb and bend it back hard."[34]
On the day of the fight, Johnny Callison was razzing Thomas for a failed
bunt attempt the night before, but Thomas chose to answer Allen instead
of Callison. He taunted Allen as "Muhammad Clay," by some accounts,
and "Richie X" by others—taunts that in either case Allen answered with
a pop to the jaw before Thomas broke a cardinal baseball rule by swinging
his bat at Allen and catching him on the shoulder.[35]

Teammates pried the two apart, but an ineluctable sequence had already been set in motion: Thomas was immediately sold off to Houston;
Allen was forbidden from discussing the incident under penalty of a $2,000
fine; but Thomas, meanwhile, freely fed his (partisan, sanitized) version to
the press. Manager Gene Mauch, too, made some rather coy remarks to the
press that not only obscured the nature of the incident and Thomas' part in
it, but also left an impression that the Phillies had unfairly and quite know-
ingly scapegoated the white veteran in deference to Allen's talent and
youth. It was here, most significantly, that the press began to tag Allen as a
"troublemaker"—an appellation that would provide a convenient media
peg for the rest of his career. "Baseball should never forget the Allen-
Thomas fiasco," says Bill White. " . . . When Dick Allen came to the big
leagues, he was a kid in love with the game. Baseball was all that mattered.
After the Thomas incident, the love was taken right out of him. There's historical significance in how that was handled."[36]

The result was that Allen came out looking unjustly favored and vaguely militant—a ready-made script for many whites, given the city's racial climate—and he was directly blamed for the departure of a popular (white) player. Banners announcing fans' unambiguous preferences—such as "We Want Thomas"—bedecked Connie Mack Stadium; *Daily News* writer Larry Merchant embarked on an anti-Allen crusade in print; one fan "sucker punched" Allen; others at the park jeered him as "darkie" and "monkey" (when he wasn't hitting game-winning home runs), and Allen recalls seeing one father pointing at him and teaching his little boy how to boo. It was soon after, too, that people started to throw things at Allen, to vandalize his home, and to harass his family. Across the balance of the 1960s, Allen was "booed mercilessly," as *Newsweek* reported, and he received "hate mail . . . so brutal that he now refuses to open anything that looks like fan mail"; "people smeared paint on his car, threw rocks and shot BBs through his windows and booed his children on the street."[37] As the *Daily News* once reported in 1967, after Allen's heroics had dispatched the Cubs, "He should have been grinning and content in the knowledge that his three-run homer in the twelfth inning won a game for the Phillies. But it is tough to grin when you come to the ballpark and there are letters calling you 'Dirty, Black Nigger.'" It was after this particular game that Allen started speaking openly about wanting out of Philadelphia.[38]

The Thomas incident may have marked a turning point for Allen and the city, but it was scarcely the only factor in that souring relationship. As Don Malcolm suggests, the "Angry Negro Problem"—a thematic convention for writing about a certain kind of athlete, from Dick Allen to Gary Sheffield—derives not only from the fact that "white Americans still are manifestly uncomfortable with demonstrative black males," but also, significantly, that they are "probably most uncomfortable with the ones who are making piles of dough."[39] (As for a bit of context on "angry Negroes": five weeks after the Thomas incident, the Phillies landed in Los Angeles just in time to witness the flames of the Watts riot.[40])

Dick Allen, emphatically, was *not* utterly unappreciated by the baseball world, and this, paradoxically, may have fueled the animosity against him in some quarters. Philadelphia had signed him for a cool $70,000 bonus, the largest ever offered a black ballplayer. Later, Allen became the highest-paid player on the Phillies (and in 1973, upon signing with the White Sox for a quarter of a million dollars, he was to become the highest-paid player in Major League history to that point). "His salary has risen faster than anyone's ever did before," remarked *Newsweek* in 1968. " . . . And his popularity has plummeted just as fast."[41] In the calculus of Philadelphia race relations—and of the nation's—these two developments may have been intimately entwined. It is not just a case of a Negro's earnings demolishing the white presumption of what would be fitting; it is also a matter of social demeanor—the white insistence upon "appropriate" black gratitude, which is to say a bit of the old-fashioned, hat-in-hand bowing and scraping. But as *Sports Illustrated* commented, on the contrary, Allen was "the first black man . . . to assert himself in baseball with something like the unaccommodating force of Muhammad Ali in boxing, Kareem Abdul-Jabbar in basketball, and Jim Brown in football."[42]

As the economics of the game shifted in the late 1960s, too, there was the volatile matter of the sheer power attaching to a player's contract: many among the white press and white fandom were troubled that the Phillies organization found even Allen's white *managers* (first Mauch, and then Bob Skinner) more readily expendable than this black star, impetuous though he was. As Jim Bouton had it in *Ball Four,* "There is a pecking order in the major leagues which goes like this: owner, general manager, superstar, manager, established player, coaches, traveling secretary, trainer, clubhouse man, marginal player."[43] Black superstar over white manager—this was a problem for many white fans in the 1960s. And while much discussion of race in baseball has focused on the suspicious paucity of black managers and team executives, the "problem" of the black super star—the tension between the racial hierarchy of the culture and the natural pecking order of the team—has been the cause of much devilment as well.

Within this alchemic mingling of circumstance, ideology, personality, and history, the media developed an iron framework for reporting on Allen's career both on and off the field: Allen was militant, a malcontent, a troublemaker, a black radical. Allen was not entirely blameless for the volume of available copy, it should be noted; but the "bad boy of baseball" label did create a media peg for stories that might have attracted no attention at all in the case of other players, black or white. (Indeed, the shock and scandal of a book like Bouton's *Ball Four* in 1970—what Bowie Kuhn called Bouton's "grave disservice" to the game—was precisely its demonstration that the game was made up pretty much exclusively of swearing, hard-drinking, tobacco-addicted, amphetamine-popping, bed-hopping, window-peeping bad boys.[44]) But for Allen and seemingly for Allen alone, a steady litany of well-publicized "transgressions" mounted throughout the '60s: the Thomas incident in 1965; a freak, off-field hand injury in 1967, broadly but baselessly presumed to be the result of either a barroom knifefight or perhaps a run-in with a lover's husband; an actual barroom brawl in 1968 (which, like the Thomas incident, began with a racial slur); and also in 1968 a few missed days of spring training, an instance of reporting late to the ballpark, and his benching by Mauch for being "unfit to play" (Allen's trouble, Mauch said, was not with "the high fastball," but rather "the fast highball"); and in 1969, income tax problems, a missed plane to St. Louis, and a missed double-header at Shea.[45]

Where silence on such matters was the journalistic norm in this cookies-and-milk era of sports coverage (Mickey Mantle was not averse to showing up at the park "unfit to play," either, for instance, as we later learned and as the press corps had surely known at the time), Allen's every move seemed to generate acres of copy. "You fellas have created an atmosphere where people who have never met me, hate me," he told reporters. Later he commented, "Even if they gave me an opportunity to tell all of my side of the story, I wouldn't take it because I just don't trust the white press in general."[46] If Allen was a perpetual story, race and racism were never an acknowledged part of that story. But the "race neutral" language of the white press makes for some interesting reading: Allen "marches to a mournful tune that only he hears, moving with an insolent grace," for example, according to the *Philadelphia Daily News;* though one might fairly ask whether it is even *possible* for a white man, in America's media cosmos, to "move with insolent grace." Further, Richie Allen is "a superstar with a built-in distaste for discipline" (*New York Times*); he is "a player of enormous talents and mercurial moods" who is "known less for his awesome batting power than for his drinking, horseplaying and habitual tardiness" (*Newsweek*); "a man who hits a baseball even harder than he hits the bottle," a "wondrously gifted misanthrope," the "chain-smoking, hard-drinking, horseplaying, perpetually late bad boy of the 1960s" (*Sports Illustrated*).[47] So infamous did Allen's movements become, that at the All-Star Game in 1969 President Nixon sent a personal message through Allen's teammate Grant Jackson: "You tell Richie Allen to get back on the job." By that same year—his last in Philadelphia, as it turned out—Allen had begun to "wish they'd shut the gates . . . and let us play ball with no press and no fans."[48]

The contrast with the *black* press could not have been starker. In 1968, at the height of his most controversial season and amid a thorough raking in the white media, for instance, a photo gallery in the *Afro-American* lovingly depicted Allen as a devoted family man ("$85,000 dad plays mom at Phils' ballpark. Richie Allen baby-sits with son between Sunday pitches").[49] After the St. Louis trade in 1970, *Ebony* directly took up the matter of the white press's racism, as "the questions continue[d]" regarding Allen: people ought to "question the questioners," the black journal protested. To question Allen "presupposes that Richie is guilty of all the bad things written about him. . . . Most of the people who hate or love Richie do so on the basis of what they've heard or what they've read in the white press." The whiteness of the press, in this equation, was as inescapably significant as the blackness of the ballplayer: "Richie Allen is black and he's proud and he has the gumption to be a proud, black man in one of America's most conservative sports. He sprouts a lush Afro that's anchored with long and wide sideburns"—"his natural and long wide sideburns were targets of white criticism in Philly for six years." After pointing out that Allen was known to read the Bible with some regularity, and that one of his infamous missed games had to do with his son's illness, *Ebony* argued that "Richie's stands on baseball's controversial issues and the fact he's black" were what marked him as a "radical." "Basically, he's just a 'regular brother,' hipped with all the jive-time routines of coolness, arrogance and a happy-go-lucky attitude."[50]

His were, indeed, the Afro and the pork chop sideburns with which *Sports Illustrated* would choose to illustrate its cover story on "Baseball in Turmoil" in the spring of the Allen-Flood-McCarver trade. Although Allen did hold out for more money from St. Louis, it is true, the "turmoil" had mostly to do, not with him—"I'll play anywhere: third, short, anywhere but Philadelphia"—but with Curt Flood, who had refused to report at all. The word "turmoil" itself, in fact, came from an exasperated Gussie Busch, the Cardinals owner: "I can't understand Curt Flood . . . or the Allen case . . . we are going through a hell of a turmoil right now." Though Busch was having his problems with the Steve Carlton contract, too, the turmoil seemed to him largely racial, apparently, and also connected to the broader social currents of 1960s America: "I can't understand what's happening here or on our campuses or in our great country."[51]

Flood's protest was, in fact, "racial," even if it was Allen who more looked the part in *SI*'s estimation. For one thing, Flood was not eager to go to Philadelphia, "the nation's northernmost southern city," as he put it, " . . . to succeed Richie Allen in the affections of that organization, its press and its catcalling missile-hurling audience."[52] And for another, as many have remarked over the years, given the bondage and emancipation motifs of the legalities involved, it was perhaps inevitable that a *black* ballplayer would be the first to challenge Major League Baseball's reserve clause and seek free agency. Flood himself begins his autobiography, *The Way It Is* (1970), with an epigraph from his brother Carl: "*Pharaoh, you better let them chillun go, honey.*" Later, noting that "the word *slavery* has arisen in connection with my lawsuit" (and conceding sardonically that "the condition of the major-league baseball player is closer to peonage than to slavery"), Flood appeals to the language of a 1949 court decision in the case of the Giants' Danny Gardella: "Only the totalitarian-minded will believe that high pay excuses virtual slavery."[53] The reserve clause/slavery analogy was neither casual nor incidental, in Flood's view: "Frederick Douglass was a Maryland slave who taught himself to read. 'If there is no struggle,' he once said, 'there is no progress. Those who profess to love freedom, and yet deprecate agitation, are men who want crops without plowing up the ground. . . . Power concedes nothing without a demand. It never did and never will.'"

To see the Curt Flood case in that light is to see its entire meaning.[54]

Elsewhere, Bob Gibson quoted Flood as likening a franchise owner's powers "to a plantation owner, allowing his players to play for him in the same way that the plantation owner allowed the sharecropper to work his land while at the same time keeping him deep in debt and constantly beholden." The slavery analogy was also clearly among the things that Gibson had in mind when, during the spring of the Flood-Allen trade, in dark jest he hung a sign above his locker, "Another happy family sold."[55]

Sportswriter Sandy Grady was tacitly acknowledging the racialized dimension of Allen's experience—not with the reserve clause, necessarily, but with the hatreds and disparagements of "The City of Brotherly Love"—when he wrote of St. Louis GM Bing Devine's having "emancipated" Allen. (In typical white press fashion, however, he also suggested that Devine had "emancipated" Philadelphia *from* Allen.)[56] And Allen, for his part, drew from the same lexicon: "You don't know how good it feels to get out of Philadelphia. They treat you like cattle. It was like a form of slavery. Once you step out of bounds they'll do everything possible to destroy your soul." "Skinner once said he could handle me," Allen later remarked, " . . . Well you don't handle human beings, you treat them. You handle horses."[57] Curt Flood might have said that; so might Frederick Douglass.

Allen headed into a slightly new era upon his departure from Philadelphia; fans never again vented the kind of hatred that Allen had seen in Connie Mack Stadium in the 1960s. Lee Vilensky's beautiful "Ode to Dick Allen" vividly captures the death grip that Allen and the white racists of Philadelphia had on one another during those years. Recalling his first ever visit to Connie Mack Stadium as an eight-year-old in 1965, Vilensky writes of the "batteries, bottles, paperweights" that were hurled in Allen's direction, and the "nigger, nigger, nigger" and "fuckin' nigger, nigger" that swirled around the stands.

> I guess it was about the seventh inning when Richie came up for his third at bat. I don't recall what he had done in his two previous at bats, but the chanting started anew. "Nigger." "Big mouth nigger." "Fuckin' nigger." "Go back to Africa, Nigger." Yes, someone actually yelled that. . . . [S]uddenly there was a crack of the bat as Richie Allen crushed a line drive over our heads. I turned around just in time to watch the ball bounce off a little eave above the top of the grandstand, then go completely out of the stadium. A shot of more than five hundred feet in distance. Not a high, arcing, majestic

home run, but a cold, vicious, angry drubbing of the ball. A loud slap. The power of it scared me. It made people quiet. Took all their air like a punch to the gut. As Richie touched home plate, the man next to me said to no one in particular: "Fuckin' nigger can hit."[58]

2. Boulder

Dick Allen and biographer Tim Whitaker stand on the diamond where decades before the Homestead Grays and the Pittsburgh Crawfords of the Negro Leagues had played, directly across from the vacant lot where Allen's boyhood home once stood. "Imaginary baseball," says Allen. "It's the purest version of the game."

> Allen tugs at his shirt sleeves and pushes his cowboy hat down on top of his head, mimicking the same routine he went through whenever he stepped to the plate against major league pitching. He takes a few practice swings with his imaginary bat.
>
> Between his feet, Allen has formed a pile of stones with his boots.
>
> He picks up one of the stones, tosses it in the air, and takes a swing with his imaginary bat.
>
> "As a kid, I used to stand right here," he tells me, "with a broomstick in my hands. When I played imaginary ball, I was always the Dodgers. I would bat stones and work my way through the Dodger lineup—Reese, Furillo, Snider, Hodges—waiting, just waiting, for *his* turn to come around."
>
> Allen pauses dramatically, then cups his hands to his mouth. "Now *battting*," he says, imitating the stadium echo of a public address announcer. "For the Brook-lyn Dod-gers . . . num-ber four-*tee-two* . . ."
>
> Dick Allen reaches down and picks up another pebble. "The Jackie Robinson stone," he says, tossing the pebble in the air and catching it, "was always the one that broke a window."[59]

When I was growing up there must have been millions of us who were right with Allen on this: that real players played real games in real stadiums was just a necessary evil so that the much purer game of imaginary baseball could take place, in lots and yards across North America, especially in the pregnant hours after dinner, as dusk edged into darkness. This scene describes much of my own childhood, though for me the Richie Allen stone was the window-breaker. (Well, our developing suburban neighborhood was still rural enough, the distances still great enough, that no windows were ever really in danger. Besides, I couldn't hit that well. But one time when I was about nine, pretending to be Juan Marichal, pitching off the side of our brick garage and mowing down the hitters 1–2–3 through the innings—a real gem—in the top of the eighth I couldn't resist giving up a home run to Richie Allen. *Num-ber fiff-teeen.* In my effort to recreate one of those awesome shots that cause opposing fielders immediately to slack their bodies and look skyward in resignation, I threw the ball too high against the wall, breaking the narrow pane of glass that ran the length of the garage just beneath the awning. Later, when my dad asked me if I knew anything about the broken window, I came *this close* to telling him Richie Allen did it.)

Why Allen would have idolized Jackie Robinson is pretty obvious, but how did *I* come to idolize *Allen?*

I had the 1965 Topps trading card of Allen—the Phillies flag in one corner, the little Rookie of the Year statuette in the other—but my real introduction to him was a hero-worshipping book for kids, *Great Rookies of the Major Leagues* by Jim Brosnan. The chapter on Allen was enough to make a huge impression on an eight-year-old, but it was not exactly calculated to do so: for example, it included Philadelphia owner Bob Carpenter's judgment, "Allen was the worst-looking infielder I ever saw. I thought he'd be killed by a ground ball." This piece of baseball hagiography also featured a four-panel sequence of photographs depicting Allen letting a grounder pass between his legs. (The caption reads, "Allen's uncertain fielding sometimes offsets his great hitting. Here he reaches for a sharp grounder, searches for the ball and then turns to watch it roll into the outfield. A Braves runner . . . passes Allen to score on the play.")[60]

When I was given the book as a gift (in 1966, I believe—the year of its publication), I adopted Allen as my hero at once. It may have been because I was enthralled by his appearance: the chapter itself goes into great detail on his powerful physique, and there is nothing in the photos of Roy Sievers, Herb Score, Frank Robinson, Tom Tresh, or Pete Rose that begins to compare with the pure poetry of form in some of the Allen photos—I see it this way even still. Or, it may have been because I identified with his much-discussed weakness as a fielder, and took special heart in the story of a player who was able to overcome his own limitations. If I were going to become a major leaguer (and who could doubt it?), my own path to glory would surely be strewn with similar obstacles, not to mention the qualms and denunciations of people like Bob Carpenter. Or it may have been that, as the fat kid with thick glasses whom everyone made fun of, I gravitated naturally toward the one figure in the book who was clearly being picked on. ("He . . . turns to watch it roll into the outfield." It might have been a few more years before I could articulate this, but even at age eight I felt some version of *hey, what the fuck, man?*) Within two years—1968—when I was three seasons into my Richie Allen worship and Allen himself was getting more and more press for his off-field behavior, I understood exactly what it was that I was seeing. This was my education in U.S. race relations.

In a 1970s routine about visiting Africa, Richard Pryor talks about meeting people who are "so black" that it makes you want to say—and here he drops his voice to an awed whisper—"*BLACK.*" My neighborhood growing up was a lot like that, except in white. It was not the militant whiteness of South Boston (or Connie Mack Stadium); it was not even the least bit self-conscious. On the contrary, the neighborhood was *so* white as to suggest and naturalize the idea that people of color did not exist at all. Which is just to say, whatever I learned about racialized relations before going away to college in 1977, I certainly did not learn by firsthand encounters. (Nearby Denver, ironically, was the AAA locale where the Minnesota Twins banished black players as punishment for dating white women.[61])

There is a longer-term history that is relevant here, because I did grow up in a liberal household in which civil rights sympathies were never in question. Since my father is a New York Jew, naturally we used to listen to Mahalia Jackson every year when we decorated the Christmas tree. He had grown up in the Bronx in the 1930s, and at age thirteen, the year he was *not* bar mitzvahed, he somehow discovered Harlem and jazz. Though his was probably not the kind of childhood that encouraged much fellow feeling with "the *shvartzes*" (to judge from my grandmother's social outlook), from those early jam sessions onward, his glimpses of Harlem and his captivation by the black aesthetic of the jazz scene translated into a very particular social sensibility—a whole way of perceiving and understanding the human virtues and various political categories like "decency." This he tried to pass on to us, along with an appreciation for Louis Armstrong. My mother, on the other hand, is a white Ohio Methodist, and her Tipp City upbringing could not have been much less white—or "*WHITE*"—than my own. But as theirs was what was called a "mixed marriage," both of my parents had some experience with prejudice—their parents', for example.

And so, with the Civil Rights movement rumbling in the distance throughout my childhood, and my parents' attention to questions of "difference" and justice remaining fairly salient, racial matters were not as far removed from my immediate experience as the demographics of my town would imply. I remember my father trying to explain the logic of King's "passive resistance" to me at a time when, as a political philosopher, I was probably too young for anything beyond "impulsive vengeance." My sisters and I got the liberal lecture on the stupidities of prejudice on the ride to Denver to see *Guess Who's Coming to Dinner.* A bit later, it became a point of bedrock principle in our household that of course one would support the Broncos' Marlin Briscoe in his bid to become the NFL's first black quarterback. ("He's not all that good," my best friend's father said, "he's just all that *black*." The opinion was offered up too gruffly not to be suspect, even to a ten-year-old.)

But what strikes me in retrospect is how *indirect* my political education was, for the most part. Straight talk like the *Guess Who's Coming to Dinner* lecture was the exception, not the norm, as was my fourth-grade teacher Miss Harms' very interesting prediction of racial retribution in the wake of the King assassination. When I think closely, I recognize that at the time I did not actually see much—or *any*—of the Civil Rights imagery that now occupies my "memory" of the era—Bull Connor's German Shepherds and fire hoses, the flames at Ole Miss, even the "I Have a Dream" speech. The balcony of that Memphis hotel I think I did see for myself on TV in 1968; but most of the rest of it is later documentary footage, not actual memory.

My teaching has been animated by Stuart Hall's dictum that social subjects "are unable to speak, to act in one way or another, until they have been positioned by the work that culture does." It is *culture* above all that outfits us to behave politically in certain ways and not in others—culture is politics by other means.[62] But rarely have I asked the question: If I was just coming to consciousness during the Civil Rights years, what was I learning and how was I taking it in? America's liberal culture was undoubtedly teaching a lot, though it may not always have been teaching liberality. The most potent message of *Guess Who's Coming to Dinner,* for instance, does not involve our common humanity across the color line, but rather a natural submission to the authority of the Great White Father (in this case Spencer Tracy): ultimately nobody can make a move without his approval. Shows like *Love American Style* and *Barefoot in the Park* taught that black is indeed beautiful—as long as it's almost white. The affable Johnny Carson taught that candor is hip and that racist stereotypes can be funny—as when he joked that there could never be a black quarterback because there were not seven white guys who would turn their backs on him at the line of scrimmage, "especially during a night game."

On the other hand, anti-authoritarianism was occupying an increasingly significant place in the dominant culture—I think of *Cat Ballou, Bonnie and Clyde, Butch Cassidy and the Sundance Kid, Easy Rider,* and a host of other films from my childhood in which bad guys were the good guys and good guys were the bad guys. Perhaps this strain in the culture outfitted me with a useful skepticism toward the media's own claims regarding the badness of the black radical; perhaps it was this strain that equipped me to sympathize with a bad boy like Richie Allen, doing battle with "the man" in the white front office and the white press. How far is it from the unorthodox authoritarianism of *The Mod Squad* to the unorthodox *anti-*

authoritarianism—consciously "raced" or not—of Richie Allen, Cookie Gilchrist, the Smothers Brothers, Jim Bouton?

During these years—confusing enough even for many adults, I am sure—baseball addressed my childhood confusions in a pre-verbal but nonetheless poetic and incandescent language. (By "baseball," I mean the whole cosmos—the games themselves, the lineups, the sports page, the fan reactions, the hypnotizing photographs, the piles of adoring books, the Topps cards, the on- and off-field lore in *Sport, Sporting News, Sports Illustrated*.) "I can't say it was because of the bombs and the Bull Connors that black players tore up the National League in 1963," writes Hank Aaron, "but I can't say it wasn't either."[63] On a particularly fierce streak in the summer of 1968, Bob Gibson, too, writes: "I really can't say, in retrospect, whether Robert Kennedy's assassination is what got me going or not. Without a doubt, it was an angry point in American history for black people—Dr. King's killing had jolted me; Kennedy's infuriated me—and without a doubt, I pitched better angry. I suspect that the control of my slider had more to do with it than anything, but I can't completely dismiss the fact that nobody gave me any shit whatsoever for about two months after Bobby Kennedy died."[64]

Aaron and Gibson might rightly have claimed the whole decade for black dominance, not just the isolated moments of 1963 and 1968. (Take the offensive statistic for total bases, the most dramatic instance: from 1960 to 1969 white players made it into the National League's top three exactly *once*—Pete Rose was third in 1968. Aaron, Banks, Mays, Cepeda, Robinson, Pinson, Allen, Williams, Alou, Clemente, Brock, McCovey, and Perez account for the other twenty-nine top-three finishes.[65]) But in any case, from the suburban picture window of Boulder, Colorado, the ball field and The Movement *read* as being intimately connected. "Baseball was socially relevant," wrote Curt Flood, "and so was my rebellion against it."[66] This is a lesson I imbibed fundamentally but wordlessly between 1966 and 1969. The hateful, swirling "nigger, nigger, nigger" that Lee Vilensky heard in Connie Mack Stadium, and Richie Allen's cold, angry drubbing of the ball in response, was a social drama that was integral, if only implicitly so, to the game-within-the-game of 1960s baseball as I watched it on *Game of the Week* every Saturday.

For one thing, while Gibson, Aaron, Allen, and others may have been playing "angry," they looked to me, above all else, to be simply *serious;* and the regular access that baseball afforded to African American seriousness was no small thing. The seriousness of King and the historic moment came across in the chatter and hum of the adult world around me and in headlines to stories that I knew vaguely about but did not exactly read. People like Sidney Poitier and Diahann Carroll also made an impression. But baseball occupied my mind 162 days of the year; and unique among the major sports, baseball games unfolded at a contemplative pace that was well-suited to conveying the force of an athlete's character—neither concealing it behind the armor of the NFL nor blurring it in the flying speed of the NBA.

"Quiet dignity" is almost certainly a racist construction—or at least a racialized one—as the phrase never appears in connection with white people, I notice; and it probably dates from a period when "quiet," from Negroes, was especially prized in U.S. culture. But nonetheless, something like "quiet dignity" *is* a part of what the 1.5 generation of black stars communicated to me, at once a contrast and an antidote to the vapid dronings-on of play-by-play announcers like Curt Gowdy and Joe Garagiola; and the "dignity" in the equation tended to keep their "quiet" from coming across as anything like accommodation. The intensity of concentration—the intensity of *mind*—evident in the expressions and small rituals of Gibson on the mound, Flood or Robinson at the plate, silently but decisively dismantled any facile cracker assertions about the brutish capacities of "the Negro." That Solly Hemus or the white fans in various Sally League locations had either failed to acknowledge this, or, perhaps, had not allowed themselves to see it in the first place, just goes to show how desperate they were.

But if baseball held the power to dislodge the slanders of racism, so did it have a tendency to generate some slanders of its own—the denigrating trope of the black athlete's "natural gift" is only one among many. "Hanging around baseball, as I have been doing," wrote Donald Hall in the 1970s, "I don't see racism in management, in coaching, or in the front office. Reading the newspapers of Detroit and Chicago and Boston and New York, I see it every day." The list of the "Most Unpopular Sports Figures, in the last decade or two," he points out, "is largely black"—a younger Muhammad Ali, Duane Thomas, Dick Allen, Alex Johnson.[67]

This is where Allen was so significant to me, not just as a personal idol but as a social emblem: the dissonance between what I felt about Allen and what the press reported about him became so taut as to snap my youthful ingenuousness, because to me Allen was clearly a figure of dignity, too, no less than Gibson or Aaron or Brock or Clemente. I was too young by about one season to catch and appreciate the Frank Thomas incident and Allen's initial falling-out with the press; but it was a stunning and deflating lesson to me when, in 1967, the media so openly questioned Allen's "claim" to have injured his hand while pushing his car, and when in 1968 and 1969, they so openly denounced him—not just as an outlier (on the order, say, of Jay Johnstone)—but as someone uncontrolled and uncontrollable, a kind of *pre-criminal,* when he missed a plane to St. Louis or showed up late to Shea. In his paean to Allen, "Letters in the Dirt," folksinger Chuck Brodsky—another white kid of almost exactly my vintage—reflects upon the racial dimension, as he saw it, in Allen's treatment by the fans and by the press: "He stood a bit outside the lines which / made him fair game for those times / Richie Allen never kissed / a white man's ass."[68] This is precisely the conclusion I came to myself, sometime around the age of ten.

Hindsight, of course, clarifies some things but hopelessly clouds others. Knowing what I now do about the 1960s, about racism, about the Movement, and about Allen himself, can I recover with any certainty the Richie Allen who occupied my imagination in 1970, when the Cardinals' road schedule and my family's summer vacation intersected for a moment at a day game in San Diego? Can I see my young self any more clearly than I see Allen? Allen would not answer, or even look up, when I called out to him from behind the Cardinal dugout after infield practice, but I had not expected it to go any differently. I bore him no grudge for ignoring me, nor did it diminish in the least the magic of seeing him in person. Did I see the situation as "racial?" Did I see myself *white* standing there—another white fan, perhaps, from Allen's point of view, who might meet his glance with an insult or an AA battery—another white boy who had been taught by some jeering peckerwood how to boo? I believe I did, because for one thing, this was one of the very first times I had ever addressed an African American directly; it is doubtful that I was unaware of my whiteness and his blackness, notwithstanding the era's liberal bromides on the virtue of being colorblind. And for another thing, even if I did not know his precise thinking on "Whitey's ways," I had figured out some things by watching Allen and his career from afar. I understood at least dimly the burden in our exchange; and, rightly or not, in an inarticulate way I felt his rebuff to concern not me, exactly, but the larger web of relationships ensnaring us both. I had entered history, in other words, and this was perhaps the first time in my eleven years that I was aware of it. At least it seems so to me now. (See figures 1.1 and 1.2.)

After the '60s crested and began to recede, the culture was hungry for emblems of reconciliation; the Richie Allen narrative was conveniently pressed into service. Following his bitter years in Philadelphia, and two years of marked underappreciation in St. Louis and Los Angeles, Allen landed in a brief dream sequence with the Chicago White Sox. Not only did he put up the kind of numbers in 1972 that the best of his early years had promised (.308, 37 HR, 113 RBI), but in Comiskey Park he found a welcoming and comfortable home. The difference, according to Allen, was White Sox manager Chuck Tanner: "He's from home and he's like a brother." (The two knew each other from the old days in Pennsylvania— Tanner's hometown of New Castle is about seven miles from Allen's Wampum—and they often called each other "Homey," which perhaps hints at Allen's intended meaning in the phrase "like a brother.") Tanner thought

1.1 Allen heads for the dugout after infield practice, ignoring my calls from the stands. Old habits die hard: note that Allen wears a batting helmet in the field, even far removed from the projectiles of Connie Mack Stadium. Photo: Jerry Jacobson

1.2 "Dick Allen and me in San Diego, summer 1970. Allen is the distant figure directly above my left hand. The glasses make me look like Pirate pitcher Bob Veale, don't you think?" Photo: Jerry Jacobson

Allen "not only the best player in the American League, but the best in the majors . . . When he's through with the White Sox, he's going to walk right into the Hall of Fame."[69] Tanner thought that Chicagoans ought to build a monument to Dick Allen.

The manager's appreciation for Allen transcended baseball by a long way. "He has a magnetism," said Tanner, "—like Clark Gable, say, or Marilyn Monroe."[70] This is an astonishing thing to say: daring to compare the appeal of a black man to the enchantment of these white icons—and one of them a beauty queen at that—strikes me as more radical in its way than anything Allen ever thought up in defiance of Whitey. This is a world, after all, where black and white *ballplayers* are rarely compared: even in the cosmos of sports talk today, Griffey might remind people of Mays, for instance, but certainly not of Mantle; and McGwire is said to have hit "with Frank Howard-type power." Orval Faubus could do no better in segregating our common conceptions of who is "like" whom; and yet Tanner spotted Dick Allen's similarities to Marilyn Monroe. We probably ought to build a monument to *him*.

From Allen's White Sox years onward, the baseball establishment fell in love with the story of its own acceptance of Allen, even if it did not quite learn to love the ballplayer himself as Chuck Tanner did. (He never did come near the Hall of Fame, for instance.) But Allen "is a man who marches to his own wry drummer," reported *Sports Illustrated* in 1972. "On the day his teammates were going out on strike, Allen signed his 1972 contract."[71] "His own wry drummer" is a far cry from the portrait of the trouble-making militant that had predominated in the coverage of Allen as a Philly. After Chicago, the press began to find something lovably quirky in Allen's history of unorthodoxies; but more important, the press seemed to find something laudable in its own warming up to Allen: it was as if, in embracing Allen, the white sports establishment could at once prove and celebrate just how far it had come. "He wrote dismissive notes to his general manager in the base-path dirt with his foot!" commented *Sports Illustrated* in tones of mock scandal in 1973. "What kind of man would do a thing like that? And why didn't anybody think of it before?"[72] Now Allen was "a team player who has bounced around . . . a mentor to the young, a seasoned veteran whom managements have seen as a discipline problem. The more you learn about Allen from outside sources," remarked *Sports Illustrated*, "the more he swims before you." Even the press's conventional disregard for Allen's point of view began to shift: as *SI* now described it, when Allen entered pro ball, "First thing, his name got changed . . . he did not care to be issued a new name by an organization."[73] Dick "Don't Call Me Richie" Allen suddenly seemed fairly reasonable.

America's favorite Dick Allen story is the one about how he got a standing ovation when he returned to the Phillies in 1975. Although he found himself "wondering where all the brothers had gone" as he looked around the Phillies' new, suburban ballpark, evidently Allen is fond of this one, too. "Things had changed," he wrote, " . . . blacks were beginning to run the city. In the old days, I represented a threat to white people in Philadelphia. I wore my hair in an Afro. I said what was on my mind. I didn't take shit. But now, like the rest of the country, Philadelphia had come around to accepting that things had changed and were going to keep changing, like it or not."[74] The movement, had, after all, accomplished some things; the logic and the accepted idioms of American race consciousness had shifted significantly; the terms of sports celebrity, too, had changed, unorthodoxy taking its place among the new orthodoxies—Jim Bouton, Joe Namath, Rosey Grier, Steve Carlton, Bill Lee. Perhaps Dick Allen had merely been a few years ahead of the curve, and there was no depth to the tragedy of his Philadelphia story after all. Many found it comforting to think so.

And yet the reconciliation narrative—the Allen/Philadelphia story, and the national healing for which it is an implied allegory—cannot plow under all the chicken bones, the bolts, and the batteries that rained onto the field in those earlier years in Philadelphia, nor can it wipe from memory Allen's whimsical sorrow songs, the letters in the dirt. Perhaps this is why the player who had integrated professional baseball in Orval Faubus' Arkansas and who had later distinguished himself as one of the most powerful hitters in the Major Leagues, expressed elation in 1987—as if finally receiving affirmation—when aging Negro star Cool Papa Bell pronounced that he indeed would have had what it takes to make it in the Negro Leagues. Inverting the conventional storyline of baseball aspiration and fulfillment, a buoyant Allen exclaimed, "He said I could have been one of them. . . . He said I had power and I could run, the two most important requirements in Negro League baseball." Even he recognized the irony in his being "a big leaguer who felt like he lost out because he never got a chance to play in the Negro Leagues."[75] This is not to paint Allen as a victim of desegregation. But his implied daydream about being "one of them," a Negro League star, does say a bit about the operations of race in the game, even two decades after Jackie Robinson had broken down the color barrier. "People said there was one set of rules for me and another for the rest of the team," Allen once said, reflecting on his image as the Phillies' troublemaker. "When I was coming up, black players couldn't stay in the same hotel or eat in the same places as whites. Two sets of rules? Baseball set the tone."[76] This is the political lesson that Allen's career had been teaching all along: desegregation did not come off as advertised.

Notes

1. Dick Allen and Tim Whitaker, *Crash: The Life and Times of Dick Allen* (New York: Ticknor and Fields, 1989), xvii; "Dick Allen," in BaseballLibrary.Com/baseballlibrary/ballplayers/A/Allen_Dick.stm; *Sports Illustrated,* Sept. 10, 1973, 105; William Kashatus, *September Swoon: Richie Allen, the '64 Phillies, and Racial Integration* (University Park: Pennsylvania State University Press, 2004), 191.

2. "Dick Allen," in BasballLibrary.Com; *Sports Illustrated,* March 23, 1970; June 12, 1972.

3. John Thorn, Pete Palmer, Michael Gershman, *Total Baseball: The Official Encyclopedia of Major League Baseball* [Seventh Edition] (Kingston, NY: Total Sports, 2001), 158.

4. Hank Aaron with Lonnie Wheeler, *I Had a Hammer: The Hank Aaron Story* (New York: HarperCollins, 1991), 334–335.

5. Bob Gibson with Lonnie Wheeler, *Stranger to the Game: The Autobiography of Bob Gibson* (New York: Viking, 1994), 224.

6. Willie Stargell and Tom Bird, *Willie Stargell, an Autobiography* (New York: Harper & Row, 1984), 168.

7. *New York Times Book Review,* April 23, 1989, Sec. 7, 36–37.

8. *Ebony,* Oct. 1972, 192.

9. Allen and Whitaker, *Crash,* 186.

10. Roger Angell, "Distance" [1980], in *Game Time* (New York: Harcourt, 2003), 208.

11. Allen and Whitaker, *Crash,* 53.

12. David Wolf, "Let's Everybody Boo Rich Allen," *Life,* Aug. 22, 1969, 50. Folksinger Chuck Brodsky's "Letters in the Dirt" is a paean to Allen and his infield writing. *Baseball Ballads,* chuckbrodsky.com, 2002.

13. Aaron and Wheeler, *I Had a Hammer,* 209. See also Jules Tygiel, "Black Ball: The Integrated Game," in *Extra Bases: Reflections on Jackie Robinson, Race, and Baseball History* (Lincoln: University of Nebraska/Bison, 2002), 104–117. Tygiel's *Baseball's Great Experiment: Jackie Robinson and His Legacy* [1983] (New York: Oxford University Press, 1997) remains the standard in the field on the early period of integrated ball.

14. David Halberstam, *October '64* (New York: Fawcett, 1994), 113.

15. Frank Robinson and Barry Stanback, *Extra Innings* (New York: McGraw-Hill, 1988), 23, 26.

16. Donald Hall with Dock Ellis, *Dock Ellis in the Country of Baseball* (New York: Simon and Schuster, 1976), 123, 128.

17. Halberstam, *October '64,* 203; Gibson and Wheeler, *Stranger to the Game,* 58.

18. Aaron and Wheeler, *I Had a Hammer,* 55, 56.

19. Aaron and Wheeler, *I Had a Hammer,* 79.

20. John Roseboro with Bill Libby, *Glory Days with the Dodgers and Other Days with Others* (New York: Atheneum, 1978), 54–55; Felipe Alou with Herm Weiskopf, *My Life and Baseball* (Waco, TX: Word, 1967), 29. (Even

so, writing in 1967 the highly conservative Alou averred that the urban uprisings were inspired by communist agitators, 103.)

21. Curt Flood with Richard Carter, *The Way It Is* (New York: Trident, 1971), 38; Samuel Regalado, *Viva Baseball! Latin Major Leaguers and Their Special Hunger* (Urbana: University of Illinois Press, 1998), 66, 67.

22. Gibson and Wheeler, *Stranger to the Game,* 52–53; Howard Bryant, *Shut Out: A Story of Race and Baseball in Boston* (New York: Routledge, 2002), 92; Hall and Ellis, *Dock Ellis in the Country of Baseball,* 134; Orlando Cepeda with Herb Fagen, *Baby Bull: From Hardball to Hard Time and Back* (Dallas: Taylor Publishing, 1998), 74–75; Kashatus, *September Swoon,* 113; Regalado, *Viva Baseball!,* 84–87.

23. Halberstam, *October '64,* 151.

24. Allen and Whitaker, *Crash,* 11–14; Kashatus, *September Swoon,* 45.

25. *Ebony,* July, 1970, 90.

26. Quoted in *Sports Illustrated,* Sept. 10, 1973, 111.

27. Bruce Kuklick, *To Everything a Season: Shibe Park and Urban Philadelphia, 1909–1976* (Princeton, NJ: Princeton University Press, 1991), 145–148; Kashatus, *September Swoon,* 9–37; Bryant, *Shut Out,* 5; David Faulkner, *Great Time Coming: The Life of Jackie Robinson from Baseball to Birmingham* (New York: Simon and Schuster, 1995), 163–164; Tom McGrath, "Color Me Badd," *The Fan,* September, 1996, 39.

28. Gerald Early, *This Is Where I Came In: Black America in the 1960s* (Lincoln: University of Nebraska/Bison, 2003), 67.

29. Kuklick, *To Everything a Season,* 155–156, 158; Early, *This Is Where I Came In,* 70–71.

30. Kuklick, *To Everything a Season,* 155–156; Early, *This Is Where I Came In,* 75–89; Kashatus, *September Swoon,* 76–80, 111–113.

31. *Sports Illustrated,* June 1, 1970, 40; Kashatus, *September Swoon,* 54.

32. *Sports Illustrated,* Sept. 10, 1973, 111; Kashatus, *September Swoon,* 82. See also William Kashatus, "Dick Allen, the Phillies, and Racism," *Nine,* Fall 2000, 151. On Allen's general mistreatment by the press, see Craig Wright, "Dick Allen: Another View" (originally published in SABR magazine), posted at www.expressfan.com/dickallenhof/docs/defense.pdf.

33. Kashatus, *September Swoon,* 80.

34. Allen and Whitaker, *Crash,* 4.

35. See "The Thomas Incident, July 1965" in Kashatus, "Dick Allen, the Phillies, and Racism," and Kashatus, *September Swoon,* 149–157; *Sports Illustrated,* Sept 10, 1973, 111; Allen and Whitaker, *Crash,* 1–10.

36. Allen and Whitaker, *Crash,* 58–59, 10; Leonard Schechter, "Richie Allen and the Use of Power," *Sport,* July, 1967, 66.

37. *Newsweek,* July 8, 1968, 52; *Sports Illustrated,* Sept. 10, 1973, 111; Kashatus, *September Swoon,* 155–156.

38. Kashatus, *September Swoon,* 172.

39. Don Malcolm, "The Angry Negro Problem," *Baseball Primer: Baseball for the Thinking Fan,* www.baseballprimer.com/articles/malcolm_2001–03–05_0.shtml.

40. Kashatus, *September Swoon,* 160.

41. *Newsweek,* July 8, 1968, 52.

42. *Sports Illustrated,* Sept. 10, 1973, 107.

43. Jim Bouton, *Ball Four* [1970] (New York: Wiley, 1990), 393; Kashatus, *September Swoon,* 189.

44. Bouton, *Ball Four,* ix.

45. This is the Richie Allen canon. See Allen and Whitaker, *Crash,* and Kashatus, *September Swoon* (Mauch quoted 166). *New York Times,* Aug. 23, 1968, 79; July 3, 1969, 35.

46. "Richie Allen is Not All Bad Boy," *New York Times,* May 18, 1969; *Ebony,* July 1970, 92.

47. Kashatus, *September Swoon,* 171; *New York Times,* "Sports of the Times," June 25, 1968; *Newsweek,* May 19, 1975, 58; *Newsweek,* Aug. 21, 1972, 83; *Sports Illustrated,* March 23, 1970, 18; April 29, 1974, 19; July 19, 1999, 19.

48. Bill Conlin, "Richie Is Beautiful. He Don't Give a Damn for Nobody," *Jock,* January 1970, 88; *Sports Illustrated,* May 19, 1975, 59.

49. *Afro-American,* July 13, 1968, 13.

50. *Ebony,* July, 1970, 89, 90, 92, 93.

51. *Sports Illustrated,* March 23, 1970, 21.

52. Flood and Carter, *The Way It Is,* 188.

53. Flood and Carter, *The Way It Is,* 139.

54. Flood and Carter, *The Way It Is,* 206; Halberstam, *October '64,* 364.

55. Gibson and Wheeler, *Stranger to the Game,* 219; *Sports Illustrated,* March 23, 1970, 22.

56. Kuklick, *To Everything a Season,* 163.

57. See "Oppositional Identity" in Kashatus, "Dick Allen, the Phillies, and Racism"; *Newsweek,* Aug. 21, 1972, 84.

58. Lee Vilensky, "Ode to Dick Allen," *Elysian Fields Quarterly: The Baseball Review,* Vol. 20, number 3, www.efqreview.com/NewFiles/v20n3/dustofthefields-two.html.

59. Allen and Whitaker, *Crash,* 40.

60. Jim Brosnan, *Great Rookies of the Major Leagues* (New York: Random House, 1966), 165–167.

61. Roseboro and Libby, *Glory Days with the Dodgers,* 232.

62. Stuart Hall, "Subjects in History: Making Diasporic Identities," in Wahneema Lubiano, ed., *The House that Race Built* (New York: Vintage, 1998), 291.

63. Aaron and Wheeler, *I Had a Hammer,* 231.

64. Gibson and Wheeler, *Stranger to the Game,* 188.

65. Thorn, Palmer, and Gershman, *Total Baseball,* 2204–2222.

66. Flood and Carter, *The Way It Is,* 16.

67. Hall and Ellis, *Dock Ellis in the Country of Baseball,* 177.

68. Brodsky "Letters in the Dirt," *The Baseball Ballads* (Weaverville, NC: chuckbrodsky.com, 2002), track 5.

69. *Sports Illustrated,* June 5, 1972, 64.

70. *Sports Illustrated,* April 29, 1974, 20.

71. *Sports Illustrated,* June 5, 1972, 64.

72. *Sports Illustrated,* Sept. 10, 1973, 107.

73. *Sports Illustrated*, Sept. 10, 1973, 108, 110.
74. Allen and Whitaker, *Crash*, 159–160.
75. Allen and Whitaker, *Crash*, 85.
76. *Sports Illustrated*, July 19, 1993, 84.

TWO

In Sports the Best Man Wins

How Joe Louis Whupped Jim Crow

Theresa E. Runstedtler

A single column cannot begin to describe the feeling of the man of color who watches a brown-skinned boy like Joe Louis, from Alabama, the most backward State in the Union, fight his way up from the coal mine and the cotton field through strength of his body and mind.

—*Ted Benson,* Sunday Worker,
reprinted in Pittsburgh Courier, *February 29, 1936*

American Hero or Race Man?

On June 22, 1938, when Joe Louis, the Brown Bomber, won a decisive, first-round knockout in his revenge match against Nazi-promoted Max Schmeling, white America embraced the black heavyweight champion as a national hero. Amid increasing reports of Hitler's imperialistic aggression and persecution of the Jews, the mainstream white press highlighted the bout's worldwide implications, claiming Louis's triumph as an American victory in the larger fight against fascism. As Heywood Broun of the *New York World-Telegram* mused, "One hundred years from now some historian may theorize, in a footnote at least, that the decline of Nazi prestige began with the left hook of a former unskilled autoworker."[1] Inspiring more than just a mere footnote, Louis's 1938 win expanded into a celebrated epic of American patriotism and democracy. Brimming with postwar confidence in 1947, Louis's close friend, Frank Sinatra, declared: "If I were the government official responsible for the job of making the rest of the world understand our national character and the ideals that motivate us, I would certainly make use of the case history of Joe Louis."[2]

However well-known the narrative of Louis as the quintessential U.S. citizen became, another story, one that white America and history have overlooked, meant more to African Americans in the 1930s: Joe Louis as Race Man. That Louis earned the customary title of "Race Man" was a mark of high distinction, since this phrase had long been reserved for men who best exemplified racial progress and leadership in areas like business, academics, and politics.[3] Writing for the *New Masses* in 1938, a skeptical Richard Wright derided the Louis-Schmeling fight as "a colorful puppet show, one of the greatest dramas of make-believe ever witnessed in America."[4] For Wright, the real significance of Louis lay not in his dubious status as a national hero, but in his ability to inspire the black masses. Three years earlier, in September 1935, when Louis garnered a swift victory over Jewish American Max Baer in front of 90,000 fans at Yankee Stadium, Wright described the "religious feeling in the air" on Chicago's South Side, where over twenty thousand "Negroes poured out of beer taverns, pool rooms, barber shops, rooming houses and dingy flats and flooded the streets." With Louis's win over Baer "*something* had ripped loose, exploded," claimed Wright, allowing "four centuries of oppression, of frustrated hopes, of black bitterness" to rise to the surface. Louis was "a consciously-felt symbol . . . the concentrated essence of black triumph over white."[5]

Wright was certainly not alone in recognizing Louis's influence as the period's iconic New Negro. African Americans' limited access to legal and political channels of protest meant that sports, and in particular boxing, became one of the preeminent mass media through which they articulated their conflict with the racial status quo. Until 1947, when Jackie Robinson joined baseball's Major League, boxing was the only professional sport that allowed whites and blacks to compete in the same arena. Moreover, in this individual sport of hand-to-hand combat, fighters emerged as contested symbols of race, manhood, and nation among the American masses. By 1933 Louis was already a fixture in the black press, supplying African Americans with the cultural ammunition to critique their persistent lack of democratic rights and dignity. Louis graced the front page of the *Chicago Defender* more times than any other black figure during the

Depression, including Ethiopian emperor Haile Selassie.[6] Not only did his life story become the focal point of sports and human-interest sections in various weekly newspapers, but his pugilistic exploits sparked larger debates about black representation as editorialists evaluated his role in racial advancement.

As the dawn of the New Negro era symbolized the race's passage into "the sunlight of real manhood," Louis's well-documented whupping of Jim Crow provided a public outlet for diverse expressions of black struggle across the socioeconomic and political spectrum.[7] The term "New Negro," meaning a progressive, politically savvy African American, initially emerged from the turn-of-the-century writings of Booker T. Washington.[8] However, black participation in World War I in tandem with the Great Migration of African Americans to northern cities like New York and Chicago had a radicalizing effect, infusing the New Negro movement with a heightened sense of militancy, urgency, and racial pride. In revisiting the Harlem Renaissance, historians have begun to expand on its traditional interpretation as a middle-class, bourgeois literary movement to uncover the various facets of New Negro activism from black theater companies to leftist internationalism.[9] The sport of boxing offered yet another arena in which New Negroes could express their racial militancy, albeit vicariously, through the hard punches and prosperous lifestyle of men like Joe Louis. Indeed, the rising figure of Joe Louis gave the masculine New Negro ideal unprecedented, mass appeal.

A detailed analysis of Louis's coming of age in his first major professional fight against Mussolini's darling, Primo Carnera, on the eve of the 1935 Italo-Ethiopian conflict, capped off with a suggestive re-reading of his well-known loss to Max Schmeling in 1936, not only uncovers how discussions of black manhood dominated both domestic and diasporic resistance strategies, but also helps to explain the historical emergence of the male sports celebrity as an integral symbol of black success in the twentieth century.[10] The Louis-Carnera match takes center stage, since most accounts have tended to downplay its significance as a matter of coincidental timing in which foreign affairs overlapped with box-office promotion. However, a close examination of the riotous celebrations Louis inspired, along with his mass representation in the black and leftist presses, photographs, fight films, and blues songs, reveals that African Americans actively fashioned him as a Race Man, using him to fight racism and fascism on two fronts—at home and abroad.[11] Taken from this vantage point, the Louis story obliges historians to expand their understandings of the New Negro's popular dimensions as a cultural conduit through which African Americans of the 1930s continued to address the interlocking questions of race, gender, nation, and class.

Biography of a Race

Triumphant tales of the young boxer's rise to fistic fame filled the pages of black and young communist publications, along with mass-circulated biographies. Even though each had a differing agenda, they all spun his life story into a kind of utopian biography of the race. While the sympathetic white writer Edward Van Every engaged in hyperbole when he claimed the boxer's life made "story book tales of fight heroes seem tame," the popular depictions of Louis's struggles from southern sharecropper to northern migrant to industrial worker to successful boxer must have resonated with the experiences of many of his African American fans.[12] Providing a mythical link that connected an oppressive black rural "past" with the promise of a prosperous urban future, the young boxer's personal story defied regional, class, and even generational boundaries to offer an accessible, yet decidedly masculine vision of collective progress.

According to the composite story that emerged in the black press, Joe Louis Barrow was born on May 13, 1914, in Lafayette, Alabama, the seventh of eight children in a sharecropping family. In 1926, Louis and his kin joined the Great Migration to the North, settling in one of Detroit's black ghettos. Soon after their arrival, twelve-year-old Louis developed his young muscles in a part-time job delivering ice to the city's wealthier citizens. Trained in cabinetry at the Bronson Vocational School, Louis later worked at the Ford plant right up until he joined the ranks of professional boxing.[13] As the papers revealed, Louis had honed his fighting skills at Detroit's Brewster Recreation Center during his teenage years. By the time he won the national Amateur Athletic Union light heavyweight championship in April 1934, the youthful pugilist had participated in fifty-four bouts, winning forty-three of them by knockout, thereby garnering the support of the African American management team of John Roxborough, Julian Black, and Jack Blackburn. Writers bragged that at twenty-one, Louis was already two hundred pounds, standing six feet, one and a half inches tall, with fifteen-inch biceps.[14] Showcasing his muscular physique, groomed hair, and boyish smile, the black press helped mold him into a statue of strength and charm that appealed to men, women, and children.

Even the *Young Worker,* an interracial communist organ, included frequent reports on Louis that tended to cast him as an exemplary African American worker. As one journalist related, "He was born in the slums of Birmingham, Ala. When only a mere lad, he carried cakes of ice to eke out a living. He worked in King Henry Ford's plant in Detroit. Always on the fringe of starvation, he learned how to struggle for self-preservation." Imbuing Louis with a black labor consciousness, the writer continued, "He can see that as a worker, he will end up just where he started from, in the slums, because of the widespread discrimination that is practiced against his race."[15] Portraying him as an everyday man with "a chance to cash in on his skillful dukes," the *Young Worker* used Louis to not only advance a positive image of African Americans to white youth, but also to show black workers that they did not have to give up their race heroes to join the communist ranks. White and black laborers both could rally around this male protagonist.

By the time Louis entered the ring against Primo Carnera in June 1935, his humble beginnings and subsequent climb to international success had taken on an epic quality, as sympathetic journalists fashioned his biography into the ultimate story of racial and economic uplift. In an era when images of bumbling Sambos, feminized male minstrels, and confused primitives still held currency, Louis's public personification of forcefulness and fairness, virility and respectability, stylishness and responsibility, resonated with popular understandings of manhood, civilization, and modernity. Thus, from the footnotes of the well-known narrative of Louis as American hero emerges not only the buried history of a black diasporic icon, but also a larger story about the intersection of gender and resistance in America's race wars.

From Uncle Tom to New Negro

Writing in the *New York Amsterdam News,* editorialist Theophilus Lewis dubbed Joe Louis a "Boxing Business Man." Lewis praised him as a model of mature focus, telling readers, "Joe Louis prefers to be Joe Louis and not what white people think Joe Louis should be. Professional boxing is his chosen road to success." As Lewis continued, "A man's success is not a playful matter—it is a serious business. He refuses to pretend it is a pastime, a sort of youthful prelude to mature living."[16] Despite the obvious passion and respect with which Louis's African American contemporaries followed his career, sports historiography, much like popular memory, has tended to overlook black representations of Louis. For the most part, scholars' focus on mainstream daily newspaper accounts has skewed their assessments of him as a moderate and even ineffectual figure of white cooptation.[17] While several historians challenge this "Uncle Tom" critique, most still emphasize Louis's contributions as a crossover American hero, without deconstructing whites' and blacks' differing perceptions of his cultural and political importance.[18] Overall, these approaches obscure the reality that various segments of black America acknowledged and even lauded Louis's accomplishments, fashioning him as a gendered expression of public resistance.

Louis's folk hero status relied, in large part, on his masculine embodiment of the period's shifting constructions of black identity and advancement. Just ten years earlier, in the opening essay of *The New Negro*, scholar Alain Locke had declared that "Uncle Tom and Sambo have passed on," and now the "American mind must reckon with a fundamentally changed Negro." According to Locke, despite African Americans' continued exclusion from the rights of full citizenship, they could still "celebrate the attainment of a significant . . . phase of group development, and with it a spiritual Coming of Age."[19] As Louis rose in the ranks of professional boxing alongside this collective rite of passage, racial progress became increasingly conflated with the redemption of black manhood.

African Americans had long deployed masculine constructions of powerful blackness to confront what historian Gail Bederman describes as the Progressives' tradition of weaving race and gender into a web of white male supremacy. According to popular, early-twentieth-century thought, one could determine a group's civilization based on their extent of sexual differentiation. In keeping with this pseudoscientific doctrine, black men and women were supposedly identical, while the patriarchal organization of the "civilized" white race signified that they were not only the furthest along in the Darwinist chain of evolution, but also uniquely capable of wielding political authority and exercising the rights of citizenship.[20] According to historian Barbara Melosh, the economic difficulties of the Depression helped to reify this overall paradigm of white male supremacy. Concerns over family stability and conflicts over female labor led to the retrenchment of white patriarchy after the gender subversions of the 1920s such as the passing of the 19th Amendment for women's suffrage, the rise of the assertive New Woman, and the racy culture of the flapper.[21] Not surprisingly, as whites continued to articulate their racial supremacy through an assertion of male control, many African Americans attempted to prove their equality using resistance strategies that embraced male dominance.

Even though the African American political and intellectual movements of the 1930s shared a common focus on promoting the legitimacy of black manhood, New Negro activists, by no means, agreed on a standardized definition of its cultural, political, and economic terms. Instead, they harnessed and shaped gendered discourses to suit not only their differing philosophical and tactical aims, but also their varied constituents. While established organizations like the National Association for the Advancement of Colored People (NAACP) and Marcus Garvey's pan-Africanist Universal Negro Improvement Association (UNIA) had long appropriated the white Victorian principles of patriarchy, propriety, industry, and thrift as the foundation for black advancement, Harlem's up-and-coming cadre of New Negro writers and poets began to challenge these rigid ideals by exploring homosocial bonds and masculine pursuits beyond the realm of bourgeois domesticity.[22] In turn, the public assertion of militant black manhood became a rallying cry for the emerging politics of collective race and class protest led by groups like the Brotherhood of Sleeping Car Porters (BSCP) and the Communist Party.[23] Whether they worked within the framework of American democratic ideals, or rejected their hypocrisy, African American activists of the 1930s used manhood as a mobilizing force.

As different sectors of black society claimed Louis as one of their own, his public representation came to embody the class and generational tensions surrounding Depression-era articulations of black manhood. On the one hand, the period's constructions of black manliness incorporated the contradictory ideals of savagery and civilization, as metaphors of battle and physical prowess existed alongside discussions of intelligence, artistry, and respectability. On the other hand, the New Negro movement also signaled a nascent shift toward a more modern sense of masculinity grounded less in middle-class notions of gentility, and expressed through recreational pursuits, the conspicuous consumption of mass-marketed commodities, and the open display of bodily might and sexual virility.[24] The popular celebration of Louis as Race Man connected these gendered imaginings of blackness with the spirit of the masses. This was not a solo performance on the part of Louis, but rather a collective spectacle involving a complex process of negotiation among his body of black supporters.

However, even as one uncovers Louis's significance as *the* quintessential New Negro of the 1930s, the inherent dangers of a masculinist critique of racism inevitably rise to the surface. Trapped in a paradox, Louis, his black fans, and members of the black press challenged white superiority by engaging the same constructions of patriarchal authority that were simultaneously confirming their racial inferiority. Not only did they ultimately legitimize existing power relations, but their male-centered modes of resistance also pushed black women to the periphery of the struggle.

Boxing's New Negro Comes of Age

When Louis celebrated his twenty-first birthday on May 13, 1935, the black press urged his African American fans to pay tribute to his work as "a sterling young fighter, a gentleman and sportsman." In calling Louis "the finest type of *American manhood*," they granted him two labels that blackness did not usually allow.[25] On the front-page of the *Pittsburgh Courier* sports section, one writer declared, "Joe Louis, you are a man now. . . . [O]nly a step across the threshold of boyhood, the hopes of a race and the best wishes of a nation are with you." Recognizing Louis's importance as an emblematic figure through which gender and race coalesced in a narrative of black progress, the writer warned the young fighter to "live a clean, honest life . . . and always remember that your very qualities of modesty and manliness are the things which bring thousands of people to see you fight."[26] In emphasizing Louis's own coming of age as a man, black journalists exposed the collective focus on questions of black manhood.

In the buildup to his bout against Primo Carnera, the black press promoted Louis's redemptive and unifying mission in what some were dubbing the "battle of the century." With bold optimism, one writer in the *Pittsburgh Courier* maintained that Louis would defend successfully "the ardent hopes of more than twelve million Americans" when he stepped into the ring at Yankee Stadium. Another pre-fight feature in the *Chicago Defender* named Louis the most "outstanding Race athlete of the past 30 years," citing his unprecedented ability to draw black fans to the box office. In the month preceding the fight, Harlem buzzed with expectant energy as African Americans of all ages kept Louis as their favorite topic. The *New York Age* even noted that "women from all walks of life, some who had never taken any interest in fights," prayed for a race victory in the ring.[27]

As widespread interest in the Louis-Carnera match cut across racial lines, many African Americans relished the fact that the black fighter's rise was revitalizing the entire boxing industry after years of sparse ticket sales.[28] In a bid to bring Louis closer to a title bout, his African American managers, Roxborough and Black, had formed a pragmatic alliance with Mike Jacobs, an influential Jewish American promoter. Jacobs held a virtual monopoly of the industry, organizing major heavyweight events in conjunction with the Hearst Milk Fund for Babies, a New York charity run by the wife of publishing magnate William Randolph Hearst.[29]

Even though Louis was already a superstar in the black press, Jacobs "introduced" the young fighter to white America. A public relations mastermind, he hired press agents like black journalist Russell Cowans to crank out daily media releases for white and black newspapers all over the country. These reports carefully constructed Louis as the epitome of white middle-class respectability.[30] While this centralized communications scheme ensured that overlapping portrayals of the "official" Louis appeared in both presses, a comparison of white and black sources reveals that writers reinterpreted and reshaped the Louis image along racial lines, often using manhood as a metalanguage for race.

While most journalists in the mainstream press certainly favored Louis to win, they were not ready to count out Carnera, even though a streak of fixed fights and messy dealings with the mob underworld soiled the veteran boxer's seven-year record.[31] Despite their high praise of Louis's technical abilities and well-mannered conduct, many white writers held reservations about his physical and mental toughness. Invoking the emasculating stereo-types of black cowardice, infantilism, and emotionality, they charged that Louis's encounter with Carnera would determine if this "beardless" boy could hold his own against boxing's big men. After all, in addition to being eight years Louis's senior, Carnera stood nearly half a foot taller and out-weighed Louis by almost 70 pounds. As one writer in the *Macon Telegraph* observed, the question of "Can he take it?" was the "one predominant note of skepticism" among the white, fight-going public.[32] Nationally syndi-cated sports columnist Grantland Rice agreed that if Louis failed to score an early knockout, the "rugged" Carnera would "outmaul" the boy to win by decision. Moreover, Rice and many of his colleagues questioned whether the young fighter would remain poised in the midst of the "terrific bally-hoo" of what promised to be one of the biggest fight crowds in many years.[33] Casting Louis as the "dusky David" to Carnera's "Goliath," white journalists wondered whether the youthful, black technician possessed the gritty manhood to defeat the roughhousing Italian Giant.[34]

As Louis's rite of passage to boxing manhood, the fight also became a litmus test for the strength and maturity of the race. However unconvinced the white press was, black writers supported Louis with great resolve, pre-dicting an easy knockout in two to five rounds.[35] The question of whether or not Louis could "take it" reportedly drew a loud chuckle from Manager Roxborough, who bragged that the young fighter had already prevailed in the face of knockdowns, a fractured knuckle, and even punches to the jaw.[36] Louis's manly battle against Carnera not only had "colored America looking to redeem its honors in the fistic world," but it took on greater im-plications as a proxy for larger racial conflicts at home and abroad.[37]

Enlisted for Ethiopia

While Louis prepared for his conquest of Carnera, another race war threat-ened to erupt across the Atlantic. Benito Mussolini's imperialistic designs on Haile Selassie's Abyssinia weighed on the minds of many African Amer-icans. From the *Courier* to the *Crisis,* articles in the black press kept read-ers apprised of the latest news on the impending Italo-Ethiopian conflict during the spring and summer of 1935. While mainstream publications tended to bury the reports of Abyssinia, the black press featured them prominently, often as front-page news. They carried not only current, but historical accounts of Ethiopia, along with human-interest stories on Se-lassie, his family, and the plight of the Abyssinian soldiers.

Ethiopia was the last independent nation on the African continent and its potential takeover had grave implications for struggles of black autonomy and equality throughout the world. In particular, the perception of a parallel between Italian fascism and United States racism served to provoke strong, public African American reactions to the looming invasion.[38] Moreover, when the League of Nations failed to come to the aid of the African country, it further emphasized the racial dimensions of the conflict, as self-interested, white governments turned a deaf ear to the pleas of their colored counter-part.[39] Given the depressed economic conditions in northern black communities like Harlem and the continued terror of Jim Crow in the South, African Americans recognized the close connections between their plight and that of their Ethiopian brothers. As poet Langston Hughes declared:

> Ethiopia, Lift your night-dark face,
> Abyssinian Son of Sheba's Race!
> . . .
> May all Africa arise
> With blazing eyes and night-dark face
> In answer to the call of Sheba's race:
> Ethiopia's free!
> Be like me,
> All of Africa,
> Arise and be free![40]

Out of the crucible of modern colonialism and fascism emerged a growing sense of black diasporic consciousness.

Many black fans saw the upcoming Louis-Carnera fight as an apt microcosm of the pending match up between Il Duce and Selassie. In the major black weeklies, stories and photos of Louis's training regimen, his victory, and the subsequent celebrations ran side-by-side with reports of the Abyssinian crisis and pictures of the Ethiopian emperor. Arguably, even African Americans who did not read the papers must have picked up on the obvious analogy. Enthusiastic discussions of the Louis-Carnera bout, from street corners and front porches to local barbershops and beauty salons, surely touched on the boxer's symbolic role as he went fist-to-fist with Mussolini's Darling. Not only had Louis become a ubiquitous folk hero by 1935, but as historian William R. Scott argues, Italy's imminent invasion stimulated an unprecedented period of black American militancy and group protest. From Los Angeles to New York, the black masses organized Abyssinian-defense loans, acts of civil disobedience, huge rallies that attracted thousands of participants, economic boycotts, and even the recruitment of volunteer combat troops.[41]

Complementing the efforts of grassroots activists, Louis became a popular outlet for articulations of nascent black nationalism, along with radical, international critiques of racism. He offered a public embodiment of the intellectual discussions of the conflict that graced the pages of periodicals like the *Crisis, Opportunity,* and Marcus Garvey's *Black Man.* Various black groups even met with Louis during his training camp to underscore the importance of his upcoming fight for black people on the world stage. Louis recalled, "Now, not only did I have to beat the man, but I had to beat him for a cause."[42] Enlisted as a fistic soldier in the fight against fascism, he promised to enact Abyssinia's struggle for black autonomy in a way that his legions of African American fans could grasp with a sense of visceral immediacy. In the spectacle of the ring, Louis's body would perform a utopian vision of not only the black American body politic, but also that of the Ethiopian homeland.

Beyond just the basic fact that Louis, a black man, would wage hand-to-hand combat against an Italian fighter, there were a number of physical and metaphorical parallels between the real and ring conflicts enabling African Americans to engage in a gendered critique of domestic racism and foreign fascism.[43] In particular, contemporary black American discourses of African redemption were suffused with the language of manly battle, independence, and honor. To black writers and political figures of the New Negro era, the colonized continent represented black womanhood, while the autonomous Abyssinian nation was a decidedly male construct. Writing to the *Negro World,* a Garveyite publication, in the lead-up to the annual UNIA convention in 1924, Irene Gaskin exhorted, "Our flag boys [the African tricolor of red, black, and green] . . . means loyalty to our country and the protection of our women in our motherland Africa."[44] Labeling colonized Africa the "motherland," she placed men at the head of both nation-building and the defense of black womanhood. Since white imperial justifications often connected a society's ability to self-govern with its degree of patriarchal order, it is not surprising that African American commentators infused both these battles for racial nationalism with an overwhelmingly masculine bent.

The conflict between Italy and Ethiopia became anthropomorphized into a duel between Mussolini and Selassie, as the black press portrayed Abyssinia's struggle to remain autonomous as a test of the tiny country's racial manhood. At a time when a boxer's moniker usually had ethnic overtones, Louis, dubbed the Brown Bomber, the Ethiopian Exploder, and the African Avenger, became a natural stand-in for the Abyssinian emperor, and by extension, black nationhood.[45] African American cartoonist Jay Jackson encapsulated this connection in a clever drawing that showed a much smaller Louis boxing against a bestial caricature of Carnera in front of Ethiopian and Italian fans, while a seat reserved for the League of Nations remained empty in the foreground.[46] (See Figure 2.1)

2.1 "Ethiopia Shall Stretch Forth," May 25, 1935. During the lead-up to his match with the Italian, Primo Carnera, Joe Louis became a natural stand-in for the Ethiopian emperor, Haile Selassie, and by extension, black nationhood. Used with permission. Source: *Chicago Defender*.

As the celebrated "Crown Prince of Fistiania," Louis was, in many ways, the ultimate "Abyssinian Son of Sheba's Race."[47] While some white journalists and intellectuals questioned the racial heritage of the light-skinned Louis and Selassie, writers in the black press embraced both men as strong Race heroes. White biographer Edward Van Every's attempts to connect Louis's athletic prowess with his tri-racial "blood strain" resonated with numerous reports in the mainstream dailies that sought to deemphasize the boxer's African roots. Although the biographer acknowledged that Louis "insists . . . the Negro predominates in his blood," Van Every stressed the possibility that Louis was "a good part white and more Indian than African."[48]

Flying in the face of such efforts to undermine Louis's role as Race Man, African American writers positioned him as the "Black Hope," arguing that Louis was a "badge of racial prestige . . . in man's most honored sphere of endeavor—the noble art of self-defense."[49] Similarly, the black press showed impressive pictures of the emperor Selassie in his full regalia, underscoring his links to the ancient kingdom of Cush and claiming him as the "King of all Negroes everywhere." One editorial in the *Baltimore Afro-American* even maintained that "one glance at . . . [Selassie's] hair" surely proved that Ethiopia was a black nation.[50] Louis and Selassie's shared African roots became a reservoir of strength, and thus, their victories in manly battle would be victories for the race on both a national and international scale.

Just as reports conflated Louis with Ethiopia's emperor, Carnera became the Italian dictator's sporting deputy. With ethnic epithets like Mussolini's Darling, the Ambling Alp, and the Vast Venetian, Carnera served as a popular platform for the fascist leader's chest-beating propaganda. Just five years earlier in July 1930, when Carnera's criminal associations had caught up with him, Il Duce had personally intervened to prevent the fighter's deportation from the United States. Moreover, when Carnera won the world heavyweight title against Jack Sharkey in 1933, Mussolini ordered a uniform of the black shirt fascisti for his boxing champion and posed with Carnera in photos that he sent to newspapers throughout the world. The fighter even addressed his leader with the fascist salute.[51]

Paralleling the Louis-Carnera pre-fight publicity, white Americans wondered whether the tiny Ethiopian nation would survive the onslaught of Il Duce's larger, more modernized forces. Despite Italy's clear military advantages, an editorial in the *Crisis* challenged Mussolini's bravado, claiming that the "last gobble of Africa" would prove to be a "bloody swallow." It charged that Il Duce and his army would have to navigate the country's treacherous terrain while facing the unpredictable guerrilla strikes of Selassie's courageous and cunning men.[52]

In the ring, Louis would have to practice and then engage a similar guerrilla strategy in order to compensate for the gigantic proportions and long reach of Mussolini's Darling. Mapped out by trainer Blackburn and perfected by Louis, the ingenious battle plan involved breaking down the

Italian's defensive stance with punishing body shots, and then moving in to attack Carnera's head. While Marcus Garvey urged his pan-Africanist brothers to "act manly, courageously, [and] thoughtfully" in mobilizing for the crisis that would come with Mussolini's invasion, the black press high-lighted Louis's strict training regimen as another confirmation that he would prevail. Although Garvey lamented that Abyssinia's lack of prepara-tion would only permit a "passionate, enthusiastic, and emotional" re-sponse to Italy's attack, the calm and conscientious Louis appeared well-equipped to conquer Carnera as he slashed his way through a host of gargantuan sparring mates.[53] Intelligence and rational discipline became in-tegral to Louis's performance of black nationhood.

Many African American journalists and politicos connected the Louis-Carnera fight to the gendered debates of savagery versus civilization in the Italo-Ethiopian conflict. Although Mussolini declared that he sought to bring progress to the supposedly backward nation of Abyssinia, black in-tellectuals like James Weldon Johnson questioned the dictator's rhetoric, ar-guing that Italy was simply after African loot. Critiquing Mussolini's violent designs, Johnson questioned the conventional, Western definition of civilization, arguing that even though Ethiopians lacked a modern infra-structure, they were at least civilized in character, with "courage, honesty, and consideration for the needs of others."[54] Drawing on similar tropes, *Pittsburgh Courier* commentator J. A. Rogers compared "Selassie, The Gentleman, And Mussolini, The Braggart." Not surprisingly, Rogers used heavyweight boxing as a metaphor for this larger battle of savagery against nobility, emphasizing Mussolini's baseness by equating his "gesturing" and "clowning" to that of the irreverent black fighter Jack Johnson.[55] In this racial and gendered reversal, Mussolini became the minstrel, as Rogers not only claimed Ethiopia as a civilized nation, but also referenced Louis's con-current role in bringing racial progress to the boxing ring.

Playing on the brutish appearance of Mussolini's Darling, along with his reputation for illegal wrestling and holding, the black newspapers' drawings and photos of the Italian Giant made Carnera appear more beast than man, while their renderings of Louis retained a lifelike appearance. Al-though white journalists and cartoonists certainly portrayed Louis in more humane ways than his predecessor, Jack Johnson, some still tended to de-pict him using Sambo stereotypes. Paul Gallico's fight-day column in the *New York Daily News* included a thick-lipped, hairy depiction of Louis chasing after Carnera. Even though Gallico predicted that Carnera would face a "shy, easily upset man mellow," the writer also suggested that the an-imalistic Louis could "go berserk" at any time.[56]

In contrast, the black press steered away from caricatures of Louis and quoted him using full sentences. Moreover, while boasting of his strength, black journalists also emphasized his kindness and generosity to his mother and family. In mid-April 1935, many black writers celebrated Louis's display of patriarchal responsibility when the fighter used one of his purses to purchase a fully furnished home for his mother.[57] Whereas the Italian Giant embodied everything that was barbaric and violent about white racism and fascism, Louis came to exemplify an exalted form of civilized black manhood, grounded in a mix of physical prowess and force of character.[58] By more than just a case of coincidental timing, Louis became a gendered metaphor of black militancy and nationalism that drew on the rhetorical power of prevailing discourses of manliness and civilization. Even if Selassie had little chance of preventing an Italian takeover, Louis would defend black honor.

The Manly Art of Self-Defense

As Louis fought for Ethiopian independence, he also fought for the dignity and citizenship rights of African Americans at home. In addition to his symbolic connections to more radical, transnational black activism, he became the focus of an interrelated debate over questions of black American manhood and the state of the race. This discursive battle in the popular media was an equally significant race war being waged on the African American home front. While he prepared for his match, black journalists shaped many of the same gendered critiques associated with the international dimensions of his fight into a domestic narrative of black progress.

Black Americans' disproportionate suffering during the Great Depression only served to highlight their continued alienation and second-class citizenship. In the South, Jim Crow segregationists still ruled by legal and extralegal means, as struggling black sharecroppers and laborers sought to combat economic exploitation, widespread disfranchisement, and the terror of lynching.[59] Many African Americans left the South in search of safety and opportunity in the North, but even the Black Mecca of Harlem experienced police brutality and high unemployment. On March 22, 1935, the famed New York neighborhood erupted into violence after rumors circulated that the white manager of a local store had beaten and killed a Puerto Rican boy. Even though several hours later the rumors were discounted, Harlem's first-ever race riot continued into the night, as African Americans expressed their frustrations through mass destruction.[60]

Against this oppressive backdrop, Louis's success became the most conspicuous argument against the continued exclusion of African Americans from the benefits of full national citizenship. Black journalists inscribed his body with the ideals of black manliness and masculinity, and they sculpted his persona into a cultural vessel in which they poured their hopes and dreams. As an editorial in *Opportunity* described, "[t]he picture of a young Negro boy working in the Ford plant at $5.00 per day ... who literally forces his way to a place where he can command a half million dollars within a single year" appealed to African Americans from "every walk of life."[61] While establishment uplifters could still embrace Louis for his respectability and productivity, a younger generation of New Negroes lionized him for his style and virility. To them, Louis was not exceptional; rather, he represented what black America could do with the chance to compete on level ground. As he climbed his way from the dirt of the cotton fields to the bright lights of the boxing ring, he linked African Americans from different classes and vocations in a story of collective progress.

As musicologist Paul Oliver argues, Louis's heroic climb from the cotton fields of Alabama to boxing fame encapsulated the appealing drama and seeming invincibility of traditional African American ballad heroes like John Henry. Indeed, Louis was the only Depression-era athlete that popular blues artists commemorated in recorded songs.[62] As a man who faced the prospect of punishment alone in the ring, he enacted through sport the same kinds of struggles confronting many of his fans. Houston singer Joe Pullman's recording, entitled "Joe Louis is the Man," was the first song to honor Louis's toppling of Carnera. Although Oliver describes Pullman's creation as a "naïve piece of folk poetry," it captured the essence of Louis as the archetypal New Negro. While revering the Bomber as "a battlin' man," it also noted that he was "not a bad dressed guy," and that even though he was "makin' real good money," it failed to "swell his head." Just as Pullman celebrated "powerful Joe" in his performance, the husky-voiced Memphis Minnie McCoy of Chicago recorded "He's in the Ring (Doin' the Same Old Thing)" as a tribute to Louis's two-fisted "dynamite." The mix of Memphis Minnie's throaty lyrics, her guitar, and Black Bob's pounding piano emphasized the indestructibility of Louis, who knocked out his opponents with remarkable consistency to the delight of his poor and working-class fans:

> When your people's goin' out tonight,
> Jes' goin' to see Joe Louis fight,
> An' if you ain't got no money gotta go tomorrow night,
> 'Cause he's in the ring doin' the same ol' thing.[63]

As a rallying point for black communities across the nation, the figure of Louis served to unite the ethereal realm of diasporic politics with the everyday troubles of African Americans.

Louis received a hero's welcome from the black community at Grand Central Station in New York City in the middle of May 1935. As the black press included photos of Louis in chic suits enjoying the finer things in life like driving brand-new cars, he moved beyond his station as prizefighter to become both celebrity and socialite.[64] His bodily display of impeccable fashion was one of the most integral aspects of his gendered performance of black pride, since it allowed him to transgress racial norms, moving beyond the ubiquitous black identity of poor worker to showcase his wealth and individuality. One black correspondent praised Louis for looking the part of fistic champion in "his street togs," while another carefully itemized the boxer's wardrobe of a "dozen suits, nine pairs of shoes, two dozen shirts, 100 neckties, ten hats, six coats and countless sweaters, zippercoats, [and] suits of underwear and pyjamas."[65] Likewise, newspaper ads for Murray's Pomade, a popular hair straightener, reinforced Louis's reputation for being not only a great fighter, but also "one of the best dressed men in America." As the text of the advertisement claimed, Louis strived to be "well-groomed" both in and out of the ring. The company encouraged the reader to support Louis and to buy their product, since doing both would enable a man to take on the young boxer's power and panache in his everyday life.[66] As the consummate New Negro, Louis reinforced his manhood through his prodigious consumption and street-hip style, offering an optimistic vision of the possibilities of black urban America.

Part politician, part pop idol, and part philanthropist, Louis spent a busy week in the Big Apple meeting with civic leaders like Mayor Fiorella LaGuardia, shaking hands with boxing legends like Jack Dempsey, and attending a series of charity benefits. Trading in his trousers for workout gear four times a day, Louis also starred in a promotional, vaudeville show at the Harlem Opera House, scoring one of the biggest draws in the history of the theater. With a kick-line of pretty dancing girls in the background, he sparred, skipped, and punched the heavy bag to the delight of packed houses. However, the respite was short-lived. With only a month left before the Carnera fight, Louis left for his training camp in Pompton Lakes, New Jersey.[67]

Black correspondents painted an idyllic picture of the countryside estate where Louis prepared for battle, emphasizing its connections to old American gentility, while also touting its modern conveniences. Celebrating Louis's role as the temporary master of the "Big House," they cloaked him in a mantle of both bourgeois respectability and technological efficiency.[68] According to local lore, George Washington had slept there, and black writers claimed that Louis now occupied the same room where the first president had stayed. Reputedly "one of the most famous fistic training grounds in the world," the camp was "[n]estled in a nature-scooped nook of the Ramapo Mountains," yet close enough to the city of Patterson to offer all of the amenities of rural and urban life combined. Although Louis spent most of his days working out, in his few moments of leisure time he supposedly enjoyed freshwater fishing, boating, golfing, and even horseback riding.[69] The training camp itself became an expression of not only Louis's nobility and modernity, but also the dignity and advancement of his people.

As the first fighter to ever rent the entire grounds for the exclusive use of his training camp, Louis ruled as lord of the estate. He retained a sixteen-man, African American entourage that included an eighteen-year-old, personal valet and the "expert dietician" Frank Sutton, a former restaurateur. In particular, Sutton, who had once served Booker T. Washington, became a popular figure in the black press reports from Pompton Lakes. Referencing the "nutritionist," black writers presented detailed accounts of Louis's disciplined, "two-meal-a-day diet," countering white reports of the fighter's supposed penchant for ice cream and tendency to overeat.[70]

Editorials in the black press insisted that African American fighters no longer needed to seek out white assistance to get ahead. Louis reputedly rejected the possibility of white patronage, saying that he would "hang up the gloves for good" if Roxborough and Black sold any part of his earnings. By this time Jacobs certainly provided much of Louis's financial backing, but black reports tended to downplay the white promoter's role, while emphasizing the influence of his black managers. Roxborough, Black, and Blackburn's tactical abilities at the negotiating table and at ringside formed an important plotline in the story of Louis's success. In true New Negro form, Louis and his black "Board of Strategy" were beating white men at their own enterprise.[71]

A steady stream of cars and pedestrians traveled to the estate to see Louis in action. In this seemingly apolitical space, showing support for Louis enabled his black supporters to publicly express their own status and worth and to gain vicariously the strength of his fists. By the middle of June, his sparring workouts had already attracted around 3,200 visitors, and as the fight drew nearer, writers predicted crowds of 1,000 per workout of mostly African American fans from all along the East Coast.[72] Alongside regular folk, professionals and celebrities made appearances. Black newspapers like the *New York Age* and the *Baltimore Afro-American* provided weekly lists of the VIP spectators—judges, sportsmen, entertainers, entrepreneurs, orchestra leaders, morticians, and politicians—who ranged from local to national elites. Many of those who saw Louis in the flesh achieved their own form of celebrity as they returned home to trumpet his prowess on the street corners and in the bars of their urban communities.[73] Attending the Louis camp became, for spectators, an expression of pride and promise.

As Louis toppled his sparring mates, his African American fans celebrated him as a polished, physical specimen of black virility. Louis embodied an undeniable, yet understated sexuality that appealed to the younger generation of New Negroes without upsetting the traditional conventions of respectability. Even though the Louis team's "official" position was that the fighter did not associate with women, black fans still celebrated his bodily perfection. As public school teacher Helen Harden recounted in a letter to the *New York Age,* many spectators visited the camp "with one purpose," and that was "to gaze on the Detroit Bomber." Harden gushed that he was simply "lovely to look at. Not a blemish on his saffron hued skin." Another black female fan refused to believe the official reports that claimed Louis would keep women out of his life until he won the world title, arguing that "Joe is a real man, after all."[74]

Although the young boxer obviously appealed to women, many articles in the white press twisted the Louis party line to unsex and infantilize the black fighter, claiming that "iceberg" Louis had "no time for women" and that his only "sweetheart" was his mother.[75] Challenging these images, the black press fashioned him as an idol of masculinity, showing suggestive photos of Louis washing himself in the shower and gazing at the camera partially disrobed. While black writers did acknowledge that Louis had no serious plans for marriage, they also reported that camp intimates swore he was a "lady-killer."[76] However, concerned with dissociating their fighter from the negative legacy of Jack Johnson, Louis's handlers kept the young man's sexual escapades with white women, along with his love of speeding cars and frivolous spending, out of the press.[77] In an era when black male sexuality connoted rape and recklessness, Louis's carefully constructed balance of physicality and decency offered a positive model of virile black manhood.

Despite the more daringly masculine aspects of his persona, Louis still stood as a paragon of manly productivity in the face of racist, white reports of his laziness. Even a sympathetic white writer like Van Every betrayed his prejudice when he claimed that Louis's trainer had to "force Joe . . . to cut out his dissipation . . . even if it infringed on his sleep."[78] In refuting these types of disparaging comments, one journalist in the *New York Amsterdam News* declared that "[n]o fighter during the past twenty years has trained with more earnestness than this Detroit boy."[79]

Following the conventions of contemporary boxing manuals, the black press provided detailed descriptions of Louis's routine, arguing that his abilities were not just "natural," but cultivated.[80] With scientific precision and utmost discipline, Louis arose at six in the morning to run in the mountains, followed by a demanding afternoon of sparring matches, bag punching, rope skipping, and bending exercises. So important was it to counter notions of black indolence that one sportswriter even maintained that Louis was a model of efficiency when he slept, taking "it as seriously as he does his fighting. No faking, no lost motion."[81] In this way, Louis's persona combined the traditional watermarks of gentlemanly respectability with the rising tide of New Negro masculinity. He became not only *the* Race Man, but also an Everyman for the race.

The New Negro and his New Crowd

Just days before the fight-date, the impending Italian invasion of Ethiopia permeated local politics as the Hearst Milk Fund contemplated canceling the Louis-Carnera bout for fear that it would inspire race riots. The Hearst announcement marked the high point in a month-long racial debate over the potential for black-Italian violence at the match. Pointing to the rioting of Harlem's black population in March 1935 and the ongoing furor over the Abyssinian crisis, white sportswriters Westbrook Pegler and Arthur Brisbane warned that a boxing match pitting a black American against an Italian fighter would furnish the fuel for racial unrest in both the stands and streets. Pegler deemed the bout a "new high in stupid judgment," while Brisbane worried that it might inspire "a fight bigger than the scheduled fight."[82]

Given Pegler and Brisbane's predictions, it became clear that not just Louis's manhood was on the line in the upcoming match, but also the collective manhood of his African American spectators. The black press responded with vehemence. Al Monroe of the *Chicago Defender* recognized white America's unease with the sudden rise of the Race Man Louis, whose burgeoning popularity was "moving 'out of control.'" He dismissed the warnings of violence, claiming that his Nordic counterparts had no intention of writing "the real facts."[83] In turn, while the *New York Amsterdam News* claimed that "Negroes today are unlikely to riot over anything less than deep-seated social injustice and economic exclusion," they also warned that "Negroes ARE likely to be forced to defend themselves against attack by whites who have been stirred by repeated comment on the possibilities of rioting."[84]

In late June, when a front-page editorial in the white *Newark Ledger* called for a boycott of the fight, the black press upped its ante. The *Baltimore Afro-American* claimed that this was a deliberate move to prevent Louis from advancing to the heavyweight championship, reporting that blacks and Italians in Newark's "hill" sections had responded with their own boycott of the *Ledger*. Linking it to larger political questions, the *Chicago Defender* placed the ultimate blame in Mussolini's lap, declaring that the dictator's shameless use of the Louis-Carnera fight as fodder for race hatred in the Italian American press had provoked the *Ledger* boycott.[85] Just as Louis's individual victory would prove his boxing manhood, so too would his black fans have a communal chance to prove their maturity and respectability as spectators. Characteristic of the period's wider questioning of the merits of bourgeois respectability alongside the rise of popular strains of more aggressive, mass politics, class tensions surfaced in this aspect of the pre-fight publicity. Recalling the controversy over Harlem's first-ever race riot in March, black journalists understood that much was at stake. Their arguments were not just defensive, but prescriptive. While Louis's win would certainly be cause for celebration, it had to remain civilized. Otherwise, his ultimate strength would remain locked in his fists, unable to transfer its impact to the larger struggle against racism and fascism at home and abroad.[86]

On the morning of June 25, 1935, the Brown Bomber and Mussolini's Darling readied themselves "to clash for the synthetic championship of two continents."[87] Despite the reassurances of the black press, the Hearst Milk Fund was taking no chances with the possibility of violence, and for the first time in New York City's boxing history, a troop of armed police would surround the ringside at Yankee Stadium as Louis and Carnera fought. Over 1,000 patrolmen and detectives would also be stationed at strategic points throughout the arena.[88]

Since the major radio networks of NBC and CBS refused to air the match for fear of potential bloodshed across the country, the 100 ticket sellers in the stadium box office had their hands full with a last-minute rush of spectators.[89] For weeks before the fight, several black newspapers had advertised organized bus trips to the event, along with special railroad rates and flights that welcomed both men and women.[90]

Under a sunny, steamy New York sky, most of the nearly 15,000 African Americans on hand to see Louis arrived long before the white spectators with ringside seats. They congregated in the right- and left-field bleachers as soon as the Yankee Stadium gates opened at five o'clock, singing, cheering, and performing ad hoc speeches during their two-hour wait for the preliminary fights. A journalist for the *New York Age* spoke with one man who had traveled with his wife all the way from Leland, Mississippi. The writer could only interpret this cotton buyer and Fisk University graduate's dedication as an example of "the spirit of enthusiasm and race pride that urged him and thousands of others from Chillicothe, Kinder Lots and many other hidden hamlets" across the country to attend the fight.[91] In addition to the lively crowds in the bleachers, black America's royalty, from politicians to professionals, and from sportsmen to entertainers like Bill "Bojangles" Robinson and Lena Horne sat closer to the ring.[92] By the time of the main event, over 60,000 spectators of all races packed the stadium, with gate receipts totaling nearly $350,000, a new high for a nontitular match.[93]

As ring announcer Hugh Balogh urged, "in the name of American sportsmanship. . . . [R]egardless of race, creed, or color, let us all say, may the better man emerge victorious."[94] As the fighters approached each other, Carnera looked like a massive beast alongside the young David. Yet, it was Louis, expressionless and calm, who commanded the center of the ring, while Mussolini's Darling danced around him. By the end of the first round, Louis had already drawn blood, cutting the Italian Giant's lip with a smashing right to the mouth. Louis continued to explode with hard body shots, followed by rights and lefts that bruised Carnera's face. Toward the end of the fifth, Mussolini's Darling looked ready to collapse, with blood streaming down his face, but Louis, still fresh-legged, blasted him with more head and body combinations. Louis rocked Carnera with a series of hard rights in the sixth round, sending Mussolini's Darling to the canvas three times. As Carnera staggered to his feet Referee Arthur Donovan called off the fight as Louis hit his target with a cannonade of punches. The crowd burst into cheers as Louis won by technical knockout, with not a mark on his face.

Even without the benefit of a radio broadcast, news of Louis's win traveled quickly. Not too far from the stadium, a phone call conveyed the result to the estimated 20,000 fans who gathered at the Savoy Ballroom in Harlem. As the *Pittsburgh Courier* reported, floods of African Americans poured into the streets from Seventh to Lenox and 125th to 145th with a carnival spirit "reminiscent of Marcus Garvey's best days." The ravages of the Depression seemed momentarily suspended as celebrants in the taverns offered up toasts to Louis, while cars with plates from as far away as the District of Columbia, Illinois, Maryland, Tennessee, Georgia, and Canada crawled and honked their way down Seventh Avenue.[95]

As the black press pointed to the relative order of the post-fight festivities as confirmation that African Americans were not as uncivilized as Pegler and Brisbane had thought, the behavior of Louis's fans became another mark of resistance. As a correspondent for the *Journal and Guide* asserted, "Contrary to unfounded anxiety expressed in some quarters, there was no sign of disorder before, during or after the fight."[96] Yet, the glowing descriptions in the black press appear to have obscured the multiple ways in which African Americans from different walks of life expressed their support of Louis.

Articles in the white dailies presented a much more raucous picture of the post-fight revelry. By reading their accounts intertextually with the black press reports, one can draw a more nuanced portrait of the vigorous celebration without much regard to hallowed respectability. One elderly, black orator named Gill Holton reputedly declared, "It [wa]s the greatest night Harlem . . . had since the riot." Officers on foot and horseback, along with those driving motorcycles and radio cars, monitored the thousands of fans that surrounded the packed Savoy Ballroom. Mounted police had to intervene when members of the crowd stormed the entrance, breaking down one of the doors and injuring a half-dozen people. When the community's honorary mayor, entertainer Bill "Bojangles" Robinson, arrived in a limousine, he made a cursory speech cautioning the throngs of fans to remain calm, but minutes later he, too, joined in the shouting as he moved down the street. Belligerent youths postured on the hoods of moving cars, yelling at the tops of their lungs, while children who should have been in bed pounded ashcans on the streets and compared their flexed biceps.[97] Even if Louis's managers advised him against expressing his jubilation in the ring, the Brown Bomber's victory gave his fans an opportunity to aggressively assert their racial pride en masse, in a way that defied conventional racial norms.

The events surrounding the Jersey City Riots of August 1935 paint an even clearer picture of this sense of militancy. According to a report in the *New York Age,* around 100 black and Italian men armed with knives, baseballs, stones, and other blunt objects engaged in a "free for all" of street fighting on August 11. A verbal dispute over the impending Italo-Ethiopian conflict and the related Louis-Carnera bout had apparently sparked a fistfight that exploded into a massive brawl, leaving four wounded and leading to eleven arrests. An emergency squad consisting of radio cars, along with police on foot with tear gas bombs, managed to quell the unrest. African Americans claimed that Louis's recent victories had heightened white aggression in the district. Yet, according to the whites involved, black youths had been taunting passers-by, demanding that everyone acknowledge Louis's superiority. After the initial clash, the hostilities almost resurfaced the next day, as two bands of white males totaling around ninety exchanged verbal challenges with a group of African American men.[98] More than just an inspiration for the writings of New Negro elites, Louis's decisive win sparked an already smoldering sense of militant consciousness among the African American masses, bringing strong expressions of black pride to the surface that defied the combined strictures of white racism and elite decency.

Brown Moses?

In addition to energizing the masses, Louis's conquering of Carnera ignited a passionate debate in the black press regarding the proper representation of the race and what constituted legitimate forms of black progress. His victory gave writers and intellectuals a symbolic slate on which they attempted to negotiate and navigate their struggle for manhood rights. For the most part, black writers never questioned whether Louis had "sold out" to the white establishment or had shirked his duties to black America.[99] Rather, they argued over whether Louis, as boxer, was a suitable male figurehead for the future of the race, both nationally and internationally. After all, with his success in the corporal realm of pugilism, Louis presented somewhat of a dilemma to the traditional politics of bourgeois uplift. Many black elites struggled to come to terms with the fact that this popular hero was gaining unprecedented notoriety and wealth through muscular achievement, rather than education and erudition. As African Americans endeavored to escape the reductionist stereotypes of black physicality that consigned most to menial labor, Louis emerged as a gendered wild card with multiple possibilities in the changing game of racial construction.

Some commentators expressed their utter joy over Louis's manly victory as a source of racial pride and progress. Dan Burley of the *Baltimore Afro-American* dubbed Louis the "Brown Moses of the Prize Ring," claiming that through his win over Carnera, Louis had become a national leader in the way that Moses brought the Israelites out of bondage. Citing the fact that Texas was now competing for a chance to host a Louis fight, along with Missouri's decision to lift its ban of interracial matches, Burley maintained that Louis was literally knocking out Jim Crow, with his wins being every bit "as good as electing a Congressman to represent us in Washington."[100]

In some respects, Louis could exert physical force and command white attention in a way that escaped his black political and intellectual counterparts. Only in the ring could a black man actually harm a white man without being arrested or lynched. Because of the ostensibly apolitical nature of Louis's triumph, many black writers, conscious of its larger symbolic implications, could celebrate it in detail without fear of reprisal. Extensive photo layouts of the Italian Giant's boxing demise splashed across the pages of many black newspapers, presenting multiple pictures of Louis standing over his conquered foe.[101]

Even though some African American journalists highlighted Louis's mix of muscular prowess and mental acuity, contending that "his cunning brain work[ed] in accordance with fast and deadly fists," others cautioned black Americans not to place their hopes in the individual, physical triumph of Louis.[102] While the *Crisis* understood his importance to the "rank-and-file," they advised black America not "to hitch its wagon to a boxer, or base its judgments of achievement on the size of a black man's biceps or the speed and power of his left hook."[103] Moreover, another editorial in the *Baltimore Afro-American* claimed that the contributions of intellectual Race Men like Carter G. Woodson and W. E. B. Du Bois, along with the legal advances in the anti-lynching campaign, were "worth a dozen successes in the prize ring."[104] Regardless of its cathartic value, Louis's win had not altered the structures of oppression in America, nor had it blazed any new paths for racial progress. Placing more weight in the potential of academic and political tactics for achieving manhood rights, they questioned the significance of sporting victories.

Falling between these two extremes, some editorialists believed that even if Louis did not bring institutional changes, he was still an appropriate role model of racial uplift, especially for young boys. While not inclined to view Louis as "a Moses of the race or as an Economic Hope," one writer for the *Journal and Guide* maintained that the Bomber's "moderation, temperance, [and] modesty" offered the "real moral in his victory, the most important thing to be proud of."[105] A few weeks after the Louis-Carnera bout, the *New York Amsterdam News* attempted to put these ideals into action, founding and sponsoring a "Joe Louis Boys Club" that encouraged youngsters to follow in the footsteps of "America's model young man." According to its advertisement, the club's main purpose was to instill the young men of the community with Louis's discipline and competitive spirit.[106] Yet, however much adults wished that young boys would emulate Louis's respectability, the teen generation had different reasons for idolizing the boxer. According to the fieldwork of sociologist E. Franklin Frazier, black youths from all classes in the 1930s admired Louis for his conspicuous wealth and hip style and drew vicarious satisfaction from his brutalizing of white opponents.[107] To them, Louis was less about uplift and more about black pride and militancy.

Ultimately, even if the heavyweight emerged as a contested symbol with little concrete effect on the realities of long breadlines and Mussolini's imperial designs, his win over Carnera still served to shine a critical spotlight on the struggles and ironies of black life. Both journalists and cartoonists in the African American press used the gendered images of boxing to formulate political critiques that drew explicit connections between foreign fascism and domestic racism. The focal point of the *Chicago Defender's* picture page showed a battered Carnera on the mat with a caption that read, "I'd rather be in Ethiopia."[108] In another particularly poignant, postfight drawing, a boxer resembling Louis became a proxy for the Brotherhood of Sleeping Car Porters, standing victorious over a dazed Carnera look-alike that had "Pullman Company, Unionism" written across his chest.[109] As a figure that embodied the deep connections between diasporic and domestic politics, Louis's victory in the ring had underlined the hypocrisy and unfairness of not only Mussolini and the League of Nations, but also white America.

Pointing to the sheer absurdity of it all, another *Afro-American* editorialist wondered what "secret of mass psychology" turned white humanity in one part of the nation into a murderous mob, while in another "they cheer to the echo a little brown boy who pummels the gore out of a big white man mountain?"[110] Louis's victory over Carnera had exposed the many-headed beast of white supremacy, while also subjecting it to a cultural barrage of strong black manhood.

Schmeling takes Sampson

Following the Carnera fight, many journalists in the white dailies suddenly became repositories of advice for Louis, offering cautionary tales of what could happen if the young fighter let amusement and overconfidence get in the way of his boxing. Bill Corum of the *New York Evening-Journal* warned Louis to stick to his "Ma" and to steer clear of the jazzy night life in Harlem. In a patronizing, almost race-baiting fashion, the writer counseled: "Don't get big headed. . . . Behave yourself." Above all, Corum reminded Louis that he was not only a fighter, but a symbol to his race.[111]

On May 16, 1936, in Lakewood, New Jersey, Louis celebrated his twenty-second birthday, along with the official opening of his training camp for the first of his two bouts against Germany's Max Schmeling. Boxing's dignitaries, from Nat Fleischer of *Ring Magazine* to World Heavyweight Champion Jim J. Braddock, honored the young fighter for his spectacular achievements over the last year.[112] However, with his next match only a month away, one of the most popular questions in the white mainstream press was whether or not Louis "could take" the pressures of his newfound fame. As yet another test of his mettle as Race Man, Louis's skirmish with Schmeling would once again become a stand-in for larger racial conflicts at home and abroad.

As Louis began his preparations, Corum's foreshadowing of the young boxer's potential downfall seemed to be coming true. Over ten pounds heavier and reputedly more interested in improving his golf game than his fighting skills, Louis appeared disinterested and sluggish during his initial practices. Even though Louis was the younger and more talented boxer, journalists from both presses wondered if his apparent smugness would cause him to falter. As Lloyd Lewis of the *Chicago Daily News* contended, "Joe Louis is the only man who can whip Joe Louis."[113]

While some writers in the white dailies continued to infer that Louis's listlessness confirmed that blacks could not handle positions above their usual station, the African American press responded with continued faith in the abilities and ambition of their New Negro of the manly art. Although one journalist in the *New York American* argued that "success and plenty" were spoiling the former "canebrake baby" turned "million-dollar corporation," most reports in the black press tended to take on a more positive view of Louis's training efforts by the beginning of June.[114]

Outside the ring, African American writers celebrated Louis's new role as husband and provider for his sophisticated, beautiful bride, Marva Trotter, thereby appropriating the gender roles of white bourgeois society. After their wedding in September 1935, the black press seized on the opportunity to refute the popular racist image of Louis as a "Mammy's boy," promoting the young couple as black America's first family. Freed from the responsibilities of her secretarial job, Mrs. Louis pursued charity work, practiced the piano, visited the beauty salon, and attended parties of New York's black society. While Marva soon gained her own form of celebrity, admired by black women for her poise, charm, and fashion sense, she assured her fans that "Joe's the boss of our family and he's always going to be so." [115] Even though economic imperatives prevented most African Americans from fulfilling these patriarchal ideals, journalists shaped Louis and his wife into a public display of healthy black American family life.

Yet, an underlying critique of Louis's decision to marry before obtaining the heavyweight title would later come back to haunt Marva after her husband's loss to Schmeling. Even before their nuptials, many of Louis's black fans made it clear that they thought his managers needed to shield him from the corrupting influences of women to protect his strength. As one editorialist in the *Baltimore Afro-American* argued, "An athlete who marries is usually no good for a year, trainers say. And this is the reason managers of Joe Louis will be shooing sweet girls away from their charge until he is champion." The temptations of female sexuality were apparently a dangerous distraction in the field of manly battle, and the editorialist went on to warn Louis' handlers not to take any chances "with some Delilah who might snear [sic] their Sampson."[116]

In addition to this sexualized, domestic plotline, the Louis-Schmeling match up became a metaphorical battle in which African Americans could combat the theory of Aryan supremacy that stripped the Jews of their rights in Nazi Germany and kept blacks from achieving equality in the United States. The African American press had already been reporting the Nazi's persecution of the Jews and its links to American racism as early as 1933.[117] Arguably, the Jewish question did not acquire the same kind of popular resonance in the black press in comparison to the Abyssinian crisis, which still continued as a featured news item even in the summer of 1936. However, it was clear that, for some sectors of the black population, the Louis-Schmeling match had both international and national implications for the race. Although the suave Schmeling did not have the same savage appeal as Carnera, the black press still invited their readers to make ethnic comparisons, offering side-by-side photos of the fighters' physical weapons, along with listings of their measurements.[118]

In contrast, white sportswriters generally ignored the international implications of the fight, since Hitler's persecution of the Jews had not yet become an issue in the mainstream daily press. Even the Nazis had little interest in promoting their ties to the match, since they assumed that Schmeling would lose.[119] In the weeks before the bout, many white American dailies appeared to put aside their national allegiances to promote the German in articles and pictures. While the text of the *Atlanta Constitution* grudgingly argued for Louis's inevitable victory over Schmeling, the southern paper's absence of Louis pictures versus its numerous, handsome photos of the German heavyweight spoke volumes about who they wanted to win.[120] Other white sportswriters were more transparent with their allegiances to Schmeling, like Pat Rosa of the *New York Post* who claimed that the prideful and industrious German would certainly give Louis the "Drifter" a run for his money. For Rosa, this test of "mind . . . over matter" would favor the talents of Schmeling.[121] Louis was not the American hero that he would later become in his rematch against the German in 1938. For many white fans, the upcoming bout was decidedly racial rather than nationalistic.

Already delayed one day because of rain, the fight took place at Yankee Stadium on the overcast evening of June 19, 1936. The poor weather coupled with a Jewish boycott of the fight made for a relatively small crowd of 45,000 spectators. Unlike the cool, lean panther of just a year ago, Louis looked thicker around the waist, while Schmeling possessed the best physique of his career. In pre-fight interviews, Schmeling revealed that he had discovered a weakness in Louis's supposedly impenetrable defense, and he intended to exploit it. Throughout the bout as Louis consistently dropped his left guard when throwing his right, Schmeling hit him with stiff counterpunches to the jaw. In the fourth round, the German fighter rocked Louis with a hard right, sending him reeling. Although Louis managed to stand his ground in the face of many punishing blows, in round twelve Schmeling smashed him with a right, sending him to his knees against the ropes. As Louis rose to his feet on the count of four, Schmeling finished him off with another stiff right. Louis dropped to the canvas and lay prostrate as if sleeping.[122]

A shell-shocked black America went into mourning. African American fans all across the country hung their heads in gloom. Their Race Man had fallen to the representative of Aryan supremacy. As one report from Louis's home base of Detroit described, "It was like a sudden death in the family."[123] With black America grieving, the white press quickly threw their support behind Schmeling, arguing that the so-called Nazi boxer had proved "[h]e was too smart for the Negro." While Grantland Rice exaggerated when he deemed the fight the "most severe beating in ring history," the *New York Post* presented a pitiful picture of the fallen Louis on his backside, accompanied by a headline that reduced him to "Just a Scared and Beaten Boy."[124] Louis's loss seemed to confirm black America's inferiority.

African American fans did not know what to make of their "Superman's" fall from grace. Rumors of doping quickly hit the black press. Another particularly vicious example of the post-fight gossip pointed the finger of blame at Marva, charging that she had distracted Louis before the match by showing him a recent love letter from her former boyfriend. In the *Black Man*, Marcus Garvey maintained that Louis had simply married too early, reasoning that the young boxer would have won against Schmeling if he were still a single man. For Garvey and many of Louis's black fans, the tragic defeat appeared to prove the liability of women in the war of the races. Their male-centered conceptions of the fight for racial equality seemed to leave little room for the meaningful participation of women. Ultimately, Garvey hoped that Louis had "learned a lesson from the fight, that when a white man enters the ring in a premier bout with a black man, he realizes that he has in his hands the destiny of the white race." Apparently Louis had not taken his role as Race Man seriously enough.[125]

On the other hand, many black fans remained supportive of Louis, pointing to his integrity and respectability even in the face of defeat. In a letter to the *New York Amsterdam News,* Sam J. Jones of Brooklyn argued that Louis had proved his manhood by showing that he could withstand prolonged physical punishment. Moreover, Jones suggested that black America take its lead from Louis in the midst of this crisis because the young fighter's denial of the rumors, along with his willingness to take responsibility for his mistakes, illustrated his true sportsmanship and dignity.[126]

While their pillars of racial manhood toppled one by one, with the Italian conquest of Ethiopia and the continuing problems of the Great Depression, some journalists in the black press worried about the future progress of the race. As one post-fight headline in the *Chicago Defender* asked, "Haile Selassie First, Now Louis; Who Next?" Louis's loss against the German fighter had managed to bring things full circle, intensifying black Americans' fears about the implications of the Abyssinian defeat at the hands of Mussolini. Depicting the instability of racial uplift in the form of a "Stool of Achievement" lying on its side with two broken legs labeled "Louis" and "Selassie," one cartoonist argued, "It can still be repaired."[127] In the wake of the Brown Bomber's defeat, Race Men across the nation called upon each other to stand up and take charge. (See image 2.2.)

2.2 "It Can Be Repaired, " June 27, 1936. Joe Louis's loss to Germany's Max Schmeling seemed to underline the uncertainty of racial uplift in the 1930s. With Louis and Haile Selassie defeated, African Americans would have to search elsewhere for viable Race Men. Used with permission. Source: *Chicago Defender.*

By the time white America embraced Louis as a national hero with his famous knockout win in his 1938 rematch against Max Schmeling, black fans, even outside the United States, had long lauded the boxer as the epitome of black pride and success. In the heart of the Nazi nation, a young Afro-German man could barely contain his excitement over Louis's pummeling of Schmeling, as he sat surrounded by white patrons in a public bar. When asked what he thought of the fight, the Louis fan responded, "In sports, the best man wins." [128] This subtle, but smug reply incensed someone to throw an iron chair at his head. Louis's victory was more than just the symbolic overthrow of Nazi fascism; it challenged the masculine foundations of white supremacy. For the young Afro-German, it was not just an American triumph, but the triumph of a fellow black man connected to him through a cultural and political identity forged in the transnational crucible of racist and fascist oppression.

Undoubtedly, Louis was neither an uncomplicated hero of American democracy nor a simple figure of racial cooptation, for the real moral of his success stands as one of the most important cultural legacies of the New Negro era. His rise as the preeminent 1930s Race Man points to the period's larger trend toward the engendering of blackness as a male construct. Despite various class and generational tensions, conceptions of black dignity, black strength, black resistance, and even the imagined black nation remained intimately connected to the imagined status of black manhood. From popular culture to academics to political organizations, the "crisis of black masculinity" moved to the forefront of discussions on racial progress, with increasingly visible and vocal calls for the "proper affirmation of black male authority."[129] While political, economic, and social equality remained elusive, the fantastic successes of African American athletes with the racial integration of U.S. professional leagues in the following decades meant that sports emerged as the ultimate, public stage for this collective project in the assertion of black manhood. Moreover, calls for black male athletes to conform to the bourgeois, patriarchal standards of respectability and productivity as "role models" for young African American men, continues to pervade current discourse on the social significance and responsibility of black athletes.

Even though the U.S. Army would soon use the figure of Joe Louis to inspire tolerance among white G.I.'s, African Americans had already laid claim to him as Race Man and budding patriarch. His model of black masculinity—one that vanquished white men, while leading black women— stayed with African Americans as they left home to fight Hitler and later returned to take on Jim Crow again.

Notes

Parts of this article were presented at the 2003 Harvard University Graduate Conference on "Performing Ethnicity" and at the 2003 Annual Meeting of the Association for the Study of African American Life and History. The author would like to thank all of those who graciously helped this piece to evolve over multiple drafts, including Glenda Gilmore, Seth Fein, Paul Gilroy, Matthew Jacobson, Amy Bass, Jeffrey Sammons, Pamela Grundy, and the members of the Spring 2002 Yale Research Seminar in American History.

1. Heywood Broun, *New York World-Telegram*, 1938, qtd. in Chris Mead, *Joe Louis: Black Hero in White America* (New York: Charles Scribner's Sons, 1985), 159.
2. Frank Sinatra, "Foreword," in Neil Scott, *Joe Louis: A Picture Story of his Life* (New York: Greenberg, 1947).

3. St. Clair Drake and Horace Cayton offer a sociological account of the "Race Man" concept in *Black Metropolis: A Study of Life in a Northern City* (New York: Harcourt and Brace, 1945). They argue that this social type developed as a means for black Americans to resist their second-class status by pointing to black superiority in particular areas of expertise. In other words, the success of the Race Man became a metaphor for the success of all African Americans (390–392). In examining the various facets of Louis's popular construction as a 1930s Race Man, this article builds on the gendered critique of twentieth-century black politics in Hazel V. Carby, *Race Men* (Cambridge, MA: Harvard University, 1998). Black feminist scholars like Carby argue against the popular practice of equating the redemption of black patriarchal manhood with racial progress, since using the Race Man as the dominant metaphor for black success tends to render black women's roles and struggles, along with the relationship between racism and sexism, largely invisible. Moreover, this association of patriarchy with progress has often foreclosed a united front against the related oppressions of white supremacy and gender inequality. Please note that I use the terms African American and black or black American interchangeably throughout this article.

4. Richard Wright, "High Tide in Harlem," *New Masses,* July 1938.

5. Richard Wright, "Joe Louis Uncovers Dynamite," *New Masses,* Oct. 8, 1935, 18–19.

6. Drake and Cayton, *Black Metropolis,* qtd. in Mead, *Joe Louis: Black Hero in White America,* 92.

7. Chicago *Whip* qtd. in David Levering Lewis, *When Harlem was in Vogue* (New York: Penguin, 1979, reprinted 1997), 24.

8. See Booker T. Washington, *A New Negro for a New Century: An Up-to-Date Record of the Upward Struggles of the Negro Race* (Chicago: American Publishing House, 1900).

9. On the Harlem Renaissance as a literary movement see Lewis, *When Harlem Was In Vogue;* and Cary Wintz, *Black Culture and the Harlem Renaissance* (Houston: Rice University Press, 1988). For research that expands the scope of the New Negro movement see David Krasner, *A Beautiful Pageant : African American Theatre, Drama, and Performance in the Harlem Renaissance, 1910–1927* (New York: Palgrave Macmillan, 2002); Mark Schneider, *We Return Fighting: The Civil Rights Movement in the Jazz Age* (Boston: Northeastern University Press, 2002); and Brent Hayes Edwards, *The Practice of Diaspora: Literature, Translation, and the Rise of Black Internationalism* (Cambridge, MA.: Harvard University Press, 2003).

10. I ground my definition of resistance in the theory of political scientist Jim C. Scott. See *Domination and the Art of Resistance: Hidden Transcripts* (New Haven, CT: Yale University Press, 1990), 8–9, 41. Louis's victories offered moments when African Americans' "hidden transcripts" of grievances could be brought into public view. Moreover, my discursive deconstruction of the variety of covert ways that African Americans articulated their notions of black representation and resistance through Louis's persona and accomplishments employs Scott's overall conception of "infrapolitics" (19).

11. My analysis draws on historian Penny Von Eschen's discussion of black diasporic activism in the 1930s. See Penny Von Eschen, *Race Against Empire: Black Americans and Anti-Colonialism, 1937–1957* (Ithaca, NY: Cornell University Press, 1997). Louis's matches against Carnera and Schmeling further demonstrate the extent to which antifascism and anticolonialism informed public debates over black identity and politics during the Depression.

12. Edward Van Every, *Joe Louis, Man and Super-fighter* (New York: Frederick A. Stokes Co., 1936): book cover. Van Every was the white sports journalist who gave Louis his first feature break in the daily press. Black newspapers like the *Chicago Defender* carried advertisements for Every's biography (see June 13, 1936, 13).

13. Fans could read about Louis in the 1935 *Pittsburgh Courier* series, "The Life Story of Joe Louis, as told to Chester Washington and William G. Nunn." Other major black press organs also included regular updates about the boxer's life outside of the ring. Also see Van Every, 34, 36, 46.

14. "Here are Details on Weight and Size of Joe Louis," *Pittsburgh Courier,* June 8, 1935, section 2, 4.

15. B. Weinstein, "Joe Louis Comes to Town," *Young Worker,* June 25, 1935. Also see "The Real Joe Louis, by his sister Eunice Barrow," *Young Worker,* December 24, 1935, 1.

16. Theophilus Lewis, "Boxing Business Man," *New York Amsterdam News,* July 6, 1935.

17. Much of the literature depicts Louis as a docile "Uncle Tom" who functioned as a "race ambassador" to white America. In these treatments, the quiet, gentlemanly Louis pales in comparison to supposedly less conventional boxers like the flamboyant Jack Johnson and draft resistor Muhammad Ali. See Othello Harris, "Muhammad Ali and the Revolt of the Black Athlete," in *Muhammad Ali: The People's Champ,* ed. Elliot Gorn (Chicago: University of Illinois Press, 1995): 56. Also see Harry Edwards, *The Revolt of the Black Athlete* (New York: Free Press, 1969); Bill Hawkins, "The White Supremacy Continuum of Images on Black Men," *Journal of African American Men* 3, no. 3 (Winter 1998): 7–18; Othello Harris, "The Role of Sports in the Black Community," in *African Americans in Sport,* ed. Gary A. Sailes (New Brunswick, NJ: Transaction Publishers, 1998), 3–14; David K. Wiggins, "The Notion of Double Consciousness and the Involvement of Black Athletes in American Sport," in *Ethnicity and Sport in North American History and Culture,* eds. George Eisen and David K. Wiggins (Westport, CT: Greenwood Press, 1994) 133–156; and Gorn, ed. *Muhammad Ali.* See Ken Burns, "Unforgivable Blackness: The Rise and Fall of Jack Johnson." USA: PBS, 2005; Gail Bederman, *Manliness and Civilization: A Cultural History of Gender and Race in the United States, 1880–1917* (Chicago: University of Chicago Press, 1995) 8–10; and Randy Roberts, *Papa Jack: Jack Johnson and the Era of White Hopes* (New York: The Free Press, 1983). In particular, Ken Burns' documentary for PBS has brought the Jack Johnson story to a mass audience on PBS. This biographical film traces Johnson's public exploits and the heated controversies they created within the context of Jim Crow America. In particular, it details Johnson's

well-publicized marriages to white women, his unapologetic enjoyment of material riches from clothes to cars, and his notorious taunting of white opponents while beating them in the ring.

18. Mead, 156–157. While Mead champions Louis's contributions to the strug-
gle for racial integration, his project investigates Louis through the eyes of
white sources. For a discussion of state-sanctioned constructions of Joe Louis
in wartime propaganda, see Lauren Rebecca Sklaroff, "Constructing G.I. Joe
Louis: Cultural Solutions to the 'Negro Problem' during World War II,"
Journal of American History 89, no.3 (December 2002): 958–983. Also see
Jeffrey Sammons, *Beyond the Ring: The Role of Boxing in American Society*
(Chicago: University of Illinois Press, 1988): 97–129; Gerald Astor, *"And a
Credit to His Race": The Hard Life and Times of Joseph Louis Barrow,
a.k.a. Joe Louis* (New York: E. Dutton, 1974); Jill M. Dupont, "'The Self in
the Ring, the Self in Society': Boxing and American Culture from Jack John-
son to Joe Louis," Ph.D. diss. (Chicago: University of Chicago, 2000); Art
Evans, "Joe Louis as Key Functionary: White Reaction Toward a Black
Champion," *Journal of Black Studies* 16, no. 1 (September 1985): 95–111;
William H. Wiggins, "Boxing's Sambo Twins: Racial Stereotypes in Jack
Johnson and Joe Louis Newspaper Cartoons, 1908–1938," *Journal of Sport
History* 15, no. 3 (Winter 1988): 242–254; and Dominic J. Capeci, Jr. and
Martha Wilkerson, "Multifarious Hero: Joe Louis, American Society, and
Race Relations During World Crisis, 1935–1945," *Journal of Sport History*
10, no. 3 (Winter 1983): 5–25. Even though several valuable works examine
Louis's black folk hero status, they still tend to overlook key questions of
gender. See A. O. Edmonds, *Joe Louis* (Grand Rapids: Wm. B. Eerdmans
Publishing Company, 1973); Lawrence Levine, *Black Culture and Black
Consciousness: Afro-American Folk from Slavery to Freedom* (New York:
Oxford University Press, 1977); Wilson J. Moses, *Black Messiahs and Uncle
Toms: Social and Literary Manipulations of a Religious Myth* (University
Park: Pennsylvania State University Press, 1982); Richard Bak, *Joe Louis:
The Great Black Hope* (Dallas: Taylor Publishing Company, 1996); Donald
McRae, *In Black & White: The Untold Story of Joe Louis and Jesse Owens*
(London: Scribner, 2002); and Thomas Hietala, *Fight of the Century: Jack
Johnson, Joe Louis, and the Struggle for Racial Equality* (New York: M. E.
Sharpe, 2002).

19. Alain Locke, ed., *The New Negro: Voices of the Harlem Renaissance* (New
York: MacMillan, 1925, reprinted 1992): 5, 8, 16.

20. Bederman, *Manliness and Civilization*, 5, 25.

21. In analyzing New Deal public art and theater, Melosh illustrates the period's
preference for constructions of rugged, white manhood in opposition to the de-
tested, feminine images of weakness and over-refinement. See Barbara Melosh,
*Engendering Culture: Manhood and Womanhood in New Deal Public Art and
Theater* (Washington: Smithsonian Press, 1991): 43.

22. See Kevin Gaines, *Uplifting the Race: Black Leadership, Politics, and Culture
in the Twentieth Century* (Chapel Hill: University of North Carolina Press,
1996), 12–13; and Martin A. Summers, *Manliness and its Discontents: The*

Black Middle Class and the Transformation of Masculinity, 1900–1930 (Chapel Hill: University of North Carolina Press, 2004), 8–9.

23. See Beth Tompkins Bates, *Pullman Porters and the Rise of Protest Politics in Black America, 1925–1945* (Chapel Hill: University of North Carolina Press, 2001), 7–12; Robin D. G. Kelley, *Race Rebels: Culture, Politics, and the Black Working Class* (New York: Maxwell Macmillan, 1994) 112–114. Bates's analysis of A. Philip Randolph's BSCP places the trade union's increasingly strident demands for the "manhood rights" of full citizenship within context of the larger shift from a "politics of civility" and white patronage to the aggressive, "new-crowd" demonstrations of the 1930s and 1940s. Moreover, as Kelley contends, the Communist International's 1928 Black Belt thesis of self-determination offered black radicals a racial platform from which to participate in the Party's masculine vision of militant, international revolution.

24. Summers, *Manliness and its Discontents*, 151–153.

25. Emphasis added; "Joe Louis Needs Boosters, Not Knockers," *Pittsburgh Courier*, May 11, 1935.

26. "Joe Louis is 'Three Times Seven,'" *Pittsburgh Courier*, May 18, 1935, section 2, 4.

27. "Joe Louis–Primo Carnera Fight Holds Spotlight," *Pittsburgh Courier*, June 22, 1935, section 2, 4; "Rise of Joe Louis is Biggest Sensation in Sports History," *Chicago Defender*, May 4, 1935; and Lewis E. Dial, "The Sports Dial," *New York Age*, July 6, 1935, 8.

28. In the early 1930s, the sport of boxing was on shaky ground, experiencing its own kind of depression. With the title changing hands almost yearly in the first part of the decade, public interest waned. Quickly becoming the sport's biggest drawing card, Louis ushered in what some contemporary authors termed the pugilistic New Deal. See Alexander Johnson, *Ten—And Out! The Complete Story of the Prize Ring in America* (New York: Ives Washburn, 1936): 245.

29. For a discussion of Jacobs' monopoly of fight promotion in the 1930s, see Richard Bak, *Joe Louis: The Great Black Hope*, 82–87. Also see Daniel M. Daniel, *The Mike Jacobs Story* (New York: Ring Book Shop, Inc., 1949). Although historian Jeffrey Sammons casts Louis's affiliation with Jacobs as an unfortunate loss for Louis and black America, it was necessary for them to align themselves with Jacobs because the promoter's influence insured that Louis would have a chance to challenge for the world title (*Beyond the Ring*, 98).

30. Mead, 53.

31. Although Carnera was a former world heavyweight champion, by 1935 his shady associations with gangsters like Al Capone, along with his participation in what many believed were fixed fights, was common knowledge in the boxing world. Moreover, his early days as a carnival sideshow act, in addition to his freakish size and frequent clumsiness in the ring, made him a kind of laughing-stock of the profession. For more biographical information on Carnera see Astor, chapter 7. Also see Clifford Lewis, *The Life and Times of Primo Carnera* (London: Athletic Publications, 1932). Lewis, in conjunction with Carnera's French manager Leon Sée, wrote this biography in defense of Carnera's already tarnished image.

32. "Joe Louis, Training for Carnera Match, Decides to Become First Beardless Heavyweight Champion," *Macon Telegraph,* June 17, 1935; Van Every, 119, 123. For a contemporary discussion of the common stereotypes of black fighters as "cowardly and unwilling to face punishment," see Robert Scott McFee, "The Rise of the Dark Stars," *Vanity Fair,* July 1935, 57.

33. "Rice Says 'Terrific Ballyhoo' Puts Big Burden on Joe Louis," *Baltimore Sun,* June 25, 1935. Also see Joe Williams, "Negro Star on the Spot, Louis by Early Kayo, Or—Carnera will Outmaul Him," *New York-World Telegram,* June 25, 1935; and Hugh Bradley, "Louis Picked to Win But He Must Start First to Stop Primo," June 25, 1935.

34. Sid Mercer, "50,000 to See Fight Tonight," *New York American,* June 25, 1935.

35. See Al Monroe, "Fight May Even End in Two if Detroiter Starts Early," *Chicago Defender,* June 22, 1935; Bill Gibson, "Brown Bomber Should Win before 6th Round," *Baltimore Afro-American,* June 15, 1935, 21; Russell J. Cowans, "Louis in Great Shape, Battle Predicted," *Pittsburgh Courier,* June 22, 1935, section 2, 4; and "Louis's Spar Mate, Six and One-Half Feet Tall, Gives Carnera 5 Rounds," *California Eagle,* June 21, 1935.

36. "Joe Louis Can Take It; His Manager Tells Why," *Chicago Defender,* June 22, 1935.

37. "New York Likes Joe Louis," Claude Barnett Papers, Part I, Series A, Reel 10, May 20, 1935, 16.

38. William R. Scott, *Sons of Sheba's Race: African-Americans and the Italo-Ethiopian War, 1935–1941* (Bloomington: Indiana University Press, 1993): 9. Also see Brenda Gail Plummer, *Rising Wind: Black Americans and U.S. Foreign Policy, 1935–1960* (Chapel Hill: University of North Carolina Press, 1996); Von Eschen, *Race Against Empire;* Joseph E. Harris, *African American Reactions to War in Ethiopia* (Baton Rouge: Louisiana State University Press, 1994); J. Diggins, *Mussolini and Fascism: The View from America* (Princeton, NJ: Princeton University Press, 1972); William R. Scott, "Black Nationalism and the Italo-Ethiopian Conflict, 1934–1936," *Journal of Negro History* 63, no. 2 (April 1978): 118–134. For contemporary explanations of the conflict and its implications for African Americans see J. A. Rogers, "Italy over Abyssinia," *Crisis,* February 1935, 38–39, 50; Makonnen Haile, "Last Gobble of Africa," *Crisis,* March 1935, 70–71, 90; and George Padmore, "Ethiopia and World Politics," *Crisis,* May 1935, 138–139, 156–157; and Charles H. Wesley, "The Significance of the Italo-Abyssinian Question," *Opportunity,* May 1935, 148; Marcus Garvey, "Barbarism in America," *Black Man,* October 1935, 8. The Abyssinian crisis was arguably the most talked-about story of foreign fascism for African Americans, as reports on the conflict continued to appear on the front pages of black newspapers well into 1936.

39. See cartoon entitled "Maybe He Bribed the Guard," *Chicago Defender,* March 9, 1935. This cartoon shows an Italian burglar robbing an Ethiopian storehouse of natural resources as a League of Nations security guard looks the other way. Also see "The League of Nations," *Chicago Defender,* March 2, 1935, editorial page; "See Mussolini Forcing a War with Ethiopia: France, England Join Plot Against Africa," *Chicago Defender,* May 25, 1935, 2.

40. Langston Hughes, "Call of Ethiopia," *Opportunity,* September 1935, 276.

41. Scott, *Sons of Sheba's Race,* 9, 59. For more detailed descriptions of popular black activism during the Abyssinian crisis, see Scott's chapters entitled "Grass-Roots Activism" and "Harlem Mobilization." For a southern perspective, see Kelley, "Afric's Sons with Banner Red" and "This Ain't Ethiopia, But It'll Do" in *Race Rebels.*

42. Joe Louis, with Edna and Art Rust, Jr., *Joe Louis: My Life* (New York: Harcourt Brace Jovanovich, 1978): 58.

43. Although journalists in the white, mainstream press also played on the international implications of the Louis-Carnera fight, they characterized the impending invasion as a wholly foreign affair with no real links to contemporary, domestic forms of racist fascism in the United States. In their reports, Louis did not function as a representative of American democracy, but rather, he took on the role of an Ethiopian auxiliary defending Abyssinia from the ravages of Italian fascism. See Westbrook Pegler, "Emperor Goes in Training for His 'Big Boy Peterson': Mussolini Takes Leaf Out of Carnera's Science of Warfare By Selecting Setup For His First Battle," *Birmingham Post,* February 16, 1935; "Police Squads to Guard Louis," *Baltimore Sun,* June 25, 1935; and John Lardner, "Can't Help Being King, Says Louis: Wins First Real Skirmish Between Men of Italy and Ethiopia," *Evening Bulletin Philadelphia,* June 26, 1935.

44. Irene Gaskin, "Boys Salute the Flag, the Red, Black, Green," *Negro World,* July 5, 1924, 10, qtd. in Summers, 100. On the male-inflected language and performance of African redemption in Garvey's UNIA, see Summers, "A Spirit of Manliness," in *Manliness and its Discontents,* 66–110. In Garveyite rhetoric, the physical space of Africa and the process of redemption both presented ideal sites for the assertion of black manhood as men took on a militaristic function while women played supporting roles. For the African Americans' gendered imaginings of Haiti, see Mary A. Renda, *Taking Haiti: Military Occupation and the Culture of U.S. Imperialism, 1915–1940* (Chapel Hill: University of North Carolina Press, 2001) 261–288. New Negro artists' rehabilitation of Haiti as "America's Africa" involved a re-reading of the Haitian Revolution as a triumphant narrative of black manhood and black pride through figures like Toussaint L'Ouverture.

45. For a list of Louis's popular nicknames see Lenwood G. Davis, *Joe Louis: A Bibliography* (Westport, CT: Greenwood Press, 1983) 202–203. Also see Mead, 50–51.

46. Jay Jackson, "Ethiopia Shall Stretch Forth—(Modern Version: His Fist)," *Chicago Defender,* May 25, 1935, editorial page.

47. Chester Washington, "Sez Ches," *Pittsburgh Courier,* June 1, 1935, section 2, 4; Hughes, "Call of Ethiopia."

48. Van Every, 24, 26, 27. One pre-fight cartoon even played up the Asian characteristics of Louis's face, touting him as "more Mongolian than Senegambian." See Burris Jenkins, Jr., "Brown Study," *New York Evening Journal,* June 6, 1935.

49. Dan Burley, "Louis Ready for Baer," *Baltimore Afro-American,* April 20, 1935, 21.

50. "Just let Italy Try it!" *Chicago Defender,* June 15, 1935; "One Look at His Hair," *Baltimore Afro-American,* April 6, 1935, 4.

51. *New York Times,* November 28, 1930, 31; Astor, 95; and *The Kings of the Rings,* produced by Jean Labib and T. Celal for HBO Home Video, 1995.

52. "No Snap," *Crisis,* March 1935, 81. Also see "Ethiopia Defiant as Italy Plans to Grab Africa," *Chicago Defender,* February 16, 1935; "Ethiopia Has 500,000 Men for Conflict," *Chicago Defender,* June 22, 1935, 1–2; "Ethiopia in Stern Reply to Mussolini," *Chicago Defender,* May 11, 1935, 1; and "Look Out, Italy," *Chicago Defender,* June 15, 1935, 1.

53. Compare Marcus Garvey's treatise on the value of preparedness with respect to the Abyssinian crisis in "Lest We Forget," *Black Man,* Oct. 1935, 4, with Louis's various training updates in the black press such as "Couldn't Take it, Ace Clark Deserts," *Pittsburgh Courier,* June 15, 1935; Russell Cowans, "Louis in Great Shape, Battle is Predicted," *Pittsburgh Courier,* June 22, 1935, section 2, 4; and Dan Burley, "Louis In Tip-Top Form on Eve of Carnera Bout," *Baltimore Afro-American,* June 22, 1935, 20.

54. Thomas O'Halloran, "Forced Civilization Hit By Educator in Talk on Ethiopia," *New Jersey Post,* October 30, 1935, James Weldon Johnson Scrapbooks, Box 7, Beinecke Library, Yale University, New Haven, CT. For other examples of the savage versus civilized debate, see Rev. E. A. Abbott, Letter to the Editor, "Mussolini and Ethiopia," *New York Age,* July 20, 1935; and "'Civilizing,' Ethiopia," *New York Age,* August 3, 1935, 6.

55. J. A. Rogers, "Selassie, the Gentleman, and Mussolini, the Braggart, Compared: J. A. Rogers Gives Graphic Comparison of Italian and Ethiopian Tactics," *Pittsburgh Courier,* August 3, 1935, section 2, 2. Garvey also concurred with Johnson's assessment of the Italian aggression, critiquing Mussolini's plans to bomb and gas innocent women and children and labeling the dictator, "the arch-barbarian of our present age." See Marcus Garvey, "The War," *Black Man,* October 1935, 1. Also see Garvey's poems, "The Beast of Rome," *Black Man,* October 1935, 4, and "Il Duce—The Brute," *Black Man,* July-August 1936, 6.

56. Paul Gallico, "At it Again," *New York Daily News,* June 25, 1935. The white dailies' infantilized, Sambo portrayals of Louis continued even after his defeat of Carnera. See Hoff, "Ink Pot-Pourri," *St. Paul Pioneer Press,* July 21, 1935; Ed Hughes, "Another Case of 'Bad Hands,'" *Brooklyn Daily Eagle,* August 17, 1935. For a more thorough discussion of Sambo depictions of black boxers, see Wiggins, "Boxing's Sambo Twins."

57. See "Joe Louis Purchases Home for his Mother in Detroit," *Chicago Defender,* April 13, 1935, 7; and Julia B. Jones, "How does it feel to be the Mother of the Next Heavyweight Champ?" *Pittsburgh Courier,* April 27, 1935, section 1, 11.

58. See "The Stage is Set," *New York Amsterdam News,* June 22, 1935, 14. In a stark inversion of the traditional savage-civilized dichotomy, a picture of the clean-cut Louis in his defensive crouch stands alongside an enlarged photo of Carnera's scowling, teeth-baring mug. For examples of cartoons that follow these conventions see George Lee, "Sporting Around," *Chicago Defender,* May 18, 1935, 15; and *Chicago Defender,* June 1, 1935, 13.

59. For comprehensive treatments of black activism for economic and citizenship rights in the South see Robin Kelley, *Hammer and Hoe: Alabama Communists During the Great Depression* (Chapel Hill: University of North Carolina Press, 1990); Patricia Sullivan, *Days of Hope: Race and Democracy in the New Deal Era* (Chapel Hill: University of North Carolina Press, 1996).

60. Jervis Anderson, *This was Harlem: A Cultural Portrait, 1900–1950* (New York: Farrar Straus Giroux, 1982): 242–244. For contemporary descriptions of the Harlem Riot, see "Machine Guns Set Up," *Baltimore Afro-American,* March 23, 1935, 1–2; "Harlem Race Riot," *Pittsburgh Courier,* March 23, 1935, 1–2; "Blame Radicals for Spreading False Rumors," *Chicago Defender,* March 23, 1935, 1–2.

61. "Joseph Louis Barrow," *Opportunity,* October 1935, 295.

62. Paul Oliver, *Aspects of the Blues Tradition* (New York: Oak Publications, 1970): 149–50.

63. Lyrics qtd. in Oliver, 152 –53.

64. See "New Buick Brings Smile to Joe Louis," *Pittsburgh Courier,* May 11, 1935. For the most part, the white dailies only included pictures of a shirtless Louis in his fighting gear. In comparison to the black press, mainstream white papers did not print as many photographs of Louis. Even though writers often made him the centerpiece of their articles, pictures of Louis often failed to accompany their words. Instead, the white press tended to showcase more pictures of Louis's white opponents, even if they were foreigners and underdogs like Carnera.

65. Al White, "New York Likes Joe Louis," Claude Barnett Papers, Part I, Series A, Reel 10, May 20, 1935, 16; and "Louis Called Best-Dressed Heavyweight," *Baltimore Afro-American,* June 15, 1935, 1.

66. *Chicago Defender,* June 22, 1935, 16. This same ad also appeared in several other black newspapers. Although some may argue that Louis's endorsement of Murrays Pomade is representative of his willingness to ape white culture, historians like Robin Kelley view "the conk as part of a larger process by which blacks appropriated, transformed, and reinscribed coded oppositional means onto styles derived from the dominant culture" (Kelley, *Race Rebels,* 168).

67. Al White, "New York Likes Joe Louis," Claude Barnett Papers, Part I, Series A, Reel 10, May 20, 1935, 16; "Defender Cameraman Follows Joe Louis Around in N.Y.," *Chicago Defender,* May 25, 1935, 17; "Joe Louis Captures New York," *New York Age,* May 25, 1935, 15. For a description of the vaudeville show, see Louis, *Joe Louis: My Life,* 54.

68. William G. Nunn, "Courier Writer Paints Word-Picture of Trip to Pompton Lakes Camp," June 8, 1935.

69. Bill Gibson, "Hear me talkin' to ya," *Baltimore Afro-American,* June 15, 1935, 20. Also see Russell Cowans, "Room Said to Have Been Used by Geo. Washington Now Used by Joe Louis," *Baltimore Afro-American,* June 8, 1935, 21; Jersey Jones, "Joe Louis's Training Camp is One of Most Modern and Ideal Spots in the Metropolitan District," *New York Age,* June 8, 1935, 8; *Baltimore Afro-American,* June 8, 1935, picture page; Lewis E. Dial, "The Sports Dial," *New York Age,* June 22, 1935.

70. See Jones, "Joe Louis's Training Camp,"8; "Sutton, Who Helped Johnson Before Title Fight, To Be Dietician In Joe Louis Camp," *Pittsburgh Courier,* April 6, 1935, section 2, 5; Chester Washington, "Visiting the Joe Louis Training Camp," *Pittsburgh Courier,* June 8, 1935; "Joe Louis Going Great on 2-Meal Diet—Sutton," *Pittsburgh Courier,* June 15, 1935; and William G. Nunn, "Courier Writer Paints Word-Picture of Trip to Pompton Lakes Camp," *Pittsburgh Courier,* June 8, 1935. For descriptions of Louis's poor eating habits in contemporary white sources, see Charles Heckelmann, "Eat and Sleep Pastimes for Bomber Louis," *Brooklyn Daily Eagle,* July 17, 1935; and Van Every, 56–57.

71. For articles on Jack Blackburn's skills as a "mastermind" trainer see "Joe Louis Going Great as He Trains for Big Bout with 'Da Preem'," *Pittsburgh Courier,* June 8, 1935; and "Joe and Jack—The Perfect Combination," *Pittsburgh Courier,* July 20, 1935, section 2, 4. For discussions of Roxborough and Black's business smarts see "Joe Louis and His Board of Strategy," *Pittsburgh Courier,* March 23, 1935, section 2, 5; "No White Managers," *Baltimore Afro-American,* June 22, 1935, editorial page; and "Joe Louis Wins," *Chicago Defender,* June 29, 1935, editorial page. According to Summers, young, black radicals of the 1930s spoke out against the traditional avenues of white patronage, even as they accepted white funds, in order to dissociate themselves from the prevailing feminized image of the dependent black man (*Manliness and its Discontents,* 234–240).

72. Van Every, 127–129.

73. Lewis E. Dial, "The Sports Dial," *New York Age,* June 8, 1935, 8; "Many Visitors at Joe Louis's Camp," *Baltimore Afro-American,* June 8, 1935, 16; and "Johnny Dundee, Claude Hopkins Visit Louis Camp," *Baltimore Afro-American,* June 15, 1935, 20; Joseph Mitchell, "Harlem Argues Itself to Sleep About Joe Louis and How He'll Tear the Stadium to Pieces Tonight," *New York World-Telegram,* June 25, 1935.

74. Harden letter qtd. in Lewis E. Dial, "The Sports Dial," *New York Age,* June 22, 1935; Julia B. Jones, "How Does it Feel to Be the Mother of the Next Heavyweight Champ?" *Pittsburgh Courier,* April 27, 1935, section 1, 11.

75. Wilbur Wood, "Louis Iceberg in Ring or Out: Bomber Abhors Flattery and Flatterers and Girls Don't Interest Him," *New York Sun,* August 12, 1935; "Mother is Louis's Only Sweetheart," *Buffalo Evening News,* July 16, 1935; Jack Miley, "Naw, I ain't got no girl 'cause I ain't got no time for women," *San Francisco Chronicle,* June 27, 1935.

76. "Famed Bomber Ready," *New York Amsterdam News,* June 22, 1935, 14; "Hear me talkin' to ya," Bill Gibson, *Baltimore Afro-American,* June 15, 1935, 20; Doc Morris, "Following Joe Louis," *Chicago Defender,* June 15, 35; and "Live Clean Life, Louis Advises Ring Hopefuls," *Baltimore Afro-American,* June 15, 1935.

77. Most biographers have pointed to an apocryphal list of Roxborough's rules of etiquette for the young fighter printed in many white and black papers to demonstrate Louis's dissociation from Johnson. According to the list, the Bomber was never to have his picture taken with white women; he was never

to go to a nightclub alone; he would not participate in soft or fixed fights; he was never to gloat over his opponents; he was to keep "deadpan" in front of the cameras; and he was to live and fight clean (Mead, 52; Sammons, 98). Yet, as Louis himself admitted in his various autobiographies, he often did things that were in direct violation of Roxborough's "list." However, the Jacobs publicity machine kept these aspects of his character out of the public eye.

78. Van Every, 56–57. After the fight, many articles continued to describe Louis as lazy and sleepy. See John Lardner, "Joe Louis Sleeps and Sleeps But He's Happy, Family Says So," *New York Post,* June 27, 1935; Margaret Garrahan, "Fame Doesn't Bother Giant Killer Louis: Joe Just Sleeps and Eats as Rest of World is Agog Over Win," *Birmingham News,* June 28, 1935; Henry McLemore, "Joe Louis May be a Whirlwind Killer Inside Ring Ropes, but Out of Them He is World's Laziest Man," *Wilkesbarre Times-Leader,* July 2, 1935; and Charles Heckelmann, "Eat and Sleep Pastimes for Bomber Louis," *Brooklyn Daily Eagle,* July 17, 1935.

79. "Famed Brown Bomber Ready," *New York Amsterdam News,* June 22, 1935, 14.

80. For examples of contemporary boxing manuals see Nat Fleischer, *Scientific Blocking and Hitting and Other Methods of Defense* (New York: C. J. O'Brien, 1935); *Boxing: A Guide to the Manly Art of Self Defense* (New York: American Sports Publishing Company, 1929); and Tommy Burns, *Scientific Boxing and Self Defence* (London: Athletic Publications, 1927). These books teach the reader how to be a skilful boxer rather than a brutish brawler.

81. Russell Cowans, "News from the Joe Louis Camp," *Pittsburgh Courier,* June 1, 1935, section 2, 4; Lewis E. Dial, "The Sports Dial," *New York Age,* June 8, 1935, 8; Gibson, "Hear me talkin' to ya,"20; and "Live Clean Life." In addition to these articles, many photos showed Louis in various stages of his training day. See "Joe Louis at Work," *Chicago Defender,* June 1, 1935, 15; and "Defender Scribe Does Road Work with Louis," *Chicago Defender,* June 15, 1935.

82. Westbrook Pegler, "Fair Enough: Plan to Stage Italian-Negro Prizefight at Very Door of Embittered Harlem is Called New High in Stupid Judgment," *New York Sun,* 1935. Brisbane article qtd. in Mead 58.

83. Al Monroe, "Speaking of Sports," *Chicago Defender,* May 25, 1935, 15. Also see "Pegler Inspires Race Riot," *Chicago Defender,* May 25, 1935; "Do They Want Trouble?" *New York Amsterdam News,* June 15, 1935; and "Columnist Spoofs Rumor of Trouble at Louis-Carnera Go," *Journal and Guide,* June 1, 1935, 14.

84. "Do They Want Trouble?" *New York Amsterdam News,* June 15, 1935.

85. "Louis-Carnera Fight Boycott is Sought by Daily," *Baltimore Afro-American,* June 22, 1935, 1; and "Uses Papers to Separate Groups Here," *Chicago Defender,* June 22, 1935, 1.

86. The Harlem Riot had exposed an existing class divide in terms of appropriate race representation and activism. In the aftermath, establishment uplifters expressed their disapproval of the riot and attempted to distance themselves from "the mob." The editors of *Opportunity* claimed that "the mob does not and

cannot reason," and that it drew its sanction from the underworld of the "irresponsible soap box orator and the street corner agitator." Thus, more civilized black leadership needed to "direct the aspirations of the Negro into peaceful channels" of protest. See "The Harlem Riot," *Opportunity*, April 1935, 102. For a general discussion of these political tensions, see Gaines, *Uplifting the Race*, 246–251.

87. Chester Washington, "Louis Favored to Win by Knockout," *Pittsburgh Courier*, June 22, 1935.

88. Jack Miley, "Riot Guns Ready at Primo-Louis Fight," *New York Daily News*, June 26, 1935.

89. The box-office stat is from Miley, "Riot Guns Ready at Primo-Louis Fight." Also see "Prejudice Kept Joe Louis-Carnera Fight Off the Air," *Indianapolis Crusader*, July 6, 1935. This was the first major fight in years that had failed to get national airplay, and the *Indianapolis Crusader* argued that networks' actions exposed their racial prejudice. Bowing to popular demand, the Michigan Network comprised of several stations managed to put the fight on air, aided by the sponsorship of Detroit's Stroh Brewery. A couple other Detroit stations also aired telegraphic reports of the fight.

90. For advertisements for organized trips see the *Chicago Defender*, June 8 and June 22, 1935; and the *Baltimore Afro-American*, June 8, 1935.

91. "Distinguished Gathering Throngs Stadium for Heavyweight Battle," *New York Times*, June 26, 1935, 24; Dan Parker, "Fans on Hand Early," *New York Daily Mirror*, June 26, 1935; "Singing, Happy Negroes Jam Bleachers To See Ring Idol Continue Win String," *Boston Herald*, June 26, 1935; and "Louis-Carnera fight drew sport fans from all over country; Gross receipts were $328,655.44," *New York Age*, July 6, 1935.

92. "Stars of Stage, Screen, Mingle with the Masses," *Pittsburgh Courier*, June 29, 1935, section 1, 4; and "List of Those at Big Bout Amazes," *Pittsburgh Courier*, June 29, 1935, section 1, 4.

93. "Louis-Carnera fight drew sport fans from all over country." The fight also broke the record for newspaper coverage, with hundreds of journalists from both presses on hand.

94. Mead, 59. The following description of the fight is based on my viewing of the fight film acquired from private collector Ken Noltheimer of Ringwise, Inc., along with contemporary white and black press reports, and secondary sources. See *New York Daily Mirror*, June 26, 1935; "Al Monroe in Vivid Story of Big Fight," *Chicago Defender*, June 29, 1935, 14; and "'Ches' Gives The Courier Readers Ringside Story," *Pittsburgh Courier*, June 29, 1935, section 1, 4.; and Mead, 59–61.

95. Floyd J. Calvin, "Harlem Goes 'Mad With Joy' as Joe Louis Chops Down Giant Opponent," *Pittsburgh Courier*, June 29, 1935, 1; and Astor, 102. Similar scenes played out across the country. In Macon, Georgia, a throng of 6,000, with an estimated 3,500 blacks, congregated in front of the press offices of the *Telegraph* to hear regular updates of the fight. In Detroit, thousands of supporters reportedly converged on the Joe Louis headquarters at St. Antoine and Beacon Streets, and in Chicago, around 10,000 fans blocked traffic out-

side the offices of the *Chicago Defender* until the wee hours of the morning. See Bobby Norris, "White or Black—He's Dynamite," *Macon Telegraph*, June 27, 1935; "Detroit Fans Believe Baer Gave up Title to Evade Joe Louis," *Journal and Guide*, June 29, 1935, 14; and "10,000 Hear Defender Broadcast of Fight," *Chicago Defender*, June 29, 1935, 1.

96. Bernard Young, Jr., "Conquest of Italian Foe is Complete," *Journal and Guide*, June 29, 1935, 2. Also see "Brisbane and Pegler," *Chicago Defender*, July 6, 1935.

97. Joseph Mitchell, "Harlem is Wild About Joe Louis, Don't Folks Here Sleep? He Asks," *New York World-Telegram*, June 27, 1935; Archer Winsten, "There's only Joy in Harlem as Joe Louis is Acclaimed"; Joseph Harrington, "Many Injured Celebrating Victory"; and "Harlem Celebrates," *Chicago Daily Tribune*, June 27, 1935. This scene is also supported by pictures and descriptions contained in the documentary *I Remember Harlem*, Schomburg Center for Black Culture, New York Public Library, Audiovisual Division, New York, NY.

98. "Race Riot Quelled in Jersey City," *New York Age*, August 17, 1935, 1, 11.

99. There is one article that warned Louis "not to get too broad in [his] sympathies" and therefore, neglect the special needs of his people and his special obligation to black America. However, this piece was the exception, rather than the rule. See Gordon B. Hancock, "A Letter to Joe Louis," *Journal and Guide*, July 13, 1935, 6.

100. Dan Burley, "Calls Joe Louis Worth Vice President or Congressman," *Baltimore Afro-American*, July 6, 1935, 16.

101. See "How Louis Smashed Primo's Defense," Pittsburgh Courier, July 6, 1935; "The Scene as Joe Louis Smashed his Way to Victory Over Giant Carnera," Pittsburgh Courier, June 29, 1935, picture page; "Through the Magic of the Speed Camera the Guide Gives you a Louis-Carnera Ringside Seat," Journal and Guide, July 4, 1935, 14; and "'David Anoints Goliath' with Barrage of Bruising Leather," Chicago Defender, July 6, 1935, 14.

102. Bill Nunn, "Perfect Fighting Machine," *Pittsburgh Courier*, June 29, 1935. Also see "Celebrities Praise Louis for Victory," *Chicago Defender*, June 29, 1935, 7.

103. "Joe Louis and Jesse Owens," *Crisis*, August 1935, 241.

104. "How Proud Should We Be of Joe Louis's Victory?" *Baltimore Afro-American*, July 6, 1935, 4. Also see "Three of a Kind," *New York Amsterdam News*, July 6, 1935, editorial page.

105. "The Moral in Joe Louis' Victory," *Journal and Guide*, July 13, 1935, 6.

106. "Joe Louis Boys Club," *New York Amsterdam News*, July 14, 1935, 4.

107. E. Franklin Frazier, *Negro Youth at the Crossways* (New York: Schocken Books, 1940, 1967), 174–185.

108. "Graphic Story of Louis-Carnera Fight Told in Pictures," *Chicago Defender*, June 29, 1935, 13.

109. Chase, "Another Joe Louis," *New York Amsterdam News*, July 13, 1935, 12. Also see "Front Page," *Chicago Defender*, July 6, 1935. In this cartoon, the artist has a black man with the words "you and me" on his back reading a

number of front page headlines like "Joe Louis Wins," "Jesse Owens Sets New Records," "Haile Selassie Defies Italy," while gruesome caricatures of the Brain Trusters, Huey Long, Mussolini, and Hitler complain that the black men have stolen their space. Once again, race progress, and even the racial subject is male.

110. William N. Jones, "Day by Day," *Baltimore Afro-American,* July 6, 1935, 4; and Ralph Matthews, "Watching the Big Parade," *Baltimore Afro-American,* July 6, 1935, 4.

111. Bill Corum, "Stick to your 'Ma,' Joe," *New York Evening-Journal,* June 27, 1935. Also see "Risko Warns Louis Against Overconfidence with Max," *New York American,* June 16, 1936.

112. Fred Van Ness, "Louis Celebrates 22nd Birthday; Cuts Cake and Gets Gold Belt," *New York Times,* May 14, 1936.

113. Lloyd Lewis, *Chicago Daily News,* June 17, 1936. For other examples from the white press that discuss Louis's poor showing at Lakewood, see "Louis Listless in Sparring with Mates," *New York American,* May 27, 1936; and Hype Igoe, "Bomber Can't Resist Lure of Golf Course," *New York Evening Journal,* June 4, 1936. For examples in the black press, see Al Monroe, "Bomber Fails to Slay 'Em in Workouts, *Chicago Defender,* May 30, 1936; and Ralph Matthews, "Joe's Camp Upset," *Baltimore Afro-American,* June 6, 1936.

114. James Cannon, "Fame and Riches May Bring About Louis' Downfall," *New York American,* June 2, 1936. For examples of positive reports in the black press, see "Brown Bomber Back in his Stride," *Chicago Defender,* June 6, 1936; "Joe Louis Impressive in Camp Workout Sunday," *Baltimore Afro-American,* June 13, 1936.

115. Thelma Berlack-Boozer, "Joe's Always To Be the Boss of the Family," *New York Amsterdam News,* June 20, 1936. For examples of Marva's exposure in the black press, see "Sunday Workout Shows Look Like Social Affair," *Pittsburgh Courier,* June 6, 1936, section 1, 9; "Harlem Elite Deluge Marva Louis with Favor!" *Pittsburgh Courier,* June 20, 1936, section 1, 9; "The Bomber's Bride," *New York Times,* June 19, 1936. For examples of white press reports that depicted Louis as a young boy under the disciplinary control of his "Mammy," see the series of articles that ran in the *New York Daily Mirror* in the early part of July 1935: "Joe's Mammy Sees Lesson in Poverty," July 6, 1935; "Joe's Behavior Mother's Care," July 7, 1935; "Joe in Church Sunday Under Mother's Care," July 8, 1935; "Mother Warns Joe of Sugar-Mouths," July 8, 1935; "Joe's Mother O.K.'s Fights," July 12, 1935; and "Mother Confident Joe Will Be Champ," July 13, 1935.

116. "Keeping the Girls Away from Joe," *Baltimore Afro-American,* July 13, 1935. For descriptions of Louis's appeal with the ladies see the series of articles in the *Baltimore Afro-American* from July 13 to August 24, 1935, that described his fan mail and the various incidents in which mobs of women rushed him for his autograph.

117. Several secondary sources offer general analyses of the connections between Jim Crow in the South and Nazi Germany. See Glenda Gilmore, "An Ethiop

Among the Aryans: African Americans and Fascism, 1930 to 1939," unpublished manuscript; Stefan Kouhl, *The Nazi Connection: Eugenics, American Racism, and German National Socialism* (New York: Oxford University Press, 1994); and Seth Forman, *Blacks in the Jewish Mind: A Crisis of Liberalism* (New York, New York University Press, 1998). For some contemporary discussions of the connections see Rabbi Stephen S. Wise, "Parallel Between Hitlerism and the Persecution of the Negroes in America," *Crisis,* May 1934, 127–129; Jacob J. Weinstein, "The Jew and the Negro," *Crisis,* June 1934, 178–179 (part 2 in July 1934 issue); "Stop Lynching Negroes is Nazi Retort to American Critics," *Pittsburgh Courier,* August 10, 1935, section 1, 3; and "American Nazis Quite as Bestial as Their German Brothers," *Baltimore Afro-American,* August 24, 1935, 6.

118. See "Powerhouses of Heavyweights Compared," and "Fighting Eyes Show Determination of Heavyweight Fighters," *Pittsburgh Courier,* June 20, 1936.

119. Mead, 92. See "Schmeling's Departure for the U.S. Practically Ignored in Germany," *New York Times,* April 16, 1936; and "Hitler Still Frowns on Max Fighting Joe Louis in U.S.," *New York American,* May 19, 1936.

120. See "It's All Part of Day's Work—In Busy Schmeling's Camp," *Atlanta Constitution,* June 14, 1936; "Can He Stop the Bomber?" *Atlanta Constitution,* June 18, 1936; "Mapping Out Maxie's Battle Plans," *Atlanta Constitution,* June 19, 1936. This same trend was characteristic of other papers like the *St. Louis Daily Globe Democrat* and the *New York Daily News.*

121. Pat Rosa, "Stolid Uhlan's Pride and Ideals May Halt Joe Louis the 'Drifter'," *New York Post,* June 13, 1936. Several reports also praised Schmeling for his hard work at training camp. See Bill Farnsworth, "Industrious Max Changes Style for Louis Bout," *New York Evening Journal,* May 13, 1936; Mary Knight, "Girl Reporter Discovers Civilized Fight Camp," *Dayton Herald,* June 13, 1936.

122. I base the above description of the fight on my viewing of the fight film acquired from private collector Ken Noltheimer of Ringwise, Inc., along with contemporary white and black press reports.

123. "Detroit, Harlem in Gloom as Idol Collapses," *Detroit Evening Times,* June 20, 1936.

124. Fred Digby, "Max in Sensational Win!" *New Orleans Morning Tribune,* June 20, 1936; "Just a Scared and Beaten Boy," *New York Post,* June 20, 1936; "Schmeling Knocks Out Louis in Twelfth Round; Most Severe Beating in Ring History, Says Rice," *Atlanta Constitution,* June 20, 1936, 1.

125. See "Continued Probe of Rumors That Bomber was Doped," *Chicago Defender,* June 20, 1936, 1; "Louis Not Doped; Love Rift Spiked," *Baltimore Afro-American,* June 27, 1936; and Marcus Garvey, "The World As It Is," *Black Man,* July/August 1936, 19–20.

126. Sam J. Jones, "He Can Take It," *New York Amsterdam News,* June 27, 1936, 12.

127. *Chicago Defender,* June 27, 1936, 19.

128. Interview with Gupha Voss recalling her father's story of the second Louis-Schmeling fight qtd. in Clarence Lusane, *Hitler's Black Victims: The Historical*

Experiences of Afro-Germans, European Blacks, Africans, and African Americans in the Nazi Era (New York: Routledge, 2002), 215. There are other examples of international attention from people of color. See "What the People Think," *Pittsburgh Courier,* December 28, 1935, section 2, 4, for a congratulatory letter from "the colored young people of Costa Rica." For a reference to purported fan mail from India, see "Fans Advise Joe Louis on Marriage," *Baltimore Afro-American,* July 20, 1935, 2. Also see "Joe Louis Beats Braddock and Is World Champion," *The Bantu World,* South Africa, June 26, 1937, 1.

129. Philip Brian Harper, *Are We Not Men? Masculine Anxiety and the Problem of African American Identity* (New York: Oxford University Press, 1996), x.

PART II:
FANS

THREE

Race and Silence
in Argentine Football

Grant Farred

Introduction

On the main highway leading from the airport into downtown Buenos Aires, a few miles before you reach the famous Avenida de Julio, the main street that goes through the heart of the city, there is a twenty-story apartment complex. Emblazoned on it in the winter of 2001 was a mural of Juan Sebastian Veron (in the colors of his then new club Manchester United, where he stayed for only two seasons), impeccably manicured goatee and all. Before the disastrous World Cup 2002 campaign, the stylish midfielder was an Argentine national hero. The image on that building is a salient one, both because of who Veron is and who he is not. That mural is a signal accomplishment for the unsettled midfielder; having struggled to put his stamp on Chelsea (the west London club that plays in the English Premier League) as he did at Lazio (of Italy's Serie A), Veron now seems increasingly likely to head back to Italy to play his club football—Inter Milan is rumored to be his favored destination. Surprisingly, in a nation that loves forwards, especially wayward, inspirational ones, here the Argentine capital chose to honor a midfielder. Moreover, Veron hails from the hinterland city of La Plata, a flat, sprawling garrison town with a strong border ethos—even though it is less than an hour from Buenos Aires. Veron's attachment to Buenos Aires, or "Baires" as it is more commonly known, is only secondary, a product of his brief stint with the city's most popular and populist club, Boca Juniors. (The other two big clubs in Baires are River Plate, arguably more middle class and, most important, Boca's biggest rival in Argentina; and Racing Club, a historically underachieving side that lacks the following of the nation's Big Two.)

In Argentine footballing history, the pantheon of national icons is dominated by forwards. The inaugural figure in this lineage is the legendary Alfredo Di Stefano, the great 1950s striker who played for River Plate before leaving for Millionarios of Bogota, Columbia. Di Stefano, of course, became internationally famous in the white shirt of Spanish giants Real Madrid, where he and Hungarian great Ferenc Puskas starred in the 1950s and early 1960s. (Di Stefano became a Spanish citizen and later represented his adopted country.) In contemporary footballing memory, however, the lodestar forward is Mario Kempes, the prolific goalscorer with the flowing black locks who was instrumental for Argentina at Copa Mundial 1978. In that World Cup, the Dutch "total football"[1] philosophy renowned for its erudition, artistry, sophistry, and interchangeability of personnel,[2] could not match the Kempes' exploits upfront. (Colloquially rendered, "total football" requires all eleven players to be equally comfortable with the ball. Apart from the goalkeeper, the infield players are expected to be able to, in a single moment, change from defender into attacker, or vice versa. Comfort on the ball, preferably at the players' feet, is the cornerstone of "total football.") At Copa Mundial 1978, Kempes was, in Uruguayan writer Eduardo Galeano's poetic terms, "an unstoppable colt who liked to gallop over the grass covered with a snowfall of confetti, his hair flying in the wind."[3] Argentina won 3–1 in extra time, mainly due to Kempes's two goals and Dutch bad luck—Rob Rensenbrink's powerful shot hit the post a minute before the final whistle in regulation when a goal seemed certain and the trophy bound for Amsterdam. But, alas for the Orangemen, deprived of their star player Johan Cruff (who refused to play in Argentina because of his opposition to General Videla's dictatorship), it was not to be.

Kempes was supported, when Argentina won their first World Cup, by the disciplined goalkeeping of Ubaldo Fillol and a defense well marshaled by the imperious center-back dubbed "El Gran Capitan," Daniel Pasarella, arguably the greatest skipper in Argentine history and later the coach of the national team from 1994 to 1998. The 1978 team was coached by Cesar Menotti, a philosophical man who believed in playing football as the "beautiful game"; his style of football, named "Menottismo," was also, he later claimed, a cultural riposte to the brutal Videla regime. Menotti was (implicitly, and aesthetically) against those who administered the "final solution": the "disappearance" of Argentine dissidents, often within spitting distance of the nation's football stadia where Copa Mundial 1978 was played.

In 1986, after the "Guerra Sucia" (Dirty War) was over, perhaps too soon forgotten by too many, and democracy restored to the nation, the pantheon of forwards welcomed its most venerable member: the goalscoring wizard Diego Armando Maradona, the very reason Argentina won the World Cup for the second time in Mexico City. Coached by Carlos Bilardo, playing a more physical game, the South Americans beat Germany 3–2, with Maradona, the forward of all Argentine forwards, laying on an exquisite pass for Jorge Burruchaga's winner.[4] Maradona is one of Juan Veron's heroes and the greatest Argentine player ever—or, some would simply say, the greatest player ever. Maradona, the demigod from a shantytown on the outskirts of Baires, star of Argentinos Juniors, Boca Juniors, Barcelona, and Napoli (the southern Italian side for whom he was at his most outstanding as a club player), would disagree with such a judgment. When asked once if he was the greatest Argentine player ever, he answered, dismissively, "No."[5] For him, that honor belonged to Di Stefano.[6] Since Maradona's descent into drugs, infamy, corpulence (and a near brush with death in April 2004), Argentina has produced, among others, strikers such as Claudio Caniggia, Gabriel "Batigol" Batistuta, and Hernan Crespo (who was for a season Veron's teammate at Chelsea), goalscorers who have all added their own twist to the definition of prolifigacy and waywardness. When set against these flamboyant countrymen, and by virtue of being a midfielder, the Veron mural in Baires represents an emblematic moment in Argentine footballing culture. In honoring Veron, was the nation metonymically paying its debts to the country's great midfielders? Or, more provocatively, did Veron represent—or could he be made to represent, as this essay suggests—a different kind of Argentine history, a culturally unprecedented engagement with the nation's racial politics (or lack thereof) as well an entirely new kind of conversation between the (postcolonial) present and the future? (Postcolonialism, the political movement by African, Asian, and Caribbean communities that successfully struggled to overthrow European colonialism—Britain, France, Belgium, the Netherlands—and secure independence for these nations after World War II, occurred earlier in Latin America. By the middle of the nineteenth century, most of Latin America had gained independence from Spain and Portugal. Argentina became a sovereign nation in 1810.) As highly unlikely as it might be, can the mural of Juan Veron (which has long since been painted over, as I found out on a subsequent visit in late 2003) be momentarily appropriated as embodiment of Argentina's black unconscious? As a symbol of its unspoken and, arguably, unspeakable, postcolonial unconscious?

Born and raised in El Mondogno, La Plata, Juan Sebastian is the son of Juan Ramon Veron. Like his son, the elder Veron played for Estudiantes of La Plata. In the 1960s Juan Ramon was a talented forward nicknamed "Bruja." Juan Ramon was called the "Witch" in part because of his hooked nose, a feature the younger Veron has inherited. The older Veron also earned his nickname because of the goalscoring "magic" in his boots, a characteristic for which the midfielder son is not quite as renowned. "Seba," as the English commentators have taken to calling Juan Sebastian, began his career with the team from La Plata at the tender age of five. Ever attuned to the history of their clubs, Estudiantes fans bequeathed the father's sobriquet to the son: the La Plata faithful baptized the younger Veron "La Brujita," the "Little Witch."

It was clear from Argentina's 2002 World Cup plans that coach Marcelo Bielsa, shockingly retained after his failure in Asia (Japan and South Korea cohosted the event), was going to run—to borrow basketball terminology—every one of his team's plays through Veron.[7] National skipper Roberto Ayala's injury was, to cast this turn of events cynically, fortunate because Veron had already been installed as the de facto captain by the Argentine public and the media. With Ayala sidelined, Veron assumed the armband and the official role of team pivot. No one, it seemed, touched the ball without looking for Veron, no matter how well or how badly he was positioned.

As no Argentine fan needs reminding, that strategy failed, in part because Veron was not accustomed to a system that centralized him without allowing him to play his natural game. Veron did not build his reputation as forager (in the mold of, say, France's Claude Makalele or Germany's Didi Hamann), the combative, effective midfielder who can win the ball and then lay it off for the creative players (Liverpool and England's Steven Gerrard is the only midfielder who can do both; and, in addition, the massively talented Gerrard can score goals himself); Veron has, rather, always been a gifted link man, playing just off the strikers, capable of hitting raking, incisive passes and occasionally unleashing the crisp shot on goal. For all his status as one of the game's preeminent midfielders, by Argentina's final game of the 2002 tournament, Veron's ignominy was complete as the gifted young Pablo Aimar of Valencia (Spain) replaced him as the Argentine playmaker. "Seba" gracefully took his place on the bench and, even when he did come on minutes from the end of Argentina's final game against Sweden, he looked a forlorn figure. Veron was aimless, adrift in a team that had been designed for him. There were moments in that final game, punctuated as it was by a pathos that rarely articulates itself on the football field or even in relation to the game, when Veron's fate recalled that of the talented black English winger John Barnes, another great admirer of Maradona.

Brilliant in his play for his club Liverpool, Barnes was expected to carry a mediocre England team for two World Cups after a breathtaking goal in 1984 at the Maracana Stadium against Brasil and an unforgettable cameo in Mexico 1986 against Argentina in the quarterfinals. In a game now known for the infamy and sublimity of Maradona's two goals, the "Hand of God" one, when he fisted the ball over the keeper Peter Shilton's head, and the breathtaking sequel where he left several English defenders hapless in his wake, Barnes was scintillating. Barnes only came on for the last sixteen minutes in the quarterfinal as substitute and he proceeded to mesmerize the Argentine defense with his jinking runs. The black winger created England's only goal and nearly made another. Like Barnes, who was criticized for his "poor" displays for the national team by the English press, Veron became, at the 2002 World Cup, yet another talented black player labeled a club level powerhouse but a failure in the international arena.

The invocation of Barnes, however, is both resonant and an ideologically inefficacious way of characterizing Veron. As Barnes made clear throughout his career and with a compelling erudition in the opening lines of his autobiography, he has always been a self-consciously black player: "Short of size and breath, the policeman kept about twenty yards behind me, trailing me for all his worth. As I continued my way through the streets of London, I knew what was going through the policeman's mind. He was convinced this black boy was heading down Wigmore Place intent on burglary. . . . Being followed after dark by the police became part of my life. . . . I had to turn down Wigmore Place—I lived there."[8] A consciousness of racism was integral to Barnes' life [9] while Veron, on the other hand, is symptomatic of Argentine society: race is a subject that Argentines almost never address. More precisely, it is that race represents an impermissible discourse: race is the social and political issue that cannot be spoken for fear of revealing the nation's racial un/conscious. It is an issue, then, that Argentina cannot accommodate. Translated into the Buenos Aires vernacular, race is *feaca:* it constitutes the act of "political relaxation." The absence of a racially conscious discourse marks a retreat from the politics of race. *Feaca* represents the deliberate limitation of discussion about the everyday economies of racial politics; especially as racial politics functions in the rest of Latin America and the postcolonial world—where race and postcolonialism are inextricably linked.

On Sunday afternoons, "Portenos" (as the residents of Baires are known) engage in a social practice dubbed "*feaca.*" After lunch they leave their homes and inhabit public spaces, many of them spacious green parks on a waterfront dotted with boats. *Feaca,* however, marks less a withdrawal from the mundane into the pleasurable than it does a disengagement with the political. *Feaca* is the act of ideological retreat. Temporally,

it takes place in that limited, imagined moment between intense domesticity, the most important meal of the week and its social accoutrements, and
the resumption of labor—the mythical, almost Fordist work week, since
this is a nation where many citizens do work on Sundays. As a metaphor,
feaca enables a broad discussion about how race, the historic silences that
mark Argentine history and culture, the discourse of postcoloniality, and
how this Latin American—or Southern Cone, to be more specific—nation's
self-imaginings can be read off the body of the black footballer.

Juan Sebastian Veron is posited as a black footballer, although he will
neither speak nor acknowledge his own racial Otherness, in order to critique the wider cultural politics of race in contemporary Argentina; or, the
absence of a politics of race. Veron is designated as "black" despite the fact
that, in Argentina, he is not recognized as such. The point of this argument
is not simply to contradict or challenge Argentina's racial categories,
though that is clearly integral to this essay, but to locate Veron disjunctively
in relation to his society: to make him racially unrecognizable to both himself and Argentina by situating him, or his physiognomy more precisely, as
"black" within the terms of postcolonial discourse. The intention here is
less to impose blackness upon Veron than it is to offer racially charged categories as a critique of Argentine exceptionalism. Paradigmatically, this
essay suggests that the Argentine postcolonial can most imaginatively—and
incisively—be understood through "futbol," the nation's most venerated
cultural practice and, consequently, the repository of Argentina's most crucial political and ideological anxieties. Sport is taken seriously here, as is evidenced by the extensive cultural history that frames and informs the
discussion (and the way in which Veron, Maradona, Boca, and River are
invoked to animate the issues), providing but a brief glimpse of the passion
that the game arouses in Argentina. Boca-River games are an intense spectacle, a battle that encompasses class and intracity rivalry, a never-ending
debate about one style of playing "futbol" as opposed to another, an instance of overidentification with a cultural institution that determines social consciousness in Buenos Aires. Everywhere an Argentine diaspora is to
be found. As a critique, this essay locates sport as the most efficaciously
way of disrupting race as Argentina's denied public fiction: the condition
that can and, therefore, must, following Oscar Wilde's dictum about forbidden love, be made to speak its complicated name through the body of
the footballer. It is a recognition, this rendering of Veron and/in his relationship to the nation (al imaginary), of the crucial ideological silences that
reside within the national passion.

Veron, as a footballer who has encountered "blackness" in its many
manifestations, in the course of his career from Latin America to Italy to
England (places where race operates differently), as a cultural icon whose

body can be identified differently because of the epistemological girdings of postcolonial theory, is read here against himself; he is read against the dominant understanding of him in Argentina; he is located as nonwhite, as the putatively black footballer who invokes that haunting specter of the nation's unconscious: not simply the blackness that marks the rest of Latin and Central America, but as the spectral incarnation of the native, the "Indian," a designation—a racialized pejorative—ascribed to Maradona at a nationally critical moment in the Napoli star's career. When Maradona returned home, disgraced, after testing positive for the banned drug Ephedrine at the 1994 World Cup in the United States, at his first match in Baires (at River Plate's stadium) he was booed and called an "Indio de mienda"—a "native" in its most derogatory enunciation (there were also "El Negras" thrown in, intermittently, just for good measure). Maradona was racilialized through indigenization, collapsing the only two categories that can bear the ideological weight of Othering in Argentine society; and this only in moments of trauma, as Maradona's failed drug test was interpreted. In that moment at River Plate's stadium, Maradona was made to bear more than the shame of the nation's defeat on its most holy terrain, the football field. He was, albeit temporarily, situated outside the nation's racial imaginary; he was denounced as having brought shame upon the Argentine nation precisely because he was not Argentine, but "native"—the indigenous subject resuscitated for postgenocidal punishment. The experience of Othering, of rejection by the nation because ethnicity has been alloyed into the source of shame, is something Veron has never endured, and Maradona alone, because of his singular cultural status, could survive. Maradona's rehabilitation did not take very long; a decade after the fact, his elevated status was clearly demonstrated by the outpouring of concern for him in April 2004 when he lay gravely ill in a Baires hospital.

Veron figures in this essay as a sports star, the national icon that, like all celebrities, resonates beyond, speaks for, and is appropriated (and expropriated) by constituencies well beyond his own cultural terrain—the Argentine and international football field. Veron is attributed, ironically invoking Juan Peron, iconic Argentine leader from 1946–55 and 1974–74 who inspired "Peronisma," as a cultural corollary to *feaca,* the quality of "Veron-isma:" the capacity not to produce or imagine radical social transformation but to maintain the silence around potentially disruptive ideological and historical issues. "Veron-isma" stands as the nonarticulation of race, racial difference, or racism in Argentine sport—and the broader society. Veron is representative—at the very least, "evocative," in current sport's sociology discourse—of the overburdened conjuncture of race, racism, (national) difference, "Indian-ness," postcoloniality, and historic silences (and silencings) in his national community.[10]

He is positioned directly in relation to (and sometimes as metonymic of) his nation so that Veron stands as more than simply a case study (though he is that, too, in moments) of the footballer who will not claim a racialized identity. (Not in his native Argentina, not in the cauldron of football racism perpetrated by the supporters of Roman clubs such as Lazio, nor in an England where there is—because of the history of racist abuse and the recent success of black players—a heightened awareness of racism.) Racial reticence, "Veron-isma," is, rather, symptomatic of the Argentine predilection for silence/silencing. According to the society's most eloquent voice, Jose Luis Borges, Argentines may be predisposed to silencing themselves: "significant of Argentine reserve, distrust and reticence, of the difficulty we have in making confessions, in revealing our intimate nature."[11] However, Borges's insights about the Argentine national character are as always keenly accurate.

In order to interrogate this phenomenon, Veron is situated as the footballer whose cultural persona provokes, indeed makes possible, crucial questions about his society—even, it should be added, as Veron and football occasionally drop out of the more focused discussion about postcoloniality: Why can Argentine society, and Veron himself, not assign him a more complex racial identity? Why does race constitute the racially unspeakable for so many Argentine constituencies? And, within Argentine discourse, what kind of structural reimagining can the designation, or, at least, the discussion about his "race," make possible? What kind of interrogative possibilities does sport, and the "futbol" star in particular in this instance, make possible for a critique of both Argentina's exceptionalism and its historically complex postcoloniality?

Argentine Exceptionalism

As other Latin American societies, from Santiago, Chile, to Sao Paulo, Brasil, from Lima, Peru, to La Paz, Bolivia, will colloquially testify, Argentina has always thought of itself not only as different from the rest of the continent, but as not being of the continent at all. Argentina, in Latin folklore, is the South American country where the inhabitants speak Spanish but think in Italian, and identify with Europe. Buenos Aires is less, as popular parlance would have it, the Paris of Latin America than it, subliminally, imagines itself as being psychically at one with the capitals of Europe. The "Portenos" live imaginatively in Paris, their psychic desire overcoming their geographical remove. Argentina is in the relationship of the *feaca* to its context. It signifies nothing so much as a deliberate disengagement from the rest of the continent—it is in Latin America but not of it. Argentina stands, in this way, as the refutation of Marxist materialism:

in and for Argentina, context—the physical place that is inhabited—means nothing, or, very little at all. So exceptional a society is Argentina that its leaders, from Augustin Justo (1932–38) to Juan Peron, the nation's self-proclaimed "First Sportsman" (and supporter of the unfancied Racing Club), would not allow the country to participate in the World Cup because it believed so inveterately in its footballing superiority. Argentina competed for the first time in 1958.

This South American society may value and appreciate the "Latin" football skills of a Di Stefano or a Maradona but there is nothing of the Samba about the Argentine style of play. This is the team of the tango: emphatic defensive thrust followed by an equally emphatic, choreographed parry, occasionally interspersed with moments of individual brilliance and improvisation. Forwards from Kempes to Caniggia to Crespo may be venerated, but the success of its teams is built on a sturdy, almost militaristic, defense. Daniel Pasarella, captain of the 1978 World Cup team, was not, coincidentally, a man with a conservative disposition, the player whose compact style inadvertently represented the glum authority of the military dictatorship. It is not surprising that Copa Mundial 1978 was most often compared, as an ideological spectacle, to the 1936 "Hitler" Olympics in Berlin. In the unself-conscious words of Berti Vogts, the West German captain in 1978, "Argentina is a country where order reigns. I haven't seen any political prisoners."[12] These were the kind of sentiments that made the Videla Junta proud.

Pasarella was the Beckenbauer of Copa Mundial 1978; Pasarella was, in his own way, as Hegel might have had it, a "world historical individual" in his capacity to represent the ideological tenor of his moment. Kempes, Ossie Ardiles, and the flamboyant Ricky Villa apart, the 1978 team had nothing of the resistant spirit of the *desaparecidos* (*"las madres de los desaparecidos,"* those mothers of detainees and victims bravely protesting the "Dirty War" against the nation's citizens that was being waged even as the World Cup was being held in, and won by, Argentina; those citizens so blithely denied by Berti Vogts) about them. "Menottismo" or not. Pasarella's was a disciplined team, inadvertently (whether they liked it or not) the *generalíssimo's* team that defeated the stylized brilliance of Dutch masters such as Neeskens, Krol, and Rensenbrink. In a telling reversal of roles, the 1978 Argentina team played like a European side, efficient with occasional bursts of inspired play, while the Dutch, with their slick passing, technical proficiency, and relaxed skill, had very much the spirit of the inspired Latin team about them. To their credit, the Dutch players refused to salute the Argentine dictators during the final ceremony.

If Argentina thinks of itself as different from, not paradigmatically or ideologically a part of Latin America, it is in large measure because it conceives of itself as an outdated, imperialist Europe.[13] Which is to say,

Argentina conceives of itself not as contemporary postmodernist, multiracial, racially and culturally hybrid Europe, the types of places where
Veron, Aimar, and Ayala currently ply their trade (frequently on European passports), but as the Europe of the nineteenth-century colonialist
project. Argentina's national self-image is, ideologically, deeply rooted in
the nineteenth century. This "long epoch" marks the moment when Argentina won its independence (1810) and the grand decades, 1852 to
1890, which saw the formation of the nation-state; the nineteenth century was also a period that saw massive European investment (especially
by Britain). Well into the first half of the twentieth century Argentina, in
a relationship only interrupted by the economic collapse of the 1930s,
"flourished as an informal component of the British Empire—smirkingly
referred to as the 'sixth dominion' by British diplomats."[14]

After centuries of being colonized, trading and culturally aligning with
various European powers (from Spain to Italy to England), and huge-scale
immigration by Europeans, in Argentina's national imaginary, its identity is
white. Not in the problematic sense offered by contemporary theorists of
whiteness in which Euro-American roots are ontologically challenged, but
rather in an Orientalist, nineteenth-century imperial sense in which an es-
sentialist, epidemiological whiteness is posited in relation to Otherness.
With its historic attachment to Europe, Argentina conceives of itself as
white because it is high cultured, literate, and racially distinct from its Latin
neighbors. Like so many understandings of the national self, Argentina's
self-perception turns upon negation. Both in the sense that it prides itself
upon not being the Other, and in that it distances its (national) self from the
social, cultural, and racial "lacks" of other South American countries. In
relation to Latin America, Argentina thinks itself more economically prosperous, more culturally advanced; it regards its infrastructure as more sophisticated, its education system more developed, and its national literature
(in which the venerated figure of Jorge Luis Borges plays a seminal role)[15]
more rich, complex and recognized in European capitals. Unlike all other
Latin American countries, Argentina has no "native" or "Indian" population. It is, by virtue of a long-ago committed genocide of its indigenous
population, white. In the national imaginary, Argentina is not like any of
its Southern Cone neighbors: Argentina is not Chile, Argentina is not Peru,
Argentina is not its near neighbor Uruguay (once an Argentine province).

Black Brasil

Most important, Argentina is not Brasil. For the best part of a century, Argentina has defined itself against its northern neighbor Brasil. Especially in

terms of race, Argentines conceive of themselves as superior to Brasilians. When Argentina plays Brasil, the stakes are immeasurably high. In Veron's terms, these matches are a "clasica," a contest in which it is not only two countries, much like an India-Pakistan cricket test, but two cultures (speaking in literally and metaphorically different languages) in competition. Argentina-Brasil football matches dramatize the multilayered contestation between two sets of values, two conflicting national identities, and two antagonistic definitions and perceptions of Latin America. In these ideologically overdetermined "clasicas," Argentine commentators, occasionally, despite the prospect of censorship or approbation from their networks or their viewers, refer to the Brasilian players as "macacos," monkeys.[16] The "macacos" designation functions as a Darwinian trope that signifies Brasilian racial inferiority. Through naming the Brasilians "macacos," Argentina marks its opponents as belonging to an earlier, less developed civilization, invoking a racial typology that has through centuries of Orientalist discourse been associated with Africans or people of African descent. Africans, as colonized and decolonized subjects, in their native continent and in the diaspora, have long been dubbed "macacos" or apes, ascribing to black subjects an inherent intellectual underdevelopment. The Argentine commentators are assigning to Brasilians a place as the racialized natives of the Conradian "jungle," or, the rain forest, to make the topographical metaphor more geographically appropriate. The Brasilians stand in symbolic contradistinction to Argentines, who trace their genealogies to Europe, be it north or south.

The "macacos" discourse demonstrates that there is a postcolonially recognizable consciousness of race—of racial difference, of racialized hierarchy—in Argentine society. It is simply a discourse of intranational difference that is determinedly externalized. It is a form of politicized speech that belongs, and applies, elsewhere, not in Argentina. Race is a discourse that has a geographical border (Brasil) as well as a psychological one (the Argentine consciousness). Neither of these borders can be permeated by race—the geographical border localizes blackness in Latin America, the national psyche is protected by an inveterate faith in its own unsullied whiteness. Argentina's is thus an expedient, selective racial consciousness; it only identifies race—blackness—when it exists outside of itself, when it can be used to define Argentina against its geographical context. Not recognizing Veron as racially discordant with whiteness is, for this reason, an ideological choice—it is the mark(/er) of his non-Brasilian-ness.

Brasil's play has, since football traveled north from the Pampas (courtesy of its exportation to Argentina by the British) to the land of the Sugar Loaf, been marked by the kind of flair, inventiveness, and freedom of expression admired the world over. Like the black cricketers of the Caribbean,

Brasilian football is identified as charismatic, flamboyant, and artistic. In Africa and in Latin American societies that identify themselves as black, football functions as a reverse, and benign, cultural Middle Passage. Brasil's skill, flair, and footballing vision, as well as its passion for playing the game with *joi de vivre,* is the diaspora's gift to the motherland. It is for this reason that Brasil's triumphs are celebrated the postcolonial world over as culturally racialized, "black" victories. The triumph not only of the subaltern, but the triumph of a "black" style, the articulate expression of a samba way of playing sport—ever mindful, of course, of the stereotypes that attach to such forms of cultural articulation. It is for this reason that the Argentines, where freedom of cultural expression is so frequently absent (although the technical expertise and defensive organization is respected and Boca Juniors often put on a sparkling show) could never serve as a model for Africa or the postcolonial world. There is nothing "black" about the way Argentina plays, the inspirational talents of Diego Maradona (when the fallen hero is racilialized and indigenized) apart.

The Racially Unmixed

Unlike the inverately mixed Brasilians, with their commingling of African, indigenous, and European heritage, Argentina's national fiction is founded upon the notion of racial purity. Argentina imagines its population to be constituted out of a blend of Europeanness—its citizens trace their roots to Italy, to Spain, and to England. This is a problematic national imagining that reflects a crucial element of the Argentine identity. It is a nation where, with the exception of courageous groups of dissenters (*"las madres de plaza de Mayo"*) and the critical movement the Madres spawned,[17] historically, the populace has shown itself able to disengage from the atrocities of the past and the present. The history and the legacy of the dictatorships, the immunity ("indulta") afforded the perpetrators of violence against the "disappeared" by the post-Junta governments of Raul Alfonsin and Carlos Menem, the memory of the "disappeared," the difficulty in prosecuting those who sanctioned the adoption of children of the *desaparecidos,* the genocide committed against the native subjects who once inhabited the now largely unpeopled province of Patagonia, those horrific events remain insufficiently addressed in Argentine society. (As important as the non- or underengagement with its past atrocities are, however, it is not at the core of its exceptionalist identity. Nations such as Australia, with the centerpiece event being the 2000 Sydney Olympics where the opening ceremony spectacularly recreated the Aboriginal past, capped by Aboriginal athlete Cathy Freeman leading the nation into the arena, frequently use sport to reconstruct themselves culturally. Argentina's exceptionalism derives from its dislocated sense of itself and its historical determination to animate and sustain that national fiction.) Those memories are glossed only rarely in public discourse; they are more likely to be glossed over, ignored, silenced into an unspeakable history. It is for this reason that there is so much riding on the presidency of Nestor Kirchner, native of Patagonia and himself detained during the "Guerra Sucia," and the only leader—to date—willing to confront directly the violences of the dictatorship. Kirchner has shown himself, moreover, prepared to bring to justice and prosecute those who committed atrocities during the reign of Videla and Leopoldo Galtieri, the latter being the leader who led the ill-fated campaign to regain the Malvinas Islands from Britain during the "Falklands" war.[18]

Because of the silence about race, Argentina can imagine itself to be putatively white, modernist European because it has never really accounted for the multiple traumas of its past. The Argentine nation can lay claim to whiteness because Otherness, the "macacos" quotient, if you will, was exterminated without a substantive public recording or engagement with that past. The struggle to produce a critique of and for the "disappeared," marks a key instance of *feaca,* a moment of collective national forgetting—the event of the Guerra Sucia and the insufficiently interrogative aftermath show how the practice of *feaca* functions.[19]

Culturally the key to the conversation about silence (and race and the repression of political memory) is the national non- or misrecognition of "La Brujita," the enactment of "Veron-isma." Physionogmically, Veron looks more Brasilian than he does Argentine. Even though, of course, Brasil has always had players who look identifiably white, such as the midfielder Juninho and the goalkeeper Marcos on the World–Cup winning 2002 team. In complexion Veron resembles the Brasilian captain Cafu; he is maybe a shade lighter than the midfielder Gilberto (now playing for Arsenal in England). It is for this reason that Veron's difference—he does not look, physically, like any of his teammates, his darkness stands out in relation to their physiognomic whiteness—marks a crucial moment of "Veron-isma." Not seeing the midfielder as black is a consequence of deliberate ideological misrecognition, rhetorical forgetting, and the paradigmatic refusal to produce a racialized discourse that attends to Veron's racial identity. There is never, from football commentators, the national press, or colloquial conversations among Argentines in general, any commentary on his racial difference. This is not because it is not epidemiologically visible, but because it has been ideologically subsumed into an incorporative, nationalized whiteness. In football terms, Maradona's indigenization after World Cup 1994 is more likely to be invoked as an instance of racialized national discourse. "Veron-isma" enables the recuperation of the black athletic body from racialized hybridity through (silent) workings of Argentine national identity, through the discourses that have strategically been allowed no vocabulary for public utterance. It is Veron's Argentine-ness that insulates him from racial epithets, it is his national citizenship that immunizes him from the Brasilian taint of the racially impure; in any case, Veron the midfielder is no Maradona the icon; in any case, unlike his hero, he only failed the nation, he never shamed it internationally; in Argentina, the price of football failure is less severe than that of shaming Argentina's collective selfhood. Veron's body, however, is a visual spectacle so unconsciously suffused with the ideology of racism that it implicitly articulates the contingency and complexity of both racist discourse and national identity. "Veron-isma" is a measure of how resolute Argentina is in its refusal to acknowledge difference among its own national subjects.

In this crucial way, Veron represents the racial pathologization of blackness, the tendency toward *feaca*, strategic and deliberate disengagement, of the Argentine nation, with its own, unrecognizable Others. It is precisely because of his blackness, its public unspeakability, and his historic silence about it, that Veron is transformed into a signal figure. In his case, "Veron-isma" facilitates self-misrecognition: the overwriting of blackness by interpellative Argentine whiteness. The denial of blackness represents not only the repression of a discourse but the very ontology of Argentineness. Through the nonacknowledgement of his difference, "Veron-isma" iterates itself as the cultural/athletic equivalent of *feaca*. The nation that will not fully, or only rarely, reluctantly engage political atrocity will, similarly, not speak its Otherness as a discourse of intranational difference. If the recognizably, identifiably black subject—at the very least, the racially hybrid subject—does not mark himself as black, does not enunciate his difference, then the Argentine nation can unproblematically construct itself as not only imaginatively, but substantively, white. The nation can emblazon itself as publicly white on an apartment building in a black body because it has made a counternarrative ideologically unimaginable.

"Veron-isma," the rendering of Veron as not putatively but ideologically white, marks the transcendence of Althusser's project of interpellation. It is not that Veron has been hailed or addressed into "whiteness." Rather, he has not needed to be interpellated: that is the ultimate triumph of the Argentine nation's racial/racist discourse. Veron, no matter his racial composition (which neither he nor any other commentator ever reflects upon, or is required to), is by ideological default always white in the Argentine public imaginary. This marks yet another articulation of Argentine exceptionalism, lending Argentina a signality in Latin American discourse in which blackness, in the form of both the native population and the progeny of enslaved Africans, is acknowledged, compels the project of nation-building through racial difference. In Argentina, interpellation exceeds and liquidates itself when it is no longer necessary to do the work of sociopolitical subject construction: when the subject is ontologized as white, when the very essence of the black subject—the black being—can unproblematically be construed as whiteness. When "whiteness" simply is. In Veron's case, whiteness can instinctively, viscerally, be read off of not his body, but his shirt, at once eviscerating the body and reifying the national shirt. The powder blue and white stripes of his Argentine national jersey are, symptomatically, the most powerful enunciations of "Veron-isma": the national cultural uniform is all that is required to mark him as not Brasilian. On the football field, more than any other venue, Argentina is not Brasil because it players are all paradigmatically white. Argentina is not Brasil because its national team players are not racially mixed. The "azul" of Argentina protects it against the "amarillo" of Brasil.

So authoritative is Argentine national marking that Veron could not only be presumed the best qualified to lead the nation, but he could do so without having his difference remarked upon. Consequently, "La Brujita" has not comprehended the salience of his own mural. The image of Veron stands out, but who he is visually—racially—cannot, will not, be afforded the same opportunity. "Veron-isma" means that he does not need to understand how, or, in fact, that, he stands out. The Argentine subject is afforded whiteness inexorably: there is nothing of the Fanonian "black skin, white mask" about Veron because to be Argentine is to be white.[20] Veron's relationship to (a peculiarly Argentine) whiteness stands in sharp contradistinction to Argentina's relationship to the rest of Latin America. In the Argentine racial calculus, to be other than Argentine is to be inveterately Other—a category that includes everything from blackness to mestizo-ness as well as racial-identity-through-national identity, Argentina's strategy for marking Brasilian-ness.

Resisting the Postcolonial

It is for this reason that postcolonial discourse, which enjoys such currency in contemporary European and North American critical discourse, has thus far had little if any purchase in Argentine thinking. The postcolonial is a concept, a historical experience, founded upon race: the oppression, exploitation, and liquidation of black and brown bodies; the resistance of those communities to European colonialism and the eventual liberation of Africa, Asia, and the Caribbean from white European rule. More important, postcolonial theory of the last fifteen or twenty years has turned its attention as much to the colonial past and its deleterious effects as to the issue of how the black postcolonial subject has reconstructed the metropolis. London, Paris, Amsterdam, Berlin, and Stockholm have over the last four decades been demographically, ideologically, and culturally transformed by the postcolonial chickens who came "home" to roost. In the process the chickens remade the metropolitan coop, not the least of which is the racial transformation of European national leagues and teams—England has many black players at club level and a few on the national side, while the national teams of the Netherlands and France are dominated by black players from Africa, the Caribbean, and Latin America.

As much as Argentina constructs itself as philosophically "European," it is at the postcolonial conjuncture where this displaced Latin American nation locates itself disjunctively in relation to the metropolis. This is the point at which Argentina disarticulates itself from imperial Europe—the postmodern postcolonial is inconceivable without the problematic of difference. Postcolonial theory cannot gain a foothold in Argentine thinking because it is predicated upon the discourse of race, and racial difference, and the complications and unattainability of pure racial identity. In an Argentine society that understands itself as cosmopolitan, the postcolonial—and, ironically, Europe, the very origin of its epistemologies—has to be rejected in part because the very conditions that transformed Europe—migrancy, gastarbeiters, the process of racial and cultural hybridization—are now increasingly manifesting themselves in Argentina. Economic migrants from Chile, Peru, Paraguay, Uruguay and of course neighboring Brasil—and Africans from places as far away as Lagos, Nigeria, who hawk in the markets of Baires—have been steadily making their way into Argentina and transforming the society. With and without its consent, Argentina is being diasporized into postcoloniality and a concomitant blackness.

Independent for almost two hundred years, Argentina is now resisting postcoloniality. It will not allow the discourse of race public utterance because, paradoxically, that will not only mark its passage to postcoloniality but will also align it with a postmodern Europe and integrate more fully economically and culturally into Latin America. In order to become postcolonial (and, postmodern), Argentina has to, in a cultural sense, return itself to its geographical context. It has to, a la Marx, come home. Anachronistic misidentification with Europe has to be resisted at this historical juncture because the metropolis is no longer distinct from the Latin American periphery. Rio and London, home to the samba and the somber, have at this moment more in common than Buenos Aires and Paris. Argentine exceptionalism becomes, through this rejection of the metropolis, an extreme condition. Conjointly, *feaca* and "Veron-isma" demonstrates the process by which the erstwhile secondary (Argentina) becomes the primary (Europe) through excessive, outdated attachment to philosophical modalities, and it also makes clear why the point of origin has to be rejected because it is no longer conceptually compatible. Most important, it shows the epistemological fallacy and the cost of postimperial Argentina exceeding postcolonial Europe in terms of its adherence to the paradigm of modernity. This is the height of Argentina's proclivity for *feaca*. Argentina becomes, through this gesture, not so much nostalgic—for an imperial Europe—but fixated in both its fealty to a mode of being and its resistance to recognizing its philosophical and historic anachronism. In rejecting postcoloniality, Argentina disconnects itself from where it is. Historically alienated from Latin America, Argentina has now taken its distance—and removed itself, in fundamental ways—from Europe. Geographically dislocated, conceptually and psychically displaced, Argentina reveals itself to be philosophically anachronistic— it belongs to an outdated notion of Europe. Philosophically, psychically, and physically isolated at the far end of the South American continent, Argentina now has to rethink its relation to both Europe and its Latin neighbors.

All too often, however, Argentina has turned in on itself in order to secure the verities and epistemological foundations of an earlier era, insisting upon claiming a past that was itself racially hybrid. The Argentine nation is fictionalizing itself once again, except that this time it is a fiction that has no currency outside of its borders; powerful and resilient though that fiction may be, it cannot postpone indefinitely a national interrogation into the purchase of "whiteness" and exceptionalism within Argentina's borders. For these reasons Veron has to be so resolutely rendered white: football is the most popular sport in the country, like it is in all of Latin and Central America, and it is in this public, international forum that the nation's self-representation must be most steadfast even as it is in danger of becoming ontologically uncertain. If blackness has no public Argentine voice, even when the body itself is black, then the nation's whiteness cannot be drawn into question. If the moment of *feaca,* the interregnum between independence and postcoloniality can be extended indefinitely, then through "Veron-isma" the engagement with the discourse of race can be further postponed.

In this extended ideological interstices, Veron's signality can be reduced to an empty cultural signifier. For as long as *feaca* remains the dominant mode of racial politics as silencing, then "La Brujita" from La Plata is simply the outstanding midfielder, the footballer who transformed his nation's perceptions of midfielders, affording them an iconic status once only lavished upon strikers. As long as *feaca* is the preeminent form of racial discourse, it will not matter that Veron is eventually displaced by Aimar, who in any case has all the flair—those flowing, unkempt, rock-star-like locks— of a forward. Except, of course, if Veron's visage is able to exceed itself and

"Veron-isma" is interrogated. If the iconic cultural figure can be transformed from the midfielder—who failed so massively in 2002 and is now struggling to rehabilitate himself—into a less benign "brujita." In Latin American footballing terms, Veron has to become aligned with Cafu and Gilberto and Rivaldo: he has to signify against himself so that he might be capable of signifying a different, racialized self that also makes possible the construction of a different Argentine racial consciousness. Intranationally, Veron has to be linked more closely (physionogmically) with Maradona the native/Indian; these differently black bodies have to be discursively aligned, made ideologically conversant.

Veron has to be disengaged from his talents and understood as a politicized visuality, as an affront to the nation, not as a confirmation of its powerfully incorporative sense of itself. His personage has to be de-lineated from his father's, a player during a different Argentine moment, but one not without its own post- (and inter-) Peronista silences. Veron has to be seen, metaphorically, if not literally (though the revealed black body at the end of the game exchanging shirts with the opposition can function as a visceral marker of difference from his teammates), without the national jersey. The once iconic midfielder must be rehabilitated, not as footballer, but as the subject of the nation's black unconscious. He must be made to stand outside the Argentine nation so that the nation might be capable of seeing itself as something other/Other than what it knows.

Argentina has to understand itself constitutively, not cumulatively—which is to say, it has to see itself as aporetic, racially disrupted, rather than continuous, racially homogenous. The silence around racial discourse has to become generative rather than an uninterrupted articulation of *feaca*. The nation must not be allowed respite from its history, it must not be allowed to stroll along the river on a Sunday afternoon but must instead be made to take steps, however sure or tentative they may be, toward postcoloniality. Argentina must be made to look toward and engage Brasil and Ecuador and Chile. Most significant, it must be made to work toward interrogating the silences of the past and the present. Argentina is a nation that has indigenized its subjects in strategic, almost cynical moments. It is, moreover, a nation that has already taken too much of a *feaca* from race.

Notes

1. "Total Football" was conceived on the training grounds of Ajax of Amsterdam under the watchful eye of Rinus Michels, nurtured by coaching acolytes such as Louis van Gaal, and brilliantly implemented and fulfilled on the playing field by the mesmerizing talents of one Johan Cryuff (especially at the 1974

World Cup in West Germany, where the "Dutch Masters" outplayed but lost, sadly, to Franz Beckenbauer's home side).

2. "Total Football" was premised on the idea that the same skills applied in all parts of the field. For this reason, coaches such as Michels and van Gaal trained their charges so that they approached the game the same way all the time, so that a forward and a defender could easily exchange positions with no reduction in the fluency of the team. Skills made players interchangeable and it took precedence over positional requirements. (Interestingly, Michels, van Gaal, and Cruyff all coached the Catalan team, Barcelona, where Cruyff also headlined as the star player in the early and mid-1970s.)

3. Eduardo Galeano, *Football In Sun And Shadow,* trans. Mark Fried (London: The Fourth Estate, 2003) 152.

4. There is considerable ideological conflict between Menotti and Bilardo, the former accusing the latter of employing a more brutal style of play that dishonors Argentina's footballing history. Menotti sees himself as the keeper of a purer style than the bruising tactics used by Bilardo in 1986. See Simon Kuper's *Football Against the Enemy* (London: Trafalgar Square, 1994) for a discussion of this coaching, intranational animus.

5. See Kuper's *Football Against the Enemy* for a fuller discussion of Maradona's evaluation of his compatriot, Di Stefano.

6. Alfredo di Stefano holds, though it is an honor that may not be his for very much longer, the record for the most goals scored by a Real Madrid player in European club competitions. The Argentine's 48-goal tally is in danger of being surpassed by a native Madridileno, and current Real skipper, Raul. It is important to note, however, that as significant as Raul's accomplishment will certainly be, he has had the opportunity to play in many more European games in the EUFA Champions League than his predecessor.

7. Bielsa resigned in 2004, soon after Argentina lost the Copa America final to Brasil in Lima, Peru.

8. John Barnes, *John Barnes: The Autobiography* (London: Headline, 1990), 1.

9. See Dave Hill's *Out of his Skin: The John Barnes Phenomenon,* a groundbreaking critique of racism in English football generally, and on Merseyside particularly. See also Hill, "Football's black past is not yet history," *The Guardian,* July 7, 2001.

10. L. Richardson, "New Practices in Writing Qualitative Research," *Sociology of Sports Journal* 17, no. 1 (2000): 5.

11. Jose Luis Borges, "The Argentine Writer and Tradition," in *Labyrinths: Selected Short Stories and Other Writings,* Donald A. Yates and James E. Irby, eds. (New York: New Directions Books, 1964), 180. It is, of course, ironic to invoke Borges in an essay on futbol since he is widely known to have hated the sport. He did, however, write a wonderful short piece on futbol as simulacra (long before Baudrillard thought of the concept) called "Esse Est Percipi."

12. Galeano, 151.

13. See David Rock, *Argentina 1517–1987: From Spanish Colonization to Alfonsin* (Berkeley: University of California Press, 1987) and Nicholas Shumway,

The Invention of Argentina (Berkeley: University of California Press, 1991) for a history of Argentina.

14. David Rock, "Racking Argentina," *New Left Review* 17 (Sep/Oct 2002): 60.

15. Jorge Luis Borges (1899–1986) is considered the most Argentine of writers. Born in Buenos Aires, Borges learned to speak English before Spanish; he lived in Geneva as a teenager, acquiring not only a B.A. at the College of Geneva but also proficiency in French and German. Borges is heralded as the definitive Argentine author because his work, though rooted in and routed through his native city, was influenced by European fiction and demonstrated the kind of universality associated with metropolitan artists. Borges is presumed to have produced an oeuvre that gave articulate voice to Argentine modernity as well as initiating the Latin American genre of fantastic realism.

16. In another instance of unreflective "macacos-ism," an Argentine "commentator decreed, 'They're all ditch-diggers, not one of them uses his head to think'" about the 1998 Nigerian team at the World Cup in France (Galeano, 212). The black body is, in the Argentine racial consciousness, always devoid of intellect, whether it is Brasilian or Nigerian.

17. The notorious "Dirty War," waged by successive military juntas between 1974 and 1983, has been written about extensively, both within and outside Argentina. See, for example, Diana Taylor, *Disappearing Acts: Spectacles of Gender and Nationalism in Argentina's Dirty War* (Durham, NC: Duke University Press, 1997); Alicia Partnoy, *The Little School: Tales of Disappearance and Survival*, trans. Alicia Partnoy (Pittsburgh: Cleis Press, 1986); and Horacio Verbitsky, *The Flight: Confessions of an Argentine Dirty Warrior* (New York: The New Press, 1996). See also Elizabeth Jelin, *State Repression and the Labors of Memory*, trans. Judy Rein and Marcial Godoy-Anativia (Minneapolis: University of Minnesota Press, 2003) for a critique of contemporary developments in Latin America, with a special focus on Argentina. U2's album *The Joshua Tree* also popularized this struggle with their song "Mothers of the Disappeared." There is also a whole body of literature on this subject written in Spanish.

18. Kirchner is the first post-Junta leader with the determination to repeal the notorious "Punto Final" and "Obediencia Debida" leyes (laws), key sections of the post-1983 Argentine Constitution that granted immunity to those who committed violations of human rights during the "Guerra Sucia" and allowed the *generalissimos* and their henchmen to escape justice.

19. It is necessary to briefly explain that this critique of Argentine "exceptionalism" is not unaware of how the "mark of whiteness" enunciates itself from Mexico City to Medellín, from Santiago to São Paulo, from Quito to Caracas, often finding complex articulations on the football field. In Chile, Uruguay, and Venezuela, to mention just three, the all too often unengaged question of the postcolonial stirs, but is often—unlike in Argentina—confronted by, and therefore contained by, the nativist and statist visions of these societies. But many Latin American countries, Brasil included—the nation that has never had a person of color as a head of state—the elite, the bourgeoisie, and the intel-

lectual left—mediate their relationship to their own black subalterns and Europe with anxious, even envious glances in the direction of Buenos Aires.

20. Veron may claim, through the tattoo on his arm, Che Guevera as his hero, but there is nothing of the political or cultural radical about him. Much of the mural's racial salience is lost in and because of the workings of Argentine nationalist discourse, so the Che tattoo functions as little more than an adornment of—black—body.

FOUR

Reading and Rereading the Game

Reflections on West Indies Cricket

Michael Arthur and Jennifer Scanlon

> But the mystery of the colonial is this: while he remains alive, his instinct
> always and forever creative, must choose a way to change the meaning
> and perspective of this ancient tyranny.
>
> —*George Lamming,* The Pleasures of Exile

As with other sports under consideration in this volume, cricket is both a
game and a source of entertainment and identity. Although largely absent
in the American sports lineup, cricket occupies a central position in the consciousness of people who lived—or whose ancestors lived—under British
colonial rule around the world. It has, as a result, always been tied to colonial and postcolonial struggles on and off the field; its fans have always
found meaning in a broad social context. In this essay, two different voices
emerge and then merge in an attempt to explore contemporary West Indian
cricket and its discontents.

Michael on Cricket

It was 1975. I was thirteen years old, and Barbadian nationalism was in my
bones. I had been given the middle name "Walton" after Errol Walton Barrow,

the father of Barbadian independence. This was a day, I believed, for me. Thousands of Barbadians, or Bajans as we call ourselves, crowded the Garrison Savannah to witness the knighting of cricketer Garfield Sobers by Her Majesty Queen Elizabeth II of England and the Commonwealth. All the dignitaries were there, some Bajans among that rank; thousands outside the Savannah listened on the radio, thousands of others watched on television from home and other locations. As for me, I had made my way to the Savannah and pushed my way through the crowd, my colonial-bred politeness challenged and then tempered by the raw energy that permeated the air. The platform, the site of the actual knighting, was located in the middle of the Savannah, and all present could see it and everything that was about to occur. Sobers arrived dressed in his suit. The Queen, as usual, wore a simple dress. The sword seemed rather thin and unremarkable, hardly matching my adolescent expectations of knightly grandeur. Sobers walked up, bowed, and knelt before her. By this time all the Bajan onlookers were silent, a remarkable accomplishment considering the fact that normally, as we say, "A Bajan's mouth has no cover." The Queen touched Gary on one shoulder with the sword, repeated the same unhurried action on the other shoulder, then issued the words: "Raise, Sir Garfield Sobers." Gary Sobers was knighted, and *she* had come to *him*, to us.[1]

Gary Sobers had emerged from the Barbados of my parents: grinding poverty, correspondingly poor educational opportunities, lifetimes of hard work and little compensation. Like many other black men in the postindependence nation, proud regardless of material circumstances, he could conceivably garner some measure of respect. But international recognition, and knighthood, the stuff of daytime play and nighttime dreams, was not normal fare on an island of only 166 square miles, our dot on the map of the world. In fact, though, Gary Sobers was not the first person to be knighted in West Indies cricket. Another Barbadian, Sir Frank Worrell, one of the three Bajans immortalized as the 3W's, along with the more recently knighted Sir Everton Weekes and Sir Clyde Walcott, had been knighted in 1964. But for many of us, this felt different. It was happening outside of Buckingham Palace, in public view, and to our hero. Sir Frank Worrell had been knighted for his immense skill, his leadership, and his contributions to the game, but Gary Sobers has been knighted because, we knew, he was, simply, the greatest of all cricketers. In 1975 that recognition was his due and ours. Sobers had, as feminist scholar and critic bell hooks would later put it about African American women, "talked back" to racism, to colonialism, to Britain, all through the game of cricket.[2] As the great critic of colonialism C. L. R. James wrote, "Garfield Sobers, I shall show, is a West Indian cricketer, not merely a cricketer from the West Indies. He is the most typical West Indian cricketer that it is possible to imagine."[3] His knighthood solidified the process that was underway since Sobers assumed the leadership of West Indies cricket in 1964. Independence followed in 1966, and although it was more complicated historically, in my mind it was all of a kind: independence, nationalism, Sobers, cricket.

I would play cricket, watch it live and on television, live out important aspects of my identity through the game and its players. Cricket readily moved with me as I grew: it was a part of my play, then my identity as a teenager interested in radical West Indian politics, then finally, my identity as a clerk at the University of the West Indies, where students, faculty, and staff came together around cricket like no other element of our intertwined lives. When I left Barbados to attend college in upstate New York, I felt the loss of many things: family and friends, sea air and sea baths, calypso music, and the shared identity that cricket provided. I followed the game with my West Indian friends and with my brother, an avid fan regardless of his decades-long tenure in New York City. But I also became friends with so many people for whom cricket appeared nothing but a game, and a terribly slow version of baseball at that. In the end, at the same time that the West Indies team seemed doomed to continual failure, I married one of these infidels, and we have both lived to tell about it.

Jennifer on Cricket

I was born in the Bronx in the house my father grew up in, around the corner from the house my mother grew up in, in an Irish neighborhood you would find unlikely to be called Country Club, but it really is, as it sprung up in the shadow of the mansions that abutted Long Island Sound. I grew up in the shadow of many aunts and uncles and in the company of a set of almost thirty cousins on my mother's side. Although my family was not a baseball family, a baseball game remains one of my salient preadolescent memories. My fifth grade teacher, Mr. Michon, took the girls in our class to a Mets game. I cannot remember exactly what precipitated the trip, but I'm guessing that, since it was 1970, it was related to nascent feminism in New York City and in us. Girls didn't play Little League in those days, and I was largely content to play hopscotch or tag endlessly in front of my house, but the trip to the game was formative. During that school year the Mets won their first National League Championship, then went on to the World Series for the first time, and our teacher believed we girls had a stake in it. I learned a lot that year: Mr. Michon's attitude about girls and sports, his love for the Mets, and his stories about Cesar Chavez and the United Farm Workers became, for me, all of a kind—and they helped develop in

me a willingness to look at discrimination and victory, and to place myself
in a larger world in and outside of school.

When I met Michael years later, in 1990, I had completed a Ph.D. in
women's history and was in the first year of a tenure-track position in
women's studies. I understood the language of politics—or so I thought. I
understood to some degree the role that sports had played in the "talking
back" process Michael mentions above. I had, after all, been in Argentina
during the semifinals of a soccer World Cup in 1986, when Argentina had
just beaten Britain, and understood very quickly what it meant to stand still
in a crowd of tens of thousands screaming "El que no salta, es un ingles,"
or "If you don't jump you're British!" I did not fully understand, though,
what Michael, and what Amy Bass and many of the contributors to this
volume have long understood; that is, the intimate, lasting, and complex relationship between sport and politics.

As anyone who knows Michael will tell you, you cannot spend much
time with him without his feeling you out on cricket. He will stoop to
drawing comparisons to baseball when desperate, but even that wasn't
enough to make me bite. I preferred the sidelines of the conversations,
somewhat appreciating the intensity of the political debates and thoroughly
enjoying the Queen-bashing that emerged in cricket lore and in calypso
music. I confess to tuning out of the conversation when Michael and his
brother Tony, or Michael and his uncle, Fred, got together to intricately critique the games, the players, the management, the culture of cricket. On
our trips to Barbados I could avoid cricket by declaring my desperate need
for beach time as we escaped the cold of northern New York. But when we
left the United States together to live in Trinidad & Tobago for a year, in
1998, I faced the omnipresence of cricket in daily life and, finally, came to
appreciate the game, if not as a sport then as a measure of contested
Caribbean identity.

Cricket, more than the weather or the complex and sordid nature of
Trinidadian politics, became the parlance that marked our interactions with
strangers. During cricket season, a generally generic "Good Morning" in a
taxicab or maxitaxi would quickly develop into an extended debate about
the legitimacy of umpire decisions and the true potential of the Afro- and
Indo-Caribbean men who by now clearly dominated the game. As Doris
Day would have declared, I surrendered. If the sport was important enough
to bring all traffic to a halt on the highways during critical moments in a
game, it was significant enough to engage me in what seemed to have become the critical question for the end of the twentieth century: What had
happened to West Indies cricket? The West Indies had for so long, as calypsonian David Rudder lamented, "ruled" the game, but could the team,
and the region it represented, again emerge victorious?[4]

Cricket: A Historical Sketch

Cricket emerged in the West Indian context as a classic struggle between the oppressor and the disenfranchised. At the end of the eighteenth century, thousands of British officers and troops landed in the islands, intent on keeping back the French. As distinguished cricket historian Hilary Beckles puts it, "These soldiers entertained themselves with bats and leather balls within garrisons while taking respite from hurling cannon balls at the French. It all developed in the heat of war as representatives of conflicting nationalisms fought bloody battles in pursuit of the national interest."[5] Absent from that description, purposefully absent as far as the British were concerned, were the Africans. Cricket became a form of cultural indoctrination to cement colonial power, further loyalty to Britain, and engender white supremacy. Barbadian planter society was particularly taken with cricket as culture. They had already defined their island home as "Little England" and "Bimshire," and remained convinced that theirs was no more than an additional British "shire," regardless of distances of kilometers and, increasingly, generations.[6]

Inevitably, cricket would become one of the grounds on which blacks made demands. Relegated to the sidelines and invited in as loyal British subjects and fans, black West Indians would eventually, as early as the nineteenth century, make African things English, English things African. West Indies cricket became, as Beckles describes it, "shaped by dialectical processes of conflict and co-option."[7] Alongside the colonial meaningmakers stood the disenfranchised colonials who "eventually claimed their right to cricket and re-promoted it as a symbol of liberating, politicized mass culture."[8] Blacks became admitted in fits and starts. First they could play but not lead the team, as the visible face of cricket had to be white. Eventually, as a result of the efforts of C. L. R. James, Frank Worrell, and others, the face of cricket became a black one.

Frank Worrell became the first black man to be appointed captain of the West Indies team, with tenure, in 1960.[9] "It took over 100 years to complete this process," writes Beckles, "and Sir Frank stood at what then seemed to be the end of history."[10] When Worrell left the team due to illness in 1963, though, Gary Sobers moved into place as the second black team leader, and history continued to be made. The Sobers generation, and succeeding generations, contested whites' rule on the field and, as James decisively put it, "beyond a boundary," through a combination of nationalism, pan-Africanism, and other related calls for social justice.[11] At the same time, though, that cricket has both benefited from and furthered social justice, it did not emerge as a pure site of postcolonial community. As Beckles puts it, cricket has a particularly dialectical quality that results from its simultaneous history of "intense ethnic contention and the nonviolent search for an idyllic area of social life."[12] In many ways, like West Indian or Caribbean identity generally, cricket blends colonial and anticolonial in a manner that defies easy definition. Perhaps that helps to explain its troubled contemporary life.

Cricket Today and West Indian/Caribbean Identity

Caribbean cricket has, as almost any fan will tell you, lost its way. In recent years teams have seemed unfocused, unprepared for play on the international level. So consistently poor has the West Indies team performed that it is now ranked eighth out of ten, surpassing only Zimbabwe and Bangladesh. Fans debate endlessly, hoping finally to locate the reasons for the team's demise and finding myriad ways to implicate the players, the management, the societies that produce the players, the region that cannot find sufficient common bond. Arguably, previous generations of cricketers, nurtured by pan-Africanism and nationalism, had a game to win, a stake to claim. The ideological discourses that pushed West Indies into the enviable position of "team to beat," and that helped foster both independence and democracy across the region, no longer seem as applicable, or even as healthy, for the future of cricket. Caribbean societies and the players emerging from these societies have moved beyond the precise set of circumstances that informed and were nurtured by specifically nationalist and Pan Africanist mentalities.

This notion, that oppression is good for the soul, and for the game, is obviously problematic. Nevertheless, it comes up again and again among cricket fans, who are indeed among its most sophisticated critics and with whom we have had many conversations on this issue. These young men, the story goes, have nothing to fight for, nothing to prove; all they care about is money and fame, not the common identity of West Indianness. "They don't understand what cricket means to us," laments a substantial fan base, a group of fans both a generation removed from the players and a generation shaped by regional aspirations. Ricky Skerritt, the West Indies manager who recently resigned, stated in his letter of resignation that he had been unable, as the newspaper account put it, "to instill in the entire team the fullest understanding of their obligations on and off the field to the people of the West Indies."[13] Players now appear impatient with the game and violate cricket's basic tenets. Just as the rapidity of U.S.-based television images seems incongruent with daily life in the Caribbean, quick cricket feels the most incongruous of possibilities. Younger fans are complicit in this dilemma, as they complain not only about unprepared players but about the game itself, which has difficulty competing on the world stage with soccer and other sports. Many cricket fans, however, also complain about cricket leadership, which they find lacking in a variety of ways. As a Bajan and an American, a therapist and a feminist scholar, an avid fan and an increasingly curious onlooker, we've been debating these issues. What, we wondered, could we learn from cultural theorists, Caribbean feminists, cricket fans flung far and wide, newspaper accounts, vital statistics? What follows is our exploration of a cricket that, by necessity, moves further away from its colonial legacies, transgresses nationalism and Pan Africanism, recognizes and acknowledges consumerism and globalization, and emerges from new regional understandings of postcolonial life.

Understanding Postcolonialism and Residual Colonialism

Cricket played an enormous role in assisting people and societies in developing healthy responses to the disease of colonial thinking and action; it facilitated political action to change desperate and demoralizing social conditions. Yet cricket facilitated the separation, one might say, but couldn't effect the divorce between colonialism and something new. One of the first tasks today is to recognize the residual colonialism that continues to pervade cricket culture. This kind of honest assessment can help move the game, and the people who invest it with so much meaning, forward. The work of George Lamming, Paulo Freire, and C. L. R. James is enormously helpful in beginning this process, in understanding the complications of colonialism.[14] All three explore the degree to which the colonized resist oppression as well as the degree to which they internalize the mindset of the oppressor, becoming on some levels the "image of the oppressor."[15] George Lamming, a Barbadian, explores the fundamental role of language in colonization: the oppressed are brought into, and limited by, the language of the oppressor. As a result, their future as well as their present becomes informed by the worldview implicit in that language and its use. C. L. R. James, a Trinidadian, writes of his devotion to things British, including and beyond language, and the degree to which the colonial mindset interferes with or precludes one's ability even to see the parameters of one's oppression. James writes about the pride and loyalty he felt toward his school, Queens Royal College, and how he lived by the code of British school system to the point where he never considered the "national question"—by this he meant independence from Britain—to have any bearing on his life. "It was only long years after that I understood the limitation on spirit, vision and self-respect which was imposed on us by the fact that our masters, our curriculum, our code of morals, *everything* began from the basis that Britain was the source of all light and leading, and our business was to admire, wonder, imitate, learn; our criterion of success was to have succeeded in approaching that distant ideal—to attain it was, of course, impossible . . . it was the beacon that beckoned me on."[16] Paulo Freire, a Brazilian, speaks of the ways in which the "prescriptions" of the oppressor become part of the actions of the oppressed; the oppressed, in many cases and contrary to expectations, tend to act much like, rather than as distinct from, the oppressor.[17]

Each of these writers attempts to dismantle colonial thinking through new forms of ideological discourse that inform freedom for all people, including the oppressors. Lamming and James deliberately use elements from the oppressor to create anew. In Lamming's case, Shakespeare features prominently in his investigations into postcolonial possibilities. For James, his own British education becomes a source for integrated understandings. Postcolonial scholar Edouard Glissant's notion of "creolization," a cultural process rooted in history as well as in the lived experiences of people in the Caribbean, speaks so well to what James encountered in his life.[18] Creolization, as postcolonial scholar Kathleen Balutansky describes it in the Caribbean context, provides a theoretical framework for understanding the mix that generates both the "subversive and transformative revolutionary activity and artistic creativity of the region."[19] Creolization demands a recognition of what, because of the historical impact of the colonial encounter, results in a "self-consciously decentered Caribbean identity."[20] In the work of Lamming and James, the continued presence of the oppressor actually facilitates the development of the new self. This dual consciousness facilitates not simply theory but action for many in the Caribbean, evident, for example, in James' instrumental role in helping Frank Worrell become the first black man to lead the West Indies cricket team.[21]

Similarly, Freire's contribution, what he calls "the central problem," is to find ways to acknowledge the presence of the oppressor in the self, reveal the mutual dehumanization that the colonial process entails, and work toward an equitable society for all.[22] This process, for Freire a "pedagogy," demands an understanding of continuums rather then clearly delineated markings of colonial and postcolonial, enslaved and free, disenfranchised and empowered. "Only as they discover themselves to be 'hosts' of the oppressor can they contribute to the midwifery of their liberating pedagogy. . . . The pedagogy of the oppressed is an instrument for their critical discovery that both they and their oppressors are manifestations of dehumanization."[23] We believe these frameworks continue to have relevance for cricket and its future in the Caribbean. The reality of life in the Caribbean is that the relationship between oppressor and oppressed continues to be felt and lived in ways worth studying. Importantly for Freire and arguably for the Caribbean, it is the oppressed who once again must take a lead in this process.

Contemporary cricket fans, in part because of a desire to find a place to locate blame, in part because of seasoned analysis, find fault with West Indies cricket management and administration. When the West Indies team went on strike on the eve of a South African tour in the 1998–1999 season, fans for the most part sided with the team, feeling that the management had not met its obligations or provided adequate leadership. While not all criticisms of the management seem fair, and it is decidedly unfair to expect cricket leadership to be more enlightened than the societies from which they come, the insights of Lamming, James, and Freire suggest some of the ways in which cricket leadership can profitably transcend the (post)colonial thinking and practices that hinder the leadership's own effectiveness. Historical thinking and long-term thinking, all exercised in a liberatory framework, offer alternative models.

One example of the ways in which cricket management has engaged in leadership infused with the legacies of colonialism is well known to cricket fans. In the 1970s, Viv Richards spent five years as the loyal vice-captain of the West Indies team. As an individual and, importantly for this discussion, as a player, Viv Richards developed and nurtured his affinity for Rastafarianism. In this, as far as cricket leadership was concerned, he had taken pan-Africanism too far. He equated Rastafarianism with his pride in being black and wore symbolic Rasta colors on the field. He made it known, to the world, that politics infused his play. His message, as Hilary Beckles explains, rang clear: "Viv Richards constituted a subsequent political argument that in spite of constitutional independence and decades of social agitation, blacks had good cause to protest their institutional and economic marginalization relative to other historically privileged ethnic groups."[24] Such blatant statements about what for many underlay all of cricket proved worrisome for cricket's leadership, a large portion of which wanted to move postindependence cricket away from the blatantly political identities that helped forge that independence and, not incidentally, winning cricket teams. When he became eligible for captain, and embodied the clear choice, many on the board felt Richards made too radical a statement; they favored the institutionalization of blacks in cricket through a more toned-down approach and presence.

The conservatives, arguably maintaining a colonial rather than regional definition of black manhood, nearly won their fight to keep Richards out of leadership. By one vote, he became captain of the team in 1980, and his outstanding record in this position only further exposed the degree to which fears about problematic black masculinity permeated decision making.[25] Several years have passed since the Richards debacle, but the question remains: To what degree has cricket leadership acknowledged the changing societies and the varieties of people and practices and ideological discourses that produce—and can potentially produce—the best players? An effective cricket leadership for the future will explore what cricket has meant, how the game and its fan base have changed, what the game can mean as the dynamics of power continuously shift within cricket and on the global stage. An effective cricket management for the future will see itself as loyal to the game, its players, and fans, but it must also, on a wider scale, further its loyalty to the societies that both provide for and benefit from the game. Thus, issues relevant to the Caribbean as a whole, particularly issues of neocolonialism, are relevant to the practitioners and stewards of cricket: continuing processes of democratization, addressing racism and class-based schisms, preparing youth to respond to the forces of globalization through a sound understanding of complicity as well as resistance. Some would argue that we place responsibility on the wrong shoulders, but, arguably, the future of the game depends in part on its leaders taking an active role as conscious and simultaneous perpetuators and transformers of residual colonial practices.

Nationalism and Pan-Africanism

For well over a century, nationalism and pan-Africanism provided a powerful philosophical, ideological, and practical framework for cricket. Blacks used cricket as the place from which to launch a struggle for freedom that took increasingly significant turns. During and after slavery and up to the period of independence, people yearned for ways to respond to racism and colonialism. Cricket provided an arena for testing both nationalist and pan-Africanist ideas. The game allowed blacks to test the limits of their physical presence, their identity as citizens, their very imaginations. Some cricket clubs, like Shannon, a club of black lower-middle-class cricketers, promoted black pride; cricketers there played "as if their club represented the great mass of black people in the island."[26] Their performance reflected the motivational power of nationalism and pan-Africanism. Identity spurred on success; success furthered what seemed singularly healthy identities. In this reciprocal relationship, as James put it, players "were supported by the crowd with a jealous enthusiasm which even then showed the social passions which were using cricket as a medium of expression."[27] This approach, not limited to Shannon or even to cricket, created links between cricket, nationalism, and pan-Africanism that remain in place but serve, arguably, in less effective ways today.

For a number of reasons, pan-Africanism fails to provide adequate motivational support, ideological foregrounding, or generational relevance today. As cricket fans will argue, young players today do not see themselves as the beneficiaries of a particularly race-based movement. They want to win, and they want to represent their countries, but at times they feel that even the regional West Indian identity implicit in the team's name, never mind a broader African-identified understanding, imposes something false on them. Players see ability, rather than race, as the premiere determinant in the game. "I am, as I have said," C. L. R. James writes, "quite convinced that the racialism I have described was in its time and place a natural response to local social conditions, did very little harm and sharpened up the game."[28] As James's quote allows us to consider, however, the precise set of circumstances that informed this mentality—the perennial in-your-face presence of white supremacy that dominated cricket as well as other forms of social life—are not present in the same forms in today's Caribbean societies. Pan-Africanism did not and does not sufficiently capture the experiences or the expectations of the many Indo-Caribbean players, although it did provide a strong impetus for their inclusion, nor does it address the global lure of the contemporary sports world, in which West Indian identity may seem less important, even less real, than global opportunities and global exposure. Pan-Africanism undoubtedly played a major role in creating a multicultural team, but it provides inadequate explanatory or actual power today.

Nationalism, too, has its limits, particularly as it is woven through with notions of maleness and masculinity. Institutional inequalities that ensured that white men would play and black men would keep the grounds eventually exploded in a nationalist response. The ensuing game, "seized by blacks and coloureds," as Beckles explains, "became the focus around which an intensive civil rights war was waged. . . ."[29] The resulting masculine framework of nationalism, which hastened independence, situated many black men in positions of significant political power, and furthered the success of the West Indies cricket team, also created societies with enormous disparities between men and women. In a blindness resulting in part from the model of nationalism that was woven from resistant and colonial ideologies, cricket left women out of the game, figuratively and literally. Women's cricket, though played, has never really developed in the Caribbean, although Viv Richards and other men identified strongly as pan-Africanists advocated for it. For many years, women were prohibited from entering the pavilions at Kensington Oval in Barbados, Queens Park Club in Trinidad, and other cricket pavilions in the Caribbean. In an interview with Hilary Beckles, one of the 3W's, Clyde Walcott, remembered that during this time his wife refused to attend any functions at these sites because of women's exclusion during cricket.[30] Even today, sports in the Caribbean means men's sports, and women play only a peripheral role in the world of cricket.

The emerging field of Caribbean masculinity studies offers important insights on constructions of gender in the region and barriers to opening up cricket, and cricket societies in the Caribbean, to full consideration of women on and off the field. In *Interrogating Caribbean Masculinities,* a 2004 collection, Linden Lewis explores Caribbean masculinity at the turn of the twenty-first century. The "culturally nationalist" masculinity he describes, which we see as exemplified in cricket, is, as Lewis puts it, "hardly the vehicle" through which gender equality can be realized.[31] Scholars in this collection as well as in *Confronting Power, Theorizing Gender,* explore the historical and contemporary complexities that have allowed the male marginalization thesis to thrive in the region. According to this argument, which feminist scholar Eudine Barriteau ultimately declares a "non theory," women have "made it," women surpass men, women, in fact, are responsible for the "crisis" of masculinity.[32] "The popular analysis of men and masculinity begins with women and remains there," writes Barriteau, "so frequently public discussions that ostensibly address issues of masculinity just quarrel about women."[33] This "quarrel about women," as Barriteau deftly describes it, continues to marginalize women as it purports to describe their successful marginalization of men.

Ironically, cricket, with its absence of women in player and leadership roles, may be the one area immune to this quarrel, and could productively serve as a space in which to explore gender dynamics, gender socialization of boys, gender pathologies that effect male success generally and, arguably, cricket specifically. New models of national or regional pride, as new models of cricket, can emerge from a sensibility that recognizes the problems of narrowly defined male identity and pays attention to the emotional lives of young men. Perhaps new models of thinking about masculinity, about speaking to boys about competition, discipline, focus, and failure could provide an impetus for a renewed cricket. Our feeling is that women, hardly the cause of the demise of cricket, have a role to play in its ascendance—as women encouraged to be full human beings who raise sons with a mentality that further purges the colonial vestiges of sexism among other disabling frames of reference.

Globalization

One of the most jarring experiences we had in Trinidad & Tobago occurred early on. We quickly became friendly with our next-door neighbors. We could communicate through our first-floor living room window to the second-floor patio where they sat on evenings, with their excellent view of the neighborhood comings and goings. After just a few days, we confronted a disconcerting realization: the children in the family had no difficulty understanding Jennifer, with her American-accented English, but they couldn't make out most of what Michael, with his Bajan-accented English, said. Their comfort not only with American English but with things American, or at least American as translated by satellite and television, informed many of our conversations. Why did Americans cry such large tears, one child wanted to know. Did Americans really get thrown in prison for giving their children "licks?" As time went on, Michael's accent grew more familiar to our friends, but it nevertheless proved a challenge in everyday conversation, and Barbados culture, and what we found as humorous and telling discontinuities between Bajan and Trinidadian life, held far less appeal than American cultural practices or idiosyncrasies. New modes of colonial indoctrination, ushered into everyday life by globalized media, informed understandings from the mundane to the profound, with cricket culture also feeling the weight.

The movement of financial, human, and cultural capital that engenders and results from globalization has interesting and problematic manifestations in cricket, since larger countries possess the capital to forge agendas beyond the control of West Indies cricket administrators. The globalization of sports has historically run counter to the interest of the region's island nations and to cricket as a keeper of consciousness for West Indian struggles for self-determination. Economically powerful nations, multinational corporations, and global sporting bodies drive globalization, and once again the West Indies seems to battle for existence, nevermind control. Cricket remains popular in many countries in the world, but the fact that it is ignored in the United States by the majority population factors into where it fits in a global sports economy and culture. It is true that cricket clubs form in immigrant communities and on college campuses, but many Americans feel they have been sufficiently globally accommodating by incorporating soccer into daily life. West Indies cricket must, as a result, understand globalization as an unavoidable reality, approached with caution and with some sense of solidarity.

In the 1980s, when the West Indies team was at the height of its cricketing power, some of its members, and other talented players not on the team, were recruited to play cricket in South Africa. The realization that global forces could dip right into the team provided fans and cricket leadership with a potentially new, and frightening, model. Yet in fact cricket leadership had had ample warning that regional and even pan-African understandings might not be enough to keep players on the team. Gary Sobers at one point decided that he would play cricket in Rhodesia, now Zimbabwe, then under the racist leadership of Ian Smith. Regardless of Sobers' own stated intention to challenge racism through sport, the incident clearly spoke to West Indian vulnerability and the need to educate players as well as the public about cricket history; it also required the intervention of three Caribbean heads of government. Certainly, as global promises and lures become more concentrated and inviting, cricket will experience difficulty maintaining a coherent, West Indian, regional identity.

A second example of the reaches of globalization was the Kerry Packer affair. Packer, an Australian television mogul, hoped to contract West Indian cricketers. He had something to offer: paying players well, introducing night cricket to draw in more fans, increasing prize monies, and providing innovative ways of filming the game. One issue rang clear in the ensuing debate about his success: the West Indian Cricket Board had not anticipated either the changes to the game or the responses of players. The idea that the West Indian player must always "be broke," as Trinidadian calypsonian Sparrow puts it, in order to bat and bowl his best, has limited resonance with modern players.[34]

Recently, the International Cricket Conference (ICC), the international cricket governing board formerly known as the Imperial Cricket Conference, has shown that it is quite interested in the issue of globalization. The first "Global Development Manager" was appointed in 1998. The ICC announced that the game must move rapidly to take advantage of opportunities for global expansion. It divided the world into five regions, each of which was allocated a full-time Development Officer, charged with the mission to take the sport to 2020 and beyond. Fortunately, the Board has not unilaterally embraced what some see as the positive elements of globalization. Many cricket fans in the region, anticipating a less than strong stance on the part of the West Indies Board, hailed the appointment of Clyde Walcott as chair of the ICC. They hoped that Walcott would bring his understanding of neocolonialism, as well as his criticisms of the ICC's predecessor, Marylebone Cricket Club, or MCC, to the fore. Marylebone, founded in 1787 in London, and eventually the world authority on cricket law, functioned, as Walcott argued, in "an imperial sort of way" that "was not good for the game."[35] But with Walcott now retired from the ICC, the Board must be mindful of the continuing issues, the unbalanced ways in which late-twentieth- and early-twenty-first century globalization has impacted upon the lives of people in the Caribbean. As feminist scholar Michiko Hase demonstrates with soccer, globalization, or the "close ties and collaboration among multinational media organizations, sports teams and sports governing bodies," threatens players' relative autonomy and even national identities.[36] Cricket administrators can benefit from paying close attention to the effects of globalization on sports such as soccer, which is even further entrenched in the process than is cricket at this point.

The commodification of athletes and of the game is certain to bear more weight in cricket as the globalization of the sport increases. Ironically enough, given the degree to which American media already permeate the islands from which West Indian cricket players emerge, that commodification may increasingly also serve as the lure of the game. As ICC chair Clyde Wolcott stated in an interview with Hilary Beckles, "Competitive sport is big business: Players are capital resources."[37] In our minds, resistance by continually and firmly situating the game in the region and its people provides a response to that globalization. One of the most effective region-building and region-affirming efforts has been at the University of the West Indies. With its three branches, in Barbados, Jamaica, and Trinidad, UWI is supported by and serves a total of fifteen countries. This regional university and the West Indies Cricket Board have undertaken an important collaborative effort, the establishment of cricket grounds on the Cave Hill, Barbados, campus and the establishment of the C. L. R. James Research Centre, a cricket research center, on the same branch campus. Players will participate at the research center, gaining an education about both the game and its history. The university, as Beckles puts it, can "provide leadership in the region until the cricket team is once more in a position to do so."[38] Alliances between sports and educational institutions in the Caribbean can help shape a new cricket by continuing the active process of decolonizing mind and body that the nationalists and their predecessors began long ago.

Conclusion

Cricket has contributed significantly to the democratization and well-being of the English-speaking Caribbean. Therefore its future in relation to globalization and other challenges must be conceived from this perspective: that of its many gifts and its enormous meaning. After many years of strength, the West Indies team lags on the world stage. The key now, it seems to us, is to keep faith with the past while embracing the future, much of which, sadly enough, lies in globalization. The Cricket Board, the players, the societies that produce and support the players, the fans abroad, we all need to find measurements of success that embrace historical, cultural, social, political, and economic realities. The game, as we all know as so much more than a game, can serve as well as be served by the region. Victories on the playing field can be matched by victories in the region; new and multiple identities of personhood, nationhood, and masculinity can and must be forged in the face of sport globalization.

The most recent indicators, however, are not promising. In a widely publicized and staggering setback, England recently defeated the West Indies in a series of matches in the Caribbean. The people of the Caribbean are wondering how the region will hold its own against the rest of the world in the upcoming World Cup. As the *Nation* newspaper puts it, what the recent losses did was to "expose just how much has to be done . . . to live up to the expectations of our own people, and especially, to dismiss the skeptics outside of the Caribbean who are already confident that we cannot handle such an assignment."[39]

As with many other aspects of cricket, the ironies loom large. At the same time that the team suffered massive defeat, West Indies team captain Brian Lara made four hundred runs, the first batsman in test cricket history to make this score. Lara also became one of a few batsmen in the history of the game to score a triple century twice at the international level. In the process, the West Indies scored the most it had ever done against England. Clearly, Lara possesses the talent that West Indians have come to expect from their great batsmen. He will certainly be considered one of the greatest batsmen ever to play the game. However, when his accomplishment is juxtaposed against the losses the West Indies has suffered during his tenure as captain and particularly during this recent tour by England, fans and critics become glum.

The defeat was as symbolic as it was real. "In 40 years of covering West Indies cricket," Tony Crozier wrote in the immediate aftermath, "I have never known the depth of frustration, hopelessness and downright anger that now exists."[40] For many fans it felt like British rule all over again, and British fans at the matches hammered that very message home with their empire-affirming chants. Even Lara's accomplishments have not sufficiently tempered the fear that, as Crozier puts it, "the decline is terminal, that the tentacles of defeatism are stifling as a love vine and that the West Indies are becoming an irrelevancy at the highest level of the game."[41] Gary Sobers and his generation of cricketers clearly provided West Indians with the psychological means to demand independence and democratic rule. It remains unclear whether Lara's victories represent another beginning—or the end of an era. Can it be that, simultaneously, Lara represents true greatness while, conversely, his teammates symbolize the fear and hopelessness and doubt in the Caribbean to struggle and win against the odds?

The upcoming World Cup of cricket in the Caribbean will provide a test of the ideas we raise here. Regional pride, coupled with "home game" mentality, is sure to renew excitement and loyalty among existing fans and entice a younger generation of fans and potential players. The event can also help secure the role of cricket in looking ahead to a more positive future for the region. The ICC awarded the West Indies Cricket Board $108US million to host the 2007 Cricket World Cup. As Prime Minister P. J. Patterson of Jamaica noted, the undertaking represents a "major commercial venture with significant spin-offs in terms of numerous commercial activities. The business community—large and small entrepreneurs—must begin from now to prepare to satisfy the expected demand for goods and services."[42] Will the West Indies Board act in a way that validates and supports the local, the societies from which the players emerge, rather than the global in this enterprise? Who will benefit most from the monies spent?

Concerns about the process have already begun to surface. Small entrepreneurs among the fans we spoke with express concern about the gatekeeping they already begin to encounter. One young man, lobbying to play a role in the World Cup and make money for himself and his local employees, felt both deflated and angry when told that security measures at Kensington Oval, a major cricket ground in Barbados, might not allow him and other small business people like him within the grounds. As C. L. R. James wrote in one of his most quoted phrases, "West Indians crowding to Test bring with them the whole past history and future hopes of the islands."[43] We hope that cricket leadership, national governments, and the demands of the people will ensure that the World Cup will benefit the citizens in economic as well as social and cultural ways. Recognition of the deep and varied roles of cricket off the field will provide the most beneficial context on the field for the World Cup and beyond. While neither cricket nor the West Indies team can simply reject the forces of globalization, or wholesale provide new definitions of regionalism, they can develop, affirm, and support positive movements for change. The West Indies team and the people of the region share rich legacies of personal pride, community advancement, talking back. As Hilary Beckles argues, in thinking about how to get where we need to go, "the greatest gift you can give is the gift of high standards."[44] The result will undoubtedly be some excellent cricket for Michael, the longtime fan, Jennifer, the neophyte, and the many fans and critics whose ideas we have revisited here.

Notes

1. Although Gary Sobers was knighted about thirty years ago, he continues to receive recognition for his role and accomplishments in cricket. Most recently, the Australian government honored him with its highest award, declaring him a "citizen of the cricket world" and appointing him an Officer in the General Division of the Order of Australia. See "Australia Honour," *Barbados Daily Nation,* April 16, 2004, http:www.nationnews.com (April 20, 2004).
2. See bell hooks, *Talking Back: Thinking Feminist, Thinking Black* (Boston: South End Press, 1989).

3. James quoted in Hilary McD. Beckles, *The Development of West Indies Cricket: Volume I, The Age of Nationalism* (Kingston: University Press of the West Indies, 1998), 175.

4. See David Rudder, "Rally Round the West Indies," a track on his recording, *Haiti* (Warner Bros., 1988).

5. Beckles, *The Development of West Indies Cricket*, 1.

6. Ibid., 5.

7. Ibid., 2.

8. Ibid., 5.

9. George Headley had led the team for one test match years earlier, but Worrell's captaincy was a turning point. See Beckles, 201.

10. Ibid., 177.

11. C. L. R. James, *Beyond a Boundary* (Durham, NC: Duke University Press, 1998).

12. Beckles, 4.

13. "No Nonsense," *Barbados Daily Nation*, March 30, 2004, http:www.nation-news.com (April 20, 2004).

14. George Lamming, *The Pleasures of Exile* (Ann Arbor: University of Michigan, 1992); James, *Beyond a Boundary;* Paulo Freire, *Pedagogy of the Oppressed* (New York: Continuum, 1999/1970).

15. Freire, 29.

16. James, 29–30.

17. Freire, 29.

18. See Edouard Glissant, *Le discours Antillais* (Paris: Editions du Seuil, 1981); and Glissant, *Poetique del la relation* (Paris: Gallimard, 1990); quoted in Kathleen M. Balutansky, "Appreciating C. L. R. James, A Model of Modernity and Creolization," *Latin American Research Review* 32, no. 2 (1997): 242.

19. Balutanksy, 242.

20. Ibid., 242.

21. As Beckles puts it, James led West Indians "into an ideological crusade that signaled the end of the ancient regime. Cricket was now in the hands of the masses who had given breath to it at critical moments" (76–77).

22. Freire, 30.

23. Ibid., 30.

24. Beckles, 183.

25. See Beckles, 95.

26. James, 55. Shannon was the club of world-famous Trinidadian cricketer Learie Constantine. The son of a sugar plantation manager, Constantine went on to play cricket, like his father, then became, as Bridget Brereton puts it, "the best known spokesman for black people" in Britain, where he was knighted and became the first black man appointed to the House of Lords. See Bridget Brereton, "Learie Constantine 1901–1971," http://www.nalis.gov.tt/Biography/LearieConstantinebyBridgetBrereton.htm (July 6, 2004).

27. James, 54.

28. James, 58.

29. Beckles, 11.
30. Ibid., 191.
31. Linden Lewis, "Caribbean Masculinity at the Fin de Siecle," in Rhoda Reddock, ed., *Interrogating Caribbean Masculinities: Theoretical and Analytical Analyses* (Kingston, Jamaica: University of the West Indies Press, 2004), 261.
32. See also Mark Figueroa, "Male Privileging and Male 'Academic Underperformance' in Jamaica," in Reddock, 137–166; Odette Parry, "Masculinities, Myths and Educational Underachievement: Jamaica, Barbados, and St. Vincent and the Grenadines," in Reddock, 167–184; Eudine Barriteau, "Assessments, Reflections, Negotiations: A Feminist Theorizing of the Future of Gender Relations in the Commonwealth Caribbean," Keynote Lecture, *Borders, Boundaries and the Global in the Caribbean Conference,* Bowdoin College, April 12, 2003; Aviston Downes, "Gender and the Elementary Teaching Service in Barbados, 1880–1960: A Re-examination of the Feminization and Marginalization of the Black Male Theses," in Eudine Barriteau, ed., *Confronting Power, Theorizing Gender: Interdisciplinary Perspectives in the Caribbean* (Kingston, Jamaica: University of the West Indies Press, 2003), 303–323; Eudine Barriteau, "Requiem for the Male Marginalization Thesis in the Caribbean: Death of a Non-Theory," in Barriteau, 324–355.
33. Barriteau, "Requiem for the Male Marginalization Thesis," 327.
34. Sparrow quoted in Beckles, 111.
35. Walcott quoted in Beckles, 187.
36. Michiko Hase, "Race in Soccer as a Global Sport," in *Sports Matters: Race, Recreation, and Culture,* ed. John Bloom and Michael Nevin Willard (New York: NYU Press, 2002), 308.
37. Walcott quoted in Beckles, 189.
38. Beckles quoted in "Saint George's University Hosts UWI's Professor Hilary Beckles (December 2002), SGU website, http://www.sgu.edu/NewsEvents.nsf/webContent/469A43E3ECBB8E3F85256CD20065BF73 (July 6, 2004).
39. Tony Cozier, "God Save the Windies," *Barbados Daily Nation,* April 4, 2004, http:www.nationnews.com (April 20, 2004).
40. Ibid.
41. Ibid.
42. "216 M Hit: ICC Perk for 2007 World Cup Hosts," Barbados *Saturday Sun,* November 8, 2003, 1.
43. James, 233.
44. Beckles, 178.

FIVE

Wa a o, wa ba ski na me ska ta!

"Indian" Mascots and the Pathology of Anti-Indigenous Racism

David Anthony Tyeeme Clark

The battle today is our own image. We are trying to reclaim ourselves.

—*Charlene Teters, 1995*[1]

This kind of racism is buried so deeply in the American psyche that it may be impossible to resolve. . . . This profound racism rises so quickly to consciousness and is expressed before the individual realizes what she or he has said.

—*Vine Deloria, Jr., 2001*[2]

When the Florida State University (FSU) football team rushes onto the playing field of Doak S. Campbell Stadium, it follows an athletic mascot wearing colored turkey feathers, riding a spotted pony, and carrying a flaming spear that he plants on the fifty-yard line with a war-whoop. While this activity unfolds on the field, over eighty thousand FSU fans chant a pseudo-Indian melody while swinging their arms together in a tomahawk chop. The FSU spectacle is a common one; resolute FSU fans recognize it as authentically Seminole, as authoritatively American Indian. For many American Indians these sorts of activities are understood as offensive, as deeply fatal to the well-being of Indigenous nations, communities, extended families, and young people. Most Native professionals and our allies comprehend them as yet another disturbing appropriation in a long and ongoing history of colonization that includes forced removals and fraudulent land transfers away from Indigenous Peoples.[3]

Countless people experience "Indians" only as mascots—as braves, Indians, redskins, savages, and warriors, as fighting Chippewas, Illini, Sioux, and Utes, as Black Hawks and Blue Jackets.[4] In every corner of the United States and accessible at all levels of competitive athletics—high school, college and university, and professional—acts that link Indians with sports amount to a pathology of anti-Indigenous racism. Three examples that represent Indians as mascots are instructive and are illustrative of the pathology of anti-Indigenous racism: the ongoing debate surrounding the professional football team in the United States capital; the favorable response to a *Sports Illustrated* publication entitled "The Indian Wars"; and reaction to an intramural basketball team in Colorado named the Fighting Whites. By assigning the term "pathology" to anti-Indigenous racism and these three examples, I mean to draw attention to a social disorder that requires intervention and correction. By "racism" in a U.S. cultural context, I mean white racial hegemony or white supremacy, a highly organized system of racialized oppression and a continuous and dynamic process of antidemocratic social control.[5]

According to Stuart Hall, people position themselves in relationship to media messages or "circuits of culture"—what I am calling "reality" and "communities of belonging"—in one of three ways: uncritical acceptance, negotiated acceptance, and resistance.[6] Through "circuits of culture," according to Hall, the lexicons and syntaxes of languages fill semantic breaches—understood as gaps in representation located between concepts being represented and the images or words or signs doing the work of representation. In the gap between a particular concept and the signs that labor to represent it, language provides passage, transporting and transmitting meaning, rendering this meaning accessible to people who then cohere around what they come to share similarly as "reality" and experience as communities of belonging. In the consumption of and participation in competitive athletics, for masses of fans and athletes in many other ways drifting apart, "Indian" mascots (understood as language) do the work of representation—they labor to fill semantic breaches located between signified concepts (certain desired qualities widely associated with normative forms of masculinity, sports, community, racial identity, and American Indians) and its signifiers (mascots, team names and logos, fan behaviors, and consumer apparel). Simply put, people invent and invigorate concepts such as "reality" and community by actively and often instinctively linking them to images, symbols, words, and signs. The idea that signs stand in to represent concepts is commonly accepted within the scientific and cultural study of language; this notion also is accepted implicitly by advocates for and foes of "Indian" mascots who struggle over precise linkages and whose meaning for those associations between concepts and signs will prevail.[7]

For individual Natives, this painful habit of associating Indians with athletic mascots hardens and softens from moment to moment, might change over time, and can be deeply personal. Countless examples could illustrate this point and suggest at the same time that Natives, like non-Natives, are complex human beings with heterogeneous desires and emotions.[8] Michael Dashner, information technology director for the National Indian Child Welfare Association in Portland, Oregon, for instance, is a father, a well-known powwow dancer and drummer, an alumnus of the University of Michigan, and a former employee in the University of Michigan's Office of Minority Student Services. He also is Indigenous, a citizen of the Bad River Band of the Lake Superior Tribe of Chippewa Indians. In his youth during the 1950s and 1960s, Dashner moved between his two Ojibwe families separated by an international boundary between Walpole Island, Ontario, and Bad River, Wisconsin.[9] As an adult, he nourishes traditional culture among his family and community members in Portland.

Responding in September 2003 to a query regarding the suitability of "Indian" mascots for college and professional athletics, Dashner offered insight into how and why individual Natives speak out about what is at stake in the mascot controversy. He identified two events that caused him "to take a firm stance against any and all Indian mascots," in his words, "after a few years of indecisiveness."[10] The first incident occurred during the September 1991 matchup that pitched the number-one ranked FSU team against the number-three ranked Wolverines. Michigan fans mocked "the FSU fight song and tomahawk chop by raising their middle finger while mimicking the chop motion and ending the FSU fight song with, 'fu-k the Seminoles'." He continued:

> The second incident happened to my family, actually my eight-year-old daughter, while attending a powwow at Central Michigan University whose mascot name is the Chippewas. We all dance and my daughter was an outstanding young girl's fancy dancer. We were having breakfast at one of the Big Boy (chain) restaurants on Main Street in this nice little town. My daughter went up to the breakfast bar for a second helping of waffles. After being gone for a few minutes she came back to the table with an empty plate and sat with her head down. After inquiring, "what's wrong?" a couple of times I noticed her wiping some tears from her eyes. With adrenalin pumping at the

thought of someone harming my little girl, I kept asking, "what's wrong?" She meekly pointed to a group of guys sitting near the breakfast bar and said, "they're so mean." I immediately stormed over towards their table to confront them on why they had made my daughter cry. As I got closer to their table I could hear them talking about the upcoming game between their school and the CMU Chippewas. My tribe is Chippewa and I'd always raised my daughter to be proud of her heritage and here were these big ignorant athletes saying things like, "we're going to fu-k up those Chippewas" and "we're going to kick some Chippewa ass today."[11] They were with the opposing team in town for the big game against the Central Michigan Chippewas.[12] The common factor in both of these cases is, a school, college, or university and all their supporters can do everything within their power to create a sense of pride for their mascot, but these supporters can not control what an opposing team will say and do regarding their mascot. I managed to get out of that restaurant with my hide still attached to my body, but with a firmly established disgust for the whole Indian mascot issue. I've become a staunch supporter of eliminating Indian mascots. My personal feelings about the whole mascot issue is that every faculty, staff, or booster who supports maintaining an Indian mascot should take some time to seriously consider if they would ever subject their own children to the kind of pain and humiliation that my daughter felt that morning.[13]

Although "Indian" athletic mascots have specific utilitarian functions, as Dashner suggests, their meaning in our everyday lives can be personal and unpleasant.[14] There is no such thing as an "Indian" athletic mascot that is a perfectly functional object without supplementary, and thus controversial, meanings. A Southeastern Oklahoma State University "Savage" and a Haskell Indian Nations University "Indian," for instance, share the same function. Both provide the connective tissue that links individuals to community but connote different things about the alumni, employees, students, athletes, and fans they represent: vanished "savages" who once embodied fierce, war-loving qualities worthy of ongoing appropriation by sports enthusiasts versus living Indians who in the present are pursuing a college education.[15] Established by an act of Congress in 1884 as a federal government Indian boarding school designed to assimilate Indian children into white culture, in 1992 Haskell was accredited as a university for students who in a typical year represent over 150 Indian nations.

Projections of meaning onto "Indian" mascots are more complex even than this example that compares Southeastern Oklahoma State and Haskell suggests. As signs that include team names and lore, fan behaviors, and consumer products, the "Savage" and "Indian" signs are rich with connotations that, for Natives, may include anticolonial rage, intergenerational trauma (or soul wounds, as some elders call it), and genocide of the mind (or internalized colonization). Thus, we can speak of "Indian" mascots as signs expressive of certain individual and group identities; simultaneously they may both bring people together and distinguish them from one another.

In what follows, three primary examples—one offered by the professional football team in the nation's capital, a second suggested by *Sports Illustrated's* assertions about Indian support for "Indian" mascots, and another provided by an intramural basketball team at the University of Northern Colorado named the "Fighting Whites"—illustrate how "Indian" mascots function as a pathology of anti-Indigenous racism.[16] The continued use of "Indian" mascots rests on the ability to wield racialized and racializing power—social, economic, and political—against actual Native peoples, while also drawing power from us. "Indian" mascots inevitably require "real Indians," like Dashner, some of whom question the legitimacy of their continued use. As the examples of the Washington team, *Sports Illustrated*, and the Fighting Whites suggest, struggles over what "Indian" mascots mean circulate from athletic venues through mass media communications— in cable news programming, popular sport journals, newspapers, and radio talk shows. As criticism moves outward from its Indigenous critics, the debate about meaning strengthens existing webs of power in which we all presently are situated. An ingrained, racist common sense that is one of the foundations (along with gender relations) for imagining and performing domination and power in the United States reaches millions in communities and homes where actual Natives have virtually no intellectual influence.

Throughout the twentieth century, Natives have spoken out in opposition to their being represented as mascots. The Chicago physician, Yavapai-Apache, Indian activist, and University of Illinois alum Carlos Montezuma, for instance, alleged that "there have been and are, a great many people using the Indians as their mascot," a practice he suggested in 1921 "may do some good to other people, [but that does] more harm than good to the Indian people."[17] Fifty years later, Dennis Banks and other media-conscious, media-savvy Indian activists moved the mascot issue as it was discussed among many Natives into broader public discourse. To make the point about the seriousness of the matter, according to Banks, the American Indian Movement (AIM) represented by Russell Means in 1970 threatened the Cleveland and Atlanta baseball clubs with the embarrassment of answering lawsuits in federal courts.[18] In 1971, just months before Natives from around the country converged on the nation's capitol to focus attention on "two hundred years of lies and empty promises our people had received from the United States," in the words of Means, seven people representing AIM, Americans for Indian Opportunity, the American Indian Press Association, the Indian Legal Information Development Service, and the National Congress of American Indians met in Washington, D.C., with

National Football League (NFL) team owner Edward Bennett Williams.[19] They asked Williams to change the team's name, amend the fight song, and eliminate offensive imagery that had been afforded legal protection by registrations filed with the United States Department of Trade and Commerce Patent and Trademark Office beginning in 1967. According to Banks, looking back on the meeting two decades later, "our overtures were rebuffed and the meeting ended in a screaming match."[20]

In 1974, Suzan Shown Harjo, who is Cheyenne and Hodulgee Muscogee, and today president and executive director of The Morning Star Institute, a national, nonprofit Indian rights organization, moved with her husband Frank Ray Harjo to the District of Columbia. Like other Natives, the Harjos were appalled when they saw how the Washington NFL franchise and their fans disparaged American Indians. At their first professional football game, which they attended after a friend gave them tickets, fans who discovered they were actual Indians pointed in their direction, poked at them, and pulled their hair as they made their exit from the stadium.[21]

For years Natives have labored to pressure the NFL team in Washington to retire its mascot. Their efforts received the broadest media coverage during a week-long, widely aired protest in Minneapolis-St. Paul accompanying Super Bowl XXVI in January 1992 that included handing out flyers, offering a free seminar on racism in sports and the media, picketing the player of the year awards dinner, and conducting an all-day demonstration on game day.[22]

Capitalizing on the momentum coming out of a protest that included between 2,000 and 4,000 demonstrators, the Minneapolis law firm Dorsey & Whitney, representing a group of seven Indigenous activists and educators that included Harjo, legal scholar Vine Deloria, Jr., and prominent Indian activist Bill Means filed a complaint in September 1992 with the Patent and Trademark Office against the owner of the NFL's Washington Redskins.[23] Six years later, in May 1998, a three-judge panel of the Trial Trademark and Appeal Board (TTAB) considered the petition. A year after entertaining testimony from each of the seven petitioners, the team owner, and expert witnesses, and after considering the findings from a telephone survey conducted for the petitioners by a market research and consumer psychologist, Ivan Ross, the three judge panel concluded that the six marks registered with the Patent and Trademark Office between 1967 and 1990 were disparaging and "may bring Native Americans into contempt or disrepute."[24] Accordingly, they ordered six registrations cancelled in a 145-page memorandum opinion issued in April 1999. The team owner appealed the decision.

Four years later, on July 23, 2003, United States District Judge Colleen Kollar-Kotelly held a hearing to address summary judgment motions filed by both sides in *Pro Football Inc. v. Harjo,* civil action 99–1385.[25] She issued her decision on September 30, 2003. Her conclusion was that the TTAB determination rendered in 1999 "must be reversed."[26]

In her decision, the federal judge dismissed evidence that could not in her estimation speak for *all* Natives. Using the "substantial evidence" standard, Kollar-Kotelly determined that the TTAB outcome was not supported by "substantial evidence" because, she reasoned, the Ross survey was not methodologically sound.[27] Ivan Ross, President of Ross Research and former professor of marketing and adjunct professor of psychology with the Carlson School of Management at the University of Minnesota, had testified through deposition before the TTAB that 37 percent of the 358 Native American adults he surveyed were personally offended by the use of the ethnic label "redskin."[28] In making her determination, Kollar-Kotelly not only attacked the credibility of the Ross survey—essentially adopting the position of an expert commissioned by Pro-Football, Inc., Jacob Jacoby— she dismissed as unpersuasive testimony provided by the linguist Geoffrey Nunberg, evidence the TTAB earlier had found convincing in rendering its judgment about the matter.[29] More important, Kollar-Kotelly adopted the logic that a "lengthy period of time [had ensued] between registration and the cancellation request" to dismiss evidence dated after the period in question, 1967–1990—which included the Ross survey—as not relevant.[30] Agreeing with the TTAB that the term "redskin" "clearly refers to [a] professional football team and carries the allusion to Native Americans," she nonetheless concluded that the claim that the term "may disparage" Indigenous Peoples "is unsupported by substantial evidence [and] is logically flawed."[31]

Thus, Kollar-Kotelly dismissed the significance—and the consequences—of the ways in which representation constitutes common sense "reality." That is, assuming an authority to speak for and otherwise represent Natives, she implied that mascots universally are not harmful and insisted (implicitly if not explicitly) that "redskin" does not have an oppressive effect. Instead, she sided with representatives of the team, who argued that loss of trademark protection would have disastrous economic consequences for the team owner. She applied a legal standard that requires Natives to uniformly agree before a federal court legitimately could intervene on their (our) behalf. Further, in her logic, Natives must not only unvaryingly agree on the matter in question, but must agree in those moments when the federal government registers a trademark, file a grievance with a federal court in a period of time that amounts to immediately in response, and furnish courts with survey data that all sides agree is scientific.

The legal firm White & Chase represented Pro-Football, Inc. before the federal court. Founded in 1901 in New York, White & Case today is one of the world's leading global law firms, with more than 1,650 lawyers practicing in 26 countries. According to Sandi Sonnenfeld, media relations manager for the firm, "White & Case regularly handles litigation and trademark matters for a wide variety of sports-related organizations."[32] Touting their legal victory in a press release on October 1, 2003, an attorney representing White & Chase, Robert L. Raskopf, claimed that Kollar-Kotelly's decision "specifically recognized . . . that the term 'Redskins' in connection with the team's marks was used in a respectful manner . . . and deserves to be recognized for what it is: the proud symbol of a famous franchise."[33] Two days later, in a press release excerpted in *Native American Times,* a nationally circulating newspaper published in Tulsa, Oklahoma, the National Congress of American Indians characterized the decision as "a victory of economic interests over the deep desire for racial healing in this nation."[34]

The grievance against the NFL team discharged in federal courtrooms, and circulated in press releases and Native newspapers, also was performed among non-Natives in the arena of official District of Columbia politics. Political maneuvering by elected representatives in the District of Columbia should be understood as responses to grassroots concerns.[35] Carol Schwartz, a Republican candidate for District of Columbia mayor in 2002, spearheaded an effort to use legislation to intervene in the commerce of racism that played out in politics locally and in mass media communications internationally between November 2001 and March 2002.[36]

In November 2001, the Council of the District of Columbia, a thirteen-member body tasked with developing legislative initiatives and budget priorities to promote the public welfare, issued a second resolution asking the owner of the NFL franchise to change his team name before the 2002–2003 season. Council members passed an earlier resolution in March 1992.[37] In January 2002, the Metropolitan Washington Council of Governments issued a resolution similar to the earlier one passed by members of the D.C. Council. Both actions precipitated by Schwartz prompted coverage in national television and print media, as well as critical reflection in the national Native media. As reported in January by one of the leading national Native newspapers, *Indian Country Today,* "On Fox Channel, Brit Hume and associated 'All Stars' pooh-poohed the whole idea of such a term being insulting. Chuckling at the mere thought of it, the pundits dismissed the issue as ridiculous or hopeless, so why bother. Tucker Carlson, on CNN's *Crossfire,* asked the inevitable question whether there weren't more important things for Indians to worry about."[38]

It was in this context of legal and political maneuvering playing out in newspapers and cable news programming that media functionaries and sports journalists working for *Sports Illustrated* and CNN intervened in the dispute over how "Indians" were represented in the United States capital by a professional football team.[39] For its over three million paid subscribers and well in excess of one billion website hits in a six-month period, the March 4, 2002, issue of *Sports Illustrated* featured a wildly colorful, arrestingly illustrated, and sensationally reported seven-page article, "The Indian Wars," concerned with what sport journalist Scott L. Price explained was a "word problem" in "today's racially sensitive climate."[40] From a telephone poll of 351 persons racially identified as "Native Americans" conducted by the Peter Harris Research Group as well as ten additional telephone interviews with persons identified as Indian activists, educators, and tribal leaders, Price suggested that in overwhelming majorities, Natives, like sport fans generally, supported using "Indians" as mascots.[41] Further, Price argued in "The Indian Wars" that activists like Harjo were out of step with the people they claimed to represent. He implied that the owner of the NFL team in the nation's capital, vocal supporters of "Indian" mascots generally, and even mascots themselves, better stood in for majority sentiment among the masses of Indigenous Peoples.[42]

It was Price's interpretation and presentation of the data, and not necessarily the findings of the Peter Harris Research Group, that resonated with mascot supporters. The findings appear to be strikingly similar to the 1996 findings of the Ross survey. Thirty-six percent of the Native respondents identified as living on reservations indicated to Harris researchers that they were offended by the term "Redskin." When asked whether they objected to mascots dressing up in Indian headdresses, wearing war paint, whooping and dancing around with a tomahawk in hand, however, 58 percent of this same group indicated that they find such behavior objectionable.[43]

The formidable impact of Price's reporting in *Sport Illustrated's* "The Indian Wars" can be identified in the ways its major findings circulated in newspapers and cable news programming. While Kollar-Kotelly concluded that a survey of 358 Natives conducted in 1996 could not lawfully be used in a federal court to speak for Natives, writers and pundits used a similar survey conducted in 2002 for CNN/*Sports Illustrated* as unimpeachable evidence. In court and in mass media communications, mascot advocates embraced the "science" of surveys either to dismiss or accept data that stood in to represent Natives.

Approving response to "The Indian Wars" voiced in newspaper editorials and columns, as well as in cable news programming, promulgated inflexible claims about what Natives think. Writing in newspapers across the country, various commentators used *Sports Illustrated* specifically to disseminate the idea that actual Native people had no problem with "Indian" mascots. Citing the market research published in *Sports Illustrated,* for instance, Scott Norvell reported for viewers of the Fox News Channel that, in his words, "the majority of them [Indians] do not think the use of these

team names and mascots contributes to discrimination."[44] In a letter to the
editor of the Decatur, Illinois, *Herald and Review,* a supporter of the University of Illinois at Urbana-Champaign athletic mascot, Chief Illiniwek, relied on the authority of the *Sports Illustrated* article to suggest that
"mascots . . . are not bothering the majority of Native Americans."[45] Some
commentators accused students who objected to the Illinois mascot of incorrectly representing sentiment among Natives. Matt Kaufman, a University of Illinois alum representing the conservative group Focus on the
Family, for example, used "The Indian Wars" to suggest for his readers that
"the anti-Chief movement is made up largely of well-to-do white kids from
the Chicago suburbs."[46] Others used *Sports Illustrated* similarly to call into
question the legitimacy of "outsiders" who questioned their continued use
of Chief Illiniwek. In a news release circulated early in 2003, for instance,
a representative of an organization "intended to provide a unified voice for
the thousands of students, faculty, alumni, and friends of the University of
Illinois that support and value the Chief Illiniwek tradition," cited "The Indian Wars" to suggest that the "Report on the Use of American Indian
Mascots" published in October 2002 by members of the Minority Opportunities and Interests Committee of the NCAA is "biased and one-sided."[47]

Other writers echoed Price's contention in *Sports Illustrated* that Native activists, educators, and tribal leaders, too, misrepresent widespread
sentiment among the masses of Native peoples. In *National Review,* for instance, John J. Miller quoted Price to suggest that Native activists see
racism everywhere and that what he called a minority of Native opinion
leaders do not speak for "the Native American population."[48] In the *Grand
Forks Herald,* a former North Dakota lieutenant governor and then professor of political science at the University of North Dakota characterized
the market research group as "a national polling organization with excellent credentials" that had "no reason . . . to conduct a sloppy poll for a national magazine." The findings, he argued, "indeed indicate that many
Indians do not share the views of the activists. . . . The anti-nickname
folks . . . should abandon the argument that they represent a majority of Indians." That position, he concluded, "has been trashed."[49] Writing under
the headline "Activists Don't Reflect Majority," a supporter of the "Indian" moniker used by the Manhattan, Kansas, high school, then under
fire, used "The Indian Wars" in a letter to the Topeka, Kansas, *Capitol-Journal* to attack the credibility of activist-scholars such as Cornel Pewewardy, a professor in the School of Education at the University of Kansas
and long a visible and vocal critic of "Indian" mascots used by Kansas
schools.[50] "[I]t's the activists—the militants and the malcontents—who oppose such nicknames and mascots," this letter writer opined, "and not the
Native American population at large."[51]

Like supporters of the controversial mascots used at the University of Illinois and the University of North Dakota, many writers used "The Indian Wars" as irreproachable authority in their attempts to end local debates in which they had a stake.[52] They suggested that the time when "activists" could shape public opinion among non-Natives was approaching its end or was already over. Matthew Cella in the *Washington Times,* for instance, referred to the market research group findings as "scientific," foreclosing any further discussion on the debate in Maryland over the future of "Indian" mascots in the state's public schools.[53] Brian Ojanpa, staff writer for the Mankato, Minnesota, *Free Press,* suggested that the market research poll commissioned by *Sports Illustrated* "wasn't some high school class project, nor one of those surveys deliberately skewed to achieve desired findings." "Anti-nickname activists," he suggested, "have been dealt a large blow."[54] The editors of the *Grand Forks Herald,* whose readers are themselves involved in an intense struggle over an "Indian"-themed athletic moniker, insisted "[that a]ctivists can't ignore and must change their strategy in response to *Sports Illustrated's* stunning survey."[55]

Thus, while in federal law, surveys cannot stand in to represent Natives, in broader cultural discourse they can, and do. A single survey with a methodology largely shrouded in mystery emerges among mascot supporters as irrefutable evidence to dismiss their pro-Indigenous opponents.[56]

Two pro-Native examples, one in California and another in Colorado, the "Fighting Whites," illustrate the potency of "The Indian Wars" for mascot supporters in their efforts to turn aside criticism. Both examples suggest that power functions through representation in ways that allow for substantial, and broad-based, public negotiations of what "Indian" mascots mean and, simultaneously, allow the re-iteration of anti-Indigenous racism.

In California, where assemblywoman Jackie Goldberg from the forty-fifth district in Los Angeles sponsored California Assembly Bill (AB) 2115 in April 2002, "The Indian Wars" stood in for some as unassailable evidence that she did not voice the concerns of Natives, but that they did.[57] Drafted by representatives from the Southern California Indian Center, AB 2115 sought to prohibit public schools from using redskins, braves, chiefs, and American Indian tribal names.[58] Debra Saunders, a self-identified conservative causes pundit in San Francisco, used "The Indian Wars" to suggest that Goldberg "sees discrimination where most American Indians don't."[59] In a letter to the editors of the *Los Angeles Times,* a reader writing late in May from Long Beach similarly used *Sports Illustrated* to suggest that while Goldberg labored in California to legislate, in his words, "'racial sensitivity' for the poor Indians, they [the Indians themselves] have better things to do."[60] A *San Diego Union-Tribune* journalist writing from

California for Missouri readers of the *Joplin Globe* on May 23—representing himself as a fan of the NFL team in the nation's capital—mentioned "The Indian Wars" to offer his view that "Indian team names actually foment goodwill toward American Indians. . . . Most American Indians understand. . . . Too bad those who presume to speak for them do not."[61]

The Alliance Against Racial Mascots, a coalition formed by the Los Angeles chapter of the National Conference for Community and Justice and the Southern California Indian Center located in Los Angeles, responded to the failure of AB 2115 with AB 858, the California Racial Mascots Act, to prohibit public schools from using certain specified ethnic labels. After failing to convince a sufficient number of assembly members to support the revised legislation introduced in February 2003, Goldberg further narrowed its scope to include only the term "redskin." Reflecting the influence of broad-based grassroots politics that included Natives and non-Natives working together, AB 858 passed the Assembly by a vote of 43–20 on January 29, 2004.[62] It passed the Senate on August 18, 44–34.[63] Insisting that "another non-academic state administrative requirement for schools to comply with takes more focus away from getting kids to learn at the highest levels," Governor Arnold Schwarzenegger vetoed the legislation on September 21.[64] In a newspaper interview, Gerald Benton, Superintendent for the Tulare Joint Union High School District "R—skins," praised Schwarzenegger and oddly framed the veto as a triumph for democracy and social justice: "This will encourage people, whether for or against this issue, that the political process works. It will encourage them to know that individuals can make a difference."[65]

Thus, in California, it appears that a grassroots mobilization of Natives and their allies countered the influence of *Sports Illustrated* in the General Assembly but not in the governor's office. This was not a victory for democracy. Citizens of Indian nations do not elect tribal representatives to represent tribal nations and interests in the California General Assembly, and must therefore convince representatives of state legislative districts such as Goldberg to represent their wishes and interests in the California General Assembly.

To the east, in Colorado, a multiracial, multi-ethnic coalition that included Natives and non-Natives attempted to influence parents, teachers, and school board members rather than pursue a legislative or legal strategy. In March 2002 when *Sports Illustrated* instructed readers that "real Indians" enjoyed being linked to the qualities associated with competitive athletics, in Greeley, Colorado, the appearance of an intramural basketball team at the University of Northern Colorado (UNC), the "Fighting Whites," generated the level of media attention necessary to counter the influence of *Sports Illustrated's* "Indian Wars." Thus, the "Fighting Whites" not only was enmeshed in a local campaign to engage residents of Eaton, Colorado, in a conversation about the education of young people and their athletic mascot, the Fighting Reds, but it also circulated through media to reinforce rather than challenge anti-Indigenous racism. At certain points of its farthest reach—Rush Limbaugh, for example—the ability of Natives and our allies to express ourselves through the Fighting Whites sign was displaced by assertions of ignorance, claims of white racial injury, and affirmations of white supremacy.

The story of the Fighting Whites begins in Eaton, a small rural Colorado town about seven miles north of Greeley, the home of the University of Northern Colorado (UNC). During the winter and spring of 2002, a group of activists used several strategies aimed at retiring the Eaton mascot—they lobbied Eaton school administrators and local school board members, conducted a telephone survey of Eaton residents and distributed their findings, made a presentation before representatives of the Colorado State Board of Education, and organized and led a protest march. Just weeks earlier, in 2001, UNC graduate student Dan Ninham and Francie Eagle-Wolf Murry, a UNC associate professor of education, launched Coloradoans Against Ethnic Stereotyping in Colorado Schools to coordinate their efforts with other progressive groups in the state. Locally, the group included additional UNC professors and graduate students, as well as Eaton staff and teachers.[66]

The racial and ethnic demographics of Eaton suggest that Indigenous Peoples are underrepresented there in terms of numbers. In July 2002, Eaton had a total population of 3,470 residents. According to 2000 United States Census data, self-identified American Indian and Alaska Native persons are less than 1 percent of the total population in Weld County where Eaton is located. White persons who do not identify as Hispanic constitute 70 percent of the total county population.[67] According to data offered by SchoolTree.org, Eaton High School has one student who identifies as Native American among a total of 436 students. Another school data source reports no American Indian students enrolled in Eaton High School.[68] Thus, "Indians" in the Eaton schools are represented principally not by Native human beings but by signs—an athletic team name and logo—with emotional significance for the substantially non-Native population.

The Eaton school mascot features a caricature of an "Indian" man with an oversized nose and wearing a feather and loincloth. The term associated with the image, the mascot "Fighting Reds," asserts an authority to teach young people about Indians. It also links school children with qualities they recognize as "Indian"; the process of weaving those children into narratives that produce knowledge about "Indians" allows them and their adult teachers and parents in moments to be the "Indians" of their imaginations. These narratives enable them to be, speak, and act as "Fighting Reds."[69]

As an educator and parent himself, as well as cofounder and member of Coloradoans Against Ethnic Stereotyping in Colorado Schools (CAESCS) and a citizen of the Oneida Nation of Wisconsin, Ninham's campaign to educate school administrators and teachers, school board members, and parents about authentic Indigenous Peoples—real Indians—began when he started graduate school in August 2000 but escalated in late fall 2001 when an Eaton physical education teacher invited him to talk with his high school students about American Indians and sports.[70] He was appalled by their ignorance and dumbfounded by the saturation of the high school campus by the "Fighting Reds" image. After the school principal and superintendent both refused to address his concerns early in 2002, like so many others across the country, they issued a statement that used *Sports Illustrated's* "The Indian Wars" to dismiss their critics' concerns.[71]

Ninham prepared a counteroffensive. First, he conducted a telephone interview with 64 Eaton households in preparation for speaking before members of the Eaton school board in February. He discovered widespread support among Eaton parents and teachers for retiring the "Fighting Reds" mascot.[72] In February 2002, he testified before members of the Eaton school board. According to Perry Swanson, writing for the *Greeley Tribune,* he provoked board members with the assertion that their mascot "is an offensive, negative, borderline racist stereotype." Francie Murry, who also spoke before the school board, reportedly told board members that CAESCS had arranged for an advertising company to design a new mascot and athletic logo. She explained that student groups at the University of Northern Colorado would hold fund-raising events to help bear the financial burden of retiring the "Fighting Reds" mascot. She expressed hope that Eaton might "be the pilot program to show other school districts what it is to change."[73]

The effort to engage Eaton adults—school administrators and teachers, school board members, and parents—according to Ninham, failed miserably.[74] Members of the school board, in his words, "closed the doors" on them and said essentially, "Don't call us; we'll call you."[75] In a March 2002 interview with Harlan Mckosato, the long-time host of the nationally syndicated weekly radio talk show "Native America Calling," Ninham framed the "Fighting Whites" as part of a "state-wide issue," a larger "campaign to address the stereotypical imagery that is being portrayed locally and specifically as the Eaton 'Fighting Reds'."[76]

In the words of the creator of the Fighting Whites and CAESCS member, Scott VanLoo, after the February school board meeting they were "shut out of real discussion" with the adults in Eaton.[77] It was in this combative context of who, or what, can represent and speak for Indigenous Peoples—mascots or actual Natives and their allies—that the "Fighting Whites" responded.[78] VanLoo took a satirical approach, transforming Eaton's

Fighting Reds into the Fighting Whites.[79] The Fighting Whites logo deploys satire in its citations to the sets of *Ozzie and Harriett* or *Father Knows Best*, to rerun episodes broadcast by Viacom on Nick at Nite that not only represent the "American family" as patriarchal, middle-class, and white but, set in a time before civil rights movements, also represent a romantic period during the 1950s when in widely circulating common sense *all* of "America," purportedly, was racially white. Through an image of a male figure with slicked-back hair, wearing a dark suit, narrow tie and big smile, with the team slogan "Every thang's going to be all white," the logo for the "Fighting Whites" projects the problem of speaking for and otherwise representing Native peoples as mascots.[80]

To the extent that interventions in the pathology of anti-Indigenous racism in athletics is ridiculed and lampooned through mass media communications or in face-to-face encounters between persons whose views are informed by competing literacies regarding racism, such symbolic matter circumscribes the range of views that enter into broad conversation. Thus, strategically embracing qualities that stereotype and racialize white men, embodied in this example as the "Fighting Whites," mascots in theory might disturb the power of the "Indian" sign in athletics by focusing on the force of symbols to elide the range of human qualities loyal subscribers claim they represent. During a classroom presentation at Colorado State University in nearby Fort Collins on March 26, VanLoo represented the issue in this way: "The Eaton basketball team, the Eaton community, is predominantly Anglo with a Native American mascot. Our team is predominantly Native American with an Anglo mascot. . . . We're shootin' hoops, and we're raising the issue."[81]

After receiving local newspaper coverage on March 6 and 10, the "Fighting Whites" promotion exploded through national and international media.[82] During the next two weeks, the Fighting Whites were an international phenomenon, with coverage by the *National Post* (in Canada) and *Edmonton Journal*, London-based *Guardian*, *New York Times*, *Boston Globe*, *Washington Times*, *Houston Chronicle*, *Los Angeles Times*, *San Francisco Chronicle*, *Billings* (Montana) *Gazette*, *Argus* (Sioux Falls, South Dakota) *Leader*, *Topeka* (Kansas) *Capital-Journal*, *Arizona Republic*, *Berryville* (Arkansas) *Star Progress*, CNN, MSNBC, the *Today Show* on NBC, and National Public Radio's "All Things Considered." Jay Leno joked about the team during his monologue on the *Tonight Show*. Team members appeared on Fox's *Best Damn Sports Show Period*.

Even Rush Limbaugh circulated the story on his syndicated daily radio show that reaches millions, transforming it into an instrument for spreading the disease of anti-Indigenous racism.[83] After reading about the "Fighting Whites" in Clarence Page's column "Fightin' Whities Mascot

Raises a Little Awareness, A Little Cash," Limbaugh told his listeners, "This is fabulous."[84] Designating the creators of the "Fighting Whites" as "innovative American injun students," the radio talk show personality suggested these students and their "liberal teachers" at the University of Northern Colorado were out of touch with "the rest of us." Acting as translator for his listeners, Limbaugh suggested, "They thought that they would give non-Injuns a dose of their own bad medicine." Citing *Sports Illustrated's* "The Indian Wars," he predicted white persons, like the masses of Natives, would not be offended, would not become "the Offended," would not "take the bait." Like others who approvingly responded to "The Indian Wars" and who, like the Eaton school administrators, used it as unimpeachable authority to dismiss the activists' concerns, Limbaugh cited the March 4 issue of *Sports Illustrated* not only to speak for Natives but also to degrade, in his words, "activists" whom he proposed "derive their living from making a beef about [names like redskins and fighting reds, and then] claim to represent their rank-and-file and they don't." Further, he used his celebrity and even appropriated the "Fighting Whites," taking it on as a self-identity, possessing it, to strike out at what he characterized as "the ongoing effort to teach certain members of our youths that the Founding Fathers were racist, slave-owning pigs."[85]

Limbaugh voiced a common counteraffirmation to the original pose, and criticism, offered in the form of the "Fighting Whites." Wrapping himself in qualities he and the editors of both the *Greeley Tribune* and UNC campus newspaper renamed "the Fightin' Whities," Limbaugh translated the meaning of the basketball mascot for those persons who, in his words, "didn't get it." He and his followers became fightin' whiteys, outspoken critics of efforts to counter racial oppression.

Claims of not understanding what was at stake in real claims of racial injury was one widely shared response to reading or hearing news of the "Fighting Whites." "Help me out here," asked one person who e-mailed the *Greeley Tribune,* "why am I supposed to be offended?"[86] "It amazes me that ethnic groups worry about that, but when they call me whitey, it doesn't offend me," another self-identified white man told a journalist for the *Greeley Tribune.* "So I have a hard time understanding where they are coming from."[87] Limbaugh and like-minded translators of racism in mass media communications reinforced these notions, these artless assertions of innocence. As uncaring witnesses to ethnic stereotyping and the pathology of anti-Indigenous racism, subscribers to Limbaugh's translation distance themselves from any ethical responsibility for understanding complex cultural issues and power differences in a multicultural, diverse society marked by the lingering residue and ongoing trauma of racism.

Said plainly, supporters of Indian mascots declare American "universal" and Indian "minor." Establishing the terms for the Indian "minor" to speak, the American universal attaches qualities to "American" and "Indian" that are difficult to disturb. Declarations of innocence, or ignorance, create conditions wherein mascot opponents must assume absolute responsibility in the matter of cultural translation—in assisting with cross-cultural understanding. Advocates for Indigenous Peoples—the Indian minor—thus are placed in positions of explaining—and reinforcing—their difference from and to the American universal.[88] Not only does this construct of universal and minor largely reinforce white racial hegemony, it also is profoundly undemocratic. It both distinguishes and solidifies the pathology of anti-Indigenous racism.

As the examples of the *Sports Illustrated* publication "The Indian Wars," and the "Fighting Whites" mascot suggest, *lived* hegemony is dynamic and powerful, constructed, defended, negotiated, *and* vulnerable to resistance and reinterpretation. Hegemony "is a realized complex of experiences," according to Raymond Williams. "In practice, that is, hegemony can never be singular. Its internal structures are highly complex, as can readily be seen in any concrete analysis. Moreover (and this is crucial, reminding us of the necessary thrust of the concept), it does not just passively exist as a form of dominance. It has continually to be renewed, recreated, defended, and modified. It is also continually resisted, limited, altered, challenged by pressures not at all its own."[89] Afflicted with the pathology of anti-Indigenous racism, the hegemony of "Indian" mascots are rewoven into narratives of racial superiority and raced differences of thought and outlook that create the conditions required for athletic mascots to represent Indigenous Peoples.

Unfortunately, not all interpretations, understandings, and counternarratives that challenge the hegemony of "Indian" mascots have equal access to mass media communications. Thus, as the examples of the struggle involving the NFL team in the nation's capital and the intramural team in Greeley, Colorado, suggest, resistance and challenges to anti-Indigenous racism often are turned aside as their meanings circulate outward through mass media away from their Indigenous critics speaking in federal courts and before local school boards. Even though it received substantial media attention, the spontaneous gathering of "Fighting Whites" is not the same as the corporate-planned or corporate-controlled spontaneity of a professional team around which fans organize in communities of belonging and that are saturated in the rights discourse of capitalism. The message from Greeley was rewritten as it circulated outward through mass media. Television and radio personalities such as Limbaugh intentionally blurred (or themselves failed to see) the bounds between these two forms of spontaneity to legitimate "Indian" mascots, to speak for the masses of Natives, and to re-negotiate how the decisions of courts, governing bodies, and "Fighting Whites" are received. Donning a renegade reinterpretation of the Fighting Whites logo, Limbaugh exploited it to literally assert himself as a fightin' whitey, fighting mad.

Limbaugh's assertions were in character with his well-known public persona. Other affirmations of anti-Indigenous racism are more subtle. Sports Illustrated's "The Indian Wars" nourished, incorrectly, the notion that the problem is one between Indians and whites, rather than between advocates for equitable justice and champions of divisiveness and oppression. What each of the examples examined here suggest—the decades-long effort to retire the NFL mascot in the country's capital city and the battle in Eaton, Colorado—is that resistance to and support for anti-Indigenous racism cannot be reduced to a racial binary: Indians versus whites. Instead, attempts to address racist representations are multiracial and aimed at social justice; they are the results of grassroots, democratic politics. They forecast possibilities for antiracist communities of belonging—for fresh ways of thinking about representation in a democratic society.

Mascots, team names, consumer products, and fan antics that link competitive athletics to selective qualities associated with "Indians" all are forms of antidemocratic, racist representation. Each form or signifier claims to stand in for and represent concepts linked to actual Indigenous Peoples (the signified) in limiting ways. Each weaves and reweaves Indigenous Peoples into already-existing universalist narratives that depict "Indians" in narrow masculine terms—as intrinsically violent, as endlessly fierce. Comprehended as expressions of gendered and raced hegemony, as representational matter, as speech and performance, *and* as perfomativity, "Indian" mascots speak for and do "Indian" in ways that pose sobering problems for cultural pluralism in an allegedly democratic society.[90] Each establishes circumscribing terms for where and how living American Indians can act and speak as United States citizens. Framed within binaries—good versus bad, as Price's "The Indian Wars" suggests—"Indian" mascots simultaneously trouble even liberal articulations of democratic representation when athletic entertainment and sport culture claims to speak, or perform, *as* someone, *for* someone, or *from* a limiting subject position.

Beyond the sobering problem of redistributing power among citizens who Vine Deloria, Jr. has characterized as "submarginal," is the haunting presence of actual and independent Indigenous Peoples.[91] Linguistically replaced as human beings by signs in athletic entertainment and in the commerce of racism that circulates through mass media, Native peoples often are paternalistically depicted as mascots, rather than in complicated ways that render us visible with all of our various faces, that represent all of our Indigenous diversity. "Indian" mascots labor to constrain the ability of Natives to represent ourselves, both symbolically and as sovereign nations; they have the oppressive outcome of subordinating independent nations to the rule of empire. The sobering, unromantic effect is anti-Indigenous racism.

Notes

1. Teters, quoted by Brenda Norrell, in "Gallup Film Festival Examines Racism of Sports Mascots," *Indian Country Today,* October 26, 1995, A1. Teters, an artist, teacher, writer, activist, and mother, is a citizen of the Spokane Nation and is perhaps most widely known for her leadership in the campaign to retire Chief Illiniwek, the notorious cheerleader for the University of Illinois at Urbana-Champaign. She was recognized on October 10, 1997, by *ABC World News Tonight* with Peter Jennings as "Person of the Week."

2. Deloria, "Forward," in *Team Spirits: The Native American Mascots Controversy,* eds. C. Richard King and Charles Fruehling Springwood (Lincoln: University of Nebraska Press, 2001), ix.

3. Among Indigenous Peoples we name ourselves, in our own languages, by terms that sometimes translate into English as "The People" or as "The Human Beings," that sometimes translate into English as entities associated with and connected to specific places, or in languages that resist easy translation into English. When using the two words "Indigenous Peoples," I am thinking of human beings who are related to thousands of distinct families, groups, kinship communities, clans, tribes, bands, councils, reservations, colonies, towns, villages, rancherías, pueblos, confederacies, and nations. This diversity troubles generalizations about how Indigenous Peoples "feel" or think about any issue, including the matter of mascots. For more on names and naming, see Michael Yellow Bird, "What We Want to Be Called: Indigenous Peoples' Perspectives on Racial and Ethnic Identity Labels," *American Indian Quarterly* 23 (Spring 1999): 1–21; and Cornel Pewewardy, "Renaming Ourselves and On Our Own Terms: Race, Tribal Nations, and Representation in Education," *Indigenous Nations Studies Journal* 1 (Spring 2000): 11–28.

4. The Cataloging Policy and Support Office of the Library of Congress added "Indians as mascots" to its long list of subheadings in May 2000.

5. Linking this pathology of anti-Indigenous racism to the social, political, and cultural abnormality of anti-Semitism, Crow Creek Dakota scholar and author Elizabeth Cook-Lynn designates it anti-Indianism. See Cook-Lynn, *Anti-Indianism in North America: A Voice from Tatekeya's Earth* (Urbana: University of Illinois Press, 2001), especially x. See also Jack D. Forbes, *Columbus and Other Cannibals: The Wétiko Disease of Exploitation, Imperialism, and Terrorism* (Brooklyn, NY: Autonomedia, 1992). I use the term anti-Indigenous racism for three reasons. First, like the designation "Indian" in cultures of politics and entertainment in the United States, the term anti-Indianism can be imprecise; Nepali nationalism, for instance, has been termed anti-Indianism. While the dynamics of both may be similar, I am not

concerned with nationalism as a necessarily counterproductive force. Second, the term "Indigenous" links antiracism struggles for social justice among Natives in the United States and North America to even broader global efforts among Indigenous Peoples. For discussions of racism as a process, see Susan Thomas, "Race, Gender, and Welfare Reform: The Antinatalist Response," *Journal of Black Studies* 28 (March 1998): 441; and Cheryl Townsend Gilkes, "From Slavery to Social Welfare: Racism and the Control of Black Women," in *Class, Race, and Sex: The Dynamics of Control,* ed. Amy Swerdlow and Hanna Lessinger (Boston: G.K. Hall and Co., 1983), 289.

6. See Stuart Hall, ed., *Representation: Cultural Representations and Signifying Practices* (Thousand Oaks, CA: Sage Publications Inc., 1997); Hall, "Subjects in History: Making Diasporic Identities," in *The House That Race Built: Black Americans, U.S. Terrain,* ed. Wahneema Lubiano (New York: Pantheon Books, 1997), 289–299; and Hall, "Encoding/Decoding," in *Culture, Media, Language: Working Papers in Cultural Studies, 1972–79,* eds. Stuart Hall, et al. (London: Centre for Contemporary Cultural Studies, University of Birmingham, 1980), 128–138.

7. Antonio Gramsci's theory of hegemony not only is helpful in making sense of the antagonism, but also in pinpointing, and understanding, the operations of noncoercive power. Unlike earlier Marxist theories of repression, Gramsci deemphasized overt state-sponsored force and instead stressed the role of public intellectuals, popular culture, and consumption in negotiating broad and spontaneous consent to rule. Writing in prison after 1928, Gramsci suggested that express attention must be devoted to the "everyday" and "common sense" when laboring to locate the instruments of domination. Antonio Gramsci, *Selections From the Prison Notebook,* edited and translated by Quintin Hoare and Geoffrey Nowell Smith (New York: International Publishers, 1971), 12, 57, 178, 195, 334, 352. Domination and the homogenizing of Indigenous voices are processes located in the state—in federal Indian law, for instance—but, as Gramsci suggests, power also is located in the business and popular culture of athletic entertainment.

8. For a more thorough discussion of identity among Natives in the United States, see Eva Marie Garroutte, *Real Indians: Identity and Survival of Native America* (Berkeley: University of California Press, 2003); and Devon A. Mihesuah, "American Indian Identities: Issues of Individual Choice and Development," in *Contemporary Native American Cultural Issues,* ed. Duane Champagne (Walnut Creek, CA: AltaMira Press, 1999), 13–38.

9. For more on Dashner, see Tara Browner, *Heartbeat of the People: Music and Dance of the Northern Pow-wow* (Urbana: University of Illinois Press, 2002), 38–45; and Mike Dashner, in *Sound of the Drum: A Resource Guide,* ed. Sam Cronk (Brantford, Ont.: Woodland Cultural Centre, 1991).

10. Michael Dashner to the author, September 8, 2003. Correspondence in the possession of the author.

11. For a discussion of the genealogy of naming people Chippewa and Ojibwe, see Gerald Vizenor, *The People Named the Chippewa: Narrative Histories* (Minneapolis: University of Minnesota Press, 1984), 13–36. As this example offered

by Dashner suggests, "Indian" (or, in this case, "Chippewa") mascots represent signifieds such as certain desired qualities widely associated with normative forms of masculinity, sports, community, racial identity, and American Indians.

12. Since the incident involving Dashner's daughter, a movement has emerged at Central Michigan University to retire the "Chippewa" mascot. See Jim Kent, "CMU ... Students Call for End to 60-year 'Tradition'," *News from Indian Country*, December 1, 2003, 11.

13. Dashner to the author.

14. The French semiologist Roland Barthes devoted his career to understanding the various meanings of objects, gestures, and practices—the signs—that surround Dashner, his daughter, and all of us in our everyday lives. It was Barthes in the 1950s who first applied semiotics, the study of signs, to popular culture—films, advertising, newspapers and magazines, photographs, cars, children's toys, and the like. For academics, this broke new ground at the time. Today, its application opens the debate over "Indian" mascots in new ways. Barthes showed that it was possible to challenge the "innocence" and "naturalness" of objects, gestures, and practices that produced supplementary meanings, or "connotations" to use Barthes' preferred term. Roland Barthes, *Mythologies,* trans. Annette Lavers (New York: Hill and Wang, 1972).

15. Southeastern Oklahoma State University and the Choctaw Nation government offices are located in Durant (pronounced Doo-rant), Bryan County, Oklahoma. During the 2000–2001 academic year, student and faculty members of the Southwestern Native American Council (NAC) campaigned to retire the "Savage" name and the "Spirit Pony" mascot, a person dressed in a blue and gold outfit with feathers and "war" paint. In response, April Brannan, the Spirit Pony mascot during 2000–2001, told the campus newspaper that, in her words, "[i]f I were Native American, I would be proud of the heritage here. . . . Savage is a tribute." Brannan, quoted by Charles Coley, in "Spirit Pony Speaks on Mascot Issue," *The Southeastern,* September 20, 2000. SOSU teams have been called "Savages" since 1921.

16. The body of scholarship devoted to critical assessments of so-called Indian mascots is growing. For sweeping treatments that draw from cultural theory, see C. Richard King and Charles Fruehling Springwood, *Beyond the Cheers: Race as Spectacle in College Sport* (Albany: State University of New York Press, 2001); and King and Springwood, eds., *Team Spirits.* See also the *Journal of Sport and Social Issues* 28 (January 2004), a special issue edited by King. Until the twenty-first century, as the voices of Native scholars increasingly have emerged in graduate programs, among university faculty, and in refereed journals and other publications, the scholarship on mascots among Natives concerned with decolonization, empowerment, and the well-being of Indian nations circulated through conversations at powwows and other face-to-face meeting grounds; in *Akwesasne Notes* (published in the Kahniakehaka Nation near Rooseveltown, New York) and *ABC: Americans Before Columbus,* the monthly newsletter of the National Indian Youth Council; and, *more recently, in newspapers such as The Circle (Minneapolis), Indian Country Today*

(Canastota, New York; formerly Rapid City, South Dakota), *Native* (formerly *Oklahoma*) *Indian Times* (Tulsa), and *News from Indian Country* (Hayward, Wisconsin), to mention only a few. Tim Giago and Cornel D. Pewewardy, to name just two of many contributors, have been writing on this subject for well over a decade. A thorough and discerning review of this scholarship has yet to be published.

17. Carlos Montezuma, "Indian Imposters," *Wassaja* 5 (January 1921): 3, 4; reprinted in *The Papers of Carlos Montezuma, M.D: Including the Papers of Maria Keller Montezuma Moore and the Papers of Joseph W. Latimer,* ed. John W. Larner (Wilmington, DE: Scholarly Resources, 1983), roll 5.

18. Dennis J. Banks, "Tribal Names and Mascots in Sports," *Journal of Sport and Social Issues* 17 (April 1993), 5–8.

19. Russell Means, with Marvin J. Ross, *Where White Men Fear to Tread: The Autobiography of Russell Means* (New York: St. Martin's Griffin, 1995), 223. The American Indian Press Association, incorporated in Denver in 1971, represented 125 Indian newspapers. See Charles E. Trimble, "The American Indian Press Association . . . a look back," *Indian Country Today,* March 28, 2003, accessed May 17, 2004, available from http://www.indiancountry.com/?1048867785.

20. Banks, "Tribal Names and Mascots in Sports," 5. Harold Gross, director of the Indian Legal Information Development Service and formerly a staff attorney for the National Council on Indian Opportunity, also met with Williams. In his testimony before the Trial Trademark and Appeal Board (TTAB) in 1998, Gross indicated that the NFL team owner agreed only to change certain of the lyrics of the team song, "Hail to the Redskins." See *Suzan Shown Harjo, et al., v. Pro-Football, Inc.,* U.S. Department of Commerce Patent and Trademark Office, Trademark Trial and Appeal Board, Cancellation No. 21,069, "Memorandum Opinion," April 2, 1999, 55–56, 59–60. The original lyrics written in 1938 by Corinne Griffith, a retired silent movie star and the second wife of then—and first—team owner, George Preston Marshall, included these two stanzas: "Scalp 'em, swamp 'em—we will take 'em big score./Read 'em, weep 'em—touchdown, we want heap more." See Corinne Griffith, *My Life with the Redskins* (New York: A.S. Barnes, 1947).

21. Harjo described this incident for Brooke Lee Foster, "She's No Redskin," *Washingtonian* 38, no. 6 (2003): 60; and also for Adriene T. Washington, "Indian Activist Tackles Football," *Washington Times,* April 26, 1999, C4.

22. Michael Freeman, "Indians Protesting Use of Redskins," *Washington Post,* January 21, 1992, D5; and William C. Rhoden, "A New View of History," *New York Times,* January 25, 1992, 31.

23. These numbers, which are notoriously low, were a media estimate. See Freeman, "Indians Protesting Use of Redskins." The seven activists and educators were Suzan Shown Harjo, Raymond D. Apodaca, Vine Deloria, Jr., Norbert S. Hill, Jr., Mateo Romero, William A. Means, and Manley A. Begay, Jr. In an interview with *The Circle,* a publication of the Minneapolis American Indian Center, Deloria explained that he and other petitioners represented a broad cross-section of American Indian culture and politics: "This is not just a disenfranchised few calling for something only a handful would agree with." De-

loria, quoted in *The Circle: News from an American Indian Perspective*, September 9, 1999, 13. Apodaca is a member of the Board of Directors for the Indian Law Resource Center and a former Governor of the Pueblo Ysleta del Sur/Tigua Tribe of Texas. Hill was Executive Director of the American Indian Science and Engineering Society for fifteen years in Boulder, Colorado, before becoming Executive Director of the American Indian Graduate Center in Albuquerque. Romero of Cochiti Pueblo is an artist whose work is collected in numerous museums; he has been a Ronald and Susan Dubin Fellow in painting at the School of American Research in Santa Fe. Means is Oglala Lakota and a cofounder of the International Indian Treaty Council. Begay was Executive Director of the National Executive Education Program for Native American Leadership at Harvard University; more recently he has been both Director of the Native Nations Institute at the Udall Center for Studies in Public Policy and Senior Lecturer in the American Indian Studies Program at the University of Arizona. Harjo narrates her view of the litigation in "Fighting Name-Calling: Challenging 'Redskins' in Court," in *Team Spirits*, eds. King and Springwood, 198–207; and Harjo, "Fighting the R-Word," *Colorlines* 3, no. 1 (April 2000): 18.

24. *Harjo, et al., v. Pro-Football, Inc.*, 125, 141, 142, 145.
25. Carol D. Leonnig, "Judge Nears Ruling in Redskins Name Fight," *Washington Post*, July 24, 2003, B7; and Jerry Reynolds, "Ruling Awaited on 'Redskins' Trademark," *Indian Country Today*, July 25, 2003, accessed August 27, 2003, available from http://www.indiancountry.com/article/1059139857.
26. *Pro-Football, Inc. v. Suzan Shown Harjo, et al.*, United States District Court for the District of Columbia, "Memorandum Opinion," September 30, 2003, 3.
27. Ibid., 42.
28. *Harjo, et al., v. Pro-Football, Inc.*, 92. Ross' methodology and criticism of it are described in ibid., 90–97; and *Pro-Football, Inc. v. Harjo, et al.*, 38–42.
29. Ibid., 17–20, 37–41. Jacob Jacoby is professor of retail management and consumer behavior and professor of marketing in the Leonard Stern School of Business at New York University. Geoffrey Nunberg is a senior researcher at the Center for the Study of Language and Information at Stanford University, and a consulting professor in the Stanford Department of Linguistics; he also is a regular contributor to the NPR show "Fresh Air." He writes commentaries on language for the *New York Times*.
30. *Pro-Football, Inc. v. Harjo, et al.*, 44.
31. Ibid., 49.
32. Sandi Sonnenfeld, "White & Case Wins Landmark Case Upholding Trademarks of Washington Redskins," press release, October 1, 2003, accessed May 13, 2004, available from http://www.whitecase.com/pr_redskins_10_01_2003.html.
33. Press release, October 1, 2003, accessed May 14, 2004, http://www.whitecase.com/pr_redskins_10_01_2003.html.
34. Jason McCarty, "NCAI Condemns 'Redskins' Trademark Decision," press release, *NCAI News*, n.d., quoted in Sam Lewin, "More Criticism of Mascot Ruling: NCAI Calls Decision a Defeat of Racial Healing," *Native American Times*, October 2, 2003. McCarty, representing NCAI president Tex Hall, was

responding to Kollar-Kotelly's assertions that "an economic cost exists when a trademark is cancelled that adversely affects prior investment in the brand" and "common sense dictates that Pro-Football will suffer some economic hardship." See *Pro-Football, Inc. v. Harjo, et al.*, 80, 81. For Harjo's response to the decision of the federal court, see Jim Kent, "Native Americans File Appeal in Washington Redskins Decision," *News from Indian Country*, November 17, 2003, 12.

35. Introduced on March 10, 1992, by Council member William P. Lightfoot who told journalists he was responding to growing concerns among American Indian people represented by the DC Native Peoples' Network; the earlier resolution stated that the team name was "objectionable," "an offense," and "racially insensitive in a multicultural society." See Alvin Peabody, "Council Passes Redskins Name Change Resolution," *Washington Informer*, March 11, 1992, 19.

36. Schwartz was a Republican Party candidate for Washington, D.C., mayor in 1986, 1998, and 2002. See "Carol Schwartz—Biographical Data," accessed August 27, 2003, available from http://www.dcwatch.com/archives/election98/schwartz–1.htm; and "Carol Schwartz, Republican Write-In Candidate for Mayor in the November 5, 2002, General Election," accessed August 27, 2003, available from http://www.dcwatch.com/archives/election2002/schwartz.htm.

37. By a vote of 12–1, the Council of the District of Columbia adopted Resolution #14–251, which stated that "[t]he name Redskins is offensive and hurtful to many Native Americans who are citizens of this nation." Members of the Metropolitan Washington Council of Governments voted 11–2 on January 9, 2002, to adopt a resolution characterizing the NFL team name in the nation's capitol as "demeaning and dehumanizing."

38. "'Redskins' Means Indians Don't Matter," *Indian Country Today*, January 18, 2002, accessed August 31, 2003, available from http://www.indiancountry.com/?1011371670.

39. Circulation of Scott Price's story on CNN during the closing moments of the Olympic games and publication of "The Indian Wars" a week later in March leaves the impression that CNN and *Sports Illustrated* assisted in a drive to discredit the actions taken by Schwartz in the two District of Columbia political bodies.

40. The subscription and website activity information are taken from Audit Bureau of Circulations, "Magazine Publisher's Statement [for *Sports Illustrated*]," June 30, 2002. Document in the possession of the author. S. L. Price, "The Indian Wars," *Sports Illustrated*, March 4, 2002, 68.

41. Michael Yellow Bird and Betty Ann Gross, two of the ten activists and educators Price quoted in "The Indian Wars," have suggested that Price reported their words out of context using only selective citations to their telephone interviews with *Sports Illustrated* functionaries. In an e-mail dated June 11, 2002, in the possession of the author, Gross wrote, "Don't let the Peter Harris research methods fool you. [T]here was nothing there, except the white people took what they wanted to hear." On the problem of the telephone poll con-

ducted by the Peter Harris Research Group, see Ellen J. Staurowsky, "A Tale of Two Surveys: An Examination of the Racial Politics Behind Public Opinion on the Question of American Indian Mascots," unpublished manuscript, 2004.

42. For an interdisciplinary reading of "The Indian Wars," see C. Richard King, Ellen J. Staurowsky, Lawrence Baca, Laurel R. Davis, and Cornel Pewewardy, "Of Polls and Race Prejudice: *Sport Illustrated's* Errant 'Indian Wars'," *Journal of Sport and Social Issues* 26 (November 2002): 381–402.

43. Harris Research Group, *Final Results,* January 31, 2002, questions 5c and 6b, quoted in Gavin Clarkson, "Racial Imagery and Native Americans: A First Look at the Empirical Evidence Behind the Indian Mascot Controversy," *Cardozo Journal of International and Comparative Law* 11, no. 2 (2003): 399.

44. Norvell is the Northeast Bureau Chief of Fox News Channel, responsible for directing the channel's coverage of New England from bureaus in Boston and New York. He also writes a column for FOXNews.com marketed as "a report from the front lines of the culture wars" entitled "Tongue Tied."

45. Miranda A. Brunner, letter to the editor, *Herald and Review,* April 10, 2002, A6.

46. Matt Kaufman, "Of Mascots and Malcontents," Boundless, May 23, 2002, accessed August 30, 2003, available from http://www.boundless.org/2001/regulars/kaufman/a0000594.html.

47. Roger Huddleston, "Honor the Chief Society Challenges NCAA Mascot Report," April 4, 2003, accessed August 31, 2003, available from http://www.honorthechief.org/news_NCAArelease.html. For a well-rounded treatment of the mascot controversy at the University of Illinois at Urbana-Champaign through 1999, see Carol Spindel, *Dancing at Halftime: Sports and the Controversy over American Indian Mascots* (New York: New York University Press, 2000).

48. John J. Miller, "By Any Other Name?" *National Review,* March 8, 2002, accessed August 31, 2003, available from http://www.nationalreview.com/miller/miller030802.asp.

49. Lloyd Omdahl, "UND Nickname Activists Can't Claim Majority Support," *Grand Forks Herald,* March 25, 2002, accessed May 14, 2004, available from http://www.grandforksherald/mld/grandforksherald/news/opinion/2933046.htm.

50. In March 1998 Pewewardy and other members of the Kansas Association for Native American Education passed Resolution 98–1 which called on "all Tribal Councils, tribal and educational organizations, the media, the individual citizens of the State of Kansas to call for the banishment of all current American Indian related mascots and logos used by public and private schools in the State of Kansas." Copy of resolution in the possession of the author.

51. Don Zahnley, letter to the editor, *Topeka Capitol-Journal,* June 17, 2002, accessed August 30, 2003, available from http://www.cjonline.com/stories/061802/opi_letters.shtml.

52. C. Richard King, "Defensive Dialogues: Native American Mascots, Anti-Indianism, and Educational Institutions," *Studies in Media and Information Literacy Education* 2 (February 2002), accessed May 14, 2004, available from http://www.utpjournals.com/jour.1html?ip=simile/issues/king1.html, examines

the practices used by schools, colleges, and universities to defend their "Indian" mascots.

53. Matthew Cella, "Many Schools Keep Indian Logos," *Washington Times,* March 4, 2002, accessed May 14, 2002, available from http://www.washtimes.com/metro/default_20023422330.htm.

54. Brian Ojanpa, "Poll Drops Bomb on Indian Nickname, Mascot Issue," *Mankato Free Press,* March 11, 2002, accessed August 31, 2003, available from http://www.mankatofreepress.com/archives/columns/bo020311.html.

55. "Editorial: Change in Nickname Strategy," *Grand Forks Herald,* March 7, 2002, accessed August 27, 2003, available from http://www.grandforks.com/mld/grandforksherald/news/opinion/2808472.htm. For the context of the struggle in Grand Forks, see Raúl Tovares, "Mascot Matters: Race, History, and the University of North Dakota's 'Fighting Sioux' Logo," *Journal of Communication Inquiry* 26 (January 2002): 76–94. Departing from sentiments expressed among other members of the *Herald*'s editorial board, Dorreen Yellow Bird suggested the market research poll might have its own problems. See Dorreen Yellow Bird, "Don't Take *Sports Illustrated* Poll at Face Value," *Grand Forks Herald,* March 9, 2002, accessed August 31, 2003, available from http://www.grandforks.com/mld/grandforksherald/news/opinion/2824341.htm. While the methodology used in the Ross survey has been examined by two courts and an expert commissioned by Pro-Football, Inc., the methodology used by the Harris group has not been made available for public scrutiny. For a thoughtful discussion regarding the telephone survey conducted by the Peter Harris Research Group, see King, et al., "Of Polls and Race Prejudice," 386–391; and Staurowsky, "A Tale of Two Surveys."

56. Citing *Sports Illustrated's* "The Indian Wars" continues among pro-mascot advocates. See, for instance, Craig Sondgeroth, "A Great Mascot," *Daily Illini,* September 9, 2004, accessed September 9, 2004, available from http://daily-illini.collegepublisher.com/news/2004/09/09/Opinions/A.Great.Mascot–713509.shtml, who cites the Peter Harris Research Group findings to confidently—and incorrectly—assert that "American Indians overwhelmingly support the Chief [Illiniwek]."

57. The endorsement of Indian nations and Indian advocacy groups in California defies this fallacious claim. See, for instance, James May, "Mascot Bill Fails for Second Time in California," *Indian Country Today,* June 23, 2003, accessed May 17, 2004, available from http://indiancountry.com/?1056374954; and Robert Gemmell, "California Anti-Mascot Bill Clears First Hurdle," *Indian Country Today,* April 8, 2002, accessed May 17, 2004, available from http://indiancountry.com/?1018184927. See also "AB 858 (Goldberg) Support List," accessed May 17, 2004, available from http://www.allarm.org/supportlist.html.

58. AB 858 Assembly Bill, February 20, 2003, accessed May 13, 2004, available from http://leginfo.ca.gov/pub/bill/asm/ab_0851–0900/ab_858_bill_20030220_introduced.html. Southern California Indian Center, Inc. is a non-profit 501 c(3) community-based organization serving the American Indian, Native Alaskan, and Native Hawaiian communities of Los Angeles, Orange, Kern and Riverside Counties.

59. Debra J. Saunders, "Home of the Brave—Oops, Scratch That," *San Francisco Chronicle,* May 12, 2002, D4.

60. Todd Fanady, letter to the editor, *Los Angeles Times,* June 1, 2002, accessed June 3, 2002, available from http://www.latimes.com/news/printedition/opinion/la–000038499jun01.story.

61. Joseph Perkins, "Let's Get Real in the Mascot Debate," *Joplin Globe,* May 23, 2002, accessed August 30, 2003, available from http://www.joplinglobe.com/archives/2002/020523/oped/story5.html.

62. According to Clea Benson, Goldberg "was able to convince her colleagues that the term Redskins was an unacceptable racial slur." Clea Benson, "School Mascot Limit Backed," *Sacramento Bee,* January 30, 2004. See also James May, "Mascot Vote Passes California Assembly," *Indian Country Today,* February 6, 2004, accessed May 17, 2004, available from http://indiancountry.com/?1076089050.

63. California State Senate, Documents Associated with AB 858 in the 2003–2004 Session, "History," in the possession of the author.

64. Arnold Schwarzenegger, to Members of the California General Assembly, n.d. Document in the possession of the author.

65. Anita Stackhouse-Hite, "Tulare Union Can Stay Redskins," *Visalia Times-Delta,* September 22, 2004, accessed September 23, 2004, available from http://www.visaliatimesdelta.com/news/stories/20040922/localnews/1280836.html.

66. Dan Ninham, correspondence with the author (telephone conversation), September 5, 2004.

67. Twenty-seven percent of persons living in Weld County in 2000, according to U.S. Census Bureau data, identified as persons of Hispanic or Latino origin.

68. "Statistics for Eaton High School," accessed September 6, 2003, available from http://www.schooltree.org/080360000476.html. According to this same data source, there are 4 elementary school students and no middle school students in Eaton who identify as Native American. In the elementary school students are referred to as "Little Braves." According to GreatSchools.net, the Eaton Elementary School student population of 344 students is 69 percent white. The middle school population of 480 young people is 78 percent white. See "Eaton Elementary School—Eaton, Colorado, accessed May 18, 2004, available from http://www.greatschools.net/modperl/browse_school/co/615/; and "Eaton Middle School—Eaton, Colorado," accessed May 18, 2004, available from http://www.greatschools.net/modperl/browse_school/co/616/.

69. For a discussion of this phenomenon of non-Natives strategically asserting "Indian" identity in mascot debates, see Charles Fruehling Springwood, "'I'm Indian Too!': Claiming Native American Identity, Crafting Authority in Mascot Debates," *Journal of Sport and Social Issues* 28 (February 2004): 56–70. See also Philip J. Deloria, *Playing Indian* (New Haven, CT.: Yale University Press, 1999); and Shari M. Huhndorf, *Going Native: Indians in the American Cultural Imagination* (Ithaca, NY: Cornell University Press, 2001).

70. Dan Ninham, correspondence with the author (e-mail), September 8, 2003. Correspondence in the possession of the author. According to Ninham, in his

words, "Scott VanLoo had the original slogan, image, and name and he rarely if ever gets credit for this." Ninham is a twenty-year educator and coach who has taught at the Oneida Tribal School and at Fort Wingate High School located east of Gallup, New Mexico. He was later head boy's basketball coach at Cass Lake-Bena High School in Cass Lake, Minnesota.

71. Ninham, correspondence with the author, September 5, 2004.

72. Ibid. Tom Trotter, a history and government teacher at Eaton High School and, according to Ninham, a CAESCS ally, reported that twelve of fifteen colleagues he asked agreed to sign a letter urging the school board to retire the mascot. See Perry Swanson, "Mascot Watch," *Greeley Tribune,* February 12, 2002; accessed September 5, 2004, available from http://gr.us.publicus.com/apps/pbcs.dll/article?AID=/20020212/NEWS/102120001.

73. Both Ninham and Murry are quoted in Swanson, "Mascot Watch."

74. In an interview with Lynn Klyde-Silverstein, others, including Scott VanLoo, agreed with Ninham, suggesting, in his words, "[Ninham and the others] finally got like five minutes of presentation time at the school board meeting. They went before an all-white male school board, did their presentation, and they kept getting

this kind of 'thanks but no thanks'." VanLoo, quoted in Klyde-Silverstein, "The Fighting Whites Phenomenon: Toward an Understanding of the Media's Coverage," unpublished manuscript, 2003.

75. Harlan Mckosato interview with Dan Ninham and Suzan Shown Harjo, "The Fighting Whities," March 19, 2002, Archives of Native America Calling, Corporation of Public Broadcasting and Koahnic Broadcast Corporation, accessed May 14, 2004, available from http://nativecalling.org/archives/2002/mar/03192002.ram; and Ninham, correspondence with the author, September 5, 2004.

76. Mckosato interview with Ninham and Harjo, "The Fighting Whities."

77. VanLoo, quoted in Rahaf Kalaaji, "Disrespectful Mascot Challenged: 'Fightin' Whites' Make the Case Before CSU Class," *Fort Collins Coloradoan,* March 27, 2002.

78. Before changing the team name to "Fighting Whites," it was designated "Native Pride"; team members were Indian, white, and Latino. According Ninham, although he did not agree with them, VanLoo and others speculated that they might use the attraction of sport culture and the influence of mass media communications to counter, rather than encourage, ethnic stereotyping. The "Fighting Whites" clearly was an effort to engage people in a conversation about racism and racial stereotyping. "It's interesting to sit around and think, what noise does a white person make?" Solomon Little Owl, director of Native American Student Services at the University of Northern Colorado, asked readers of the Denver-based *Rocky-Mountain News.* "When you say that about a white person, you realize how ridiculous the whole idea of having people as mascots is. This is our way of making that point." See Little Owl quoted in Joe Garner, "'Whities' Mascot About Education, Not Retaliation," *Rocky Mountain News,* March 12, 2002, accessed March 13, 2002, available from http://www.rockymountainnews.com/drmn/state/article/0,1299,DRMN_21_

1026337,00.html. Another Indian member of the team, Ray White, told a Denver television audience that, in his words, "It's not meant to be vicious, it is meant to be humorous. . . . It puts people in our shoes, and then we can say, 'Now you know how it is, and now you can make a judgment'."

79. The "Fighting Whites" was not the first effort that used satire in an attempt to break through the hegemony of athletic mascots, what Todd Bordeaux, who, with Robert Peaslee, in 2000 founded the fantasy Native American Football League, referred to as "in your faceism." See Julie Shortridge, "Native American Community Announces Formation of 'Native American Football League'," *Ojibwe News,* March 10, 2000, 1; and Duane Stinson, "Native American Football League Spoofs Team Mascots," *The Circle,* November 30, 2001, 9.

80. Examples of this point are numerous. Following a classroom lecture in 2003 during which I labored to suggest that some American Indians use—and even prefer—the ethnic label, Native American (see Yellow Bird, "What We Want to Be Called"), one racially self-identified young white man responded in writing with this rap: "I find this misappropriation of the term 'Native American' to be a direct assault on *my* Native American culture and institutions, including our beloved Constitution and the fact that America, in its short 212 year history, has created the most dynamic, innovative, prosperous and free society in the history of the world." This young father is not alone. Charlton Heston, for instance, asserted his right to the name "Native-American" in what has become a widely cited rant against what he termed "political correctness" delivered at the Harvard Law School Forum in February 1999. "For me," Heston confidently asserted, "I'm a Native American, for God's sake. I also happen to be a blood-initiated brother of the Miniconjou Sioux. On my wife's side, my grandson is a thirteenth generation native American . . . with a capital letter on "American." Heston, "Winning the Cultural War," speech delivered at Ames Courtroom, Austin Hall, Harvard University, February 16, 1999, accessed May 14, 2004, available from http://www.law.harvard.edu/students/orgs/forum/heston.html.

81. VanLoo quoted in Kalaaji, "Disrespectful Mascot Challenged."

82. The first article ran on Wednesday, March 6, on page 2 of UNC's student newspaper, *The Mirror.* Four days later, a story ran in the local paper, the *Greeley Tribune,* also on page 2.

83. For broader treatment of this matter, see Bruce E. Johansen, "Putting the Moccasin on the Other Foot: A Media History of the 'Fighting Whities'," *Studies in Media and Information Literacy Education* 3 (February 2003); and Klyde-Silverstein, "The Fighting Whites Phenomenon."

84. Clarence Page, "Fightin' Whities Mascot Raises a Little Awareness, A Little Cash," *Seattle Post-Intelligencer,* March 19, 2002, A19.

85. Rush Limbaugh, "Caucasians Slow to Take Offense," March 19, 2002, accessed August 31, 2003, available from http://www.rushlimbaugh.com/home/folder/031902.guest.html; Limbaugh, "Hasta La Vista, Speedy Gonzalez," March 27, 2002, accessed August 31, 2003, available from http://www.rushlimbaugh.com/home/ folder/03_27_02.guest.html. And, yes, Limbaugh

actually enunciated the word "Injun" carefully to stress his point that the substance of the complaint signified by the "Fighting Whites" was, in his words,
"politically correct claptrap."

86. Quoted in Page, "Fightin' Whities Mascot Raises a Little Awareness."

87. Julio Ochoa, "Reaction to Whities Mascot Varies," *Greeley Tribune,* March 17,
    2002, accessed August 31, 2003, available from http://www.greeleytrib.com/
    apps/pbcs.dll/article?AID=/20020317/NEWS/103170033.

88. For a broader discussion of the problem posed by discursive constructions of
    "universal" and "minor," see David Palumbo-Liu, "Universalisms and Minor-
    ity Culture," *differences* 7, no. 1 (1995): 188, who argues that universalism
    "erases contingencies of time and space, history and location, and with the
    same gesture elides its operations of domination, projecting instead the ap-
    pearance of being democratic."

89. Raymond Williams, *Marxism and Literature* (New York: Oxford University
    Press, 1977), 112.

90. A good deal of critical theory in recent years has centered around performa-
    tivity, most notably and widely read discussions as Jacque Derrida, "Signature
    Event Context," in *Margins of Philosophy,* trans. Alan Bass (Chicago: Univer-
    sity of Chicago Press, 1982); Judith Butler, *Gender Trouble: Feminism and the
    Subversion of Identity* (New York: Routledge, 1990); and Butler, *Bodies That
    Matter: On the Discursive Limits of "Sex"* (New York: Routledge, 1993). In
    brief, performativity, a consequence of complex and multidimensional cita-
    tional processes, is the suggestion that doing something is also saying some-
    thing, and vice versa. Mascot and fan antics, as well as team logos, cite and
    stand in for something that came before. They do Indian. And they do Indian
    in the present. For a recent effort to read the performative of race in sports, see
    the essays in John Bloom and Michael Nevin Willard, eds., *Sports Matters:
    Race, Recreation, and Culture* (New York: New York University Press, 2002),
    especially John Bloom and Randy Hanson, "Warriors and Thieves: Appropri-
    ations of the Warrior Motif in Representations of Native American Athletes,"
    246–263. For a discussion of when and how doing something is saying some-
    thing, see Andrew Parker and Eve Kosofsky Sedgwick, eds., *Performativity and
    Performance* (New York: Routledge, 1995).

91. Vine Deloria, Jr., "Marginal and Submarginal," in *Indigenizing the Academy:
    Transforming Scholarship and Empowering Communities,* eds. Devon Abbott
    Mihesuah and Angela Cavender Wilson (Lincoln: University of Nebraska
    Press, 2004), 16–30.

PART III: AESTHETICS

SIX

Backfield in Motion

The Transformation of the NFL by Black Culture

Joel Dinerstein

Nearly every aspect of our national pastimes has been transformed by African American participation and protest, style and aesthetics, physical gesture and emotional expression—a social fact suggesting that African Americans create permanent changes in American sports once they attain a certain critical mass. African Americans constitute more than 80 percent of NBA players and 65 percent in the NFL. That basketball is deeply embedded in black culture is common knowledge: the sport's transformative elements over the last forty years—the jump shot, slam-dunk, fast break offense, and defiant self-expression—make pre-1965 b-ball, with its running hook-shots and two-handed set-shots, look like a diagrammed pickup game. But football was equally transformed by black culture in the 1970s in aesthetic, athletic, expressive, and performative ways, yet this is an untold story that remains a sideline to the AFL-NFL merger and the rise of Monday Night Football. In fact, the sport seems embarrassed by the changes: How else to assess the "illegal celebration" penalty of the 1980s except as the illegal use of black culture? As historian Alan H. Levy notes in *Tackling Jim Crow*, "Many head coaches of the 1970s (and all were white) sought to clamp down on it [black culture]," since they were "unduly threatened by matters of identifiably and self-consciously black behavior that lay outside their ken and control."[1]

In the 1970s, football provided the nation with some of its most mainstream and celebrated exemplars of aesthetic excellence. This seems a forgotten fact, buried in consciousness by a nation that wants to forget the social failure embodied by O. J. Simpson, the premier symbolic hero of sports integration and one of the great running backs in NFL history. In 1970, less than a year after Simpson turned pro, author Ralph Ellison affirmed the elements of an African American cultural aesthetic alive in *all* American culture—in sports, music, dance, humor—in his famous *Time* magazine essay, "What America Would Be Like Without Blacks." "Without the presence of Negro American style," Ellison wrote, "[American] sports would be lacking in the sudden turns, the shocks, the swift changes of pace (all jazz-shaped) that serve to remind us that . . . the real secret of the game is to make life swing."[2] Bursts of rapid flows—of words, music, feet—over syncopated beats characterize not only jazz and hip-hop oratory, but break dancing, tap, the Charleston, stride piano, the crossover dribble, stepping. Sudden turns, swift changes of pace, the jazz practice of improvisation within set patterns, opening up pathways for self-expression to make any game "swing"—all these aesthetic elements were present in the *open-field running style* of African American running backs and wide receivers as they began to dominate college and pro football offenses after the civil rights movement helped end gridiron segregation.

In the early 1960s, the NFL was approximately thirteen percent African American, but many major universities in the South—including Texas, Alabama, Arkansas, Kentucky, and most of the Southeastern Conference (SEC)—refused to play any team with African American players until the late 1960s. It took a warning from the Justice Department in 1967 to force the SEC's last holdouts to "dismantle their racial ramparts or to face the withdrawal of federal funds."[3] The year before in college basketball (1966) the all-black team of University of Texas-El Paso (then Texas Western) shocked the all-white University of Kentucky to win the NCAA Championship. College football has an analogous contrast: O. J. Simpson won the Heisman Trophy in 1968 by the largest margin of victory in the trophy's voting, while the last all-white squad to be voted number one in the college rankings was the University of Texas Longhorns in 1969.

Consider the startling shift in Heisman winners that began a few years later. Between 1973 and 1983, every Heisman winner was a running back—and all but one African American—in a distinguished list of future hall-of-famers that included Tony Dorsett (1976), Earl Campbell (1977), and Marcus Allen (1981). The previous ten years (1963–73), seven of the ten winners were quarterbacks, all of them white; the other three were black running backs.[4] This juxtaposition of white quarterback and black running back becomes even more significant given that most coaches believed blacks lacked both the intelligence and the leadership ability to lead offenses.

As the third black running back to win the Heisman in the 1960s, O. J. Simpson was the first to frame it in terms of racial and cultural empowerment as a kid from the projects of San Francisco. "I knew I needed to be recognized," the former gang leader said in 1969. "People who grew up in my environment need recognition." The two black previous winners— Ernie Davis (1961) and Mike Garrett (1965)—relied upon assimilationist rhetoric and subsumed all politics to tropes of teamwork. "I'm not interested in the racial game," Davis announced, "all I want to be is a success. I don't feel the Redskins would be making a case of me like Jackie Robinson."[5] Yet by the end of the decade, the new African American running back style emerged concurrently with racial pride, the black power rhetoric of Malcolm X and the Black Panthers, the cultural rebellion of the Black Arts Movement, and the proud embrace of black culture at the level of music, dance, fashion, and language. As James Brown chanted in the tagline of his number one hit on the black charts in 1969, "Say It Loud, I'm Black and I'm Proud."

The crucial transition figure was Jim Brown of the Cleveland Browns, perhaps the dominant NFL player between 1957 and 1965. Sportscaster Bob Costas sums up Brown's legacy: "5.2 yards per carry [career average], never missed a game, won the rushing title every year but one when he was in the league . . . you have to pick Jim [Brown] as the greatest running back in history." A punishing power-runner with great speed and balance, Brown carried a tough, defiant attitude on and off the field that confounded all white expectations of a black athlete. Brown's open-field running was characterized as a "rhythmic gallop," and he claimed to enjoy *hitting* would-be tacklers, not evading them—the opposite of O. J.'s fluid hipshake-and-spin. His expressive style was thus heavy, driving, powerful, and aggressive. In fact, his two signature "moves" (gestures, really) were unrelated to running. After a hard hit, he would stand up with a cool, exaggerated slowness—as if to make sure everyone was aware of his importance to the team and his indestructibility—then simply hand the ball to the referee nonchalantly. He would then saunter back to the huddle (he was always the last man back) and duck his head in for just a second, suggesting that no play could start without him. With these gestures, Brown called attention to his value to the team; it was as if he believed social equality, dignity, and toughness needed to be performed publicly before issues of aesthetic artistry could be addressed. Consider perhaps that the Georgia-raised Brown embodied the discipline of the civil rights movement with a more assertive, defiant tone, and that it was a necessary prelude to the more expressive, individual style of the Black Arts Movement embodied by the

Californian, O. J. Simpson. Michael MacCambridge writes in *America's Game* that it was through athletes like Brown that management and fans "learn[ed] to accept the modern black athlete on his own terms."[6]

So what do I mean by a running back's "style" or "aesthetic"? In *Elevating the Game* (1992), cultural critic Nelson George declared the advent of a "black athletic aesthetic" in basketball that has transformed the sport since the late 1960s. That aesthetic includes improvisation, a player's signature style, and "intimidation through improvisation." An example of the latter element—a combination of skills, style, surprise, and intensity—would be the slam-dunk, an act in which a player "personalize[s] the act of scoring." African Americans invented the slam-dunk, and the act itself is embedded in a black athletic aesthetic: (1) a dunk is rarely planned through a set play (it's an improvisation); (2) most athletes have a signature dunk (self-expression); (3) the slam-dunk is often used to punctuate a strong move to the hoop, throwing the ball down in a celebratory yell (intimidation). George singled out Magic Johnson—who has never been considered an in-your-face player—for consistently combining "flamboyance with intensity" to such a degree that he "intimidate[d] through his improvising."[7]

In "The Case for an African American Aesthetic," American Studies scholar Gena Caponi-Tabery theorized a performative set of elements valued across music, dance, and sports: individual improvisation and stylization; rhythmic complexity; call-and-response; engagement of the community; and social commentary through irony or satire. Likewise, George claims that a "distinctive African American ethos" informs the fields of music, comedy, and sports, and that it is understood by athletes, artists, performers, and the African American community of fans. Echoing Ellison's claims of a generation earlier, George points out that "rapping, sermonizing, and soloing . . . all manifest a particular—and shared— African American aesthetic." Nearly all African American scholars find aspects of this aesthetic transferable at a conceptual level from music and dance to sports. George locates a "musical analogy" between the black athlete and "the African American musician's affinity for the saxophone" at the individual level, and, at the group level, he suggests that "certain African Americans execute their court magic with a funky attitude akin to that of the race's greatest musicians." Todd Boyd has expanded upon this notion by calling basketball "a contemporary version of jazz" in his short essay, "From Bebop to B-Ball.[8]

Renowned playwright August Wilson claims simply that black Americans "do not share the same sensibilities" as Euro-Americans. "The specifics of our cultural history are very much different. . . . We have a different way of responding to the world. We have different ideas about religion, different manners of social intercourse. We have different ideas about style, about language. We have different aesthetics."[9] In *Swinging the Machine* (2003), my study of African American swing culture between the world wars, I identified a modernist African American aesthetic in music and dance that emphasized a dynamic of *controlled power* within the individual. In other words, during the black migration, individual musicians and dancers communicated the need for, and created aesthetic expressions for, an *energized modern body* that stylized the mechanical rhythms of industrialization into new music and dance forms. Such cultural innovations were picked up by youth cultures around the globe: swing music and dance pervaded urban dancehalls from New York and Chicago to Paris and Prague, and notably functioned as forms of rebellion inside Nazi Germany (as dramatized in the 1993 film *Swing Kids.*[10]

In contrast to the scholarship that focuses on the construction of a "performed blackness" derived from the theatrical tradition of blackface minstrelsy and first theorized in Eric Lott's *Love and Theft,* scholars of African American culture such as Nelson George, Robin D. G. Kelley, Gena Caponi-Tabery, Shane White, and Graham White refer to African American *cultural practices.* Minstrel-derived frameworks assume cultural formations based primarily in constructions of "the Other" by the dominant society; such models presume a white audience with an agenda of difference when looking at black bodies that can only result in objectification, commodification, or exoticization. But such models run aground when faced with African American culture created by and for African Americans, and fail to address this crucial question: What happens when whites aspire to African American expressive style without condescension or mockery?

When Euro-Americans admire, imitate, or strive to learn from African American performance—from its aesthetics, style, and kinesthetics (physical gesture)—Michael Eric Dyson calls this process the "pedagogy of desire." A theologian and race scholar, Dyson coined the phrase to theorize Michael Jordan's global impact as a "public pedagogue," an aesthetic exemplar who communicates "[the] elements of African American culture" in performance, and who, in competition, embodies an athletic tradition that "symbolically ritualize[s] . . . the ongoing quest for mastery of environment and [the] vanquishing of opponents within the limits of physical contest."[11] I would argue that, for better or worse, the most admired and imitated *human body-in-motion* in global popular culture is the African American male body (in sports, music, and dance)—yet few cultural critics find such a social fact worthy of analysis. Certainly there are elements of essentialism and primitivism in this admiration, as well as a projection of difference onto the Other, but in imitating African American moves—whether on the dance floor or the playing field—Euro-Americans express their need and desire to master modern environments through dynamic engagement as modeled by black Americans.

Football's New Individualists

With regard to professional football, the African American aesthetic returned elements of style and individual affirmation to a game predicated on set formations and teamwork. Historically, this makes sense for two reasons. First, football emerged as a national sport in the industrial period and has always been culturally indebted to a rigorous division of labor, top-down planning, sublimated aggression, and militaristic rhetoric; a pendulum swing toward freedom and individual style in the game was long overdue. Second, in the 1960s, a cultural battle between self-expression and mass conformity was central to what was then called "the generation gap"; certainly not all changes were due to African American influence.

We need only look at the moment when the AFL shocked the NFL with its first Super Bowl win in 1969. The flamboyant, urbane, long-haired, anti-establishment playboy "Broadway Joe" Namath guaranteed a win in the face of a betting line that made his New York Jets seventeen-point underdogs—the kind of boasting and old-school trash-talking disapproved of by the staid, authoritarian NFL embodied by the crewcutted Johnny Unitas and the Baltimore Colts. Both Namath and Unitas were charismatic team leaders and carried themselves with authority, if in different styles; both were great passers and pocket quarterbacks. But Namath led an offense more geared to passing than any football team in history—a key aspect in the transformation of the sport—and only the year before became the first quarterback to pass for more than 4,000 yards in a season. Some football scholars consider Namath the primary cause of the AFL-NFL merger, since the older league could not afford to lose such talent to a rival league.

Namath was white but his style and personality heralded the arrival of the African American influence in the NFL; in fact, his resistance to the sport's militaristic ethos—his long hair, late-night partying, and straight talk—symbolized the refusal of a younger generation to carry the image of the team off the field. Ironically, Namath played for the all-white University of Alabama teams in the early 1960s under the legendary discipline of Paul "Bear" Bryant, and he was the Crimson Tide's star quarterback when Governor George Wallace attempted to block the enrollment of African Americans there. Much of the all-white team participated in racist name-calling and pranks, but Namath, raised in rural Pennsylvania, distanced himself from all racist acts on campus. In New York in the late 1960s, Namath was one of the few white football players who casually socialized with black players at meals, on the road, during workouts, or partying. "Namath was cool," his biographer declares simply, a sentiment apparently shared by players, fans, women, and scholars across the color line. To *be cool* in the black cultural sense of the 1960s had different connotations than the term does now—it meant that a person possessed poise, a signature style, and a reliably defiant individuality.[12]

In contrast to Namath's cult of personality (and sexuality), the black running back style was indebted to the aesthetics and moves of a tradition: the African American dance tradition. The fundamental elements of this tradition differ from Euro-American physical expression in several ways, which is why dance scholars can easily identify and distinguish African dances from Balinese dances or Hungarian ones. First, African-derived dance has a quintessential energy nexus located in the hips that explodes outward through the legs, as Marshall Stearns first theorized in his definitive *Jazz Dance* (1968).[13] Second, dancers usually begin from a crouch, not erect, which creates a lower, more dynamic center of gravity. In contrast, the European dance tradition emphasizes an erect carriage and the upper body—think of the waltz or the Irish jig. Within a European tradition of physical movement, sinuous hip motion was considered lewd, perverse, and coarse until quite recently—hence the widespread panics that greeted several African American dance crazes of the twentieth century (the shimmy, the lindy, the twist, the grind). Hip-shaking snakes through twentieth-century popular culture as a distinctive element of African American physical expression, admired for its rebellious and sensual elements only when white faced by performers from Mae West to Elvis to John Travolta to Madonna.

More to the point here, in football and basketball, hipshakes and hipfakes often precede explosive bursts of speed. As 1978 Heisman winner Billy Sims of Oklahoma (later of the Detroit Lions) characterized his running style: "I'm sort of like a Corvette—built low to the ground, accelerates pretty good, and when I'm in full gear, I'm lean and gliding."[14] The black running-back style emphasizes a dynamic of lower-body control, fast footwork, and an aesthetic of acceleration. Sims' comparison to a Corvette is telling; his style is similar to many black running backs (not all, of course), and recently a sports announcer employed the same imagery to describe Kansas City Chief kick-return specialist Dante Hall after a touchdown in a January 2004 playoff game. The announcer first explained that Hall aspired to be a race-car driver and that Dick Vermeil, the Kansas City coach, coveted sports cars. He then praised Hall accordingly: "Dick Vermeil can only hope that his sports car can corner and change direction like Dante Hall—[and] have his sense of timing." By the time O. J. Simpson joined the Buffalo Bills, halfbacks like Gale Sayers and Leroy Kelley already represented the African American style of open field running. Simpson's importance was not in creating this new style, although he combined speed, evasion, and power in dramatic, fluid fashion; he was instead its most famous and charismatic exemplar. It was Simpson's aesthetic power, USC's high profile, and the charged racial tensions of the 1960s that made it clear African American running backs were bringing something culturally innovative—from within black vernacular culture—to the game of football.[15]

Watching old tapes of running backs from the 1920s to the 1950s reveals how much more dependent rushing plays were on blocking formations and raw power than on the improvisatory flights of cut and spurt, spin and reverse field, back-up and end-around. Earlier NFL runners nearly always followed blockers down the field and rarely broke into the open. The cuts against the grain were gradual, not sharp; the movement was more continuous even when changing directions; headfakes seem lame and clumsy to modern eyes; it was rare for a runner to fake out defensive players with a quick shake and shimmy. Moreover, there were good reasons why a fast back did not waste his time honing his open field moves: it was common for defenses to try to put a team's offensive weapon out of the game through serious injury. Football's archetypal offensive formation in the late nineteenth century was the "flying wedge"— "a charging juggernaut of blockers and linked arms"—and it was meant to injure would-be tacklers. In 1906, there were 18 deaths and 159 serious injuries in college football, and President Theodore Roosevelt called the nation's coaches to the White House to implore them to lessen the sport's violence. One indirect result was the legalization of the forward pass, a maneuver then considered both a less rugged and less manly way of moving the ball, a perception that did not totally diminish in the NFL until the early 1960s.[16]

Professional football is war in the form of play, a game of military maneuvers. It can be seen as the public display of coveting ground and then conquering it through power, grit, intelligent planning, and hard, grinding work. To speed by the defense or soar passes over it long seemed outside the fighting "manly" spirit of the sport. In contrast, the performance continuum of African American culture is motivated by the affirmation of individual style within the rules of the game. The new running-back style did not emerge suddenly; the boundaries of sports and dance in African American vernacular culture began blurring in the 1930s, when dances followed basketball games and vice versa. In that decade, the black running-back style surfaced for one moment in the national spotlight and then submerged for nearly three decades of college gridiron segregation.

Back to the Future

How shocking was it to encounter the rapid tempo shifts, radical dips and turns, and disruptive flows of "the black athletic aesthetic" in the 1930s? Those who watched Iowa's Oze Simmons run between 1934 and 1936 left some clues. In Simmons' first full college game, the sophomore halfback ran for 166 yards against Northwestern, and reporters grasped for metaphors. Simmons left defensive players "fumbling at his twinkling heels most of the afternoon, clutching at empty spaces," wrote the *Chicago Tribune*. African American reporter David Kellum celebrated the interracial goodwill generated by his performance, as "all races and nationalities arose from their seats as one, and proclaimed Oze Simmons, Iowa's slippery, elusive, and sensational new football thunderbolt, for his dazzling individual exhibition." The white press declared Simmons "the black jackrabbit of the prairie states," while the black press created new nicknames for Simmons almost weekly—"the Ebony Eel, the Texas Tornado, the Sepia Sprite, . . . the Hula-Hipped Hawkeye Hog Hide Handler." Black Chicago claimed Simmons and the Iowa Hawkeyes as their own, and the games became "pilgrimages for black America." A full-page profile in the *Chicago Defender*, the nation's premier black newspaper, proclaimed the hardworking Simmons "The Joe Louis of Football."[17]

Ohio State's coach, Francis Schmidt, identified the distinctive aspects of Simmons' running style in a 1935 article in the *Saturday Evening Post*. Schmidt was stunned that Simmons would suddenly stop in the middle of a play, and then reverse field. "As the tackler advances, Oze . . . holds the ball right out in front of him in one hand, and then breaks to the right or left at incredible speed, or even pivots like a basketball player and turns his back to the tackler." Simmons also apparently taunted defenders with an in-your-face gesture, holding the ball out and "wav[ing] it to the front and side, almost in the face of the tackler," as one sportswriter described it—a dangerous display of confidence that carries a high risk of fumbling (which he did often). Coach Schmidt remembered a specific moment in the Ohio State-Iowa game when one of his linebackers reached for the ball Simmons offered and "Oze grinned, flashed to the left and raced straight past him. This colored boy has raised *shiftiness* to a new level . . . and he's probably the most dangerous punt receiver in America in the past ten or fifteen years." The pun on "shiftiness" here enables Schmidt to capture Simmons' speed, elusiveness, and hip motion while simultaneously accusing him of not quite playing fair.[18]

Here's another sportswriter on "Ozzie's technique": "He runs as if he were climbing stairs—golden stairs maybe—packs the ball in one hand, and when a tackler grabs at him he goes into a convulsion *near the hip line* which would do justice to Gilda Gray in her most supple moments."[19] The writer here makes two comparisons to dancers working within an African American tradition. Gilda Gray was one of the most popular stars of the Ziegfeld Follies throughout the 1920s—a white woman—and known in particular for her signature shimmy (featuring torso undulation and shoulder shaking) and the "Voodoo dance" (featuring sinuous hip motion). Gray was one of many dancers who *white* faced black dances for theatrical revues and their elite Euro-American audiences; *that she was white does not change the fact that these were black dances*. The "climbing stairs" metaphor is certainly a reference to Bill "Bojangles" Robinson's famous stair dance, then his act's showstopper and the centerpiece of that year's Shirley Temple–Bill Robinson vehicle, *The Littlest Colonel* (1935).

The aspects of African American cultural style that comprise "Ozzie's technique" are clear from these fragmented reports: speed, acceleration, sudden changes in tempo; self-expression and flamboyance; quick cuts and spin moves; improvisational decision making; hip "convulsions" and shoulder movements indebted to the African American dance tradition. "In the 1960s, [Oze] Simmons would have been denounced for 'showboating,'" Michael Oriard reflects in *King Football*. "Today, he would be recognized simply as a black running back." In 1973, nearly forty years after Oze Simmons's fame, sportswriter Dan Jenkins employed similar dance imagery to describe the five-foot-nine, one-hundred-seventy-three pound Johnny Rodgers of Nebraska in *Sports Illustrated*: "Seemingly every Saturday he manages to invent *a new repertoire of dance steps* with the ball which leave . . . TV audiences and his own hoarse following mercilessly agog at the wonder of it all." In 1972, Rodgers won the Heisman Trophy; in the 1930s, Simmons could not even get elected team captain. Not only was he put out of action several times by various Big Ten defenses but by his senior year, his teammates stopped blocking for him, a then-common way to register dissent against a player's ego, or possibly to make a racial statement.[20] Oriard suggests that Oze Simmons represented the emergence of "an incipient black [football] style . . . during the Jim Crow era" at the intersection of dance and athletics.[21]

There are analogies to basketball in the 1930s as well, a decade in which African Americans began experimenting with the jump shot. White basketball coaches immediately condemned it as too individualistic and too flamboyant (in today's vernacular, "too street" or "too black"), a declaration by management that successfully prevented its development for nearly thirty years. Such an aesthetic judgment masks an underlying racial, cultural, and economic logic: the shot was simply outside the perceived "white" skill set. The same process ran its course with the slam-dunk in the 1960s—"the stuff" was ruled illegal in college, thought to be only within the capabilities of extremely tall African American men such as Lew Alcindor (aka Kareem Abdul-Jabbar). Such declarations are a form of culture war. Why did professional coaches who might prize individual achievement and innovation effectively stigmatize brilliant individual innovations in expressive style and aesthetic mastery? For two reasons: (1) it took power away from the coaches; (2) the innovators were black. When a white basketball player plays in a black style—e.g., Pistol Pete Maravich, Jason Williams—that player often becomes instantly, enormously popular.[22]

Airing It Out

Running backs won all the Heismans between 1973 and 1983 because college football was still primarily a running game. However, African American wide receivers were equally responsible for bringing the black athletic aesthetic to football. In the late 1960s, (white) quarterbacks began to pilot wide-open aerial offenses searching out increasingly fast and elusive—and usually African American—receivers for long bombs. This began in the early 1960s in the AFL and peaked in the early 1980s, when 400+ passing yards per game became commonplace for quarterbacks such as Dan Fouts or Joe Montana.[23]

The turn of the 1970s was a high-water mark for wide receivers bursting the deep seams of defensive secondaries with a self-conscious sense of finesse and elegance. Paul Warfield (Miami), Homer Jones (NY Giants), Bob Hayes (Dallas), Gene Washington (SF 49ers), Lance Alworth (San Diego), Don Maynard (NY Jets), Isaac Curtis (Cincinnati), Warren Wells and Cliff Branch (Oakland), Otis Taylor (Kansas City)—each of these receivers averaged 20+ yards per catch for at least two years, a marker rarely reached today.[24] In the AFL formerly colloquial terms such as "wide receiver" and "flanker" became codified. A brand-new vernacular term—the "wideout"—marked a receiver who lined up far off the line, suggesting that his speed and moves after the catch were as big a threat as his hands, strength, or efficiency of his pass patterns; the wideouts were the "fastest, showiest, and most graceful players on the field." By the late 1970s, one sportswriter could call the next generation of wide receivers—Lynn Swann, James Lofton, and John Jefferson—football's new "rugged individualists." Here was the sport's new "cowboy," "pioneer," or "antihero," the game-breaker every kid wanted to be, football players who were "leapers . . . acrobatic players who . . . added a basketball-like dimension to catching the ball." One receiver called his position "a performing art," and analogies to dancers—"balletic," "graceful," "floating"—became common sportswriting tropes; this "razzle-dazzle game" was a new dimension for a sport known more for its raw aggression. Lynn Swann's childhood idol was Fred Astaire; Jerry Butler of the Buffalo Bills claimed "wide receivers are more like artists or actors than other players. They're free spirits."[25] I am by no means dismissing the skills and achievements of great Euro-American receivers such as Fred Biletnikoff (Raiders) or Cris Collinsworth (Bengals), but only pointing out that with the exception of tight ends, most receivers of the late 1970s (and since) have been African American.

The transformation of pro football offenses to the passing game was developed overwhelmingly in the AFL and called by players "airing it out." The Chiefs were the first teams to consistently gain more yardage through passing than rushing (now the norm), and 80 percent of the deep threats listed above worked in AFL offenses. With the exception of Roger Staubach and the Dallas Cowboys, AFL teams pioneered the passing-centered offense over a generation: Namath, Daryle Lamonica, Bob Griese, Len Dawson, Kenny Stabler, Terry Bradshaw, Ken Anderson, Dan Fouts. As early as the league's first two seasons (1960 and 1961), the commitment to an aerial attack marked a difference with the ground games that dominated the NFL; in fact, many veteran NFL coaches condemned the aerial offenses of the AFL as amateurish, and often derided it as "basketball" (i.e., not a "serious" game). But they had to eat crow and adapt. When the Super Bowl began in 1967, the NFL expected to remain the superior league for the foreseeable future. Yet between 1969 and 1981, the AFL won eleven of thirteen Super Bowls and the Dallas Cowboys (using an AFL-style offense) the other two.[26]

What had happened in the AFL? For the first time, football became as much about speed, style, mobility, and improvisation as it had always been about power, network, and ball-control. As a newer league, the AFL had less tradition to buck—in terms of coaching and veteran players—and engaged in bidding wars to secure the best talents in the college drafts of the 1960s, who were increasingly African American. New offensive weapons created a more dynamic locus developed around the scrimmage line; the football mind slowly changed from an ideal of set formations to *sets of options* predicated on constant motion. The rushing quarterback became necessary to offenses that required more mobility due to increased backfield and upfield speed—symbolized by the "multiple offense" developed by Kansas City Chiefs' coach Hank Stram, often called the "floating pocket."[27] The deep-threat wide receivers were a crucial element in the Steelers' offense, the development of the Cowboys' shotgun offense and, later, the "run and gun" style of the San Diego Chargers and the Buffalo Bills.

The final stage of development of the wide-open passing offense was made possible by a 1978 rule change that defensive players derided as the "can't hurt 'em" rule, also called the "one-chuck" rule. Until this ruling, defensive backs could harass a receiver at any time except when the ball was in the air; the new ruling meant defensive backs could only bump and run receivers once within five yards of the scrimmage line. Passed in response to the gratuitously violent hits laid upon wide receivers such as Lynn Swann or Isaac Curtis by Jack Tatum of the Raiders or Jack Lambert of the Steelers, linebackers and defensive backs (and many coaches) thought the rule demasculinized the sport. Commissioner Pete Rozelle was aware of the popularity of the aerial offenses, however, and was then negotiating a new TV contract for the NFL. Nielsen ratings showed that fans responded to the more explosive offenses; the ruling marked a pendulum shift away from the game's violence.[28]

In many ways, the history of football in the 1970s parallels basketball at the institutional level: the AFL forced changes in the NFL similar to those the ABA brought to the NBA. Each sport became "increasingly, a black game" in the 1970s, as sportswriter Phil Patton reflected in *Razzle-Dazzle* (1984), although "this fact was necessarily tiptoed around in the press." The black aesthetics of the ABA—exemplified by Dr. J.'s Afro-blowing aerial slam-dunks—helped transform and funkify NBA ball in the 1980s after the leagues merged. Basketball developed into "a game of constant excitement, speed, and acrobatic grace," Patton reflected, and these were "exactly the [same] virtues that professional football would seize on to accomplish its own revitalization."[29] In the 1970s both sports became more exciting, and in the process, experienced increased power and revenue from television and advertising; owners in each sport were forced to concede power to individual players. These infrastructural changes, arising from various economic and cultural factors, still mask the fact that the ABA-NBA and AFL-NFL mergers represented the triumph of black culture in both sports.

If the symbolic gesture of this shift in basketball was the slam-dunk, in football it was the touchdown dance. To this day, only African American players dance after touchdowns and players take pride in performing a signature dance move. Credit is generally given to Kansas City Chief receiver Elmo Wright for performing the first celebration dance in 1973, although the most memorable may be the rubber-legged dance of Billie "White Shoes" Johnson, the punt returner and receiver with the Houston Oilers; significantly, both played at one time in the AFL. Individual expressions of braggadocio and celebration, crowd-pumping and body bumping, simply did not exist before the 1970s.

If the slam-dunk enables basketball players to bring passion, intimidation, style, and self-expression to the exact moment of scoring, then black football players have found ways to celebrate immediately afterward. Besides the touchdown dance, there's spiking the football (credited to Homer Jones of the New York Giants, 1965), the jump into the stands (the "Lambeau Leap"), and my personal favorite, the sudden cut-motor stop and dinosaur walk into the end zone after a long pass or interception runback (sometimes credited to Deion Sanders). There have been team celebrations as well, such as the Atlanta Falcons' "dirty bird dance" or the Denver Broncos' "Mile High Salute." All of these celebratory gestures were created by African Americans, just as the recent spate of end zone stunts were planned and executed by black wide receivers (e.g., New Orleans Saints' receiver Joe Horn's cellphone call after a touchdown; Terrell Owens, then of the San Francisco 49ers, autographed a football after scoring by taking a pen from his sock).

For Euro-American players and coaches in the 1970s, touchdown dances seemed to connote a lack of emotional self-control, a feminized sense of the male body, and unnecessary self-expression or wildness; i.e., the act itself is antithetical to the sport's valorized ethos of teamwork and traditional white masculinity. In African American culture, however, the individual achievement *reflects back on the community;* in other words, African American athletes often find ways to share the moment of scoring with a real or perceived audience. "The virtuosic individual performance is a social act, inspiring the team and the community," Caponi-Tabery suggests. Nelson George recalls from childhood a day he watched a slam-dunk on the playground so incredible and from such an unlikely source—"that slam-dunk—dramatic, unexpected, fantastic"—that for him, that "moment" was the game. "Who won? Who cared?" he reflected.[30]

Many African American athletes have a different attitude toward cultural and self-expression than Euro-Americans. To take one example, in the late 1960s, the Rams' legendary defensive line, the "fearsome foursome" of Rosey Grier, Deacon Jones, Merlin Olsen, and Lamar Lundy performed publicly as a Motown-style singing group, "The Fearsome Foursome." These were some of the toughest, strongest, seemingly meanest defensive athletes in the NFL performing sensitive soul ballads in bright-colored tuxedos. The band reluctantly had to drop Olsen, the only Euro-American of the four, because he couldn't master the choreographed dance moves behind Grier (which were not especially difficult); after Olsen left, they performed as "The Fearsome Threesome."[31] This doesn't mean white men can't dance, but instead that cultural desire creates kinesthetic shifts; consider how effectively Eminem or Jason Williams or John Travolta demonstrate black moves within white bodies. My central point here is simply that African Americans consider sports, dance, music, language, and humor along a continuum of performance and not as segregated aspects of play, theater, masculinity, thought, display, or seriousness.

African American celebration dances emphasize self-expression and levity in a game based on turf war and played in full battle regalia; in a sense, the act of dancing tempers football's relentless aggression. The celebration dance is simultaneously an act of self-expression, an appeal to fans, and an act of cultural resistance. The subtext? "Hey, *I* scored for *us*—oh, and lighten up." Why this particular celebratory act in this sport? The football helmet creates a certain facelessness that prevents fans from seeing players' emotional expressions and reactions; it also allows for an effacing of race and face that often leads to my students' surprise when I mention that two-thirds of the NFL is black. Only physical self-expression can distinguish an athlete wearing a helmet and uniform. By way of contrast, because basketball players are the only team athletes who play without any face covering at all—they are also the least dressed—we see the full range of emotional expression on their faces, not to mention the expressive markers of headbands and haircuts and tattoos.

Again, for African American athletes, music, dance, self-expression, dynamic physical gesture, and signature athletic style exist on a cultural continuum, not as separate realms of performance. It would still be unusual to see a Euro-American football player, after scoring a touchdown, spin the ball away slowly on the ground then wiggle his ass to celebrate his achievement, then hipshake his lower torso right and then left while walking away—and, often enough, have some of his teammates join him in the dance. In a recent game, wide receiver Terrell Owens of the Philadelphia Eagles spun, shook, and powered through the league-leading Baltimore Raven defense for an eleven-yard game-winning touchdown, and then punctuated the score with a touchdown dance that seemed to specifically mock (or signify upon) Raven linebacker Ray Lewis' dance. Asked to comment directly, Owens smiled broadly and dissembled, calling Lewis a good friend and declaring simply: "He's a highlight film, like I'm a highlight film. . . . If I score, everybody knows I'm going to try to do something exciting."[32] For African American athletes, it's all the same plane of the game: get the job done, celebrate, strut your (personal) stuff.

In its continued aversion to levity, individual style, and African American culture, the NFL maintains its role in upholding the sport as gladiatorial battlefield. In the early 1970s, the increasing presence of African American players and influence of African American culture occasionally provoked enmity among veteran white football players; it was culture war. One legendary encounter took place over the cultural style and politics of the handshake in 1970. All-Pro middle linebacker Mike Curtis of the Baltimore Colts advanced to midfield to shake hands with the opposing team's captains and, extending his hand to the African American defensive captain, he shouted, "Regular, damn it, regular!"[33] He meant let's do the "normal" handshake, not the soul-shake (fingers up, palms slapped, thumbs hooked). Curtis' message? You (blacks) adapt to us (whites, "regulars")—not we to you. However, in various aspects of cultural expression and physical gesture in American culture, the reverse is often the case.

I am using football as a lens here to shed light on the resistance of Euro-Americans to recognizing the depth of their appropriations and adaptations of black culture as mainstream *American* culture: kinesthetic shifts in sports; moves and grooves in walking and dancing; new slang; tropes of humor. To take another set of examples from this period, African Americans rarely get their due regarding their impact on the specific physical gestures that embodied the cultural revolution of self-expression in the 1960s and '70s—from hip slang to rituals of meeting and greeting (such as the soul-shake) to the thousand-and-one dances that helped ground American bodies during an age of high-flying Space Race rhetoric and Cold War nuclear anxiety. Considering a specific set of contributions—*a specifically African American aesthetic* of stylistic and expressive aspects—remains anathema to the fantasies of aggression, power, and teamwork in contemporary football consciousness.

Selling Aggression, Effacing Finesse

To judge by the promotional graphics for football on CBS and Fox, as well as the NFL's own ads, the networks and the league have conceded to basketball the aesthetic elements of grace and flow, bypassing the finesse of Jerry Rice, Marshall Faulk, and Dante Hall (to take a few examples) to sell equal opportunity aggression. When Fox signed on with the NFL in the 1990s, the network's promotions located the essence of football in raw power and naked aggression. Their ads emphasized the gladiatorial persistence of offensive players breaking the plane of the goal line, quarterbacks blindsided by blitzes, the ephemeral moment of a pass reception immediately followed by a nasty hit. The ads for the short-lived XFL went even further in riffing off the muscular bluster of the World Wrestling Foundation, intercutting brutal hits with the joyous promise, "No fair catches." So let basketball have humor, flash, and expressive power—and all those tattoos, erratic headcases (Allen Iverson, Dennis Rodman), and defiant bad boys. Here in Football-Land, we still understand teamwork, the greater good, and the place of violence in securing the land.

In contrast, the NBA markets itself by focusing on players' faces as they nakedly express spontaneous emotional response to game events. Faces front-lit in the midst of dazzling slam-dunks that combine power, persistence, and personal style; faces stylized into dispassionate no-look blankness that turn explosive bursts of downcourt running into fluid, intuitive passing faster than the eye can follow; quick defensive swats from gargantuan men wearing masks of now archetypal defiance. In ads for the NBA, players on the bench fall all over each other in celebratory laughter or in mock-shock at an unbelievable individual shot, pass, or block. Such levity is almost impossible to imagine with regard to the NFL, where humor is still often punished—one sportswriter recently mocked it as the "No-Fun League"—as selfishness. It is no surprise that kids today choose to emulate basketball players—to be like Mike or Kobe or Jason Kidd—as a result of the camera's emotional revelations. Whereas in the 1970s, football players were the corporate spokesmen of choice—O. J. Simpson for Hertz, Joe Namath for Noxzema shaving cream, Ben Davidson and Mean Joe Greene for Schick and Coca-Cola, respectively—basketball players have dethroned them as pitchmen for sneakers, soft drinks, and corporate image.

Current ad campaigns for football focus either on fandom or traditional rough masculinity: good-time men, big-breasted women, the sacrament of beer to lubricate the game's bloodlust. You would certainly never find out from NFL mythography (or its marketing, which amounts to the same thing) that the aesthetic ideal globalized by Michael Jordan—the explosive, fluid, improvisational *body-in-motion*—was jump-started by O. J. Simpson and the black running backs and wide receivers of the 1970s. It would be hard to imagine an ad campaign focused on black culture in football akin to the recent Nike campaign featuring a fictional ABA team and trading on '70s nostalgia for that league's loose style of play, individual razzle-dazzle, and Afro hairstyles—all propelled by a funky soundtrack and booty-shaking cheerleaders. A retro campaign imbued with both nostalgia and a certain surreal poetic justice, the ad's tagline for Nike sneakers— "There since 'back in the day'"—suggests "the day" is the moment African American aesthetics and style transformed professional basketball. (Of course, Nike sneakers were not even around on that particular day.)

It might be useful to consider the nation's three major team sports as useful metaphors of American historical consciousness: baseball is the agrarian game, football the industrial game, and basketball the electronic (postindustrial) one. Baseball is informed by nostalgia for the pastoral, and its manicured fields harken back to myths of rebirth and fertility, the renewal of spring, and the boys of summer. Films like *Field of Dreams, The Natural,* and *Bull Durham* build upon agricultural symbols: a cornfield, a special tree from which to forge a bat, "Woman" as natural landscape and muse. In contrast, basketball is an urban game that exemplifies the shift from modernity to postmodernity. It was once a more industrial game of set plays and set shots—with a clear division of labor among guard, forward, and center— but now professional basketball teams feature multitasking players at every position and aspire to an aesthetic of perpetual flow. This is an *electronic* aesthetic: speed, flow, instantaneous communication, an airborne ideal, multitasking athletes. A symbol of this shift might be the triple-double, a statistic so named for a player who puts up double-digit numbers in assists, rebounds, and points scored in a single game (e.g., 25 points, 10 assists, 17 rebounds). The triple-double did not exist until the 1980s because players kept to their roles in the division of labor among guards, forwards, and centers. More important, the slam-dunk has shifted basketball's metaphorical landscape from the ground to the air in the cultural imagination and in the vernacular—as recent basketball films for kids illustrate (Air Jordan begat *Air Bud, Lil Mike,* and *Space Jam*).

Football, however, remains the symbolic battlefield of war, and its cultural imaginary is hard work, sacrifice, discipline, toughness, teamwork, and traditional aggressive masculinity. All of these elements receive due respect from recent Hollywood films—*Remember the Titans, Any Given Sunday, Jerry Maguire*—but each of these films, unlike the NFL, also engages African American culture in some way. African American athletes are shown not only with regard to racism, difference, and the struggle for social equality, but often as agents with a separate aesthetic agenda with regard to humor, dance, language, and style. The best example concerns Rod Tidwell, Cuba Gooding, Jr.'s character in *Jerry Maguire,* who represents athletic excellence, black pride, and black cultural expression simultaneously. Director Cameron Crowe takes the character's more confrontational emotional style seriously and grants him both a celebration dance and his own personal slang ("kwan" for coin, "show me the money"). At one point Tidwell mocks Jerry Maguire (his agent) because he "can't dance"— Tidwell sees this as a *weakness* of masculinity, in terms of flexibility, freedom of movement, and the ability to laugh at one's self (i.e., to cut up or play the fool).

Yet the real world of football allows for no such ethnic recognition, if we consider the recent fines to Joe Horn and others for their end zone stunts, and their vilification by fans, coaches, and many sportswriters. There have been four major fines in the past year for "excessive celebration," but it is no longer assessed as an onfield team penalty—the individual (African American) transgressor has to pay the fine in cold, hard cash out of his own pocket. Apparently the sanctity of football and the team must be maintained: *this game is war by other means, Son,* and that's nothing to laugh about. As one New Orleans sports columnist succinctly titled his reaction, "NFL Should Allow Players A Little More Individuality."[34]

Humor moderates aggression, and yet, with their revved up pregame shows and ramped-up graphics, every year CBS and Fox inch closer to the WWF's style of power and braggadocio. This rawer shade of celebration, primal roaring, and self-expression is embraced as much by African American football players as by Euro-Americans. The mixture of WWF and hip-hop has produced a hybrid style of aggression, trash-talking, and machismo where the strands are intertwined. There's no need to call it white or black or multicultural, and besides there's no one rushing to claim it as "culture," or any group's "culture"; in many ways, it has eclipsed public memory of the distinctive cultural and aesthetic contributions of African American players.

That O. J. Simpson was the first African American athlete to be a spokesperson for a national corporation speaks to both a particular moment of hopeful integration and the desire of Euro-Americans for African American locomotion. In the enormously popular ad campaign for Hertz car rentals in the 1970s, Simpson used his open field running skills to dash through airports, as if his athletic aesthetic—of speed and spin, hurdle and hipshake—would enable consumers to catch planes when they were late. The corresponding "white" integrationist ad of the 1970s was the classic, long-running Miller Lite "tastes-great / less-filling" ad campaign that framed football players as regular guys at the bar, as if to enhance the consumer's masculinity with their presence and comic eagerness to brawl. In the 1970s, regardless of the presence of Euro-American finesse players and African American defensive brutes, in the cultural imagination, football's white masculinity was associated with aggression and power while its black masculinity was portrayed in terms of speed, style, evasion, and improvisation.

When African Americans create a new mode of football or basketball, or a new rhythmic idiom and its accompanying dances, such cultural innovation and expression emerges from a vital African American aesthetic tradition created by and for themselves. The process by which these performative innovations almost always become global *American* culture—from jazz to tap to funk, from hip-hop to high-fives to the slam-dunk—is something scholars need to excavate more closely. The tradition of the black body on stage as exoticized or commodified Other is only one part of a complex story of framing African American athletic achievement. When Charlie Keil declares simply, "Blacks create the new moves and grooves of every generation," who can dispute this claim? That Americans neither seem to care about, understand, or wish to celebrate all the African American moves and grooves that make football (and American life) swing suggests an anxiety of influence at the deepest levels of our society and culture.

Notes

1. Alan H. Levy, *Tackling Jim Crow: Racial Segregation in Professional Football* (Jefferson, NC: McFarland, 2003), 154.
2. Ralph Ellison, "What Would America Be Without Blacks?," *Time*, April 6, 1970, repr. in *Going to the Territory* (New York: Vintage, 1986), 104–112.

3. John Sayle Watterson, College Football: *History, Spectacle, Controversy* (Baltimore: Johns Hopkins University Press, 2000), 318–320; John T. Brady, *The Heisman* (New York: Atheneum, 1984), 154–157. For a few exceptions to the monolithic segregation of college football in the South before the 1960s, see Patrick B. Miller, "Slouching Toward a New Expediency: College Football and the Color Line During the Depression Decade," *American Studies* 40, no. 3 (Fall 1999): 5–30.

4. Brady, *The Heisman*, 140–215.

5. Simpson and Brady quoted in *The Heisman*, 157, 134.

6. Michael MacCambridge, *America's Game* (New York: Random House, 2004), 107–110, 164–167, 201–203; Bob Costas quoted in Larry Swartz, "Biography—Jim Brown," www.sportsplacement.com/brownbio.htm. Brown was equally outspoken off the field, as when challenging the racism, segregation, and double standards of the Cleveland Browns as a corporate organization in 1960: "If they don't invite us to the parties and events with the pretty white girls, then we won't go to those community functions, that boring, political shit, where they want to make us look like one happy family. If we can't go to . . . the fun stuff, then we won't do the fake stuff." Brown quoted in MacCambridge, *America's Game*, 202. Many thanks to Clark Dougan for his recollections of Jim Brown and for suggesting this line of argument.

7. Nelson George, *Elevating The Game:The History and Aesthetics of Black Men in Basketball* (New York: Simon & Schuster, 1993), xiv-xxi.

8. Gena Dagel Caponi, ed., *Signifyin(g), Sanctifyin' and Slam Dunking* (Amherst: University of Massachusetts Press, 1999), 9–13; George, *Elevating The Game*, xiv, xvii, xix, xxi; Todd Boyd, *Am I Black Enough For You?: Popular Culture From the Hood and Beyond* (Bloomington: Indiana University Press, 1997), 111–116; an earlier reference to basketball as "visual jazz" appears in Jeff Greenfield, "The Black and White Truth About Basketball," in Caponi, *Signifyin(g)*, 373–378.

9. August Wilson quoted in George, *Elevating the Game*, xv.

10. Joel Dinerstein, *Swinging the Machine: Modernity, Technology, and African American Culture Between the World Wars* (Amherst: University of Massachusetts, 2003).

11. Michael Eric Dyson, "Be Like Mike? Michael Jordan and the Pedagogy of Desire," in Caponi, *Signifyin(g)*, 408; see also Dinerstein, *Swinging the Machine*, 290–291.

12. Mark Kriegel, *Namath: A Biography* (New York: Viking, 2004), 237–238; MacCambridge, *America's Game*, 250–252. On African-American male cool as formed in jazz culture, see Joel Dinerstein, "Lester Young and the Birth of Cool," in Caponi. *Signifyin(g)*, 239–276.

13. Marshall Stearns and Jean Stearns, *Jazz Dance: The Story of American Vernacular Dance* (New York: Macmillan, 1968).

14. Billy Sims quoted in Brady, *The Heisman*, 188.

15. A dominant society has no motivation to celebrate cultural achievement by an oppressed group unless it is responding to political strife or declarations of cultural independence—which is how a period marked by vernacular phrases such

as "Black Power," "Black is Beautiful," or "Say It Loud, I'm Black and I'm Proud" needs to be understood.

16. Phil Patton, *Razzle-Dazzle: The Curious Marriage of Television and Professional Football* (Garden City, NY: The Dial Press, 1984), 163–164; Watterson, *College Football*, 64–98.

17. All quotes here are from Michael Oriard, *King Football: Sport and Spectacle in the Golden Age of Radio and Newsreels, Movies and Magazines, the Weekly and the Daily Press* (Chapel Hill: University of North Carolina Press, 2001), 302–307, 319–327.

18. Oriard, *King Football*, 319–320.

19. L. D. Hitchkiss quoted in Oriard, *King Football*, 319–320.

20. Oriard, *King Football*, 320, 307; Dan Jenkins quoted in Brady, *The Heisman*, 172, emphasis mine.

21. Oriard, *King Football*, 319–327.

22. Gena Caponi-Tabery, "Jump for Joy: The Jump Trope in African America, 1937–1941," *Prospects: An Annual of American Cultural Studies* 24 (1999): 521–574.

23. Patton, *Razzle-Dazzle*, 159–161, 163–189.

24. See NFL statistics online, www.Pro-Football-Reference.com.

25. Patton, *Razzle-Dazzle*, 165, 175–177.

26. Patton, *Razzle-Dazzle*, 164, 167.

27. Patton, *Razzle-Dazzle*, 149, 166–168.

28. Patton, *Razzle-Dazzle*, 158–162.

29. Patton, *Razzle-Dazzle*, 152.

30. Caponi, *Signifyin(g)*, 5–7; George, *Elevating the Game*, xiv; see also Dinerstein, "Lester Young and the Birth of Cool," 253–258. To take another example, when black players began mouthing "Hi Mom" to the cameras after scoring touchdowns in the 1970s, sportswriters and coaches singled out this seemingly neutral action as "selfish" and unsportsmanlike; it seems more likely they just wanted to share the moment with their mothers.

31. Oriard, *King Football*, 322.

32. Judy Battista, "Owens Breaks Some Tackles and Burns More Bridges," *New York Times*, Nov. 1, 2004, online edition.

33. Oriard, *King Football*, 364.

34. "King Kaufman's Sports Daily," Salon.com, Dec. 17, 2003; Lynn Zinser, "A Tough Call on Touchdown Celebrations," *New York Times*, Dec. 16, 2003, D1; "Last Call," *New Orleans Times-Picayune*, Dec. 18, 2003, D1, 6; John DeShazier, "NFL Should Allow Players A Little More Individuality," *New Orleans Times-Picayune*, Dec. 18, 2003, D1, 6.

SEVEN

The Harmonizing Nation

Mexico and the 1968 Olympics

Eric Zolov

A tourist arriving in Mexico City in the early summer of 1968 would have found the city awash in color, an air of expectation and optimism everywhere palpable as the country finalized last-minute preparations for the staging of the Olympic Games that fall. Yellow, blue, and pink banners framing a white peace dove lit up major thoroughfares. Throughout the city, numerous commercial billboards had been replaced with photographs of cultural and physical activity related to the Games; in one corner, a superimposed dove of peace was clearly visible. Other enormous images featured caricatured line drawings of school children, a family portrait, and anonymous faces in a crowd set against a background of hot pink and vibrant yellow. "Everything is Possible in Peace," they proclaimed in a multitude of languages. Along a designated "Route of Friendship" that extended across the southern part of the city, large abstract sculptures by artists of international renown, made of concrete and painted in various bright colors, could be observed in various stages of completion. The country's official logo for the Games—"MEXICO68"—whose evident Op Art influence was designed to evoke a moving, modernist feel, was omnipresent, as were the hundreds of young *edecanes* (event hostesses), whose uniformed miniskirts and pants suits were emblazoned with a graphic representation of the logo. The viewer could scarcely have avoided the sensation of a city, a country on the verge of something spectacular.

Today, however, the 1968 Mexico City Olympics are generally remembered either for the tragic massacre of unarmed students on the eve of the Opening Ceremony or, alternately, for the image of silent protest by black athletes Tommie Smith and John Carlos at their awards ceremony five days into the Games. Moreover, these memories tend not to overlap. For Mexicans, images of repression have overshadowed all other aspects.[1] For Americans, the 1968 Olympics have been largely telescoped into a single image of black-gloved defiance.[2] Lost in this narrowing of historical memory is a recollection on one hand of the shared sense of optimism during the period leading up to the Games and, on the other, of the challenges—both material and promotional—Mexico faced as the first "developing nation" to host an Olympics.

Since the days of the dictator Porfirio Díaz (1876–1911), Mexico has faced the burden of exchanging an international reputation for banditry and backwardness (inherited from the chaotic dissolution of the nation-state following independence from Spain) for one of progress and civilization.[3] During the reign of Porfirio Díaz relative political stability and a surge in economic growth laid the foundations for a more favorable, even conceited outlook by Mexican elites and foreign observers. French, British, and U.S. cultural influence accompanied their economic investments and thus helped to shape an impression of the capital, at least, as faithfully emulating the metropolises.[4] An incipient *indigenista* strategy—that is, the glorification of Mexico's pre-Hispanic past, albeit in the context of a repression of Mexico's indigenous *present*—also shaped the language and policies of state-sponsored nationalism. By linking an indigenista aesthetic with the regime's modernizing capitalist outlook, Díaz had looked to establish a cosmopolitanism worthy of respect among the world's leading nations. In the course of the revolutionary violence from 1910 to 1920, this project effectively collapsed. Nonetheless, the pre-revolutionary regime had established the basis for a post-revolutionary definition of nationhood in which indigenous (i.e., non-Western) culture was granted a central place in the quest for modernity.

From the ashes of revolutionary upheaval came a renaissance in artistic expression and folklore appreciation, a movement that not only valorized but romanticized indigenous culture while elevating certain aspects of regional mestizo (i.e., Spanish-Indian racial mixture) culture into iconic referents of national belonging.[5] The outcome of this nationalizing process was a more coherent sense of shared belonging among Mexicans[6]; it was also a deeper respect (at times, even awe) by Americans for Mexican culture. Writing about the impact of a special exhibit of Mexican muralist art presented in the United States during 1930–31, for instance, Helen Delpar notes that "instead of being a backward country full of bandits as many imagined, [Mexico] was now seen as a nation of culture."[7] The "vogue of things Mexican" that Delpar discusses reflected the beginnings of an important shift in the U.S. reception of Mexican nationalism, which included a new valorization of the nation's indigenous past and, to varying degrees, its present as well. It also pointed to the Mexican state's leveraging of representations of mestizo and Indian culture as central components of its domestic and international diplomacy.

During the 1950s scores of U.S. travelers and potential investors flocked to Mexico, eager to take advantage of an inexpensive vacation that promised modern comfort alongside the thrill of an encounter with the "exotic." As one American observer noted in early 1953, "Politically, the country has never been more stable. The intense activity all around, the big building program and flourishing private enterprise point up a new era coming."[8] The sense of progressive economic *movement,* moreover, had broader ramifications on foreign perceptions of a changing Mexican character. Slowly disappearing, for example, was the derogatory association of the Mexican "siesta" with sloth. Thus whereas a *New York Times* article from 1946 referred to Mexico as a country "where the siesta spirit is prevalent"[9] a decade later another writer felt confident in proclaiming that Mexico was "waking up after a long siesta": "Mexico proved herself a loyal ally in World War II. Mexico proved herself just as loyal a friend in the free world's defense against communism. . . . Mexico can no longer be caricatured as a poor peon, clothed in rags, having his mid-day siesta in the sun. Mexico is waking up!"[10]

With the Mexican economic "miracle" of "stabilizing development" (low inflation backed by a stable peso) producing average annual growth rates of 6 to 8 percent throughout the 1960s, the image of Mexico as the "land of 'Blood and Merriment,' of fighting cowboys and ragged Indians" was giving way, according to the perspective of one Mexican editorialist, to a "more optimistic" image of the nation.[11] The selection of Mexico City as the site for the 1968 Olympics evidently confirmed as much, for it was the first time the Olympics were scheduled to be held in a newly industrializing country. For most Mexicans, the Games clearly symbolized an important step up into the club of "first worldism." As one writer noted, "Mexico will be the point of observation for all the nations on Earth."[12]

Still, Mexico's "underdevelopment" was (and remains) an inseparable discursive component to perceptions of the nation abroad. This was especially true during the 1960s, when Mexico held out for many the hope of fulfilling modernization theory's expectations that third world countries would advance along the spectrum of democratic, capitalist development by allying with the United States.[13] It was thus inevitable that Mexico would be judged by foreign assumptions and stereotypes regarding the nation's

"progress" and continued "backwardness." Such notions arguably were en-
coded in spoken and unspoken references to the country's racial composition: its majority Indian and mestizo populations (guided by a small,
European-descended elite) were still presumed to be a burden on the nation's
development, imposing limitations to the country's organizational and industrial prowess. The organizers of the 1968 Games were well aware of this
tendency to associate Mexico (and nations in the "third world" more generally) with "disorganization" and thus desired to control the terms of representation to the best of their ability. In short, aside from the complex
logistical and financial considerations, Mexico faced the equally important
challenge of demonstrating to the world that the country was indeed an appropriate choice to host the 1968 Olympic Games: that its "underdevelopment" was not a liability but an asset in a world marked increasingly by
racial and national conflicts between the "first" and "third" worlds.

To meet this challenge, the Mexican Organizing Committee (MOC) for
the Olympics, through various aspects of visual and performative culture and
in its public relations, put together a comprehensive marketing approach that
leveraged the nation's perceived strengths—its connections to a European
(Iberian) heritage and harmonious melding of racial and ethnic groups; its
revolutionary tradition and spirit of liberalism in an era of political intolerance—while simultaneously reconfiguring (and "erasing") its alleged weaknesses—its overwhelming Indian presence and the continued influence of
"backward" colonial traditions (such as machismo); its blatant poverty and
a reputation for being politically and socially "disorganized." A central element of this strategy was the promotion of the so-called Cultural Olympics—
a year-long, comprehensive series of artistic, musical, theatric, and other
cultural events beginning in January 1968. By examining a series of promotional aspects associated with these events, what we will come to better understand is how the Cultural Olympics played a central role in fomenting
popular support for the staging of the Games within Mexico, while serving
an eminently important function in shaping perceptions abroad regarding the
"appropriateness" of Mexico to serve as Olympic host.

A unifying theme behind the Cultural Olympics was the idea of Mexico as a land beyond racial and domestic conflict, a "harmonizing nation"
transcendent of internal divisions. In a world increasingly characterized by
political and social conflicts, Mexico was marketed as an embodiment of
the highest ideals of Olympic harmony. At the same time, these efforts en-
compassed a manifest anxiety to demonstrate that the nation was no longer
a "land of *mañana*" but the "land of tomorrow," one truly capable of han-
dling its Olympic responsibilities. Mestizaje (i.e., the outcome of racial and
cultural mixture) was still regarded in the Anglo world as a sign of "impurity" (and thus a metaphor for disorganization and "non-Western" capa-

bilities). A central component to the promotional strategy of the Cultural Olympics thus was to rework the negative stereotypes associated with Mexico's dominant mestizo identity by seeking to transform the notion of racial "mixture" from something derogatory to something positive. Hence, the nation's "Indian" (read darker) component was positioned within a static romanticization of "folkloric authenticity"—no longer a burden to the nation's progress—while the country's "modern" (read whiter, European) face was celebrated as the forward-looking embodiment of a new cosmopolitanism.[14] Mexico's racial difference—as a nation of "mixed" racial heritage—was thus simultaneously highlighted yet erased: a picturesque notion of the country's indigenous traditions was to be celebrated while the lived reality of Mexico's poor, made up almost entirely of indigenous and darker-skinned mestizos, was completely ignored. The outcome nevertheless was to create an impression, for foreigners at least, of the evident harmony of diverse racial and ethnic groups all sharing a common national identity. This "harmonizing" of diversity would become a powerful symbol of Mexico's claim that the nation had found the successful formula for peaceful coexistence.

From Optimism to Anxiety:
The Aftermath of the Selection
of Mexico City to Host the Games

Contrary to expectations, Mexico City was the surprise victor in the vote by the International Olympic Committee (IOC) at Baden-Baden, Germany, at its October 1963 meeting.[15] Although a fuller accounting of the decision-making process still awaits historians, the records left behind by Avery Brundage (president of the IOC) are extremely helpful in understanding some of the important factors that impacted the final vote. "Both Detroit and Lyon were handicapped by NATO actions barring East Germans," Brundage later reflected in a series of confidential observations to himself in the wake of the decision. "The peculiar United States foreign policy for the last thirty years, which has lavishly spread hundreds of millions of dollars throughout the world but has left a lack of confidence abroad in the United States, did not help Detroit," he added.[16] Brundage's evident resentment of the ramifications of Cold War politics on sport was juxtaposed with his early and outright embrace of Mexico City as preferred choice for the 1968 Games. This bias was revealed, for example, in a private letter following the vote to Mexican José de Jesús Clark Flores, a member of the IOC since 1952 and with whom Brundage had a close working relationship. "I may say that there are many who are still stunned ... at the success of Mexico,"

Brundage wrote, adding: "I understand that I have been criticized in certain quarters for leaning too far in the direction of Popocatepetl [i.e., the famed snow-capped volcano once clearly visible from the capital], but I don't think any harm was done."[17] In the wake of the decision, Mexicans would soon grapple with the significance of this unprecedented achievement.

An open celebration in Mexico followed the vote at Baden-Baden, but the euphoria of victory was short lived. For the next three years, the country was increasingly wracked by political controversy related to a central question: How could a developing nation realistically afford the expense of hosting the Olympics? Winning the bid had been the obsession of out-going president Adolfo López Mateos (1958–64), a populist in economic and political matters and an avid athlete himself. His successor, Gustavo Díaz Ordaz (1964–70), on the other hand, was a fiscal conservative who soon "felt he had been saddled with [the Olympic responsibility] by the previous administration."[18] For López Mateos—who successfully angled to become Chairman of the Mexican Organizing Committee shortly after he finished his term as president—Japan's massive investment of some 2.7 billion dollars to refurbish Tokyo in preparation for the 1964 Games was a model Mexico might emulate. This brash vision of leveraging the Olympics to highlight Mexico's developmental prowess, however, threatened to reopen latent political divisions over national development priorities. A raging debate over costs and the feasibility of hosting the Games shortly ensued. Thus the respected left-wing newsmagazine *Siempre!* editorialized at one point, "Mexico is clearly not in a condition to buy prestige at such a price."[19]

A second question also surfaced throughout the foreign press as the debate over costs intensified. Though generally worded in coded language, the implicit racial assumptions were nevertheless transparent. Could Mexico, still considered by many to be a "land of *mañana*," be counted on to organize an international event of such vast magnitude? Little more than a year following Mexico's victory at Baden-Baden, an editorial in the *Detroit News* criticized the country's "failure to hustle and bustle over the blessed event," barely hiding a subtext that the country's purportedly entrenched *mañana* attitude remained a liability.[20] Delays in construction (tied to the debate over financing and ensuing political disputes between the MOC and the Díaz Ordaz administration) also helped rekindle a preexisting debate concerning the alleged dangers of Mexico City's altitude (7,415 ft.) on athletes, a concern that had nearly doomed the country's chances in 1963. "At least half a year is needed to adapt to the oxygen-poor air," Copenhagen's *Extra Bladet* bemoaned, suggesting how "thin air" itself had become a metonym for underdevelopment, as if to suggest that even the country's air was not developed enough![21] As rumors circulated abroad that Mexico might bow out, Art Lentz, executive secretary of the U.S. Olympic Committee, optimistically told the press: "We could end up with the Games right back here in the U.S."[22]

Thus what was supposed to have been a golden opportunity to showcase the "new Mexico," threatened instead to divide the body politic and embarrass the nation's leadership precisely at its moment of developmental glory.[23] Two years after winning the bid, there were still few material signs of advancement to quell the chorus of foreign critics. At one point, according to a Mexican investigative report, by late summer 1965 President Díaz Ordaz was ready to "throw in the towel" altogether.[24] Although Brundage himself remained optimistic, the political stalemate between the MOC and the government was affecting morale both in and outside Mexico. By the following summer, Mexico faced not only the pressing reality of financial restraints but also the more abstract problem of credibility. If something was not resolved shortly, the country appeared poised to forfeit playing host altogether.

The sought-for resolution came in an unanticipated fashion. In late June 1966, former president Adolfo López Mateos announced that he was stepping down as chairman of the MOC. The official explanation was an urgent health concern, though others suspected clashes with President Díaz Ordaz over costs also played a role.[25] Immediately, Díaz Ordaz appointed the nation's leading architect, Pedro Ramírez Vázquez, at the time vice president in charge of construction within the MOC, to head the Organizing Committee. Ramírez Vázquez was neither a sports enthusiast, nor did he have any direct links to the International Olympic movement. Yet, he was a "man of the system" whose insider-outsider status was precisely what Díaz Ordaz believed necessary to shake up the MOC.[26] Barely a week after his appointment, Brundage sent Ramírez Vázquez a letter emphasizing the urgency of the image problem: "Unfortunately, because of the fact that all problems have not yet been settled and because of the altitude, there has been considerable unfavorable publicity. It is harmful both to Mexico and to the Olympic Movement. Journalists, as you know, are always seeking sensation and something to criticize adversely. The best answer is constructive action on the part of the Organizing Committee."[27]

In a press conference shortly after his appointment, Ramírez Vázquez announced in unequivocal terms that Mexico would stage an Olympics "that was not onerous for the country. . . . We will do nothing that cannot be fully justified in terms of its social utility in the life and development of our country."[28] Hence forward, the idea of an "Olympics of the cheap"[29] took hold, with planning shifted away from Adolfo López Mateos' push for expenditure, toward an emphasis on efficiency, utility, and display that would build upon Mexico's inherent advantages without forcing it to match those of Japan. Brundage himself was by then advocating as much, urging the Mexicans not to view the Olympics as "a competition in spending money" and to "stage the Games in a Mexican manner."[30] Under the direction of Rámirez Vázquez, planning took on a pragmatic emphasis marked by recognition of the country's—and the city's—resources as well as limitations. In the end, the country's $176 million investment amounted to a fraction of that expended by Japan on the 1964 Games.[31] Still, it was hardly an insignificant sum for a nation with pressing rural and urban development needs. Indeed, challenging the regime's choice of economic priorities would later become a rallying point for the student-led protests that erupted on the eve of the Games.

Organizing a Cultural Olympics

Almost immediately, Ramírez Vázquez announced that the MOC would launch an ambitious, broad-based cultural and visual arts program that came to be known as the Cultural Olympics. This program was integral to Ramírez Vázquez's overall strategy to reenergize Mexican support for the Olympics following nearly three years of divisions and doubts and thus "redistribute the expectations, responsibilities, and objectives for the Olympic year."[32] At the same time, however, the Cultural Olympics would also serve the equally important function of shifting the terms of debate abroad. The latter challenge was perhaps best encapsulated in an unfortunate and evidently flippant remark made by a member of the Mexican Organizing Committee in 1964 to a reporter (following inspection of the Tokyo Olympics) and repeated often in the U.S. press: "We are not sure we can guarantee the organization of these games. But the weather will be nice."[33] The remark was costly precisely because it resonated with racialized U.S. and European stereotypes of Mexico lying in the "disorganized South," despite the erroneousness of that assumption (Mexico City being anything but "tropical"). Brundage made an explicit acknowledgement of this image problem in public remarks to President Díaz Ordaz at a meeting of the IOC held in fall 1966 in Mexico City: "[A]s you know, sometimes Mexico has had the reputation of being the land of *mañana*. I kept time with my watch and everything was perfectly coordinated and happened just as [you] had programmed it. We are not going to worry about the Olympic Games."[34] In follow-up letters, however, Brundage repeatedly underscored "the necessity of constructive publicity."[35] He later reiterated, for instance, "Mexico can lose all the intangible benefits which come from staging the Olympic Games if the publicity is not favorable."[36]

The idea of a cultural component was nominally part of the Olympic charter, yet Mexico was the first host country to turn an emphasis on culture into an integral aspect of the Games themselves. Mexico's "Cultural Olympics" program involved twenty separate spheres of activities (mirroring the twenty athletic contests), and ranged from exhibitions of modern scientific advances, to a graphic arts program, film, dance, music, poetry, and theater productions. There was also a "youth camp" and an international sculpture competition.[37] The Mexican state had vast experience in organizing cultural events, and the MOC, working on a tight budget, managed to pull together an incredible array of presentations from around the world. The final program totaled some 1,500 events (over 550 of which were dispersed throughout the republic) and incorporated the participation of many of the country's leading artists and intellectuals, not to mention the hundreds of students, journalists, and state bureaucrats who each came to play a role. "The goal," explained an article in *Saturday Review,* was to foment a "total 'cultural presence,' [through a] program expressing the theme of peace in a world 'where the old are still burying the young.'"[38]

Five components characterized the Cultural Olympics as conveyed to the public. First, there was the iconic use of the peace dove and other references to Mexico's "peace-maker" role in international affairs. Second, was the elaboration and dissemination of an official logo that conveyed a cosmopolitan, "forward-looking" sensibility. Third, there was the elevated presence of women as participants, suggesting the country's "modern" values. Fourth was the elaborate staging of folkloric performances, culminating in the arrival of the Olympic flame at the pre-Hispanic site of Teotihuacán, which underscored the country's cultural "authenticity" but also Mexico's unique commitment to racial and ethnic harmony. Finally, there was the liberal use of bright colors in general, thus reinforcing a popular association with Mexico as a festive yet exotic land. As part of a broader strategy to rally enthusiasm for the Games abroad as well as among the Mexican populace, these components became key reference points in public discussions and promotional literature. Together, they comprised a vision of Mexico in which the nation became a land, on one hand, whose international traditions demonstrated profound tolerance of political difference while, on the other, a place where indigenous cultural traditions were framed by and interfaced seamlessly with a forward-looking embrace of modern values. Collectively, they worked to reorient domestic and foreign opinion away from questioning the practicality of Mexico as host toward viewing the nation as an ideal location during a moment of international discord.

The first component, the promotion of a direct association between Mexico and world peace, was without question the most pervasive. Mexico's boasted "independent position with respect to the major world powers,"[39] despite its rhetorical aspects, had played an important, if not decisive, role in the IOC's 1963 Baden-Baden decision. Indeed, in a world characterized by superpower rivalry where the "third world" and Latin America in particular were increasingly portrayed by the media as points of global conflagration, Mexico had managed to navigate around the major ideological fault lines of the Cold War, most notably with regard to revolutionary Cuba. Alone among Latin American nations, Mexico had resisted U.S. pressures to sever its diplomatic relations with Fidel Castro's Cuba. At the same time, Mexico became increasingly central to U.S. strategic relations with Latin America, even secretly passing information about Cuba to U.S. authorities. Thus, Mexico was able simultaneously to defend its "revolutionary" credentials while underscoring its allegiance to liberal principles, including capitalist-led development.[40] Both former president López Mateos and current president Díaz Ordaz invoked the stance of Mexico as "peace maker" often and it readily became a leitmotif for the Games.[41] As *Excélsior,* the nation's leading newspaper, editorialized in reference to Ramírez Vázquez's plans, the cultural element "will carry to all nations a true reflection of the spirit of Mexico, which aspires to the elevation, harmony, and balance of humankind, [and] projects [those aspirations] toward international understanding and collaboration, peace and justice."[42] One example of how these ideas were promoted internationally was in the commissioning by the MOC of an ambitious documentary film project titled, *La Paz* that would explore "peace" in its biological, anthropological, psychological, historical, and sociological dimensions. Significantly, the rationale for funding the film was that the subject matter was "very in line with the norms of fraternity and peace that have distinguished Mexico's actions internationally."[43]

The most prominent manifestation, however, was the universal display of the silhouetted white dove of peace, which became a central icon of the graphics arts program. Rámirez Vázquez later recounted the icon's origins in the organization of "a contest to come up with a dove design that would symbolize peace without resembling the Holy Spirit or the one done by Picasso."[44] The simple yet elegant final design was meant to symbolize the "fraternal coexistence among all peoples of the world"[45] and, in short time, became an important feature in virtually all aspects of official promotion for the Games. As a later commemorative volume describes:

> The symbol of peace became a constant image along principal thorough-fares, as well as along wide tree-lined avenues, narrow streets, residential areas and in working-class communities. Giant plastic sheets with the white figure of the dove of peace superimposed on rose, yellow, green or blue backgrounds also graced [Olympic] installations. . . . Complementing a similar campaign of billboard advertising, tens of thousands of stickers bearing the

symbol of peace were placed in display windows and business establish-
ments, in study areas and on transportation media. Mexico City was covered
by symbols that accentuated both the universal desire for greater understanding among all peoples and the underlying objective that constituted the
spirit of the Games.[46]

In conjunction with this display was the elaboration of an official motto for
the Games: "Todo es posible en la paz" (Everything is Possible in Peace),
which found its way onto billboards and numerous other spaces. It was a
phrase that Mexicans undoubtedly identified with former President Benito
Juárez's revered statement, "El respecto al derecho ajeno es la paz" (Respect for the Rights of Others is Peace), and which formed the basis for the
nation's celebrated noninterventionist stance. Mexico's historical ideal was
grafted onto that of the Olympic movement and celebrated for all to see.[47]

A second component of this promotional strategy was the creation and
dissemination of the Olympic logo itself, a psychedelic, Op Art image
meant to epitomize the nation's cultural heritage and cosmopolitan aspirations. As an internal memorandum discussed, in reference to the graphic
arts program in general and for the official logo in particular, images used
to promote the Mexico City Games should "spring forth from needs and
express the grave uncertainties of our epoch, based in Mexico's origins, customs and ways of being and that maintain, at the same time, consistency
and uniformity."[48] Rooted, on one hand, in Huichol indigenous design, yet
at the same time clearly influenced by the avant-garde Op Art aesthetic then
in vogue, the MEXICO68 logo achieved a truly unique fusion of cultural
sensibilities.[49] Even today, the image retains much of its original resonance
and invokes the vibrant optimism of an earlier era. Ironically, given the significance of the image for Mexico's self-representation, the final design of
the logo was created by two foreign graphic artists: Lance Wyman, of the
United States, and Peter Murdoch, his British associate. Their participation
resulted from an invitation by Eduardo Terrazas (head of the Graphic Arts
Program for the Cultural Olympics) to join in a design contest for the
graphic arts program. The fact that non-Mexicans would be considered as
part of the design team (at that point, Wyman and Murdoch were still technically competing for the commission) was a clear indication that Ramírez
Vázquez was eager for new perspectives that would help break through the
tired stereotypes by which Mexico was traditionally labeled.

Arriving in Mexico for the first time, Wyman recalled how he and
Murdoch "were given free rein" in terms of ideas. "The only thing I remember as a guideline was the sleeping man with the sombrero did not
properly represent Mexico."[50] Indeed, Rámirez Vázquez later explained
that publicity needed to go beyond the "charro [i.e., Mexican mariachi]

and all that, because that's typical, its picturesque, but it doesn't convey confidence as far as a capacity for organization."[51] Clearly, the logo needed to convey the cosmopolitan, "Mexico of tomorrow," not the sleepy image of a "Mexico of *mañana.*" For the next eleven days Wyman and Murdoch struggled with different concepts, constantly returning to the Mexican streets, markets, and, in particular, to the new Museum of Anthropology to garner ideas. "We wanted something that would clearly relate the Olympic games to Mexico," Wyman explained to a reporter at the time. "One way of doing this would be to use a recognizable element such as the Aztec calendar, or typical Mexican folk art forms."[52] But that would have based the final imagery in a folkloric element at the expense of highlighting the modern connotations of hosting the Games. Wyman later recalled that they were "starting to sense panic" when suddenly the design came to him: "I hit on the idea of generating the 68 number forms from the geometry of the five Olympic rings. From there I developed the letter forms of MEXICO and the logo was born."[53] What emerged would be both quintessentially modern yet rooted in Mexican visual tradition. Wyman said of the design: "The 5 rings to the 68 to the MEXICO'68 was a very natural progression that was preceded and influenced by many visits to the Museum of Anthropology to study Mexican pre-Columbian design and Mexican folk art, by taking in the vitality and aesthetic of the Mexican markets, and by the influence of "Op" art and the powerful work of Bridget Riley and [Victor] Vasarely."[54] A writer would later describe the visual impact of his ideas as "Quetzalcoatl doing the Op Art twist."[55]

Asked recently to reflect on the impact of his efforts on foreigners' perceptions of the Games, Wyman described the role of the graphic arts in terms that directly reflected Rámirez Vázquez's own stated objectives: "I suspect the logo and the entire design program gave a sense of being organized and dealing with the responsibilities of hosting the games despite some of the difficult things that went down during the preparations."[56]

At the same time, a third discursive component to the Games focused precisely on the significance of "folklore" and "cultural heritage" to national belonging and international harmony. Yet the open celebration of traditional cultural practices ultimately served to underscore the *modernity* of Mexico by framing those practices within carefully scripted performances largely confined to a paying audience of foreign visitors. When he initially announced the cultural program, Ramírez Vázquez envisioned an equal celebration of "folkloric" and "modern" aesthetic sensibilities, thereby underscoring and simultaneously validating the composite nature of humanity in an era of rapid modernization. To this end, each nation would be asked to bring "jointly with their athletic delegations" two works of art: "one representative of any one of its brilliant cultural stages

7.1 Graffiti-covered sculpture along the "Ruta de la Amistad" in present-day Mexico City. Photo: Eric Zolov.

of the past; the other, the best of its contemporary art."[57] The sum total of these contributions would provide nothing less than "an overall view of universal art, and, through it, both man himself and the footprints he has left on the sands of time."[58] However, in practice the Cultural

Olympics' emphasis on formal presentations of culture (whether as art-work, dance/theatre, or otherwise) contributed to the common perception at the time that a sharp line divided "traditional" from "modern" cultural practices. Such perceptions were not only contrary to lived reality, in which the line between "traditional" and "modern" was much more blurred, but furthermore contributed to an artificial romanticization (or, reification) of the "traditional" as something utterly distinct from the "modern," an Other to be admired for its "authenticity"—yet no longer regarded as a burden or threat to development—at a moment when the tide of capitalist modernization was rapidly transforming local cultures across the planet.

One significant example of such formal representation of traditional (or "folkloric") cultural performance was through dance. In Mexico, re-gional dancers would be brought to the capital to "allow us to show our visitors the full scope of our popular traditions."[59] Ramírez Vázquez an-nounced that participating nations would also be invited to send their own dance groups to perform: "These events will not only help to make all our respective traditions better known by the others, but it will also make the participants in the athletic events feel the warmth of their presence with their own native customs, costumes, and popular art, helping to keep their morale and their spirits high, which in turn will undoubtedly lead them to better performances on track and field."[60]

Newspaper commentary following the announcement applauded the opportunity to showcase Mexico's folkloric traditions. "The sentiment, color, rhythm, and originality of our regional dances . . . will give an accu-rate projection of the immortal side of Mexico,"[61] one paper editorialized. Mexico's Ballet Folklórico—which Brundage once described as "a spectac-ular advertisement that could not be improved, for your country"[62]—was envisioned playing a special role through the creation of a "Ballet of the Five Continents." The celebration of national "folk cultures" thus not only highlighted Mexico's commitment to the broader theme of the Olympics as a peaceful meeting of humanity, but reinforced an image of Mexico—for it-self and, especially, for the world—as a cosmopolitan yet culturally inte-grative nation-state. This sentiment was aptly captured in a commemorative volume later produced by the Mexican Organizing Com-mittee: "Folklore, a common heritage, implies community. It can exist only in a harmonious, stable, society, one in which life has a meaning and the world a sense of order."[63] The controlled, stage-managed display of "folk-lore" thus directly contributed to the implicitly racialized language of a "Mexico of Tomorrow" by underscoring the nonintrusive nature of "folk tradition" to the broader goals of modernization that Mexico would ably demonstrate in the staging of the Games themselves.

Perhaps the supreme reflection of this strategy was in the symbolic reenactment of the meeting of Old and New Worlds carried out through the arrival of the Olympic flame. Although organizers dismissed as mere coincidence the fact that the Opening Ceremony fell on "Día de la Raza" (literally, "Day of the Race" otherwise known in the U.S. as Columbus Day), the importance of the date could hardly be overlooked.[64] The flame itself traversed the same route traveled by Hernán Cortés (via the port of Veracruz), and was carefully timed to arrive the night before the Opening Ceremony (October 11th) at the ancient city of Teotihuacán where "twenty thousand spectators watched in awe [as] three thousand dancers . . . revived the ceremony of the 'New Fire'—a ritual performed by ancient Mexicans [sic] every 52 years."[65] The symbolism of this carefully choreographed spectacle conveyed a clear rewriting of the conquest itself: Erased was the violence of subjugation in order to highlight the nation's "heritage" and the birth of the mestizo as the harmonious new subject of this meeting of two distinct worlds. Thus, "race" was emptied of any political content. Here, the indigenous and the European ways were presented as harmoniously fused, the conquest itself transformed into a celebration of cultural difference and syncretism. Paradoxically, the performance simultaneously objectified the indigenous by conflating the wide range of Mexico's native cultures (both living and defeated) into a singular image associated with the Aztec—commonly ascribed in nationalist narratives as constituting the nation's "primordial" essence.

A fourth discursive component was delivered through images of the "liberated" Mexican woman. Foreigners writing about Mexico still generally regarded the country as a *machista* society, a place where middle-class women were routinely denied access to social mobility by men who "throw up invisible walls to keep [them] quietly at home, away from the dangers and achievements of the competitive world."[66] This machismo was directly associated with traditional values seen to be rooted in a "backward" Spanish culture. Such images of female second-class citizenry clearly contradicted official language emphasizing the "modernizing nation"; highlighting the new, "modern" role of women in Mexican society became part of the broader promotional campaign of the Games. One example of how this transpired was in the realm of fashion, namely the required uniforms for the 1,170 event hostesses (*edecanes*), the majority of whom were evidently young women, recruited and specially trained to greet visitors. The idea in designing these uniforms, as Ramírez Vázquez later explained, was to create a style that "looks good on a girl who's chubby, or one who's skinny, or tall . . . that will identify [her], so that all the world will recognize that, well, she is an *edecan*."[67] American reporters (overwhelmingly male) certainly noticed the visible presence of these *edecanes,* such as the journalist who praised the "[p]retty girls in psychedelic miniskirts."[68]

This use of vanguard fashion suggests the ways in which women—and especially, middle- and upper-class, generally lighter-skinned women—were specifically recruited to present an image of a modern Mexico, not only as a land "young," "beautiful," and "inviting"—here, continuing a marketing strategy dating to the 1940s—but now also as a country where traditional machismo no longer circumvented social mobility.[69] Avery Brundage himself highlighted the "open" role of Mexican women as a sign of the nation's modern coming of age, writing in his diary of the Olympics: "Mexican girls parade in their little cars around the [athletic] village to look for a contact with athletes they want to entertain. . . . This is something that in Spanish-speaking countries had never been done before!"[70]

Another way in which the image of the "modern woman" was used during the Games was in the selection of the twenty-year-old Mexican hurdler, Norma Enriqueta Basilio (a light-skinned *mestiza*), to carry the Olympic flame to its final destination for the Opening Ceremony. The question of whom "should carry the Olympic torch arriving at the stadium" was at the top of the list of issues raised by Ramírez Vázquez as soon as he took over as Chairman of the MOC.[71] In an internal memorandum, Ramírez Vázquez underscored that in Japan an athlete "born the same day as the explosion over Hiroshima" had been chosen as torchbearer.[72] Clearly, he sought someone of like symbolic value. As historian Amy Bass writes, "The first woman to light the Olympic flame, the farmer's daughter presented an image that emblematically spoke to an increasingly feminist political tenor in Mexico, simultaneously symbolic of both the preservation of a rural heritage and a quest for modernity."[73] This sentiment was reflected in a letter to Brundage a year later by a man in Ohio who wrote, "I saw her [Basilio] light the fire [for the Opening Ceremony] on T.V., and I will never forget that short but epochal and beautiful feat. . . . Ever since I saw her, I have had the compunction to find out who she is and let her know how I feel about her 'First in the World' accomplishment."[74] Basilio thus helped invoke those images associated with the "new Mexico" favored by the public relations team of the MOC: a nation young, vibrant, inexorably *moving forward* and yet fortified by the uniqueness of its cultural and racial heritage.

Finally, a fifth component central to the promotion of the Cultural Olympics was the deliberate and liberal use of bright colors in all aspects associated with the Games. This was true not only in the graphic arts programming in general—where promotional materials showed the evident influence of Andy Warhol's Pop Art aesthetic—but in the explicit transformation of the city itself. As notes from a brainstorming session concerning the recently finished Olympic Village made clear, one way to confront the "aesthetic problem" of the new building complex—which according to the notes had the "aspect of a strong fort"—was "to make one forget by [using] splotches of color." "A painted fence is no longer a fence," the group concluded with a slight hint of irony.[75] In other examples, huge expanses of pavement surrounding the Aztec and Olympic Stadiums were painted in bright pink, orange, and blue hues, emulating the MEXICO68 design and thus, in effect, transforming the stadiums into giant Op Art performance pieces.[76] "The plaza in front of the Olympic Stadium is awash with magenta and orange waves," an article in *Life* described, "a spectacular test of the paint to be applied to some city streets."[77] "Wherever the visitor looks all is color,"[78] Ruben Salazar later wrote in the *Los Angeles Times*. Even the walls of the poorer neighborhoods bordering the area of the Olympic Village (in the southern part of the city) had been painted in "shocking pink, purple and yellow—temporarily hiding the misery."[79]

Although the "mañana" label remained as an entrenched benchmark against which to measure Mexican readiness, by the spring of 1968 a new tone literally set in bright, psychedelic colors cast perceptions of the Olympic organization in a more forgiving light. Soon the media latched onto the idea that Mexico was "creating an atmosphere of the ultimate fiesta,"[80] a trope Ramírez Vázquez himself heartily endorsed. "We Mexicans are by character 'great fiesteros,'" he was quoted as saying in the U.S. media, "so our Olympics will be a big party for the world."[81] Certainly the question of organization was in the forefront for at least some U.S. officials, as revealed in a February 1968 internal memorandum sent by the Legal Attaché of the FBI in Mexico City to FBI Director J. Edgar Hoover: "There is a danger that Mexico's 'manana' policy of procrastination will result in frantic efforts at the last minute to get ready."[82] Yet while the "mañana label" no doubt remained for various skeptics, in public referencing of the Olympics in the media there was a notable shift as the date of the Games approached. One example of this was a story that spring in *Saturday Review* in which the inevitable question, "Will Mexico, land of mañana, be ready on time?" was used as the central narrative frame.[83] (The interrogation appeared directly in the article itself and was repeated for emphasis as a photo caption.) Upon reading the story itself, however, one quickly discovered that "the question that has been asked so condescendingly ever since Mexico was awarded its first Olympic Games at Baden-Baden in 1963" was mistaken; the Olympics were, in fact, coming together on time.[84] In refuting the "mañana label," moreover, the article focused almost entirely on events organized under the rubric of the Cultural Olympics. In another example, a story appearing that summer in the *New Yorker* noted that "In every possible way, [the Mexicans] are using their great talent for display . . . to prove that 'Mexico is no longer the land of *mañana*' . . ."[85] After describing the various events of the Cultural Olympics, the article concluded, "It should all look splendid on color television."[86]

Despite Mexico's various efforts to transcend the negative connotations of the term *mañana,* the notion of staging an Olympics in a "developing country" brought with it a degree of inherent uncertainty and perhaps even mild risk. Travel writings, for example, frequently warned about drinking the water and eating food on the street. On one hand, such warnings reinforced racist associations of Mexicans with dirt, disease, and disorder. On the other, however, by including such warnings within stories that heralded "the biggest fiesta since the Greeks got together at Olympia,"[87] as one writer for *Saturday Review* proclaimed, the impact of such negative associations was arguably reduced to the level of trivialized exotica one should anticipate when crossing the border. This was especially true for those who chose to drive to the Olympics, a preferred choice for many. "The drive will be an *adventure,*" emphasized *Sports Illustrated;* "Something different will happen each day."[88] This description was literally placed in the context of bright colors when the author described how he inadvertently had his car painted purple by street children in an apparent misunderstanding of the words "cuidar" (to watch over) and "pintar" (to paint). Another article in *Look* similarly narrated: "Everything in this strange country is *strange,* to Mexican as well as to foreigner, and there is some little twist to the most "ordinary" event. . . . To us, Mexico seemed not only "foreign" but almost completely unpredictable. The absence of order in the European or American sense is what exasperates. It is also what delights and rejuvenates."[89] To enjoy this, as the motorclub aficionado Dan Sanborn put it, one had "better be able to roll with the punches." "Any old ladies better stay home!," he admonished, perhaps only half in jest.[90]

By the spring of 1968 Americans appeared thoroughly enthused about the prospect of Mexico playing host to the Games. So, too, did most Mexicans.[91] Few would have anticipated the eruption of a massive student movement shortly thereafter, a movement that used as a rallying point latent concerns about the wisdom of hosting the Games. As a result of the ensuing violence, by the eve of the Opening Ceremony the public relations strategy emphasizing Mexico's unique contribution to international peace, racial harmony, and cosmopolitanism so assiduously constructed by the MOC over the past two years lay largely in tatters.

This is not the place for a detailed discussion of the student-led movement, the definitive history of which, at any rate, has yet to be written. In short, following somewhat murky origins in a series of seemingly minor protests and scuffles with police at the end of July, by September the government found itself facing wide-scale protest by many youth as well as working- and middle-class supporters throughout the capital. Ostensibly, the protesters challenged the validity of hosting the Olympics though in fact their attacks were aimed more at the authoritarian nature of Mexican society than against the Games per se. Significantly, student protesters reappropriated graphic elements used by the Organizing Committee to convey their outrage at government hypocrisy and repression. For example, the MEXICO68 image often appeared on posters next to caricatures of Mexican symbols of repression (such as the hated *granaderos* or riot police). One particularly effective poster used the image of a tank with Olympic rings for the tread, in a clear desire to transform Wyman's original concept. "In the end," writes Tim Rohan, "Wyman had provided the students with a visual language for dissent that spoke volumes. The tools of the oppressors became the language of the protestors."[92]

In another example, white doves of peace silhouetted on walls throughout the capital were splattered with red paint, their message of peaceful coexistence openly subverted. As one foreign journalist expressed, in the context of the recent repression the images now suggested that of "a bleeding heart."[93]

Following the massacre of unarmed protesters on October 2 that put a definitive end to the demonstrations, the headline for a travel article in the *Washington Post* warned, in an ironic twist on a familiar theme, "At Olympic Time, Mexicans Worry About Manana": this time, literally the post-riot *mañana* and whether the Olympics would be held at all.[94] State Department analyses of the events stated confidence in the Mexican security forces' ability to "control the situation," while nevertheless capturing the essence of the problem: "What does worry Mexican officials is the image projected by the disturbances and the impact on the Olympics in which they have so heavily invested."[95] This theme was repeated elsewhere. "Yet if people here are relieved that the spectre of *mañana* has temporarily been exorcised," wrote a reporter for *Sports Illustrated,* "they are still a bit shaky over *ayer*—yesterday."[96] Although Brundage quickly reassured the public that the Games would continue (along with the State Department, he remained confident in Mexico's security apparatus), the sense of wonderment and color was irrevocably clouded. "[I]t is hard to be in Mexico City now and think just of fun and games,"[97] one author wrote. On the opening day of the Olympics the *New York Times* ran a large, front-page photograph showing the Aztec stadium surrounded by soldiers. Neither the giant Alexander Calder sculpture nor the psychedelic swirls that enveloped the stadium were rendered visible.[98]

Conclusions

Hosting the 1968 Olympics was supposed to herald Mexico's entry into the "first world" club of nations, a public relations jubilation that would mark the nation's coming of age. Increased tourism, investment, foreign accolades, and an animated nationalist spirit were all part of the "intangible benefits," as Brundage had once articulated, anticipated in return for successfully playing host. Many, though not all, of these benefits were canceled out by the violence on the eve of the Games. For Mexicans, the Olympics would be forever marked by that violence—some remaining firmly convinced that it was the students (or international communism) to blame, others regarding the government as the culprit. Rather than images of vibrant color, younger Mexicans are raised with the perspective of an Olympics framed in the grainy reality of black and white photos featuring student protest and government response. The tremendous logistical accomplishments and artistic fervor that were a direct outgrowth of planning for the 1968 Games and Cultural Olympics are today either overlooked, or hastily dismissed. The brightly painted sculptures along the "Ruta de la Amistad," meant to symbolize the nation's progressive traditions, are now silent, defaced, peeling tombstones of a modernist moment defeated. (See Figure 7.1)

By contrast, contemporary U.S. history texts on the 1960s inevitably include a black and white image of that famous gesture of fisted defiance by Smith and Carlos. The photo itself conveys a sense of solemn, principled conviction; easily masked is the fact that these athletes were booed and forced to return home.[99] For Americans, this image came to symbolize the humanity of African American struggle. At the same time, it also marked an important transitional moment in the Civil Rights movement when a belief in nonviolent struggle (heralded by Martin Luther King, recently assassinated) would shortly be eclipsed by the influence of a more radical approach advocated by the Black Panthers. The "power salute" by Smith and Carlos was and remains a contested image that has come to symbolize the unfulfilled promises of American justice and equality for all. The Olympics themselves, however, are subsumed in this image as mere background text, a platform for the enactment of such bold protest testimony. Mexico is not "represented" anywhere in the photo and it would be easy to overlook the actual site of the Olympics as particularly relevant.

Throughout the 1960s Mexicans struggled on two fronts: on one hand, against the hypocrisy of a political party *cum* government whose practices mocked a public façade of democratic process and respect for human rights; and, on the other, to overcome the sense of marginalization and denigration that located Mexico as a nation still "developing." Accepting the challenge of the Olympics created an opportunity for the ruling regime to displace domestic criticism, while recasting entrenched stereotypes regarding Mexican "efficiency" and "stability" in a new light. Arguably, the strategy worked, as evidenced by the growing public support and foreign enthusiasm as the date of the Games approached. The challenges posed by the student movement, however, changed everything. As a result of the protests and ensuing state repression, Mexicans and foreigners alike were reminded that beneath the psychedelic, Op Art twists of MEXICO68 lurked a grittier reality of economic inequalities and political authoritarianism that a highly orchestrated public relations strategy and celebratory spectacle alone could not make disappear.

Notes

*   Support for research came from the Provost's Office of Franklin & Marshall College. On this and earlier drafts, I wish to acknowledge the generous and constructive commentary of numerous persons, including Rachel Adams, Amy Bass, Emmy Bretón, Robert Holden, Ariel Rodríguez Kuri, Anne Rubenstein, Arthur Schmidt, and commentary by participants of the Washington Area Seminar of Latin American Historians (2001). A slightly different version of this essay was published in *The Americas* (October 2004).

1. The historiography on 1968 in Mexico is vast and continues to expand, especially as new access to government documents becomes available. With very few exceptions, however, virtually all of the literature focuses on the question of state repression and student protest to the utter exclusion of the broader cultural context of this period. The recent historiography from the Mexican perspective includes, Sergio Aguayo Quezada, *1968: Los archivos de la violencia* (Mexico City: Editorial Grijalbo/Reforma, 1998); Raúl Alvarez Garín, *La Estrela de Tlatelolco: Una reconstrución histórica del Movimiento estudiantil del 68* (Mexico City: Grijalbo, 1998), Julio Scherer García & Carlos Monsiváis, *Parte de Guerra: Tlatelolco 1968* (Mexico City: Nuevo Siglo/Aguilar, 1999); Carlos Montemayor, *Rehacer la Historia: Análisis de los nuevos documentos del 2 de octubre de 1968 en Tlatelolco* (Mexico City: Planeta, 2000). Important exceptions to this trend include Ariel Rodríguez Kuri, "El otro 68: Política y estilo en la organización de los juegos olímpicos de la ciudad de México," *Relaciones* 19 (Fall 1998): 109–129, Jorge Volpi, *La imaginación y el poder: Una historia intellectual de 1968* (Mexico: Era, 1998); and Eric Zolov, *Refried Elvis: The Rise of the Mexican Counterculture* (Berkeley: University of California Press, 1999).

2. The definitive discussion of the Carlos and Smith protest salute and its legacy in the United States is Amy Bass, *Not the Triumph but the Struggle: The 1968 Olympics and the Making of the Black Athlete* (Minneapolis: University of Minnesota Press, 2002).

3. The following four paragraphs are drawn from an earlier essay, "Discovering a Land 'Mysterious and Obvious': The Renarrativizing of Postrevolutionary Mexico" in Gilbert Joseph, Anne Rubenstein, and Eric Zolov, eds., *Fragments of a Golden Age: The Politics of Popular Culture in Mexico Since 1940* (Durham, NC: Duke University Press, 2001), 236–239.

4. See, for example, Edward M. Conley, "The Americanization of Mexico," *Review of Reviews* 32 (1905): 724–725; Mauricio Tenorio-Trillo, "1910 Mexico City: Space and Nation in the City of the Centenario," *Journal of Latin American Studies* 28, no.1 (February 1996): 75–104.

5. Alex Saragoza, "The Selling of Mexico: Tourism and the State, 1929–1952" in Joseph, et al., eds., *Fragments of a Golden Age*, 91–115.

6. For an excellent discussion of how a common, nationalist discourse of belonging was negotiated see Mary Kay Vaughan, *Cultural Politics in Revolution: Teachers, Peasants, and Schools in Mexico, 1930–1940* (Tucson: University of Arizona Press, 1997).

7. Helen Delpar, *The Enormous Vogue of Things Mexican: Cultural Relations between the United States and Mexico, 1920–1935* (Tuscaloosa: University of Alabama Press, 1992), 146.

8. Robert Scott Burns, "Simpatico, Senor! [*sic*]," *Travel* 99, May 1953, 15.

9. Milton Bracker, "'Beisbol' Hits a 'Jonron' Down Mexico Way," *New York Times Magazine,* June 9, 1946, 21.

10. "Mexico—Waking Up After a Long Siesta," *Scholastic* 68, April 5, 1956, 11. This was a reassessment that was also being extended to the rest of Latin America, as reflected in a U.S. government-produced guidebook for enlisted servicemen: "Latin American countries long ago were dubbed the 'lands of mañana' (tomorrow) to signify the leisurely tempo for which Latins have been noted for centuries. But in recent years the meaning has changed. Today, modern progress is transforming most of the countries south of the border and has made them truly 'lands of tomorrow.'" (*South of the Border* [DC: Government Printing Office, 1958], 3.)

11. "Proyección de México."

12. "Promoción para México y las Olimpiadas," *Jueves de Excélsior,* June 20, 1968, n.p.

13. Michael E. Latham, *Modernization as Ideology: American Social Science and 'Nation Building' in the Kennedy Era* (Chapel Hill: University of North Carolina Press, 2000).

14. This strategy continued a trajectory dating to the late nineteenth century. See Mauricio Tenorio-Trillo, *Mexico at the World's Fairs: Crafting a Modern Nation* (Berkeley: University of California Press, 1996); Zolov, "Discovering a Land 'Mysterious and Obvious'."

15. The meeting was originally to be held in Nairobi, Kenya, but was changed at the last moment due to conflict over South Africa's participation. Mexico won on the first round of voting, with the final tally as such: Mexico (30); Detroit (14); Lyon (12); Buenos Aires (2). Press reports later suggested that Mexico received all eight votes from the Soviet Bloc, an allegation never verified one way or the other. For recent historical treatments see Rodríguez Kuri, "El otro 68";

Kevin Witherspoon, "Protest at the Pyramid: The 1968 Mexico City Olympics and the Politicization of the Olympic Games" (Ph.D. Diss., Florida State University, 2003).

16. "Observations on the Selection of Mexico City as the Host for the Games of the XIX Olympiad in 1968 (Confidential)," November 12, 1963, Avery Brundage Collection (hereafter: ABC), Box 178, "Organizing Committee, 1962–65"; Richard Espy, *The Politics of the Olympic Games* (Berkeley: University of California Press, 1979), 76–82.

17. Avery Brundage to General Clark, November 13, 1963, ABC, Box 52, "Gen. José de J. Clark Flores, 1962–1965."

18. Terrance W. McGarry, "The Real Nitty-Gritty on the 1968 Olympics," *The News* (Mexico City), September 26, 1966, 21. Located in ABC, Box 139, "Newspaper Clippings, 1961–69." Enrique Krauze writes: "In economic matters, Díaz Ordaz had always shown great responsibility. . . . Under López Mateos, he had opposed Mexico's bid for the Olympic Games, expressing doubts about the cost to Mexico or the benefits it would supposedly bring to the country" (*Biography of Power: A History of Modern Mexico, 1810–1996,* translated by Hank Heifetz [New York: Harper Collins, 1997], 680–681).

19. Quoted in McGarry, "Real Nitty-Gritty."

20. Pete Waldmeir, "Mexico Lagging on Olympics; Detroit Told it Has Chance," *Detroit News,* January 13, 1965. Located in ABC, Box 178, "Press Department, 1968." See also, Kevin Witherspoon, "Thin Air and Lofty Dreams: The Altitude Controversy and the 1968 Olympics," paper presented at the American Historical Association, Washington, D.C. (January 2004).

21. Beatrice Trueblood, ed., *Mexico 68,* vol. 2 (Mexico City: Miguel Galas, SA, 1969), 14.

22. Waldmeir, "Mexico Lagging." Among the various rumors that surfaced during the 1968 Student Movement was one that suggested the student protests were actually sponsored by disgruntled Olympic organizers in the United States, who pined for a way to force the Games back to Detroit. I thank Amy Bass for bringing this point to my attention.

23. Zolov, "Discovering a Land 'Mysterious and Obvious,'" 235.

24. Horacio Quiñones, *Buro de Investigación Política,* August 23, 1965. Located in ABC, Box 139, "Mexico: Newspaper Clippings." According to the informant cited by Quiñones, on learning of the estimated costs for the Olympics Díaz Ordaz reportedly stated: "Señores, si esto es lo que nos cuestan las olimpiadas, tiro el arpa."

25. McGarry, "Real Nitty-Gritty." Adolfo López Mateos suffered from migraine headaches throughout his presidency. An operation in July 1966 revealed he had seven cerebral aneurysms. Although he survived, over the next three years he gradually lost control over his body and consciousness. He died on September 22, 1969, "ignorant of the silence and pain of his country" and the outcome of the Olympic Games he had so avidly pursued. (Krauze, *Biography of Power,* 664.)

26. Ariel Rodríguez Kuri, "Hacia México 68: Pedro Ramírez Vázquez y el proyecto olímpico," *Secuencia* 56 (May-August 2003): 47. Among the major

architectural achievements credited to Ramírez Vázquez were the recently constructed Museum of Anthropology and the "Aztec Stadium," slated for completion in time for the Olympics.

27. Avery Brundage to Pedro Ramírez Vázquez, July 24, 1966, ABC, Box 178,
"Organizing Committee, 1966."

28. Manuel Seyde, "'Una Olimpiada no Onersa para el País y Ningún Gasto sin una
Plena Justificación Social,' Dijo Ramírez Vázquez en su Discurso Ayer," *Excelsiór,* November 4, 1966. Located in ABC, Box 139, "Newspaper Clippings."

29. Rodríguez Kuri, "Hacia México 68," 39.

30. Avery Brundage to Pedro Ramírez Vázquez, November 1, 1966.

31. See Rodríguez Kuri, "Hácia Mexico 68," 63. Kuri's chart showing comparative Olympics financing is extremely useful. In examining the twelve Olympic
Games from 1936 to 1988, Rodríguez Kuri found that the Tokyo Games
(1964) were by far the most exorbitant. Japan spent more than thirteen times
that spent by Mexico and more than double the next highest figure—the
Games in South Korea in 1988! See also Joseph L. Arbena, "Hosting the Summer Olympic Games: Mexico City, 1968," in Joseph L. Arbena and David G.
LaFrance, eds., *Sport in Latin America and the Caribbean* (Wilmington, DE:
Scholarly Resources, 2003), 133–143.

32. Ródriguz Kuri, "Hacia México 68," 53. Internal MOC documents indicate
that plans for a significant cultural component were already under consideration by spring 1965. Nevertheless, Ramírez Vázquez elevated this component
to the status of a "dual Olympiad," with virtually equal status as the sporting
events themselves. See for example, José Clark to Lic. Agustín Yáñez (Secretario de Educación Pública), March 24, 1965, Comité Olímpico Internacional
[Hereafter COI], Gallery 7, Box 41, Folder 146, Achivo General de la Nación
[Hereafter AGN].

33. "Mexico City's Olympic Feats," *Fortune* (March 1968): 149.

34. "Versión Taquigráfica y Traducción a la Audiencia que El Señor Presidente de
la República Licenciado Don Gustavo Díaz Ordaz Concediera a los Honorables Miembros del Comité Olímpico Internacional," October 22, 1966, ABC,
Box 82, "Meeting of the Executive Board, Mexico City, October 22, 1966."

35. Avery Brundage to Ramírez Vázquez, November 1, 1966.

36. Avery Brundage to Pedro Ramírez Vázquez, November 28, 1966, ABC, Box
178, "Organizing Committee, 1966."

37. Trueblood, ed., *Mexico 68,* vol. 2, 275; Rodríguez Kuri, "El Otro 68";
Rodríguez Kuri, "Hácia México 68," 54; Pedro Ramírez Vázquez, "Mexico's
Cultural Olympics," *Americas* (October 1968): 15–19.

38. Frank Riley, "Of Poets and Pole Vaulters," *Saturday Review,* March 9, 1968,
58. See also "Programa General de los XIX Juegos Olímpicos," press release,
November 3, 1966, COI, Gallery 7, Box 41, Folder 4, AGN.

39. Beatrice Trueblood, ed., *Mexico 68,* vol. 1 (Mexico City: Miguel Galas, SA,
1969), 106.

40. Eric Zolov, "Toward an Analytical Framework for Assessing the Impact of the
1968 Student Movement on U.S.-Mexican Relations," *Journal of Iberian and
Latin American Studies* 9, no. 2 (December 2003): 41–68.

41. An internal memorandum of the MOC listed the specific instances in public speeches where President Díaz Ordaz referenced "concepts... of peace." ("Conceptos del Sr. Lic. Gustavo Díaz Ordaz, Sobre 'La Paz'," n.d., COI, Gallery 7, Box 41, Folder 32, AGN.)

42. "Humanismo Olímpico," *Excélsior,* November 5, 1966. Located in ABC, Box 139, "Mexico: Newspaper Clippings."

43. Luis Aveleyra Arroyo de Anda to Lic. Don Hugo B. Margain, September 10, 1966, COI, Gallery 7, Box 41, Folder 121, AGN. Among the prominent (and, interestingly, left-wing) figures that eventually collaborated were Pete Seeger and Dalton Trumbo. Despite the money and efforts put into this production it is not clear what became of the film itself or if it was ever realized.

44. Sergio Rivera Conde, "El Diseño en la XIX Olimpiada. Entrevista al arquitecto Pedro Ramírez Vázquez," *Creación y culture,* 1, no. 1 (July-August 1999): 33.

45. Beatrice Trueblood, ed., *Mexico 68,* vol. 4 (Mexico City: Miguel Galas, SA, 1969), 732.

46. Ibid., 731–735; "El Diseño en la XIX Olimpiada," 33.

47. The drawings were done by Mexico's well-known caricaturist Abel Quezada, who was specifically recruited for the campaign.

48. "Departamento de Ornato Urbano," n.d., COI, Gallery 7, Box 41, Folder 27, AGN.

49. The Huichol Indians populate an area in North Central Mexico and are widely known for their "psychedelic" artistic representations of dreams through a ritual consumption of peyote, which induces hallucinations. "Optical Art is a mathematically-oriented form of (usually) Abstract art, which uses repetition of simple forms and colors to create vibrating effects, moiré patterns, an exaggerated sense of depth, foreground-background confusion, and other visual effects." During the 1960s the term "Op Art" was coined to describe the work of a growing movement of painters led by Victor Vasarely and Bridget Riley who developed a unique style using Optical Art methods (www.artcyclopedia.com/history/optical.html, accessed on September 22, 2004).

50. Lance Wyman, e-mail communication with author, October 16, 2001.

51. Rivera Conde, "El Diseño en la XIX Olimpiada," 28.

52. Arthur Solin, "Mexico 68: Graphics for the XIX Olympiad," *Print* (May/June, 1968), 3.

53. Lance Wyman, e-mail communication with author, October 16, 2001. Curiously, Ramírez Vázquez recalls the evolution of this graphic quite differently and claims that it was his insight to draw the connection between Huichol design and Op Art. See Rivera Conde, "El Diseño en la XIX Olimpiada," 28.

54. Lance Wyman, e-mail communication with author, October 16, 2001.

55. Tim Rohan, "Games Plan," *Wallpaper* (September 2000), 158.

56. Lance Wyman, e-mail communication with author, October 16, 2001. For a discussion of the shift in direction in promotional strategy for the Olympics see Rodríguez Kuri, "Hácia México 68," 51–52.

57. Report by Mr. Pedro Ramírez Vázquez to the Executive Board of the IOC, Mexico City, October 22, 1966, 2. ABC, Box 82, "Meeting of Executive Board, Mexico City, October 22, 1966."

58. Ibid.

59. Ibid.

60. Ibid.

61. Gustavo Rivera, "Cancha," *Novedades,* November 4, 1966. Located in ABC, Box 139, "Mexico: Newspaper Clippings." The original Spanish reads: "a dar una proyección real del Mexico inmortal . . . una fiel imagen de lo nuestro."

62. Avery Brundage to Pedro Ramírez Vázquez, April 1, 1967, ABC, Box 178, "Organizing Committee, 1967." The Cultural Olympics's year-long schedule was inaugurated on January 19, 1968, with a performance of the specially choreographed "Ballet of the Five Continents," directed by Amalia Hernández (founder and artistic director of Mexico's famed "Ballet Folklórico") and with music by Mexican composer Carlos Chávez. For a discussion of the Ballet Folklórico's role in Mexican promotion abroad see Zolov, "Discovering a Land 'Mysterious and Obvious.'"

63. Trueblood, ed., *Mexico 68,* vol. 2, 419.

64. Rodríguez Kuri, "Hacia México 68." "Raza" is a difficult term to convey in English, for while it literally translates as "race" (in a biological sense), it is often used—especially in this context—to convey a notion of cultural solidarity and even fusion, i.e., mestizaje. To say, "Viva la raza" ("Long live the race") hence invokes a notion of Latin American (and often, Mexican/Chicano) distinctiveness from the Anglo/European world.

65. Trueblood, ed., *Mexico 68,* vol. 4, 627. The original budget estimate for costs involving the flame ceremony was 620,000.00–700,000.00 pesos. The final cost, however, was twice that amount: 1,403,834.93 pesos. ("Festival en Teotihuacan para recibir la Antorcha Olímpica," October 31, 1967, COI, Gallery 7, Box 41, Folder 13, AGN; "Memorandum," October 25, 1968, COI, Gallery 7, Box 41, Folder 354(1), AGN.)

66. Allen Rankin, "Born to Dance," *Reader's Digest* (October 1963), 235.

67. Rivera Conde, "El Diseño en la XIX Olimpiad," 35.

68. Ruben Salázar, "Wonderland of Color Welcomes Olympics," *Los Angeles Times,* October 13, 1968, 8. Located in ABC, Box 177, "XIX Olympiad, Mexico City – U.S. Press, 1968–69."

69. For a discussion of how gender was a key element of tourist marketing in the 1940s see Saragoza, "The Selling of Mexico." For a discussion of gender conflicts and public discourse in middle-class Mexico during the 1960s see Eric Zolov, *Refried Elvis: The Rise of the Mexican Counterculture* (Berkeley: University of California Press, 1999).

70. Avery Brundage, Personal Diary of the Olympics, 18. ABC, Box 84, "A. Brundage's Trip to Mexico City, September-October 1968."

71. "Memorandum," Pedro Ramírez Vázquez to Luis Aveleyra Arroyo de Anda, September 19, 1966, COI, Gallery 7, Box 41, Folder 114, AGN.

72. Ibid.

73. Bass, *Not the Triumph but the Struggle,* 106–107.

74. John Leinbaugh to Avery Brundage, December 16, 1969. ABC, Box 178, "Organizing Committee, 1969–70."

75. "Brain Storming," May 9, 1968, COI, Gallery 7, Box 26, Folder 41, AGN.

76. For images see Trueblood, ed., *Mexico 68*, vol. 4, 306–357.

77. "A Well-Designed Warm-Up for the Olympics," *Life*, May 17, 1968, 57.

78. Salázar, "Wonderland of Color."

79. Ibid.

80. Riley, "Of Poets and Pole Vaulters," 60.

81. Pan Dodd Eimon, "Olympic-Sized Fiesta," *The American City* (August 1968), 14.

82. Legat, Mexico City (80–103) to Director, FBI, February 29, 1968. Located in FBI file, "1968: Mexican Olympics" at the National Security Archive in Washington, DC.

83. Riley, "Of Poets and Pole Vaulters," 57. An article in *Sports Illustrated* listed various problems facing the Games including "the stereotype of the Mexican peasant, slumped against the wall, sombrero down to shield his eyes from the work left undone" (John Underwood, "Games in Trouble," *Sports Illustrated*, September 30, 1968, 46).

84. Riley, "Of Poets and Pole Vaulters," 57.

85. Christopher Rand, "Letter from Mexico," *New Yorker*, June 29, 1968, 68.

86. Ibid., 86.

87. David Butwin, "The Games, the Boycott, the Problems," *Saturday Review*, June 22, 1968, 39.

88. "¡Vengámos [sic], Gringos!," *Sports Illustrated*, June 17, 1968, 69. Emphasis in original.

89. George B. Leonard, "A Different Journey on the Eve of the Olympics," *Look*, September 3, 1968, 42–44. Emphasis in original.

90. "¡Vengámos Gringos!," 75.

91. Volpi, *La imaginación y el poder*, 23–28.

92. Wyman was evidently unaware of this at the time and only learned of the students' use of his images in 1985, when he gave a lecture at the UNAM. Rohan, "Games Plan," 158.

93. Salazar, "Wonderland of Color," 8.

94. Morris Rosenberg, "At Olympic Time, Mexicans Worry about Manana," *Washington Post*, October 13, 1968, H1.

95. White House Memorandum, "Student Disturbances in Mexico City," William G. Bowlder to LBJ (Secret), July 31, 1968, National Security Archives, Washington, D.C.

96. Kahn, "Sporting Scene," 221.

97. Ibid., 226.

98. *New York Times*, October 13, 1968, 1.

99. The Mexican government had in fact offered to extend standard tourist visas to Smith and Carlos following their expulsion from the Olympic team. However, the pressures were so great that they soon left the country on their own account. See Bass, *Not the Triumph but the Struggle*, 268–269.

PART IV:
FUTURES

EIGHT

Courtside

Race and Basketball in the Works of John Edgar Wideman

Tracie Church Guzzio

In 1973, following the publication of his first three novels, John Edgar Wideman informed interviewer John O'Brien that he was working on a book about basketball. It seemed a natural direction given Wideman's background. As a former star on the University of Pennsylvania's basketball team, Wideman balanced his athletic talents with his scholarly and creative pursuits. His university academic record culminated with a Rhodes scholarship. A stellar achievement by anyone's measure, Wideman's success was even more exceptional given his family's economic status. Growing up on the troubled streets of the Homewood section of Pittsburgh, Pennsylvania, informed his skills both as a player and as a storyteller. A two-time winner of the PEN/Faulkner award for fiction, Wideman has established a career noted for its unflinching portraits of the often violent realities associated with the African American community. Many of Wideman's novels and autobiographical pieces consider both the triumph and tragedy of urban African American families and the racism that continues to impact their daily lives. His first novel, *A Glance Away,* was published in 1967 at the height of the civil rights movement. *Hurry Home* and *The Lynchers* followed in 1970 and 1973, respectively.

Following his brother Robby's arrest and imprisonment for murder, Wideman's career took a new direction. Though his fiction had been laced with autobiographical elements before, Wideman's work in the next decade shifted its focus directly on "family" stories: tales of his Homewood neighborhood, of his grandfather, his mother, his brother, aunts and uncles, and the slave past. *The Homewood Trilogy*, as the next three books in Wideman's career would later be called, were published in 1981. The last novel of the three, *Sent for You Yesterday*, won Wideman his first PEN/Faulkner award. Each work in the trilogy emphasized the importance of keeping past traditions alive in African American families in order to combat the sometimes nihilistic quality of contemporary African American life. Wideman suggests in these novels that the stories African Americans tell about themselves—fictitious or not—are just as powerful and as meaningful as those recorded in the historical record, which usually has excluded honest portraits of African Americans.

In the opening of the second book of the trilogy, *Damballah*, Wideman includes a letter to Robby. The letter tells Robby that the stories included within are designed to "tear down the walls" of his prison cell. The book heralds the work *Brothers and Keepers*, which had much the same mission. Published in 1984, this autobiographical work examined Robby's life and the events that led to his imprisonment. It also criticizes American institutions of racism, especially the penal system within the context of Wideman's family stories and the history of African Americans. In *Brothers and Keepers*, Wideman seeks to understand the cultural and historical forces that helped to destroy Robby's life, and in doing so Wideman reconciles himself to his past and his family. Wideman structures the work primarily as conversations between him and his brother. But a section is also narrated by his mother (a "fictional" voice) and one solely by Wideman. Each strand of the work illustrates Wideman's commitment to allowing all voices and all stories to be heard, a multivocal characteristic found in most of his writing. The book brought Wideman to national prominence. To a lesser degree Wideman examines some of these same issues in works like *Philadelphia Fire* and *Fatheralong*.[1] But in these works, Wideman reflects on the incarceration of his son, Jake, and the loss of young black men to prison or violent death in general. Throughout his career, however, whether in his fiction or in his autobiography, Wideman has endeavored to illustrate America's cultural and historical attitudes to African Americans, especially in terms of the concept of "black masculinity."

Since 1967, Wideman has published a total of fifteen books and numerous essays. His novels and collections of stories, as well as his nonfiction, have garnered him several prestigious awards, including the MacArthur Fellowship, and secured a place for him in any study of serious American fiction. However, it took more than twenty-five years for Wideman to produce his promised work on basketball, *Hoop Roots*. Basketball sketches did appear in 1987 in the novel *Reuben* (a basketball scout is one of the main characters) and in 1998 in *Two Cities,* a work that uses the basketball court as a space of love and hope for a newly acquainted man and woman. In his memoir, *Hoop Roots,* Wideman examines the problematic history of African Americans in this country through his family ties and through basketball. Thus, readers may view the effects of race in America in the context of a genealogical autobiography and a chronicle of African Americans in sports. The memoir is divided into various sections, much like *Brothers and Keepers.* Here, however, Wideman attempts to capture various stages of his life from youth to middle age and the role basketball played in them. He also includes historical and fictional accounts— "basketball stories"—and a more academic or critical voice that attempts to analyze basketball as a cultural phenomena. Another multivocal work, the book, published in 2001, met with favorable reviews, but like other Wideman works requires a great deal of its reader. This is not a linear narrative; the postmodern, fractured, jazzlike style is not what many readers might expect to find in the genre of memoir.

Throughout the memoir, as well as in other shorter pieces that address basketball, Wideman attempts to illuminate the historical and cultural intersections of race and sports in America. But as a former college basketball star—and as the father of Jamila Wideman, former Stanford University point guard and WNBA player—Wideman offers a unique perspective on the ways that race still complicates his love of the game, in many of the same ways it has haunted his creative and scholastic achievements and jeopardized the lives of his family.[2]

As a site of understanding and reconciliation with the past in Wideman's world, basketball functions as an expressive space that Wideman uses to play, to criticize, to celebrate, to analyze African American experience. Wideman suggests that the sport creates this space for many other African Americans as well. And though basketball, or "hoop"—especially the playground variety—is arguably growing in the urban culture's consciousness as America's "game," it is still most popularized and dominated by African Americans. The hoop game—its style, its energy, its form—is a kinetic, athletic representation of African American expressive culture.

Paradoxically, for Wideman, basketball operates both as a celebration of African American culture and as a sign that white America still equates African Americans primarily with athletic ability. White, middle-class America largely supports the merchandising of basketball, yet the images marketed by Madison Avenue are primarily those of African American athletes. In American sports, the viewing public has furthered long-standing representations of black masculinity and physicality, building on the animalistic representations of the black male body that, historically, have been the site of both white consumption and fear. Wideman suggests in his work that these images have framed or "caged" African American masculine identity. In *Hoop Roots*, Wideman inscribes basketball as a possible form of resistant expression that addresses and refutes stereotypes of black masculinity and reveals the spurious nature of even the notion of such a cultural construction as "black masculinity"; here basketball operates in much the same way writing has done for him. At the same time, for Wideman, basketball is an African American art form that celebrates family, unites the community, and reflects the unique character of African American culture; nevertheless the sport is also a metaphor for the complex attitudes toward race in America. Wideman professes in *Hoop Roots* that he wants to do with writing what Michael Jordan has done with basketball, to "become a standard for others to measure themselves against."[3] This linkage of writing and basketball structures the work and may ultimately disappoint, and even annoy, readers of the book. Fans of the game expecting a work about basketball, or at least a thorough cultural analysis of the sport, will believe that Wideman has, no pun intended, dropped the ball. Instead, Wideman proffers meditations on his personal relationships, family, and an exegesis on race in America, much like he does in many of his novels and works of nonfiction. Like his other works, *Hoop Roots* requires a great deal of even the most intrepid reader, but like a classic piece of jazz or a good playground hoop game, the book captures the voices of everything at play. This is really a book about expression in its many forms—love, play, and especially writing. Wideman reminds us that whether in the pulpit, the juke joint, or on the basketball court, African Americans have always found unique, sometimes coded, avenues of self-expression in order to prove their humanity, their grace, their soul.

One of the most historically successful ways that African Americans have liberated themselves from racist portraits drawn by whites has been through autobiography. Often an autobiography is the only major work an African American author may produce. These moments of literary self-expression—whether they describe the poverty of urban youth of Claude Brown's *Manchild in the Promised Land* or the spiritual and political rebirth of Malcolm X—stand as testimonies against the often silenced lives of African Americans. This is especially true of the slave narrative. Popular as both a literary genre and a political document, antebellum slave narratives portrayed the lives of ex-slaves to the masses of America in a way that questioned, and even sometimes countered, the prevailing notions of African American identity. Beginning with the narratives of ex-slaves such as Olaudah Equiano and James Gronniosaw, African Americans fought the silence enforced on them by slavery. Legally, and often violently, enforced illiteracy maintained the image of blacks as mentally inferior and thus clearly designed to be regulated to the less-than-human status of slavery. As the genre of the slave narrative developed through the pens of talented writers like William Wells Brown and Frederick Douglass, black male subjectivity expressed in abolitionist rhetoric became the surest way to directly engage the image of the silent black male body.

Autobiography has also been the means to counter other negative associations with the black male body, especially those that defined black men by their sexuality or physicality, implying they were rapists or mere animals. Even in the earliest slave narratives, ex-slaves recorded that whites looked at them as mules, cattle, breeders, or pets. And by the time of post-Reconstruction, white, southern politicians and writers revised the image to include barbaric animal sexuality. Most notably in Thomas Dixon's *The Clansmen* (the inspiration for the film *The Birth of a Nation*), African American males were defined by their predatory hunger for white women and the threat to white purity and superiority. African American male writers have engaged this image as well through autobiography, either by criticizing the history of these portraits, such as Eldridge Cleaver does in *Soul on Ice,* or by expressing themselves beyond their physical associations, emphasizing their intellect or creativity, as Richard Wright does in *Black Boy.*

Using the autobiographical framework, Wideman tries to accomplish a similar redefinition of the African American male in *Hoop Roots.* Drawing on his own experiences as a basketball player, Rhodes scholar, and successful novelist, Wideman aims to illustrate that the black man is more than his physical associations: he is also a father, a lover, and a writer and thinker to be reckoned with. Basketball is another method to regain ownership of one's individual African American identity, just as autobiography has proven to be in the past.

Wideman's analysis of basketball scrutinizes the conversations of sociologists and media analysts alike over the past decade, especially in regards to "hoop dreams"—a version of the American Dream that sanctifies the game as the path out of the ghetto. These "hoop dreams," redolent in the popular culture, enforce the racial paradigm of black physical prowess versus white intellectual pursuits. Wideman argues however that it is precisely this rhetoric of blackness and whiteness that helps maintain racial division. In writing about his own life, Wideman forges a different black male image: his own status as a writer, professor, and athlete contests the stereotypical view of black masculinity. His pursuits have been both intellectual and physical, and in all, he has consciously addressed the images and stories that others have constructed about African American life—this was what drew him to writing: "I need writing because it can extend the measure of what's possible, allow me to engage in defining standards."[4]

Another way that Wideman has contested the limited images of black masculinity is by constructing a role for himself as a public intellectual. As

a contributor to magazines and journals ranging from the *New Yorker* to
Esquire, Wideman has commented widely on politics and race, especially
on African Americans and sports. Sometimes his essays have described his
love of basketball or his joy at seeing his daughter play, but he has also
written about and/or interviewed Michael Jordan and Dennis Rodman.[5]
These moments are clearly paradoxical for Wideman: in the midst of celebrating the player or the sport, he also criticizes the culture and the country for its attitudes toward race. This is apparent even in an interview
Wideman conducted with actor Denzel Washington on the eve of the release of Spike Lee's film *He Got Game.* Titled "This Man Can Play," Wideman emphasizes Washington's celebrity, his creativity, his intelligence, *and*
his ability to play basketball. As a writer and critic of the game, Wideman
embraced the public intellectual role again in the interview, reflecting on
sports, film, black actors, and fatherhood. More than just being the man
who got the job because he used to play basketball, Wideman uses the conversation to question and to transcend stereotypical images of black male
identity. Consequently, both Washington's and Wideman's voices offer a
less limited picture of African American life between the pages of a mainstream magazine like *Esquire.*

Wideman breaks from the interview format several times to analyze
basketball in American society: "in the case of hoop, the game I love, the
big picture includes irony, paradox, pain, poor drug-ridden communities
blasted by unemployment, sudden violent death, imprisonment, the slow
erosion of health and prospects, affluent communities of spenders wildly
consuming, addicted to possessions, communities connected mostly by the
overarching dog-eat-dog ethos reigning from top to bottom of the economic scale."[6]

Wideman takes this piece beyond the typical celebrity interview, seizing
the opportunity to be heard about race and sports, which here are inseparable in Wideman's observation. In the estimation of many poor, African
American youth, the promise of the NBA contract, a highly improbable
dream at best, is the means of escape from poverty, drugs, and despair. As
a product of American society, Wideman reiterates what many others argue
elsewhere—that basketball reflects the racial divide that has plagued the
country for centuries. It "also functions to embody racist fantasies, to prove
and perpetuate essential differences between blacks and whites, to justify
the idea of white supremacy and rationalize an unfair balance of power,
maintained by violence, lies, and terror, between blacks and whites."[7]

It is this racial division that Wideman endeavors to analyze in *Hoop
Roots* while simultaneously honoring the sport that he loves so much. This
may be one of the ways that he differs from other writers on race and
sports: while Wideman holds the game up to scrutiny, his personal reflec-

tions of basketball suggest a bygone era and a return to a love of the possibilities the game offers beyond the fame and the paycheck. This isn't just cultural criticism; this is autobiographical confessional. He describes the book as an attempt to "explain to myself the power of playground basketball, its hold on me, on African American men, the entire culture."[8] For Wideman, basketball also furnishes a space to create an identity of one's own, apart from the identity that others have constructed for you. This is especially true of African American males whose lives have been the subject of stories forced on them by the white hegemony.

Still, much of the work is devoted to a critique of the black male athlete in the white mainstream. Possibly the most difficult balancing act in the book, Wideman negotiates this analysis at the same time that he both professes his love of the game in his own life and praises it as an African American art form. Indeed at times it reads as though two different men were writing the book. Wideman's own "double-consciousness" regarding the sport may stem not from *his* own but rather *our* own cultural ambivalence regarding sports and race in America. Despite the abundance of African American sports figures—heroes in the eyes of even middle- class white America—African American males continue to be defined in a negative manner. Even Wideman's creation of his own identity as a writer is foregrounded by the revelations about his family's violent past and accounts of the violence that has marred the African American community, including the lives of basketball players.

Throughout *Hoop Roots* Wideman describes the intertextual relationship between race in America and the history of the game. The tale of basketball is obviously also the tale of racism in America. Wideman, in this vein, equates the marketing and managing of basketball metaphorically with slavery. The game, for example, used to be played behind metal cages—hence players are called "cagers"—and today, he argues, the African American athlete is "caged" by the appropriation of his body for sport and for advertising. He cautions players: "don't allow anyone to steal your body or rent, buy, disembody, tame, virtualize, shrink, organize, defang it."[9] At the same time, Wideman projects into the text positive images of the black body and self to counteract the stereotypical images of male blackness. Those images, Wideman realizes, are the burden of Western history. As Maurice O. Wallace illustrates in his study, *Constructing the Black Masculine,* the black male body became a depository of the West's "darkest places," a "walking palimpsest of the fears and fascinations possessing our cultural imagination."[10]

The image of blackness as ugly, animal, sexually violent, and even illiterate can be found in the earliest cultural representations of colonization and new world slavery. The character of Caliban from William Shakespeare's play *The Tempest* is a forefather of such representations. Wideman uses the Prospero/Caliban relationship from *The Tempest* occasionally in his work, connoting the cultural enslavement that African Americans still find themselves subjected to. Wideman uses Caliban's problem with learning and speaking Prospero's language, especially to critique white attitudes toward race and difference. Control of the body, as well as the rhetoric or the "story" of African American life, illustrates the cultural construction of African American identity that Wideman so urgently wants to dismantle. Since Caliban can only express himself through Prospero's tongue, he exists only through Prospero's voice. The manner in which black men have been constructed in Western thought is what critic James Coleman calls "Calibanic discourse."[11] The white ownership of the African American image, especially of black males, continues to impact African American identity today.

In both *Hoop Roots* and in a *New Yorker* article on Dennis Rodman, Wideman uses the Prospero/Caliban trope to install the images of master/slave relationships and silent black male bodies that he sees operating in the NBA. Players are silent performers that are condemned when they speak up, act out, or talk back. In the essay on Rodman, Wideman compares the player's battles with NBA commissioner David Stern to the Prospero/Caliban conflict. Rodman's body was clearly on display—tattooed, dyed, and pierced—during the years he played in the league. Wideman argues that Rodman wrestled for control of his body, reacting against its silencing by the NBA, namely by Stern.[12] Stern, because of Rodman's popularity and talent, needed the silent, black body to "rule his island."[13] Wideman asks what seems to be a rhetorical question: "Why does Rodman's refusal to allow his identity to be totally subsumed by a game offend people?"[14] The answer is clearly that America is more comfortable with, more historically accustomed to, a silent, unadorned, physical black self.

In *Hoop Roots,* Wideman cautions playground hoopsters not to let the NBA "kidnap" and "whitewash" them.[15] The rhetorical allusions to slavery and colonization here indicate Wideman's cautionary motive. What may be at stake for young players is ownership of their self-expression. In the NBA, players' skill, as well as their creative and expressive talents, are controlled by a white consciousness on the court and in the media. Their blackness will be marketed for pleasure and entertainment, and their bodies will become material for someone else's story as Caliban has been in Prospero's tale—a relationship that Prospero notes in the play's last scene: "This thing of darkness I acknowledge mine."[16]

The use of blackness, particularly the employment of black male bodies, to symbolize the exotic, the Other, has enslaved African Americans in a silent melodrama, Wideman's work suggests. This "racial gaze" has promoted America's negative attitudes toward urban African American existence, turning men and women into the statistics recorded in the media and social programs as evidence that "black life" is bankrupt. Welfare, drug use, unemployment, crime, punishment, even teenage, single motherhood become associated with this stereotype of African American life. As Greg Tate suggests in the introduction to *Everything But the Burden: What White People Are Taking from Black Culture,* the influence of such cultural constructions has had a sweeping impact on the real lives of African Americans: "The African-American presence in this country has produced a fearsome, seductive, and circumspect body of myths about Black intellectual capacity, athletic ability, sexual appetite, work ethic, family values, and propensity for violence and drug addiction. From these myths have evolved much of the paranoia, pathology, absurdity, awkwardness, alienation, and anomie which continue to define the American racial scene."[17] But as most of the essays in Tate's book point out, white America is nevertheless transfixed by blackness at the same time it remains unaware that this very idea of blackness is culturally constructed. White America's popular culture, its modes of expression, its style is indebted to African American tradition even though the lives behind such production are invisible to the mainstream. Nowhere perhaps is this more apparent than in the world of sports.

While the stars of the NBA receive wealth, fame, and accolades almost beyond measure, the majority of the young men that pin their futures to basketball will fall short of their dreams of success. In *Hoop Roots,* Wideman juxtaposes an analysis of a superstar like Michael Jordan with the lives of young men whose lives are lost to the streets, including his own nephew, Omar. Omar, the son of the imprisoned Robby, was shot to death—execution-style—by three men following a barroom fight in 1993. Omar's death highlights Wideman's personal pain found throughout the book, but the loss also signals those silent, invisible black bodies used and then neglected in the American consciousness, becoming a social scientist's statistic. While at the funeral of Omar, Wideman runs into Ed Fleming, a hometown boy who had a fairly successful career in the NBA in the 1950s. Nevertheless, Wideman reminds us that Fleming's success had not shielded him from the effects of racism on his own life. He carries "visible scars or the invisible ones" with him, particularly because Fleming belonged to an era when his dark skin clearly represented a threat. Wideman argues that Fleming's

> body type and color [was] a stigma, a danger to the bearer for five hundred years in racist America. Convict body, field hand body, too unadulterated African, too raw, too black, too powerful and quick and assertive for most whites and most colored folks to feel comfortable around until Michael Jordan arrived and legitimated Ed Fleming's complexion and physique, mainstreaming them, blunting the threatening edge, commodifying the Jordan

> look, as if the physical, sexual potency of a dark, streamlined, muscular body could be purchased, as if anybody, everybody—Swede, Korean, Peruvian, Croat, New Englander—could be like Mike.[18]

Seeing the former NBA player in the funeral home reminds Wideman of recent stories he has heard about Fleming, especially an altercation at the school where he coached—an altercation that left him severely beaten. In this instance, Fleming's physical presence, his "body" could not protect him from the violence of the urban neighborhood. Nor did Fleming's fame or success remove him from such a situation.

The association between Wideman's dead nephew and the beaten athlete resonates in Wideman's critique of race and sports in America. Both men, residents of the neighborhood, are unable to escape its violence and its perpetual lack of opportunity—even in the case of Fleming. Omar and his "crew" sought marginalized and violent ways to define their manhood. Unable to find an identity as a young, black man beyond the limited choices prescribed for him in America, Omar took to the streets, ultimately paying for his decision with his life. Fleming's flight from the ghetto, through sports, and his later decision to return as an educator and coach, did not shield him from physical violence. Even if he stayed away from Homewood, his identity in racist America will always threaten his safety. Both men's blackness condemned them despite the different paths they took in life. Seemingly, only a star like Jordan seems to negate such racial constructions.

But even Wideman begins to question whether or not Jordan can "defy gravity" when it comes to race in America. While Jordan is imminently popular throughout America, his iconographic status might actually reinscribe attitudes in the culture toward the black male body. Even though black and white kids alike might want to "be like Mike," few African American boys will ever come close to achieving his level of his success, while white Americans will be content to engage in a cultural racial masquerade, satisfied to act "like Mike" or popular rap stars without having to live their racial realities in America. As Wideman states: "Buy Jordan or be Jordan. Very different messages."[19] Wideman compares the "commerce in images of blackness" to American slavery, suggesting that "black bodies still occupy the auction block."[20] Writer Michael Eric Dyson makes a similar pronouncement when he argues that Jordan's body has become a "cultural text" for America.[21] Jordan's image is separated from his individual identity, constructed and promoted to entertain, to purchase. Consequently, the popularity of the sport and of its stars continues the legacy of racial commodification.

It is on the neighborhood playground, Wideman suggests, that players may be the freest from a marketplace definition of the black male body.

Here strangers, families, friends, fathers and sons can play the game in the purest sense—as a sign of individual expression and communal identity. The playground emerges as a site of communication and possibility in the silent African American world. It offers men a place to connect beyond their family in the wake of racism and urban despair. It is here that a "counterreality is dramatized. Playing hoop, African American men act out a symbolic version of who they are, who they want to be."[22] Wideman romanticizes this urban space in *Hoop Roots* almost to the point of nostalgia. It appears that it is only here that the black male body is free from the definitions that others have given it. When Wideman brings his lover, Catherine, to a game, she neglects to see this association. He believes that the failure results from differences in culture (she's European) or gender, or that he hasn't had proper time to explain the game to her. It is more likely that the game does not have the symbolic importance to her that it has for Wideman. Here men choose their names, their court titles. They define their identity.

This section of the book, titled "The Village," offers the most mixed of Wideman's responses to basketball. What begins as a desire to share a beloved pastime with Catherine and a celebration of the game ends as an indictment of America and its attitudes toward race.

Interwoven in the history of the sport is the history of slavery and racism. As he does in his novels, Wideman interrogates in this chapter the ways in which history has codified racial construction. However, Wideman has a more difficult time negotiating his examination here. His meditations move back and forth between his neighborhood, history, Carnivale, the dress of NBA players, the game he's currently watching, minstrelsy, and the beginnings of basketball in Springfield, Massachusetts. The epigraph that opens this chapter illustrates the "separation, segmentation, and division" of African art. While Wideman's observation of the playground game implies individual and communal unity, the characterization of art indicates something else. By the end of the chapter, Wideman is unable to reconcile these different and opposing perceptions of African Americans and sports.

This also happens to a lesser degree whenever Wideman talks about his family. As a young man Wideman begins to escape his trying family situations by running to the courts. He finds solace there during the time that he cares for his ill grandmother. Though Wideman has said elsewhere that the playground has operated as a space to bring the community together, in this case, his relationships with his family seem fragmented further by his trips to the court. He even admits that he left behind the women in his family in order to find connections to other men, fathers, brothers on the playground. His own emerging identity as an adult is dependent on this separation. Yet this action echoes stereotypical representations of African American males and their absence from the household. This is, by Wideman's account, one reason why he has sought male connection on the courts in the first place. Here he seeks to find a masculine self, modeled on the men that are playing basketball. It also seems noteworthy that he brings Catherine back to his home playground as a means to explain his past, his identity, to her. The creative expressions that he has seen elsewhere in his culture—at church, in music—are also illustrated in the games taking place. The solo flights and team unity embody young Wideman's need to develop his voice and find companionship outside of his home life—to discover what it means to be a man in the midst of a household of women. Everywhere on the court Wideman encounters the ways basketball provides men with their sense of self in a world that seems intent on stripping them of their masculine identity. The dress, the walk, the trashtalking all connote a ritual drama of manhood. Even slam-dunking rises beyond a test of physical prowess and "showboating" skills to represent a masculine symbol.[23] But in accepting this vision of manhood, is Wideman paradoxically embracing the racial stereotypes of the black male body? Clearly, Wideman is attracted to the types of expression that he sees displayed on the court, but he also emphasizes the ways the game helps men find their masculinity.

As a budding writer, the young Wideman believed that the unique game-playing styles of the "hoopsters" were examples of individual creative expression. In *Hoop Roots* he often digresses from the description of a particular game or player to a story about his family or an acquaintance. Playground ball and storytelling are synonymous for Wideman as ways to combat the negative and limited portraits of African American life. One of the most prevalent and damaging images of African American masculinity, as discussed earlier, has been the association between the black male body and sexual violence. Often portrayed in history and in the American consciousness as the sexual predator, black men have borne the burden of American preoccupation with blackness as a sign of animalism. Black men have rarely been portrayed outside of their own community as loving husbands and partners. They have paid for such characterizations—in some cases with their lives, as the history of lynching illustrates.

Basketball serves elsewhere in the book as a means to tell positive stories about the African American family—Wideman also uses the game to fashion an image of the African American male in a healthy and loving sexual relationship. His love of the game is something he wants to share with Catherine, but it also serves as a way to share stories of his past with his lover. Basketball frames his youth, his relationships with his mother and grandparents. All of these autobiographical moments are essential to understanding his character, but he is unable to simply relate them to his partner. To share his inner life, Wideman has to speak through the game, showing again that he believes that basketball is a form of artistic expression. He considers their intimate interaction a "verbal ball game." He admits the metaphor doesn't quite work, but reveals that when he went to the courts as a young man he was seeking love and acceptance. He explains to Catherine: "Homewood boys and men running to the court to find our missing fathers. Playing the game of basketball is our way of telling stories, listening to stories, piecing a father together from them. Practicing bittersweet survival whether we find fathers or not. Recalling your stories, telling mine. I'm practicing survival again. Remembering what's lost. Remembering my stories can't save you."[24]

The image of the vulnerable, loving man emerges here as a refutation of the black sexual brute. It is also not the first time that Wideman has used the game as a central trope in a romantic relationship. The novel *Two Cities* follows the relationship of Robert and Kassima, two wounded lovers whose "courtship" parallels Robert's experiences on the playground "court." Wideman revels in the wordplay, as when he notes that this is a "rebound" relationship. In many ways the novel is a fictional mirror of "The Village" section of *Hoop Roots* and also uses the playground as a site of connection and reconciliation. In both works, racism's impact on African American manhood complicates and even destroys love relationships—Kassima has lost sons and a husband to the streets—reminding us again that Wideman's personal life is the lens by which he examines the culture and history of America.

The basketball court in *Two Cities* is a site of both love and urban violence. Robert invites Kassima to watch him play a game, a place where he can display his manhood. More than an arena for mere showmanship, it is a space where Robert feels in control in a world where he clearly has no real power. Kassima acknowledges: "Nothing he could do would make me love him more. Loved him enough. More than enough. More than enough to last us both forever and ever and he should have understood but they never do. I don't need him to be any better than he already is, but men don't understand love is love and if it's love it's enough. Men always got to prove something. Or have you prove something to them. So I walked up to the basketball court that day against my better judgment just to be with him because he asked me to. Why do men have to pretend they are better than they are?"[25] Even though Robert is a kind, gentle man and a loving protector of the world-weary Kassima, he only feels like a powerful man when he is playing the game. Here he can confront the failures he sees in himself as a man and the limited identity he has been handed by society. He sacrifices his sore, aging body to prove to himself and to Kassima that he's more than the chances he's been given. He tries "to be something he's not. More than he needs to be. Someone he doesn't need to be."[26] Robert's desire to prove himself results in a fight with a young hoopster—who has brought a gun to the game. Shot, but only wounded by the boy, Robert realizes that even on the court the violence and despair of the urban world can intrude. And even here someone else can try to define who you are: Robert is called "old nigger" by the youth that shoots him.

The identity of the African American community might be most secure, but not completely, in such spaces where cultural expression can take place. The neighborhood playground court is, in Wideman's estimation, such a space. As he tells us in *Hoop Roots,* the court in Homewood, where he grew up, was named Westinghouse, after one of the European founders of the city. Wideman argues that the space should be renamed after one of the neighborhood's inhabitants—men who played on its blacktop. This naming process is a crucial aspect of the maintenance of communal identity, as it has been in forging individual African American identities. Thinking about the players that have helped shape the neighborhood court, Wideman offers the name "The Maurice Big Mo Stokes/Eldon L. D. Lawson Memorial Playground" as an alternative to Westinghouse. The name marks the contributions of both the celebrated and the unknown players from the community. The career of NBA star Maurice Stokes is juxtaposed in the text with stories of the nearly anonymous L. D. Lawson. Though their successes might seem completely opposite of one another, both men met similar fates.

Lawson had a promising playground career as a youth, but impatient for the fortune and fame that he believed would come his way, he turned to a life of crime and violence. His story reflects the loss of the dreams and the despair of young men in the urban community. Now in prison, his body has been ravaged by diabetes, leaving him without legs. He is caged both by his body and by society. Stokes, on the other hand, was a star in the NBA. A Rookie of the Year, Stokes appeared to be on his way to fulfilling his dreams. But his career was cut short as well when he was injured on the court. Stokes played on even after the injury and soon after fell into paralysis. Wideman suggests that Stokes' body, "his large, darker presence" was sacrificed for the sport and the team. He spent the rest of his life in bed, imprisoned in his body. In the biographies of both Lawson and Stokes, definitions of identity and success rest on their physical self. Unable to transcend the damaged body, both men are left to be remembered by the game they played.

Telling these stories of the players of the game, those known and unknown, Wideman enacts a ritual designed to illustrate basketball's artistic expression and to celebrate the past. Basketball helps frame African American experience in this country: both in the ways that it reflects the problems of racism and in the ways it helps its artists name their experience. In one of the sections of the book called "Who Invented the Jump Shot?" Wideman worries that the academic panel that has been assembled to answer this question will rewrite history, excluding the unique contributions that African American culture has made to the sport, and by extension to America. Unless African Americans can find a space—whether a court or a blank page—to tell their story, in their own voice, their identities will continue to be owned and appropriated by someone else, as their bodies and their lives once were.

Notes

1. *Philadelphia Fire* (1990) interweaves autobiography and fiction in its account of the bombing of the MOVE house by Philadelphia police in 1986. The novel explores the theme of lost sons by interposing the search for an orphan of the bombing with Wideman's own personal tragedy: the imprisonment of his youngest son, Jake, for murdering a fellow classmate. Published in 1996, *Fatheralong* follows Wideman and his father as they journey to the South. Wideman's personal meditations also structure this work; at the same time he analyzes the impact of race on the lives of African American men. There are few book-length studies of Wideman's work. In fact, the critical examination of his writing as a whole is slim. See James Coleman's *Blackness and Modernism: The Literary Career of John Edgar Wideman* (Jackson: University Press of Mississippi, 1989) and Bonnie Tusmith's edition *Conversations with John Edgar Wideman* (Jackson: University Press of Mississippi, 1998).
2. Jamila Wideman played for Stanford University's team in their Final Four season of 1997. She was also drafted as a point guard in the inaugural season of the WNBA's Los Angeles Sparks.
3. John Edgar Wideman, *Hoop Roots* (New York: Houghton Mifflin, 2001), 13.
4. Wideman, 13.
5. See for example "Playing Dennis Rodman," *New Yorker,* April 29, 1996; "My Daughter the Hoopster," *Essence,* November 1996; "Michael Jordan Leaps the Great Divide," *Esquire,* November 1990.
6. Wideman, "This Man Can Play," *Esquire,* May 1998, 71.
7. Wideman, *Hoop Roots,* 167.
8. Wideman, 163.
9. Wideman, 180.
10. Maurice O. Wallace, *Constructing the Black Masculine* (Durham: Duke University Press, 2002), 2.
11. James Coleman, *Black Male Fiction and the Legacy of Caliban* (Lexington: University Press of Kentucky, 2001), 3.
12. David Stern condemned Rodman for his on-court antics and flagrant fouls, levying numerous fines and suspensions against the player during his very celebrated years as a Chicago Bull. At the same time, Stern kept Rodman in the

news, thus ensuring that the viewing public would tune in to see what Rodman might do (or tattoo) next.

13. Wideman, "Playing Dennis Rodman," 94.
14. Wideman, 95.
15. Wideman, *Hoop Roots*, 189.
16. Qtd. in Wideman, "Playing Dennis Rodman," 95.
17. Greg Tate, *Everything But the Burden: What White People Are Taking from Black Culture* (New York: Broadway, 2003).
18. Wideman, *Hoop Roots*, 40.
19. Wideman, "Michael Jordan Leaps the Great Divide," 389.
20. Wideman, *Hoop Roots*, 41–42.
21. Michael Eric Dyson, "Be Like Mike: The Pedagogy of Desire," in *Signifyin, Sanctifyin and Slamdunking: A Reader in African American Expressive Culture,* ed. Gena Caponi (Amherst: University of Massachusetts Press, 1999), 408.
22. Wideman, *Hoop Roots*, 164.
23. Wideman, 246.
24. Wideman, 134.
25. Wideman, *Two Cities* (New York: Houghton Mifflin, 1998), 61.
26. Wideman, 66.

NINE

The Stepping Stone

Larry Holmes, Gerry Cooney, and *Rocky*

Carlo Rotella

On June 11, 1982, Larry Holmes defeated Gerry Cooney in a heavyweight title fight that turned out to be boxing's last great black-white cultural event of the twentieth century. If you want to talk to Holmes about it now, you call the offices of Larry Holmes Enterprises in Easton, Pennsylvania. The secretary puts you through to his business manager, who determines whether it's worth the boss's while to talk to you. If all goes well, you make an appointment to call Holmes—or visit in person—during business hours later in the week. If Holmes has to go on the road for a promotional appearance, as he often does, it all takes longer. To reach Cooney you call the offices of the Fighters' Institute for Support and Training (FIST), the organization he founded to help boxers make the transition to life outside the ring. FIST has good intentions, but no real money yet. The cheerful woman who answers the phone gives you Cooney's cell phone number without bothering to find out what you want; you leave a message on his voice mail, then he calls you back from his car sometime and you talk as he drives around New Jersey, usually at night.

The one-time adversaries have become friends, but it still matters that Holmes won and Cooney lost, that Holmes is rich and Cooney is not, that Holmes held the heavyweight championship for seven years and Cooney never did. During the long, bitter runup to their fight, it seemed to matter most to just about everybody that Cooney is white and Holmes is black,

but they both have tried to put that particular aspect of their encounter behind them. They would like to think that they are better, wiser men than
they were back then.

"Everything connected with the Cooney fight was race, race, race," as
Holmes put it in his autobiography.[1] That's the one thing almost everybody
knew about the fight in 1982, and that's how it is still remembered. The
most widely accepted version of this received wisdom (codified and restated
recently by a documentary in HBO's "Legendary Nights" series) has Don
King, who handled Holmes, and Mike Jones and Dennis Rappaport, the
Long Island real-estate men who handled Cooney, "turning it into a racial
thing" in order to make more money. Cooney sees it that way now: "They
did that, the guys managing me, and Don King. It had nothing to do with
me; I never felt it that way, never thought about it that way, didn't see it
that way. I have nothing good to say about them." Another version of the
received wisdom blames American culture, not the promoters, for "turning
it into a racial thing" because that's what Americans do to boxing matches
and anything else—sports, music, trials, elections, social class—that can be
made to fit the bill. Holmes sees it that way now: "I realize what kind of a
world we live in. I know this is a white man's world. I know they gonna
come first. I know white people wanted Cooney to kick my ass, and black
people wanted me to kick his ass. That's the way it is."

Everything connected with the Holmes-Cooney bout seemed to be
Rocky, Rocky, Rocky, too. That *Rocky* and its sequels somehow framed the
fight's meaning is the second thing that almost everybody knew about it at
the time, and this assumption still shapes popular memory of it. For some,
Cooney was "a real-life Rocky." For others, Cooney embodied the delusive
Rocky fantasy, a revival of the old White Hope formula that calls for a
white challenger to contest the heavyweight title—a traditional apogee of
manhood—whenever it is held by a black man. The fighters themselves participated in fitting the Rocky template over their fight. Asked by Howard
Cosell to predict the outcome, Cooney said, "I'm going to win. Did you see
Rocky II? When his wife is in a coma, she lost the baby, and she says 'Win!
Win!'" After he lost to Holmes, Cooney said to Cosell, "There's always
room for *Rocky II,* right?" (Rocky, having lost an honorably close decision
to the champion, Apollo Creed, at the end of *Rocky,* wins the rematch at
the end of *Rocky II.*) Looking back on the way he felt as he prepared to
fight Holmes, Cooney now says, "It was like the Rocky story being lived."
Holmes did not invoke Rocky as often as Cooney did, but directly after the
fight Holmes did declare, "I have killed all the critics. Rocky, Sylvester Stallone, *Time* magazine, *Sports Illustrated*"—an odd list of critics, headed by
the fictional character who loomed over the bout, the actor who played
him, and two magazines that put Cooney and/or Stallone, not Holmes, on
their covers before the fight.[2]

The two items of received wisdom converge as elements of one item: Rocky served as a primary vehicle for articulating the fight's racial meaning. Rocky-and-race begged—still begs—to be employed by those seeking to make sense of Holmes-Cooney, and the longer cultural history of the heavyweight title makes Rocky-and-race seem like just the tool to use. There's Jack Johnson vs. Jack London and red-blooded racialism, Joe Louis vs. Nazi and American versions of racial order, Muhammad Ali vs. The Man and the legacy of the colonial world-system . . . you know how it goes. The empire strikes back against the black champion with Rocky Balboa, as it did before against Johnson with Jim Jeffries and Jess Willard, against Louis with Max Schmeling and Rocky Marciano (even though it was Ezzard Charles, a black man, who actually took Louis's title and was never forgiven for it by some black fight fans), and against Ali with Joe Frazier and George Foreman—two black heavyweights who, according to the crazed logic of sport and race, have been made out by some observers as surrogate White Hopes.

But the ingrained familiarity of turning to Rocky-and-race makes the move suspect, at least to me. This suspicion comes in two parts.

First, "race, race, race" too often proves to be a graveyard of analytical thinking. Americans in general and commentators on culture in particular have grown overused to assuming that when you have reduced a subject to "race, race, race" your work is done and there is no need to devote further thought to the matter—a bad habit that prevents an argument from even attempting to do justice to its subject's full complexity. Think of it this way: Do Don King, Mike Jones, and Dennis Rappaport constitute the interpretive company you want to be keeping? All three harped on racial drama as the fight's meaningful content. King, favoring the direct approach, would say things like, "It's a white and black fight. Any way you look at it, you cannot change that," and then he might add something about how it might be too bad, but that's the way it is. Jones and Rappaport, taking the more indirect approach, talked about "Mom, apple pie, and Gerry Cooney," but their keynote slogan, "Not the white man, but the right man" (in which the rest of the slogan pretty much cancels out the "not" and the "but"), cast everything else they said as an oblique restatement of King's central selling point.

Writing yet one more account of Holmes-Cooney that stops thinking when it has reduced the subject to "race, race, race" would amount to joining in on the promoters' fun, albeit in a deploring and superior sort of way, and I see exactly no point in doing that. The promoters did it to make money (and it worked); the rest of us do not even have that excuse. As an analytical tool, "race, race, race" is a stepping stone, a midpoint and not an endpoint. Especially when it comes to boxing, which most academics (when they think of it at all) are only too eager to reduce to racial drama

and little else, I think of "race, race, race" as a trialhorse, the sort of oblig-
atory analytical opponent you have to get past to find out how far you can
really go. "Race, race, race," in other words, is like Tex Cobb in the 1980s
or Bert Cooper in the 1990s: an opponent against whom it can be easy to
look good (and nearly impossible to look great) because, while he may
seem imposing, he stands lumpishly in front of you and eats your best
shots, which makes you feel like a world-beater and entertains the crowd,
too. Bear in mind, though, that you take on a trialhorse only because you
want to get to the trickier, rougher, more accomplished opponents waiting
beyond him.

Second, if you go back and actually watch the Rocky series, you may
be surprised to find that Rocky-and-race is of limited and decaying analytical utility even when applied to the movies from which it supposedly derives.[3] If you pay close attention to the movies, as I will do after I've paid
close attention to the fight itself, you will find that the deeper you go into
them, the clearer it becomes that "race, race, race" is a trialhorse, a stepping stone on the way to addressing other matters—like the fit between the
local and the cosmopolitan—that increasingly command the movies' primary attention.

With the help of Holmes and Cooney, who have been talking to each
other for years about their fight and who talked to me about it on the
phone, I want to look again at the Holmes-Cooney fight and the Rocky
movies to see what each can tell us about the other and about the utility
and limits of "race, race, race." Holmes and Cooney speak of the Rocky-
themed furor of signification that surrounded their bout as if it were a
storm, a madness, that overtook them, swept them up, and then passed,
leaving them to begin the long process of fashioning a perspective that takes
"race, race, race" into account without collapsing into yet another rendi-
tion of it. Now *that's* the interpretive company we ought to be keeping.

The Fight

The fanfare from *Rocky* played while Cooney, the challenger, made his ring
walk in a satiny green robe with a peaked hood. Close by him, wearing the
green and white of his corner, were Victor Valle, his trainer, and Mike Jones
and Dennis Rappaport, who had orchestrated his swift passage to contest-
ing the heavyweight championship of the world. Jones and Rappaport cultivated a reputation as fast-talking operators—they were known as the
Wacko Twins, and liked it—but when it came to selling boxing and bullshit
in wholesale lots they were not yet in the class of Don King, who was promoting the fight. They were closing in on him, though. They had negoti-

ated at least an even-money split of the biggest purse of all time—their challenger stood to make up to $10 million, the same as the champion—and they had succeeded in positioning Cooney to win the title and become the biggest boxing star since Muhammad Ali, which would allow them to dictate terms to everyone, including King.[4] If their guy won this fight, they would be sitting pretty.

Once Cooney was in the ring, Holmes, the champ, entered. The sound system played his familiar ring walk theme, the Philadelphia soul anthem "Ain't No Stoppin' Us Now." His trainers were Eddie Futch and Ray Arcel—wise old men, one black and one white, cumulatively 152 years old, each of them having forgotten more about boxing than Valle, Jones, and Rappaport together could ever hope to learn. Holmes and his crew, in red and white, fairly raced down the aisle to the ring. Jesse Jackson, looking fit and visibly stimulated by the intensity of the crowd's and the media's attention, jogged briskly among them, just ahead of the champion and just behind the men bearing aloft his belts. Jackson's presence helped to mark— that is, market—the event as serious business with an import extending well beyond sport.

Don King was already in the ring, wearing a white jacket with a boutonniere, his pshent-like 'do in fine vertical form. Oozing unclean vigor, tall but a little hunched in a manner that suggested vulture or wolf, he was clapping his hands and smiling his eternal Old Scratch smile, which makes him look as if he has just materialized in a cloud of acrid smoke and will shortly be presenting a receipt for a shrieking victim's immortal soul. His work was largely done; he had already made a killing on the promotion. All that was left was for the fighters to do the manual labor and the suffering.

Jones, Rappaport, Jackson, and especially King were all figurative sons of P. T. Barnum, brothers under the skin in a way that transcended differences of race, creed, and class background. But you did not need their fine-tuned noses for action to sense the significance and profit crackling in the air that night. A marathon card of fights was about to culminate in a confrontation between a black man and a white man for the heavyweight title of the world. The promotion featured what were then the richest live gate, gross receipts, and combined purse in the history of boxing. Caesars Palace had erected a 32,000-seat temporary arena just for this event in its parking lot, and the casinos were hauling in a prodigious take on their gambling floors. Television cameras lingered on celebrities collected at ringside: Farrah Fawcett and Ryan O'Neal, Jack Nicholson, Lola Falana, Kareem Abdul-Jabbar, the aging Joe DiMaggio, the twenty-one-year-old Wayne Gretzky—and, of course, Mr. T, who played Clubber Lang, the monster out of Chicago who first defeats Rocky Balboa and is then defeated by him in *Rocky III*.[5] The movie had opened just a couple of weeks earlier. Cooney had recently shared the cover of *Time* with its star, Sylvester Stallone, who posed in character as Rocky, a likeable slugger who comes out of nowhere to become heavyweight champion.[6]

Those present felt that the nation, primed by the Rocky movies' evocation of a half-remembered history of heavyweight title fights with larger cultural significance, was watching over their shoulders. Even people who usually expressed no interest in boxing had taken notice of this bout, and taken sides. *Who do you like in the big fight?* The question had an old-school resonance, evoking an era of streetcars and horse-drawn wagons, the *Police Gazette,* men in hats. The question had largely fallen out of use since the 1950s, but it was in the air again, mostly because Cooney—a soft-spoken, dark-haired, third-generation Irish guy from County Suffolk, Long Island—had followed the path to center stage mapped for him by the Rocky movies. *Who do you like? The brother, or the guy who looks like Rocky?* Much of the popular side-taking appeared to be proceeding along racial lines. It helped, too, that Cooney had been winning fights with all the abrupt, melodramatic one-sidedness of a movie montage sequence depicting a dangerous challenger's ascent to a title shot. He had caved in Ron Lyle with a body punch and knocked him out of the ring in the first round, and he had reduced Ken Norton to a half-crushed bug in just fifty-four seconds. Lyle, Norton, and the cutie-pie technician Jimmy Young—by far the three best opponents Cooney had faced—were in steep decline when he beat them, but that did not mitigate the galvanizing effect on the popular imagination of ten-second sportscast clips in which Cooney blasted them out. As far as most people were concerned, Norton was the pumped, scowling stud who had broken Ali's jaw and played the he-man slave who gets it on with a white woman in *Mandingo,* and Cooney had nearly killed him.

The Holmes-Cooney bout was a major cultural event, and it had that status *before* the fight occurred (as opposed to, say, the fight in which Mike Tyson bit Evander Holyfield's ear, which made its way *after* the fact into office chat and late-night talk show monologues). But, let us not forget, it was also a boxing match.

Holmes, one of the very best heavyweights of all time, was perhaps at the peak of his considerable powers when he stepped between the ropes to fight Cooney. At thirty-two years old, Holmes still had most of the quickness and flexibility of youth, and he was rich in experience. His record stood at 39–0, he had already defended his title eleven times, and he had beaten Earnie Shavers (twice), Norton (when Norton was still a heavyweight to be reckoned with), and Ali, among others. Weighing in at 212-1/2 pounds, Holmes entered the ring stronger and more confident than ever. He went into any fight intending to wear out the other man with a steady jab and good defense, to "make 'em drunk, then mug 'em," as he always says, not to stand there like a fool and trade haymakers. He knew that Cooney, who had never fought past the eighth round, could not stay with him for fifteen rounds. It was close to 100 degrees in the ring, a hot evening in Las Vegas made hotter by television lights. Holmes, as he saw it, did not need Futch and Arcel to do much more than keep him well iced and watered. "All I needed them to do was just keep me cool," he says now. "I already knew how to win the fight."

Cooney, for his part, never really had a prime—he came up too fast and, after fighting Holmes, declined even faster—but he was as good on that night as he ever was. He entered the ring with a record of 25–0. At twenty-five he was seven years younger than Holmes, and at 6' 6" he was three inches taller. The two men's reaches and chest measurements were about the same; at 225–1/2 pounds, Cooney was really not much bigger than Holmes. A converted lefthander, Cooney looked to the casual observer like a pure puncher, but he had the makings of a pretty good boxer, too. His best punch was a crushing left hook, but his long left jab was developing into a versatile weapon and his straight right was becoming an effective complement to the hook. Between his quick knockouts of Lyle and Norton and his managers' insistence on going for a title shot without first eliminating other young contenders, he had accrued just over one full round's worth of actual fighting experience in the previous two years—a recipe for rust—and he had not fought or sparred with enough expert fighters to gain a first-rate fistic education. Still, despite inexperience and a weak corner, he had picked up enough elements of craft to give him confidence that his impressive talent had begun to ripen into a mature style. That, combined with faith in his natural punching power, made him feel unbeatable. "It was the first time in my career," he recalls now of the Holmes fight, "when I wasn't nervous going into a fight."

Okay, back to the racial hype. Boxing tradition holds that the challenger enters first and is introduced first, but on that night—for the first and only time that anybody could recall—the ring announcer introduced the champ first and the challenger second, which meant that Holmes had to settle for a brief round of applause, punctuated by audible boos, that gave way to a swelling, sustained ovation for Cooney. Holmes, impassive, stowed the insulting reordering of ring introductions in a mental pigeon hole along with other slights: the even-money split of the purse, *Time*'s decision to put Cooney and Stallone on its cover, *Sports Illustrated*'s decision to put Cooney on its cover and Holmes on an inside fold, and the news that Cooney's dressing room, and not Holmes', had been equipped with an outside phone line so that he could receive a congratulatory call from President Reagan if he won.

The ring introductions, marking the end of the pre-fight runup, were the last touch in the process of framing the bout in context. Promoters, sportswriters, op-ed types, fans—all of them, not only those who wanted the fight to be about racial potency but also those who deplored such tribalism, had done their parts to invest it with meaning. This was the kind of fight that editorialists wrote about. Opinions, predictions, and critiques of the hype proliferated not just on sportscasts but on late-night talk shows, not just in *Sports Illustrated* and daily papers' sports sections but in *Time* and on op-ed pages, not just in *Esquire* and *Jet* but in *Christianity Today* and *New African*. The fact of the fight's perceived significance became the story. Holmes-Cooney was about black and white, or it was about the shocking or not-so-shocking persistence of black-and-white thinking, or it was about how such thinking obscured the purity of sport or the impurity of boxing. The story ended up being about the fight being about all of these things, and all these things reduced to just one thing.

Now that it was time to box, the pre-fight drama had come to an end, or at least had reached a pause in which Holmes and Cooney could mix it up in peace, so to speak, before the post-fight analysis began. That Cooney was white might help explain how he had gotten a shot at the title with so little on his résumé, and it helped explain why everybody was so excited about the fight, and it certainly helped explain why the principals were making so much money—all of which Holmes had pointed out in his usual blunt public manner over the previous few months—but for the next hour or so the tribal affiliations that mattered most would be stylistic: boxer and puncher.

Holmes knew he was a better boxer than Cooney was a puncher, and he knew Cooney had not yet developed a complete boxing style, either. The only green on Cooney that mattered now was inexperience, not the talismans of Irishness in which he was draped. Holmes expected to stick and move as usual and grind down another promising young challenger; it would be just another day at the office. Cooney, for his part, had elements of various fight plans and contingencies in his head. He had to be ready to pace himself for fifteen rounds, but he also had to press from the outset to get at Holmes and begin pounding his body, taking away his legs and his wind. And what was he going to do about Holmes' jab? Move to his left? Counter with his right? Try to out-jab him? Spend defensive energy on exerting his own offensive pressure? Whatever else he was trying to do at any given moment in the fight, Cooney also had to remain alert for the puncher's main chance, an opening that might allow him to finish it with a big left hook or two. Since he had never been in with anybody anywhere near as good as Holmes, he was not sure what to expect.

The fighters met in the middle of the ring for ritual instructions from the referee, Mills Lane. Holmes gave Cooney his pre-fight look, an affectless stare that said *You're a job and I'm going to do you*, rather than *I'm gonna kill you, motherfucker.* Cooney looked down, uninterested in eye contact, as if his opponent was just a heavy bag to pummel. When the referee was done, the fighters touched gloves. Before they turned to go back to their respective corners to await the bell for the first round, Holmes said, "Let's have a good fight."[7]

And, surprisingly, they did. For twelve-plus rounds, Holmes fought a master-boxer's fight, jabbing steadily and crossing hard rights over the jab, moving to his left to negate Cooney's left hand, patiently disassembling the challenger's game. At first, Cooney did not fight enough of a puncher's fight. He had been listening to everybody say that he couldn't go the distance, and he was overly preoccupied with pacing himself. But after Holmes put him down in the second round with a one-two right on the button, Cooney seemed to shed his initial reluctance to go all-out. "I got dropped," Cooney remembers, "and I said to myself, 'What the *hell* am I doing *here?*'" It is not clear whether he means what he was doing on the canvas or what he was doing in the ring with the best heavyweight in the world. Either way, he arrived at an inspiring answer: trying to punch this guy's lights out before he punches out mine. He got up and got to work, rising to the occasion as he fought far past his limitations. He hurt Holmes with left hooks to the body and surprised him with the quality of the jabs and the sneaky rights he used to set up the hooks, but Holmes did not allow the challenger to know it and take heart from knowing it. "He had a lot of power and long-ass arms, and he threw the jab," Holmes says now. "You gotta make him feel it ain't nothin'. He didn't know his jab was as good as it was. I had to hide it from him."

Holmes, implacable as ever, cut up Cooney's face and wore out his will, beating the force and fighting sense out of him. It took Holmes a few rounds to establish command of the fight, and Cooney had his moments throughout, but the dynamic of the fight soon became the champion patiently taking apart the challenger and the challenger trying to find a way to stop him. Cooney, body punching with increasing desperation, landed several low blows, including a flagrant one in the ninth round that caused Holmes and every man who was watching the fight to double over, but Holmes stayed after him. Mills Lane penalized Cooney three points for the low blows, which gave Holmes a big added advantage on the judges' scorecards, but the champion did not intend to let the fight go the full fifteen rounds anyway. No need to give the judges a chance to job him out of a decision. By the thirteenth, Holmes had his man drunk and ready to be mugged. Cooney, like a lot of brave souls on the wrong end of a beating, had been reduced to a single defeatist resolve. "All I was thinking by then was, 'Let me show him he can't hurt me.' It was dumb, but I was inexperienced, and I had a couple of real estate guys in my corner."

Holmes was hitting Cooney whenever he wanted, staggering him, hurting him, finishing him, when Victor Valle, the only one in Cooney's corner who knew anything about boxing, jumped into the ring to save his fighter. Lane stopped it at 2:52 of the thirteenth. It turned out to be a very good fight, actually, although that's not what people remember about it.

The Movies

In *Rocky* and its sequels, a cycle of five male weepies (a sixth movie, a Broadway show, and a derivative reality show produced by Sylvester Stallone are in the works as of this writing), the training sequences matter more than the fights because they suggest what is at stake in the ring. The principal motif of the series is the spectacle of Rocky running, not Rocky fighting; from the standpoint of making meaning, the runup to a fight matters more than the fight itself, which mostly serves to confirm and enact whatever content the movie has already deployed to frame it. The Rocky movies teach audiences to respond to the appearance of their hero in training gear—and the familiar opening notes of the musical themes that accompany the training sequences, like "Gonna Fly Now" and "Eye of the Tiger"—as a cue to be alert for bedrock meaning.

This tendency of the Rocky movies conforms with a more general cultural habit. Even people who know nothing about boxing recognize the stock figure of the running fighter from repeated sightings in movies, on TV, in literature, journalism, and advertising. Rising early, wrapped in hooded sweats, he (and, more recently, she) throws punches in the air to keep his arms loose as he runs past tenements or rowhouses or bungalows or housing projects, through parks, along the waterfront and the tracks. The running fighter has become a cliché because he carries a powerful set of meanings and a powerful assumption *about* meaning: just as the run shapes the fighter's body, the world through which he runs shapes his fighting self and suggests what will be at stake when he enters the ring. In addition to fighting for a payday, he represents constituencies and narratives rooted in that landscape—on both the local scale (a neighborhood, city, or region) and the more general (a class, a nation, a people). The running fighter prepares for a contest that will advance a larger story or principle, that will exorcise or perhaps just exercise demons. All of this content resides, at least latently, in the relationship between fighter and landscape: each figures the other's import.

Since 1976, the paradigmatic running fighter, the one who fixed the image in cinematic amber for posterity, has been Rocky Balboa. It is easy to think of the Rocky movies' training sequences as being about the construction of a

White Hope, but as you go deeper into each movie and the whole cycle, the White Hope element becomes more and more obviously vestigial, buried ever deeper in the signifying routines of movies more interested in teasing out the relationship between the local and the metropolitan, the national, the global. The running fighter and the content associated with him are usually assumed to have a local accent, to be lived with special force in *my* neighborhood, in *my* city, by *my* tribe . . . and not *yours*. But the tribal conceit encounters a potential contradiction when the running fighter, whose imbibing of local virtues supposedly equips him to win fights, makes a name for himself and becomes a national or international figure. This contradiction, not racial essence, turns out to be the Rocky series' primary subject matter.

Rocky's first training sequence, in which Rocky arises at 4am on a frosty morning and drinks five raw eggs before setting out for an uninspired run, frames his departure with a long shot down a classic South Philly row-house block. That vista, like tenements in New York or bungalows in Chicago, has compressed within it the history and resonances of the urban village and the ways of life it housed—more particularly, the neighborhood orders fashioned by Italians and other immigrants and their descendants in the high-industrial period between the Civil War and the mid-twentieth century. We catch another emblematic glimpse of the urban village in the movie's third running sequence, when Rocky runs through South Philly's Italian Market, which still retains a whiff of the horse-and-wagon commercial district.

That atavistic whiff also pervades the larger landscape revealed by his runs, which trace the arteries and ligaments of the industrial city in which the urban village thrived: railroad and streetcar tracks, the working waterfront, a neighborhood landscape signposted by the ethnic parish church, the saloon, the boxing gym. Only the factory is missing, although the meat warehouse where he trains and later works stands in for the memory of it. The training sequences make a thumbnail sketch of the remnants of a world made by hinterlanders—immigrants and migrants—who gathered in American cities to work in factories. Especially for white ethnics, the urban village served as a staging ground for subsequent moves into the middle class, to the suburbs, away.

The story of the rise and fall of the urban village is also the story of a traditional heartland of boxing. The rise of American fighters to dominance in the early twentieth century, especially in the heavyweight division, roughly paralleled the rise to global power of the United States. In boxing and empire, America supplanted Great Britain, and the successes of American boxers served as indicators of larger prowess. The great industrial capitals of the Northeast and Midwest were also world capitals of boxing in the first part of the century, and the deindustrialization of these cities in the

latter part of the century contributed to the decline of the urban village's
dominance in boxing. Gyms and the local halls that staged club fights went
the way of the factory, the Italian or Polish social club, the saloon with saw-
dust on its floor and old world language and smells in its atmosphere.[8]

Rocky and its sequels want to suggest that some potency remains in the
urban village and its indigenous working class, which once upon a time produced fighters, singers, and gangsters as well as manufactured goods. When
the urban village becomes a nostalgic artifact, a romantic ruin of its former
self, it becomes the Old Neighborhood—and Rocky's from the Old Neighborhood. *Rocky* caught and held the fancy of audiences, in part, because it
proposed that even as late as the 1970s, after suburbanization and deindustrialization and ethnic assimilation and upward social mobility and urban
redevelopment had leached away most of the urban village's traditional vitality and turned it into the Old Neighborhood, it could still deliver an old-
school champion to respond to new-order challenges from the ghetto, the
barrio, the third world, and other complex facts of postindustrial life.

This is often what people are talking about when they say that the
Rocky movies are "about race." And I suppose the movies *are* "about
race," but only on the way to being about a romance of immigrant-ethnic
identity in which black people serve as supporting characters. The first
three Rocky movies (the three released before Holmes-Cooney) might appear to be about kicking a black champion's ass, but they are more about
earning his respect as an equal. They dream not of reclaiming the no-
longer-white city but of fully inhabiting it. An obvious irony shadows that
aspiration, since white ethnics still dominated the governance and business
of American cities, especially old manufacturing capitals like Philadelphia.
After all, Frank Rizzo was mayor of Philadelphia in 1976, when *Rocky* was
released. But part of Rizzo's appeal resided precisely in the way he allowed
white ethnics to reckon with the ironic distance between the continuing fact
of their political dominance and the feeling of dispossession that hounded
them—the feeling of having lost or abandoned the urban village, or of
being besieged in its fortified ruins.

Early in *Rocky,* the bartender at the neighborhood dive, watching
Apollo Creed arrive in all his smack-talking glory at the airport in Philadelphia on TV, wonders where all the real fighters—that is, fighters from the
urban village—have gone. "All we got these days is jig clowns," he laments.
Rocky responds, "You callin' Apollo Creed a *clown?*" as if the "jig" part
were incidental. The "jig" part is not incidental—it can't be—but it is not
ultimately what matters most about Creed in this movie. It matters more
that he is not from the Old Neighborhood but is opulently rich and famous
and cosmopolitan, that he holds the heavyweight title and the claim to superior manhood that traditionally goes with it, that he dominates the air-

waves, invading Philadelphia and even the neighborhood bar by way of the television set.

Another way to see Rocky's training sequences as about something other than "race, race, race" is to consider who, and therefore what, he trains to fight. Now, you may well be thinking, "Isn't Apollo Creed obviously supposed to be Muhammad Ali, and isn't the fantasy of beating Ali always at heart a racial one?" My answer: a short Yes and a longer No.

It does not take much effort to identify Creed, Rocky's antagonist in the first two movies (and his pal in the third and fourth), as a fictional avatar of Ali. Like Ali, Creed is a heavyweight who moves like a middleweight, a virtuoso of celebrity in the television age, a showman who points with gloved hand while delivering mock-poetry. Creed may not be the antinomian social critic that Ali was in the '60s, but by 1976 neither was Ali. He was already well into his twilight phase, making the transition from being an unhittable personification of disorienting cultural change to being America's much-knocked-around and half-loved-to-death fuzzy bunny, revered in great part because he was soaked through with nostalgia for the 1960s.

The movie similarly makes it easy to identify Rocky "The Italian Stallion" Balboa as a fictional avatar of Rocky Marciano, the champion of the 1950s who still enjoys special status as the white-ethnic urban village's last great heavyweight. Marciano is an archetypal running fighter, a hard worker rather than a fortuitously gifted athlete. He matters most, the story goes, because he hardened himself to outlast more gifted opponents by training harder than they did, especially by running through the streets and parks of his hometown, Brockton, Massachusetts—fueled, the story goes, by the fabled Brockton work ethic, the ethnically supercharged carbs in his mother's pasta, and a burning desire to avoid ending up in the shoe factories where his father labored.[9]

Mick, Rocky Balboa's trainer, pointedly remarks more than once in the movie that Balboa reminds him of Marciano, and Balboa's training techniques—running with bricks in hand, punching sides of meat, chasing a chicken (in *Rocky II*) to improve quickness—reference Marciano's improvised methods and their resonances of blue-collar labor. Balboa keeps a picture of Marciano by his bedside, next to his pet fish. When Balboa says, "How you doin', Moby Dick?" he seems to be talking not to the fish but to the fight world's undefeated, undisputed White Whale, on whom has been loaded the whole elegiac content of what was lost in the long, slow aging out of industrial urbanism, especially as it was lived by white ethnics.

Rocky Balboa fulfilled in fiction the prayerful wish arising in certain quarters for Rocky Marciano—who retired in 1956 and died in a plane crash in 1969—to return and give Ali a taste of old-school manhood. After Ali took care of various foreign contenders and Jerry Quarry, further plausible white

challengers had to be conjured by semiotic voodoo (hence Frazier and Foreman as surrogate White Hopes) or spun from fictional cloth, which made possible Marciano's imagined return to the ring.[10] *Rocky* was not the first attempt
to imagine a Marciano-Ali fight. In 1969, seven years before *Rocky* and just
months before Marciano's death, a Miami promoter named Murry Woroner
convinced Marciano and Ali to participate in the filming of a staged "computer fight." Woroner claimed that he had programmed the protagonists'
strengths and weaknesses into a computer that impartially determined the
course of the fight, but all he did was script scenes of mock fighting, which
they then acted out: Ali jabbing and circling, Marciano stalking and occasionally pinning Ali to the ropes with a flurry. Both men were out of shape:
Ali, then twenty-seven, had not fought in two years because the sanctioning
bodies of boxing had barred him from the ring and stripped him of his title
after he refused to be drafted into the military; Marciano, forty-five, had not
fought in fourteen years and had to become a running fighter once more to
make the movie, training hard to shed fifty pounds of fat. Ali, the better actor,
threw half-speed punches and made faces, amusing himself by dislodging
Marciano's toupee. Marciano seemed to take the sham more seriously, but his
bigger punching motion made it easier to see that he was faking. They play-
acted a variety of endings, in some of which Ali won, but when Woroner assembled and released the film he had Marciano knocking out Ali in the
thirteenth round. Ali hammed his way through the finale like a trouper.[11]

Marciano *had* to win Woroner's "computer fight"—not just because
the result was as likely as any other, and not just because he had died relatively young only a few months before. ("Having Ali beat him right then,"
a fight sage recently suggested to me, "would have been like pissing on
Rocky's grave.") In that anxious moment, many people who held Ali's politics and public manner against him also valued Marciano as a child of the
Depression and as a World War II-era patriot—a familiar type from the Old
Neighborhood—who might reimpose what felt increasingly like a lost sense
of everything in its place and a place for everything. And yes, some large
subset of these people felt that a camera-friendly black dissenter had to be
defeated by a white regular guy whose authenticity resided not only in his
resonance of blue-collar work but also in his media-unsavvy, tongue-tied
parochial manner: Marciano sounded like Sylvester the Cat, and he shared
that cartoon character's bottomless capacity to take a beating and come
back for more.

But more than simply telling a story of white over black, the computer-
fight charade both reaffirmed and pined for the potency of tradition in the
face of a flourishing new order. It became the cultural work of the old-
school, working-class tough guy Marciano, and his avatars, to stand up to
the intimidatingly cosmopolitan Ali and all he represented. To reduce an

imagined struggle between the local and the cosmopolitan or between the 1950s and the 1960s to "race, race, race" is to be a little bit right at the cost of being much more deeply wrong.

The struggle between localistic tradition and new-order cosmopolitanism would be one subtextual story in *Rocky*, too, although with more emphasis on elegy and less on the need to beat Ali. It was necessary only that Rocky Balboa go the distance. He would not have to beat Creed and defend the championship until he became a box-office winner featured in multiple sequels, and by then his reasons for beating Creed had little to do with kicking a black champion's ass.

Those sequels make an increasingly strong argument for not reducing *Rocky* to a simple—or even a complicated—racial allegory. *Rocky III,* the episode in the series that was still playing in theaters when Holmes and Cooney fought in 1982, made it especially clear that race was a stepping stone, not the endpoint of meaning-making.

After Rocky beats Creed at the end of *Rocky II,* he becomes the wrong kind of running fighter, lapsing into bad training habits that bespeak a bad relationship to his home ground and what it stands for. When *Rocky III* begins, he is fighting all over the world, he trains in a fancy hotel, and he has moved to a mansion far from the rowhouse blocks of South Philly, which means he is ready to take a fall. Meanwhile, the challenger, Clubber Lang, played by Mr. T, runs through the streets of his neighborhood on the South Side of Chicago and works out in a grubby improvised gym. The conventional calculus of authenticity dictates that Lang has to win; Rocky can only defeat him in the rematch by getting right with that calculus. With South Philly out of reach in his wake, getting right means getting back to somebody else's basics. Under the now-retired Creed's guidance, Rocky moves into Creed's old neighborhood, in Los Angeles. There he runs on the beach and, in Creed's old gym, learns the stereotypically black boxing virtue of fluid movement to go with the stereotypically white boxing virtue of being able to take three punches in the face in order to land one good one to the body, all of which leads to his defeat of Mr. T in a parody of Ali's victory over Foreman in Zaire. The lesson here is that getting back to *any-body's* basics will do, as long as they allow you to fashion a fighting self by exposing it to the hard knocks native to a particular locality.

This principle informs the longest and weirdest stretch in the series to date, in *Rocky IV,* when our hero moves to the USSR to train for his fight against the Siberian giant, Drago, who has killed Creed in the ring. (It is worth pausing here to line out an analogy to the real-life situation in the early 1980s: let's say Ali, the flamboyant former champion, had tried a comeback and Cooney, the White Hope contender, had killed him in the ring; then Holmes, the reigning champion and Ali's former adversary, would be responsible for avenging Ali. So at this point in the series, for those still keeping score at home, Creed=Ali, Drago=Cooney, and Rocky Balboa=Larry Holmes. Got it?) Setting Drago's high-tech workouts in a laboratory, *Rocky IV* samples two latter-day Frankenstein tropes, the Nazi mad doctor and the steroid-enhanced Eastern European athlete, to figure the White Hope as a crewcut blond supervillain. By contrast, Rocky, now the organic people's hero who must bring down the cynically constructed Nordic superman in order to avenge his fallen soul brother, conducts low-tech workouts at a farmhouse somewhere in movie Siberia, an abstract, white-out landscape vaguely associated with peasantry. Rocky runs through deep snow, startling a team of horses pulling a wagon. He lifts rocks, chops down trees, drags a sled in a harness, and does sets of presses with a cart in which his wife and cornermen are sitting to provide extra weight. He has not just returned to the Old Neighborhood, he has gotten all the way back to the Old Country and, in his training methods, to the kind of work done by imaginary great-grandfathers from the true village that preceded the urban village. If it is not *his* Old Country, that's a technicality: he increasingly stands for fungibility, not essence, so anybody's Old Country or Old Neighborhood will do.

At the end of the training sequence, when Rocky climbs a remote mountain of the kind you see in SUV ads, he has come about as far from South Philly as he can get. He upholds American honor in a fight with explicitly geopolitical meaning—both fighters appear wrapped in flags—but after winning it he makes a blinky universalist speech. In the next and (so far) last installment, *Rocky V,* he will lose all his money in a dime-novel disaster and return to South Philly, but the transformation has been completed: Rocky, having already gone metropolitan and national, has now gone cosmopolitan and global. As such, he has become a shapeshifting vampire of localisms. Just by running through his opponent's Old Neighborhood, he makes himself more authentically from there than the opponent can ever be.

And that, in the end, is the crowning irony of Rocky's career. Because he runs diligently enough and trains hard enough, he wins fights, earns a title shot, and therefore enters the big time, which creates a potential contradiction in the way the movies think. On the one hand, the more local fighter must be the more potent by virtue of more intimate access to the wellsprings of meaning that constitute a fighter's edge in these movies. On the other hand, winning a fight because you're so damn local means becoming a media star, winning audiences in lots of localities, going global.[12]

How does Sylvester Stallone, perhaps underrated as a narrative theorist, finesse this contradiction? One answer lies in one more way to read the training sequences: that is, to consider where Rocky ends up. In the definitive training sequences of *Rocky* and *Rocky II,* he ends up at the top of the steps of the Philadelphia Museum of Art in Center City. In *Rocky III,* the city places a statue of him at the top of those steps. And the very last we see of Rocky in *Rocky V* is a shot of him running up those steps with his son, who wants to show him the Picassos inside. In his notes on the making of *Rocky,* Stallone modestly urges us to read it as an allegory of his own career—how he got to be a great artist, like Picasso, only more, you know, buff. He wanted to make a movie that was also "my particular story," about "my inability to be recognized. I felt Rocky to be the vehicle for that kind of sensibility. So I took my story and injected it into the body of Rocky Balboa because no one, I felt, would be interested in listening to or watching or reading a story about a down-and-out struggling actor/writer. But Rocky Balboa was America's child. He was to the '70s what Chaplin's Little Tramp was to the '20s."[13] In the body of Rocky, Stallone sets out running from South Philly and ends up at the intersection of art, celebrity, and the big money.

Rocky served as Stallone's calling card, opening the way for a career as an international movie star. He blew up as big as Ali; maybe even bigger. It worked so well, and Stallone played such a major role in Hollywood's blockbuster-centered phase of globalization in the '80s and '90s, that other accounts of local heroes rooted far from South Philly—for instance, the Indian movie *Ghulam,* a blend of *Rocky* and *On the Waterfront*—freely draw upon Stallone's persona to imagine the defense of principles that Stallone could never have imagined when he was scheming to become Rocky and then Rambo. Becoming a star, figured visually on the metropolitan scale as a run from South Philly to the Art Museum, requires a trajectory anchored in the local. Any of several localities will do; our hero just needs to start from *somewhere* so he can trace a dramatic arc that reaches from an Old Neighborhood into the white-out abstract space of the global mediascape.

The prototypical figure modeling this arc was, of course, Ali, who started out as the Louisville Lip but left that identity far behind as he became the first true world champion and the first athletic star to take full advantage of television. The Rocky movies are not reducible to a domestic fantasy of beating black champions, and they are not just about imagining a vital reconnection with the urban village. They are also, and more deeply, about defeating Ali in order to *become* him, a model cosmopolitan of the television age, and Stallone uses whatever comes to hand to accomplish the task—including locality, a quaintly potent principle that can be compressed into a neat package and taken or sold, like a pill, to gain advantage in the heroic struggle to make it big. That, and not the priorities of neighborhood, tribe, and "race, race, race," might be the ultimate consequence of Rocky Balboa.

The Wise Men

Like Rocky Balboa and Apollo Creed—and perhaps like Rocky Marciano and Muhammad Ali, who are reported to have gotten along well during the filming of Murry Woroner's "computer fight"—Larry Holmes and Gerry Cooney started out as adversaries in a racial drama but eventually became friends in a way that reduces "race, race, race" to subtext. The seeds of the friendship may lie in Holmes' final pre-fight words to Cooney in the ring, or in the gestures he made afterward. "I told him that night, after the fight: don't quit," says Holmes. "I told him in person, right there: if he'd fought anybody else, he'd be heavyweight champ of the world." Holmes says now that Cooney could have become not only a champion but a great fighter. "If he'd waited a few months, he'd a beat me. If he'd had a few more fights before fighting me, if he'd fought me five fights later in his career, he'd a beat me. He would have improved, and I'd a been older. He was strong, great hook, good jab." (A grain of salt is in order here: Holmes always talks up the men he beat, to make his victories over them seem all the more impressive. I think Holmes would have beaten Cooney whether they fought in June of 1982 or a year later or five years later or tomorrow, no matter who Cooney had fought in the interim.) When he and Cooney met for a live interview on *Good Morning America* a few hours after the fight, Holmes told him, "Everyone gets beat, and sometimes losing makes you an even better fighter. Hell, you're only twenty-five years old."[14]

But Cooney and his corner did not turn the defeat into a useful boxing lesson. He did not quit right away, but something had gone out of him. He went around abjectly apologizing, over and over, to all the people he had let down, and he promised he would do better next time, but it took him many months to get back into the gym. He did not work steadily at his craft and he stopped improving as a fighter; those around him were not equipped to reverse his decline. Cooney began a long sojourn in booze, cocaine, and bad company. Two attempted comebacks ended catastrophically: he was stopped by Michael Spinks in 1987 and poleaxed by George Foreman in 1990. Holmes says, "The white peoples killed him. Can I say that? Well, it's true. It's like when I got home after the Olympic Trials"—in 1972, when he lost to Duane Bobick—and people said, 'That white boy kicked your ass.' That's what white peoples did to him after he fought me. 'Damn, Gerry, that nigger kicked your ass.' It got to his head. Then you want a drink, maybe smoke something."

Cooney agrees with Holmes that their fight might have turned out differently if he'd had a better fistic education. He says, "With the tools I had, I did great. Holmes was an all-time great. I would have to have had five more fights to be really ready." He blames Don King and the Wacko Twins for holding him back. "I trained with Tim Witherspoon a couple of times, but I needed to *fight* these guys to develop my talent. King wouldn't let me at them because I didn't sign with him." He means that he could not get fights with fellow contenders like Witherspoon, Greg Page, or Michael Dokes, as opposed to the ringworn trialhorses used by Jones and Rappaport to pad his record. His handlers, angling for a shot at Holmes, did not want to risk Cooney's perfect record by matching him against other promising heavyweights. When I asked him about Jones and Rappaport as managers, Cooney made a disgusted noise. "They couldn't stand each other, and I was in the middle. They wouldn't get me the fights. Tell you the truth, I never learned how to fight until I was done as a fighter. It all happened so fast, I never got the chance to experience it."[15]

During the buildup to their fight, made longer and testier by a postponement after Cooney suffered a training injury, Holmes and Cooney said unflattering things about each other. Cooney was always careful to make it personal, as opposed to racial. His line was that he had respect for Holmes as a fighter, but not as a man, and that he was disappointed in Holmes for participating in turning their fight into a racial thing. Holmes, for his part, pursued the opposite strategy, which meant that he spent a lot more time talking explicitly about race than Cooney did. Using a formula borrowed from Ali, he emphasized in particular that Cooney had "the complexion to get the connection," that he was a White Hope who had been given a title shot and preferential treatment he had not earned (including an outsize cut of the purse, which burned the money-minded Holmes like hellfire). Much of this backchat between the fighters amounted to promotional business as usual, but Holmes and Cooney now express regret for what they said about each other. More than that, they both seem to regret the callowness of their understanding in 1982 and the single-note quality of the promotion of their fight; they both want to demonstrate the intellectual and moral progress they have made, the distance between themselves and "race, race, race."

Looking back on the buildup to the fight, now more than two decades behind him, Holmes sees himself out of balance, too angry, too caught up in the trivial. Feelings were running high then, and Holmes felt he had to take the brunt of them. People were calling his house to threaten him, harassing his family with cherry bombs, messing with him on the street. Somebody shot up the windows of his restaurant. In his autobiography, he describes himself as becoming paranoid in reaction, and overly fixated on race: "I took to carrying a gun because the gunshots and cherry bombs meant there were some real crackpots out there. But the big problem was that I began to get leery of white people just because they were white. That's what I mean about the atmosphere getting poisoned. I began to think, 'What do they think about me?' I began to imagine I could read their minds, and naturally what I read was prejudice. If I came across a white man who said, 'I hope you beat Cooney, Larry,' I thought he was just being sarcastic and making fun of me."[16] He found it harder, too, to draw a line between strangers and the white people he knew. Much of his extended family was white, as were many of his colleagues, employees, friends, and neighbors, so Holmes had ample opportunity to display a surliness so comprehensive that it disturbed even himself.

But Holmes' bad feelings did not reduce to "race, race, race." He was extraordinarily touchy not only about the upcoming fight with Cooney but about being a reigning champion who still had to get out from Ali's long shadow and win his own comparable acclaim. Holmes resented Cooney's sudden celebrity—not just because he felt that Cooney was famous for being white, but also because he resented the fact that Ali, whom he had effectively put out to pasture with a one-sided beating in 1980, still enjoyed much greater celebrity than Holmes would ever achieve. Holmes had also received death threats after beating Ali in 1980, and Ali sure as hell was not white.

Holmes, who was still working out a public manner with which he could be comfortable, felt too much under Ali's influence to suit himself. Notoriety makes for bigger purses, so Holmes obligingly played to the crowd with Ali-like tactics: inventing nicknames for his opponents, grabbing the ring microphone after a fight to tell everybody how great he was, explaining to the TV cameras that a black man couldn't get a fair deal. But the Ali-style posturing never fit well with Holmes' character. Plainspoken but fundamentally modest, committed to work and family (rather than Ali's touchstones, play and performance), Holmes was an exemplary man of the Lehigh Valley, a resolutely local industrial belt in eastern Pennsylvania that lies only an hour by car from New York and Philadelphia but figuratively a thousand miles from both. Lehigh Valley-place names—Easton, Bethlehem, Allentown—carry the tang of diligent labor, not showbiz flash, and Holmes, unlike Ali, never moved out of the town where he grew up. Holmes, always introduced as "The Easton Assassin," did not look comfortable miming the brand of winking blowhardism and political theater that Ali had made synonymous with being heavyweight champion.

Holmes has always had a basically economic view of the world, but over time he has grown farther into it. He's no less outspoken now than he was in 1982, and he frequently sees the world in black and white, but he does not have much Ali left in his manner. After defeating Cooney, and directly after he claimed to have "killed all the critics," Holmes said, "I'm very sorry to not be what you expect. I'm not Muhammad Ali. I'm not Joe Louis. And I'm not Leon Spinks either. But I wasn't born to be these people. I was born to be myself, Larry Holmes."[17] Becoming his own man entailed putting some distance between himself and three archetypes of the black champion that never suited him: the flamboyant political celebrity, the well-behaved credit to his race, the unlettered street buffoon.[18] The ideal persona Holmes had in mind for himself was more like workingman-cum-businessman. He wants to be remembered not only as one of the very best heavyweights of all time, but also as a fighter who invested his purses wisely, took care of his family, and spoke his mind not just to pimp his fights but to cut through the doubletalk and hypocrisy of public life.[19]

Now, having more squarely inhabited his preferred persona for the better part of the two decades since the Cooney bout, when Holmes looks back on all the crazy pre-fight talk about *Rocky* and race war—not only the things he said, but also the Wacko Twins' and Cooney's provocations, the death threats, the paranoia—he sees just a condition in which to do business. In the end, for him, the racial reading of the fight provides a stepping stone to the economic reading. "The whole black and white thing," Holmes says now, "that's okay on a business perspective. Anything a black person says that's sensitive, he gets in trouble, but I understand." Beyond race can be found the content that matters most: "He was getting a chance to fight me for the title because he was white, and I welcomed the opportunity. Thank God for Gerry Cooney! I'd a had to fight fifty black men to make that much money."

Once he put behind him the madness of the buildup to their fight, Holmes could feel compassion for Cooney. It began during the fight itself. During the thirteenth round, as he put the finishing touches on the beating he was administering to the swaying, nearly helpless challenger, Holmes found himself thinking, "Man, why am I doing this to another man?" Perhaps the truest measure of his feeling for Cooney can be found in the fact that Holmes, who does not like to give up a penny without getting fair value for it, later lost $10,000 betting on Cooney against Spinks and Foreman.[20] That is a lot of money for Holmes, a shrewd judge of boxing and character, to willfully throw away on what for him amounts to the ultimate romantic gesture of friendship. Holmes, who stood in line for government cheese when he grew up in a big fatherless family in a fading mill town, always had a more acute sense of the bottom line than did Cooney, who had a father (albeit a monstrous one) and grew up in a solidly working-class family in Huntington, Long Island. As Holmes sees it, Cooney did not have that sense of the bottom line to steady him when they both found themselves caught up in the cultural tempest attending their fight. Fighting for the pride of white America, or to placate the ghost of an angry father, provided weak motivation for Cooney against Holmes, who regarded the fight as a job of work that, if properly done, would lead to more big paydays.

Cooney, for his part, has arrived at a basically therapeutic view of himself and the world. He has talked and talked over the years about his father, a hardhanded, bitter ironworker who plays the lead role in the psychodrama of his life. Cooney's most repeated line on the subject goes like this: "I grew up in a household where I learned five things from my old man. You know what they were? You're no good, you're a failure, you're not going to amount to anything, don't trust nobody, and don't tell nobody your business. When I lost to Larry Holmes in 1982, I felt all five of those things smack me right across the face. Had to deal with 'em."[21] Everything else passes through the filter of coming to terms with his father. When Cooney describes falling in with the Wacko Twins, for instance, he tells the story as a parable of replacing one bad father with two bad ones. "My father had died. I was eighteen years old, goin' around, meeting with this guy and that guy, trying to figure out what to do. Somebody set me up with Jones and Rappaport, and I went to Queens, to their real estate office, and they started telling me what they would do for me. When you grow up in a really dysfunctional family, you attract dysfunction. They just made it prettier, sound better, but it was more of the same."

Cooney treats his entire boxing career and the dark period afterward as a single traumatic episode, continuous with his childhood, from which he has finally emerged into a new life. In recent years, since sobering up, he has founded FIST, a nonprofit organization that offers medical, financial, and educational assistance to fighters negotiating the transition from boxing to regular life, and he has returned to the gym as teacher and enthusiast. "I wanna tell you this," he says now, "and I wanna tell you this right. I'm a very lucky man. I love the life I have. If I'd won the heavyweight title, I wouldn't be here. It was too fast. And I love boxing now. I spar thirty, forty rounds a week. I'm a different fighter, too. Now I make you miss, *then* make you pay. Have some fun. Boxing can be about just enjoying what your body can do."

Like Holmes, when Cooney looks back on himself in the months before their fight he sees a younger man out of control. But Cooney's lack of control extended into the fight itself, and beyond. He was poorly supervised by his handlers, unready as a fighter, hauling around unexorcised demons. He refuses, as he did then, to entertain even a suggestion that the race-obsessed atmosphere colored his thinking about the fight, but he does admit to disliking Holmes at the time. "I was angry at Holmes 'cause I thought he was being a jerk. He was angry, and I understand it. He was in Ali's shadow, couldn't get the recognition he deserved, and then I came along and they put me on the cover of *Time*."

That was long ago. Now Holmes contributes to FIST, and the two former adversaries hang out together. In 2002, when Holmes (who as of this writing has still not officially retired) fought a minor celebrity and barnstorming fatman seventeen years his junior known as Butterbean, Cooney was at ringside in Norfolk, Virginia, with Joe Frazier, Earnie Shavers, and Leon Spinks, cheering on the fifty-two-year-old Holmes to an easy victory. Cooney now regards the hard words that passed between him and Holmes in 1982 as part of the larger trauma of growing up dysfunctional, and he treats the furor surrounding the fight as just another reservoir of anger and bad feeling to confront, process, and put behind him. He has come to see the fight's racial meaning as merely the most unwelcome part of the expectation that was loaded onto him by angry dysfunctional people: Jones and Rappaport, Don King, the American public, and of course the younger Cooney himself. He failed to carry the load and it bore him down, starting him on his long decline toward rock bottom, which he had to reach in order to recover. For him, the racial reading of the fight provides a stepping stone toward a therapeutic reading of his whole life.

Now that they are well into middle age, both fighters can look back on the moves they made or did not make in reckoning with the Rocky movies' central problem—not "race, race, race," but rather the disorienting jump in scale from the local to the cosmopolitan. Cooney knows he blew it. He did what he could, but he lost touch with his hometown and with his own inner balance. No longer a local hero, he never found his feet as a cosmopolitan star. "I kept a bunch of friends I grew up with, they traveled with me a lot, but I grew up in hotels. From eighteen on. I used to miss seasons. It would be summer, I would leave, I would come back, and it would be winter." In two different interviews held right after being beaten by Holmes, Cooney, on the verge of tears, responded to questions about how he felt by saying that he had "been away from home a long time." In other words, Cooney made the mistake Rocky makes in the beginning of *Rocky III,* but since his life was not a scripted fantasy—or rather, since it was at the time a fantasy scripted by handlers who took little interest in his long-term well-being— he did not manage to reground himself in the world until it was too late to save his career. One might see his friendship with Holmes and his periodic visits to Easton, though, as a modest real-life version of Rocky's regrounding himself in Creed's old neighborhood. Maybe those movies aren't as dumb as they seem.

Holmes, on the other hand, never left Easton, mightily resisting the pull of the cosmopolitan. After a fight, he packs up and rushes back home (lingering, if the fight was held in or near a casino, only long enough to play some late-night high-stakes blackjack). He generally does not leave Easton unless there is money in it for him, and he brings his paychecks right home and socks them away in the bank, in municipal bonds, or in the array of real property he has amassed around town. He could have lived anywhere in the world once he made his millions, but he believes that staying in Easton prolonged his career and safeguarded his fortune. Easton, he told me a few years ago, is a "quiet, beautiful" town where you can raise "regular kids" who "don't think they are better than other people" (a one-sentence synopsis of the Lehigh Valley's fundamental ethos). And the modest pace of life helped him stay in shape and save his pennies. "You can go out for a beer or whatever, but most nights after ten o'clock it's time to go home. Plus, there are no Joneses to keep up with." Asked at a press conference a few years ago why he was still going strong in the ring well into his forties, especially when the great Ali had been sadly over the hill at the age of thirty-eight when Holmes beat him, Holmes said, "Ali burned the candle at both ends. I never did. Thanks to Easton, my lifestyle has been at a minimum."[22]

Among the greatest heavyweight champions—a peer group consisting of Louis, Ali, Jack Johnson, Sonny Liston, Jack Dempsey, Marciano, and perhaps a couple of others—Holmes stands out as the one who best sustained his entire wherewithal, physical and financial, over the long haul.[23] He is also the one who most insistently sustained his connection to the locality that produced him. Rocky Balboa, who lost touch with South Philly and only moved back when he was broke, would be proud or envious of Holmes' continuing connection to Easton, even if Sylvester Stallone might see Holmes' localism as having restrained him from making it as big on the global scale as he might otherwise have done.

I asked Cooney if he had Rocky on his mind *during* his fight with Holmes, considering all his talk about Rocky before and after. He said, "Nah, I was too busy. It's just a great movie." When I asked Holmes if he had Rocky on his mind during the fight, he said, "No, but when I was in training, people was talking about Rocky, yeah. All the white folk, it made it hard to go in the lobby of the hotel." As Holmes saw it, Rocky-and-race and Don King's and the Wacko Twins' inflammatory talk and just about everything else became irrelevant bits of extracurricular business when the bell rang. Okay, I said, but what if the fight had gone the distance and the judges had robbed you and given the decision to Cooney and made all those Rocky-crazed fans happy? In fact, it looks like just such a robbery was well under way when Mills Lane stopped the fight in the thirteenth. Despite Holmes' clear advantage in a majority of rounds, two of the three judges, Duane Ford and Dave Moretti, had scored the fight so that Cooney would have been ahead on their scorecards when it was stopped, were it not for the points he lost to low blows. Even with the deductions, Ford and Moretti had the fight close enough that if Cooney had lasted the distance and staged a surge in the final rounds he might have been gifted with a draw or even a split-decision victory. Could Rocky and the associated extracurricular business have been working on the judges' minds? "Well," said Holmes, "you know they give too much credit for being the aggressor and all that. Really, though, I don't give a shit about Duane Ford." He also said, "Beauty is in the eye of the beholder," and there was a trace of something in his voice—amusement, maybe, or contempt—that I couldn't quite place. I could not tell if he meant that the judges preferred sluggers to boxers, or white men to black men, or the ending of *Rocky II* to the ending of *Rocky*.

Notes

* All quotations from Larry Holmes and Gerry Cooney, unless otherwise attributed, are drawn from telephone conversations I had with them between May and October 2003. My thanks to them, and to Amy Bass, Brendan O'-Malley, Charles Farrell, Mike Ezra, Gary Moser, Brian Moore, and Tina Klein for expert readings and comments on drafts of this essay.

1. Larry Holmes with Phil Berger, *Larry Holmes: Against The Odds* (New York: St. Martin's, 1998), 201.

2. Holmes, *Against the Odds*, 211.

3. Watching the Rocky movies end-to-end can get to be a chore, I know, especially when "Eye of the Tiger" kicks in, Stallone's star persona achieves the fullness of its self-regarding amplitude, and you begin to reel from the mounting punishment of writing, direction, and boxing sequences that start out sort of endearingly oafish and grow ever less endearingly so as the sequels pile up. Hey, tough it out. Nobody said that the study of popular culture is all fun and games.

4. Holmes claims now that he made no more than $7.5 million before payouts to Don King and others (and perhaps $5 million after), and speculates that Cooney did better, perhaps even two or three million dollars better. Most authoritative estimates put Cooney's purse at $8.5 million. In our conversations, Cooney would not or could not confirm that number.

5. Mr. T., aka Lawrence Tero, aka Lawrence Tureaud, did muscle work before he made it in Hollywood. He was employed as a bodyguard for Leon Spinks in 1980 when he nearly came to blows with Larry Holmes during an altercation at a banquet for Joe Louis.

6. Stallone visited Cooney's final workout, but he does not seem to have been present on fight night.

7. Both Holmes and Cooney remember that Holmes said, "Let's have a good fight." When I return to the moment on videotape, crowd noise and a semidefeated microphone make it impossible to determine exactly what he said. It could have been "Let's have a good fight," but it might have been "Gonna be a good fight" or "Gonna have a good fight." If it was either of the latter, then Holmes' pre-fight line acquires another subtext: Cooney had never been in a good fight with a first-rate heavyweight, and Holmes, who had plenty of them on his record, was reminding Cooney that he was out of his depth and about to have a new, uniquely difficult experience.

8. I have written in greater detail about the intertwined histories of boxing and industrial cities in *Good with Their Hands: Boxers, Bluesmen, and Other*

Characters from the Rust Belt (Berkeley and Los Angeles: University of California, 2002), especially in chapters 1 and 4.

9. For more on Marciano and Brockton, see Rotella, *Good with Their Hands,* chapter 4.

10. Chuck Wepner, a white club fighter whose valiant effort in defeat when fighting Ali provided the proximate inspiration for Sylvester Stallone to write *Rocky,* falls somewhere between Quarry and a fictional challenger. He had no chance to win, but he did provide some drama. In November 2003, Wepner announced that he was suing Stallone for a cut of the profits generated by the Rocky franchise over the years.

11. This result followed a pattern Woroner had established years before when he staged a fantasy radio tournament of all-time heavyweight champions. Marciano won that tournament, too, by knocking out Jack Dempsey—not Joe Louis—in the finale. Woroner had Cassius Clay eliminated in the preliminaries by Jim Jeffries, giving Jeffries the win over a black champion he failed to earn against Jack Johnson.

12. Rappers trying to make it big have to finesse this particular local-global whipsaw all the time. Rocky Balboa—who says "yo" all the time to mark himself as a guy from the neighborhood, a habit he shares with rappers who were not even born yet in 1976—encountered it first and may well have showed them the way.

13. An excerpt from *The Official Rocky Scrapbook* (Putnam, 1977) posted on ESPN's website at http://espn.go.com/page2/s/stallone/011207.html.

14. Holmes reports his encounter with Cooney at the post-fight interview on *Good Morning America,* conducted by Howard Cosell, in *Larry Holmes,* 212. Cosell was just awful, as usual, when he covered the Holmes-Cooney bout. Some would say that his worst moment of the night came during his call of the action itself, when he barely and belatedly noted that the fight had ended, but I vote for a moment that came soon after, when Cosell opened his immediate post-fight interview with Cooney in his locker room by saying, "You seem so depressed." When Cosell interviewed Holmes in his locker room after the fight, the champion stared straight ahead and replied in a seething monotone, plainly counting the seconds until he would be free of Cosell's company.

15. The Wacko Twins deserve a word in their defense here. Cooney had flaws that a good fighter, especially an energetic young fighter, could exploit. It is unlikely that he could have fought his way up through the ranks of heavyweight contenders—Witherspoon, Page, Dokes and the like—with his record, confidence, and health intact. His handlers matched him against Holmes before he was ready, true, but on the other hand he might never have been ready for Holmes, and they did succeed in parlaying his perfect record and White Hope status into the largest possible payday. From a promoter's point of view, they may well have handled Cooney perfectly, extracting maximum profit from minimum risk.

16. Holmes, *Larry Holmes,* 201.

17. Holmes, *Larry Holmes,* 211. Holmes offered slightly variant versions of the line several times in post-fight interviews.

18. Holmes will not say it out loud, but Ali's physical decline strengthens the case for the superiority of Holmes' belt-and-suspenders approach to boxing and life.

19. Holmes wants to be remembered, also, for something other than his own encounters with Marciano's ghost, which has haunted his career. First Holmes had to beat not one but two variations on Marciano, Gerry Cooney and Rocky Balboa, in 1982. Then, in 1985, he lost an extremely debatable decision to Michael Spinks in Las Vegas to fall one victory short of matching Marciano's perfect lifetime record of forty-nine professional victories without a loss. After the fight, Holmes testily reminded questioners in the press that he was a much better technical boxer than Marciano. The phrase he used—"To be technical, Marciano couldn't carry my jockstrap"—yearned to be misunderstood. It caused an uproar and will live on in fight-world lore as the perfect example of what not to say to the press after you lose a questionable decision.

20. Holmes, *Larry Holmes,* 210 and 212.

21. Cooney gave me a couple of versions of the line over the phone in our conversations, and one can find others in various interviews; this particularly polished version comes from an interview he taped for HBO's "Legendary Nights" documentary about his fight with Holmes.

22. Holmes offered his opinion about Easton and celebrity during interviews I conducted with him and a pre-fight press conference I attended in the mid-1990s, from which I quoted at greater length in "Three Views of the Fistic Summits from College Hill," *South Atlantic Quarterly* 95.2 (1996), 281–320 (see especially 303).

23. One might argue that George Foreman, too, has done exceptionally well in preserving both his fighting ability and his fortune over the long haul, but Foreman does not belong with Holmes in the first rank of heavyweight champions. Holmes reigned longer than any champion except Joe Louis; Foreman was inconsistent, lost important fights in his prime, and did not hold his titles for long.

Contributors

MICHAEL ARTHUR is Counselor and Multicultural Consultant in the Counseling Services Center of Bowdoin College and a native of Barbados, where his love and knowledge of cricket became solidified at a young age. He is pleased with his wife Jennifer's progress in becoming a proper cricket fan.

AMY BASS is Assistant Professor of History and Honors Program Director at The College of New Rochelle. She is the author of *Not the Triumph but the Struggle: The 1968 Olympic Games and the Making of the Black Athlete,* and is currently writing on the 1960s battle over designating the birthplace of W. E. B. Du Bois a national landmark. She has served as a research consultant for NBC television for the broadcasts of the Atlanta, Sydney, Salt Lake, and Athens Olympic Games. A recovering Red Sox fan, she is currently trying to find a new source of agony after the World Series in 2004.

DAVID ANTHONY TYEEME CLARK is Assistant Professor of American Studies and faculty member of the Center for Indigenous Nations Studies at the University of Kansas. He is currently working on two books: *Roots of Red Power: American Indian Protest and Resistance, From Wounded Knee to Chicago,* and, with Cornel Pewewardy, *Counting Coup: Looking Forward to the History of "Indian" Mascots.* Because of his belief that indigenous decolonization politics surge through the languages of music and performance, he listens to musical artists like Blackfire, especially the song "Exiled [in the land of the free]."

JOEL DINERSTEIN is Assistant Professor of English at Tulane University. His book, *Swinging the Machine: Modernity, Technology, and African-American Culture Between the World Wars* (2003) received the 2004 Eugene M. Kayden Book Award for best new book in the humanities published by an American university press.

GRANT FARRED is Associate Professor in the Literature Program at Duke University. His most recent work is *What's My Name? Black Vernacular Intellectuals* (2003) and his forthcoming book is entitled *Long Distance Love: A Passion for Football.* He is a lifelong fan of Liverpool Football Club in England.

TRACIE CHURCH GUZZIO is Assistant Professor of English at the State University of New York at Plattsburgh, where she teaches courses in African American literature, literary theory, and film. She is currently revising a manuscript on John Edgar Wideman, and is also working on a project about the figure of the "double" in African American literature and culture.

MATTHEW FRYE JACOBSON is Professor of American Studies, History, and African American Studies at Yale. His publications include *Old World Bound* (2005), *Barbarian Virtues* (2000), and *Whiteness of a Different Color* (1998). He is currently working on a cultural history of the Civil Rights era, *Politcs by Other Means,* an investigation that began with his reflections on Dick Allen's career as "Richie."

CARLO ROTELLA is Director of American Studies and Associate Professor of English at Boston College. He is the author of *October Cities: The Redevelopment of Urban Literature, Good with Their Hands: Boxers, Bluesmen, and Other Characters from the Rust Belt,* and, most recently, *Cut Time: An Education at the Fights,* which received the L. L. Winship/PEN New England Award and was a finalist for the Los Angeles Times Book Prize. He contributes regularly to the *Washington Post Magazine* and *The American Scholar;* his work has also appeared in *Harper's, DoubleTake, Raritan, American Quarterly,* and *Critical Inquiry.* He is a member of the Boxing Writers Association of America, which is sort of like the American Studies Association or the Modern Language Association, only more inclined to esoteric dispute featuring the free use of "dirtbag" as both adjective and noun.

THERESA RUNSTEDTLER is a doctoral candidate in African American Studies and History at Yale University. Her dissertation examines boxing from the 1880s to the 1930s as a cultural lens through which to view popular conversations on race, ethnicity, gender, empire, and biopolitics. She received her B.A. from York University. Before attending graduate school, she danced and acted professionally, studied Radio and Television Production at Ryerson University, and worked in the public relations department of a Canadian national sports network.

JENNIFER SCANLON is Associate Professor and Director of Gender and Women's Studies at Bowdoin College. Among her many publications, she is the author of *Inarticulate Longings: The Ladies' Home Journal, Gender, and the Promises of Consumer Culture* (1995) and editor of *The Gender and Consumer Culture Reader* (2000) and *Significant Contemporary American Feminists: A Biocritical Sourcebook* (1999). She was a Fulbright Senior Scholar at the Centre for Gender and Development Studies at the University of the West Indies in Trinidad and Tobago, 1998–1999. A lifelong Yankee fan, she barely survives living in Red Sox territory.

ERIC ZOLOV is Associate Professor in the Department of History at Franklin & Marshall College and associate editor for *The Americas: A Quarterly Review of Inter-American Cultural History.* He is the author of *Refried Elvis: The Rise of the Mexican Counterculture* (1999) and co-editor and contributor to *Fragments of a Golden Age: The Politics of Popular Culture in Mexico Since 1940* (2001), and *Rockin' Las Américas: The Global Politics of Rock in Latin/o America* (2004). He is also coeditor of the classroom reader *Latin America and the United States: A Documentary History* (2000). Currently he is researching and writing on the impact of the Cuban revolution on Mexican political culture and U.S.–Mexican relations during the 1960s.

Index